VISUAL QUICKSTART GUIDE

QuarkXPress 5

FOR MACINTOSH AND WINDOWS

Elaine Weinmann
Peter Lourekas

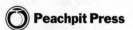

Peachpit Press

For Alicia

Visual QuickStart Guide
QuarkXPress 5 for Macintosh and Windows
Elaine Weinmann and Peter Lourekas

Peachpit Press
1249 Eighth Street
Berkeley, CA 94710
510/524-2178
800/283-9444
510/524-2221 (fax)

Find us on the World Wide Web at: www.peachpit.com

Visual QuickStart Guide is a trademark of Peachpit Press,
a division of Pearson Education

Cover design: The Visual Group and Nathalie Valette
Interior design and illustrations: Elaine Weinmann and
Peter Lourekas

Colophon

This book was created with QuarkXPress 4.11 on a Power
Macintosh G4 dual 500 and a Power Macintosh G4 450. The
primary fonts used are New Baskerville, Gill Sans, Franklin
Gothic, Lithos, Officina, and Futura from Adobe Systems Inc.

Permissions

Definitions on page vi from *The Oxford Encyclopedic English
Dictionary,* 1991, edited by Joyce M. Hawkins and Robert Allen,
reprinted by permission of Oxford University Press.

Notice of Rights

Notice of Liability

ISBN 0-201-35491-8

9 8 7 6 5 4 3 2 1

Printed and bound in the United States of America

Our thanks to

Nancy Aldrich-Ruenzel, publisher of Peachpit Press

Cary Norsworthy, senior editor

Marjorie Baer, executive acquisitions editor

Victor Gavenda, senior technical editor

Gary-Paul Prince, promotions manager

Keasley Jones, associate publisher

Lisa Brazieal, production coordinator

And the rest of the terrific staff at *Peachpit Press*

Glen Turpin, communications manager at Quark Inc., and the beta team, who kept the alphas and betas flowing and answered our technical questions

thepowerxchange.com, for supplying us with information about Quark XTensions

Nathan Olson, freelance writer, for helping us revise Chapter 21

Karen Reichstein, Maureen Forys, and *Kate Kaminski,* for updating and testing the keyboard shortcuts

Leona Benten and *William Rodarmor,* proofreaders

Steve Rath, indexer

Polling All Instructors

We'd like to hear your opinion. Our books are getting so big that something's gotta go. Please send us a note at: peterandelaine@peachpit.com with your suggestions about what we should include—or leave out—of our next editions of this book or, of our other Visual QuickStart Guides on Illustrator and Photoshop.

Thank you!

quark[1] /kwaːk/ *n. Physics* any of a group of (originally three) postulated components of elementary particles Quarks are held to carry a charge one-third or two-thirds that of the proton Many predictions of this theory have been corroborated by experiments but free quarks have yet to be observed. In a sense, quark theory recapitulates at a deeper level efforts earlier this century to explain all atomic properties in terms of electrons, protons, and neutrons [coined by M Gell-Mann, 1964, from phrase 'Three quarks for Muster Mark!' in James Joyce's *Finnegans Wake* (1939)]

quark[2] /kwaːk/ *n.* a type of low-fat curd cheese.

From The Oxford Encyclopedic English Dictionary, 1991, Oxford University Press

Table of Contents

Note! New or substantially changed features are listed in **boldface**. In addition to the changes we have noted, there are dozens and dozens of new sidebars, introductory paragraphs, and other improvements throughout the book—more than we could note.

Chapter 2: **Startup**

Chapter 3: **Get Around**

Table of Contents

Chapter 7: **Typography**

Chapter 8:
New chapter!

Tables and Tabs

Chapter 10: **Multiple Items**

Chapter 11: **Pictures and Text**

Chapter 12: **Lines**

Chapter 13: **Style Sheets**

Chapter 14: **Master Pages**

Chapter 15: **Color**

Chapter 20: **Libraries**

Chapter 24: **XML**

New chapter!

Table of Contents

The Basics 1

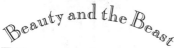

"Beauty! I've starved myself since you forgot about me. Now at least I shall die in peace..."
"Live!" cried Beauty. "And let us marry. How could I live without you, my dearest Beast?"

1 *A text box with a frame*

2 *Text on a path*

3 *A picture in a picture box (with a delicate .5 point frame)*

4 *A picture in a box without a frame*

What is QuarkXPress?

QuarkXPress is a page layout application. A page layout application is a central gathering place for text, pictures, lines, and tables, all of which together compose a page or series of pages. QuarkXPress can be used to produce anything from a tiny hang tag for a line of apparel to a multiple-volume encyclopedia. A finished document can be output on a home laser printer (newsletter, party invitation, etc.), output on a high-end imagesetter for final printing by a commercial printer (book, magazine, brochure, etc.), or exported for online viewing.

This chapter is a reference guide to the basic QuarkXPress features. In the remaining chapters you'll learn how to actually build pages and page elements.

The QuarkXPress building blocks

■ To place text on a page, you must type or import text into a rectangular or irregularly-shaped **text box 1** or along the edge of a Bézier **text path 2**.

Similarly, to place a picture on a page, you must first create a container for it, whether it's a simple rectangular or intricate Bézier **picture box**. Then you can import a picture into it. If you want the border of a text or picture box to print, you must apply a frame to it **3**–**4**.

A **line** can be straight or curved, and functions as a decorative element. And a **table** holds a checkerboard of cells; each cell can contain text or a picture.

■ A text box, text path, picture box, table, or line is called an **item.** The picture or text a box contains is called its **contents**.

A picture or text box can also be rendered **contentless**, after which it functions strictly as a colored shape.

■ Tool selection is the first step in many of the instructions in this book. To create an item, for example, you'll use an item creation tool, such as the Line tool or the Rectangle text box tool.

To move a whole item or a group of items across a page, you'll use the **Item** tool ■, since you'll be working with the overall container.

To copy/paste, delete, or restyle text or a picture after it's input or imported, you'll use the **Content** tool, since you'll be working with the contents of, not the outside of, the container.

For some tasks the Item and Content tools are interchangeable. For example, the Content tool can be used to reshape or resize items, or select multiple items. The Item tool can be used to import a picture.

■ An item or its contents must be **selected** before either one can be modified ■–■.

■ The readouts on the **Measurements** palette vary depending on which tool and which kind of item are selected (■, next page). The left side of the palette displays information pertaining to an item—a picture box, text box, text path, table, or line—if that item and the Item or Content tool are selected. Item information includes dimensions and location on the page.

The right side of the Measurements palette displays content information about a picture or text, such as its size, if that item and the Content tool are selected (■, next page). The right side of the Measurements palette displays line style and width information if a line and the Item or Content tool are selected. The palette is blank when no items are selected (■, next page).

The two workhorse tools

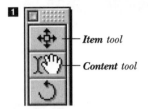

Item *tool*

Content *tool*

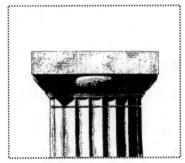

■ *A picture box that is **not selected***

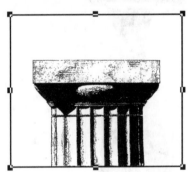

■ *Eight handles display when a box is selected.*

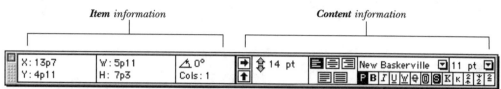

1 *The Measurements palette when the **Item** tool and a **text box** are selected*

Item *information*   Content *information*

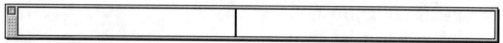

2 *The Measurements palette when the **Content** tool and **text** are selected*

3 *The Measurements palette is **blank** when **no** items are selected. Select an item to make the palette light up.*

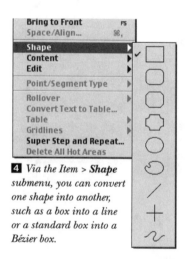

4 *Via the Item > **Shape** submenu, you can convert one shape into another, such as a box into a line or a standard box into a Bézier box.*

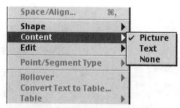

5 *Using the Item > **Content** submenu, you can change a text box into a picture box, or vice versa, or make either one contentless.*

If it's not one thing it's another

Our first encounter with QuarkXPress was in 1988 (ancient history, in the software world), and we were impressed with its precision, but frustrated by the inflexibility of its parent/child architecture. New items were drawn inside—and constrained by—existing items.

Now QuarkXPress is as flexible as it originally was brittle. Not only can you place an item anywhere, you can turn just about anything (text box, text path, picture box, or line) into something else **4**–**5**. If you're brand new to QuarkXPress (or are chronically indecisive), just ignore this aspect of QuarkXPress for the moment. But just to whet your appetite, these are a few of the easy conversions you can make:

- Change a text box into a picture box, a line into a box or a text path, and vice versa.

- Make a text or picture box contentless—capable only of being recolored or resized (the contents of either kind of box are deleted during the conversion).

- Change a standard box into a Bézier box or Bézier line, or vice versa.

- Change a text character into a picture box.

Pet Living

The magazine for Pet Lovers

December 2002

A transparent text box on top of a picture box

SPECIAL HOLIDAY ISSUE
Kibble Snacks for Kwanzaa

Helping your Pet Cope with Holiday Depression

Cat Treats for Chanukah

BOWSER

Type on a Bézier path

A Bézier picture box with a frame

A line

Decorating the Doghouse

Schnauzer Strudel

PLUS

Cake Decorations

The Best Pet Gifts

The QuarkXPress building blocks: **Picture boxes, text boxes, text paths, lines** *(and tables).*

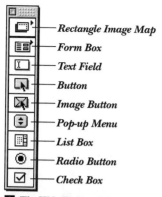

— *Rectangle Image Map*
— *Form Box*
— *Text Field*
— *Button*
— *Image Button*
— *Pop-up Menu*
— *List Box*
— *Radio Button*
— *Check Box*

1 *The Web Tools palette*

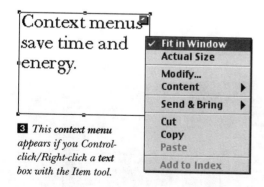

2 *A QuarkXPress Web document page viewed in a browser*

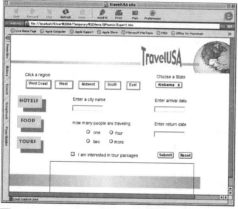

3 *This context menu appears if you Control-click/Right-click a text box with the Item tool.*

Print documents and Web documents 5.0!

The Web features of QuarkXPress 5 **1**–**2** represent a major new addition to the program, and we cover them in Chapters 19 and 24. As you learn how to create print documents, starting with the next chapter, Startup, bear in mind that most, but not all, of the features that are used to create print documents are also available for creating Web documents.

TIP Text features that are not available for Web documents are listed on page 124.

You can build a Web page in QuarkXPress using editable HTML text; rasterized text; pictures; tables; interactive elements, such as image maps and rollovers; buttons; and forms with text entry fields and check boxes. When your Web document is finished, you can preview the page using whichever browser is currently installed in your operating system. In a print document you can create boxes, lines, text paths, and tables; in a Web document, you can create all of the above, plus forms and form controls.

Context menus 5.0!

In QuarkXPress 5, many commands and features can be accessed using context menus, saving you energy and mousing time **3**. The choices on a context menu will vary depending on whether the pointer is over the pasteboard, rulers, a blank area, a picture box, a text box, a text path, a line, a table, or a palette.

In the Mac OS, you have a choice of two preference settings for context menus. Choose Edit > Preferences > Preferences, then click Application–Interactive on the left side of the dialog box. If you click Control Key Activates: Contextual Menu, then all you have to do to open a context menu is Control-click. If you click Control Key Activates: Zoom instead, you'll need to Control-Shift-click to access context menus. In Windows, it's simpler: Just Right-click (no preferences setting).

The QuarkXPress screen: Mac OS

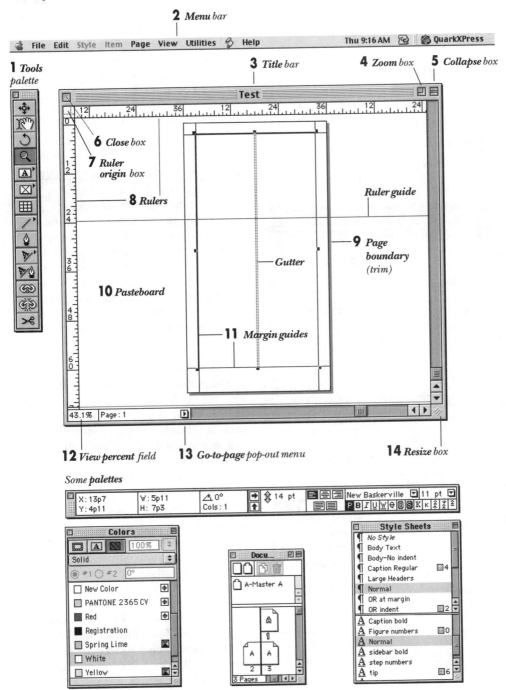

2 *Menu* bar

File   Edit   Style   Item   Page   View   Utilities   Help   Thu 9:16 AM   QuarkXPress

1 *Tools palette*

3 *Title* bar   **4** *Zoom* box   **5** *Collapse* box

Test

6 *Close* box
7 *Ruler origin* box
8 *Rulers*

Ruler guide

9 *Page boundary* (trim)

Gutter

10 *Pasteboard*

11 *Margin guides*

43.1%   Page : 1

12 *View percent* field   **13** *Go-to-page* pop-out menu   **14** *Resize* box

Some palettes

X : 13p7   W : 5p11   △ 0°   14 pt   New Baskerville 11 pt
Y : 4p11   H : 7p3   Cols : 1   P B I U W ⊕ ⊚ S K K

Colors
100%
Solid
#1 #2   0°
New Color
PANTONE 2365 CV
Red
Registration
Spring Lime
White
Yellow

Docu...
A-Master A

A
A   A
2   3
3 Pages

Style Sheets
No Style
Body Text
Body–No indent
Caption Regular   4
Large Headers
Normal
OR at margin
OR indent   2
Caption bold
Figure numbers   0
Normal
sidebar bold
step numbers
tip   6

QuarkXPress Screen (Mac OS)

Key to the QuarkXPress screen

1 *Tools palette*
Most of the palettes are opened from the View menu: Tools (and Web Tools), Measurements, Document Layout, Style Sheets, Colors, Trap Information, Lists, Layers, Profile Information, Hyperlinks, Index, Sequences, and Placeholders. Library palettes are created and opened via the File menu. Many of the commands found under the menu bar can be accessed more quickly from the Measurements palette. Palettes that are open when you quit/exit QuarkXPress will reopen when the application is relaunched.

2 *Menu bar*
Press any menu name to access a list of dialog boxes, pop-up menus, commands, and features. XTensions are also accessed via the menu bar.

3 *Title bar*
A document's name is displayed in its title bar. Drag anywhere in the title bar to move the document window.

4 *Zoom box*
Click the zoom box to enlarge the document window to full-screen size; click it again to restore the window's previous size.

5 *Collapse box*
Click the collapse box to shrink the document window to just its title bar; click it again to retore the window's previous size.

6 *Close box*
Click the close box to close the currently active file.

7 *Ruler origin box*
Drag from the ruler origin box to reposition the intersection of the horizontal and vertical rulers, also known as the zero point. Click the ruler origin box again to reset the zero point to the uppermost left corner of the page.

8 *Rulers*
You can choose inches, inches decimal, picas, points, millimeters, centimeters, ciceros, or agates as the default measurement increment for rulers and entry fields. In a Web document, you can also choose pixels. Choose Show Rulers or Hide Rulers from the View menu. Non-printing guides, which are dragged from the vertical and horizontal rulers, are used for aligning and positioning objects.

9 *Page boundary*
The edge (trim size) of the page.

10 *Pasteboard*
The pasteboard functions as a scratchboard for creating page elements or as a holding area for storing page elements for later use. Web documents don't have a pasteboard.

11 *Margin guides*
The non-printing margin guides are displayed for layout purposes only. Choose Show Guides or Hide Guides from the View menu.

12 *View percent field*
The zoom level of a document is displayed, and can be modified, in this field.

13 *Go-to-page pop-out menu*
Display a document or master page by choosing it from this menu.

14 *Resize box*
Drag the resize box to resize the document window.

The QuarkXPress screen: Windows

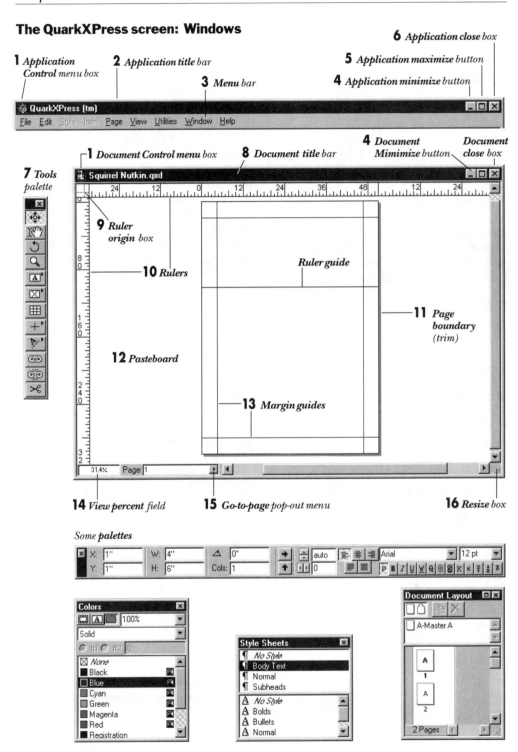

1 *Application Control menu box*

2 *Application title bar*

3 *Menu bar*

6 *Application close box*

5 *Application maximize button*

4 *Application minimize button*

QuarkXPress (tm)

File Edit Style Item Page View Utilities Window Help

1 *Document Control menu box*

8 *Document title bar*

4 *Document Mimimize button*

Document close box

7 *Tools palette*

Squirrel Nutkin.qxd

9 *Ruler origin box*

10 *Rulers*

Ruler guide

11 *Page boundary (trim)*

12 *Pasteboard*

13 *Margin guides*

31.4%   Page: 1

14 *View percent field*

15 *Go-to-page pop-out menu*

16 *Resize box*

Some **palettes**

X: 1"   W: 4"   ⌀ 0°   auto   Arial   12 pt
Y: 1"   H: 6"   Cols: 1   0   P B I U W Q O S K K

Colors   100%

Solid

○ #1 ○ #2 0°

⊠ None
■ Black
□ Blue
■ Cyan
■ Green
■ Magenta
■ Red
■ Registration

Style Sheets

¶ *No Style*
¶ Body Text
¶ Normal
¶ Subheads

A *No Style*
A Bolds
A Bullets
A Normal

Document Layout

A-Master A

A
1

A
2

2 Pages

Key to the QuarkXPress screen

1 *Application (or document) Control menu box*

The application Control menu box commands are: Restore, Move, Size, Minimize, Maximize, and Close. The document Control menu box commands are: Restore, Move, Size, Minimize, Maximize, Close, and Next.

2 *Application title bar*

The application title bar contains the name of the application. If a document is maximized, the document name appears in the application title bar.

3 *Menu bar*

Press any menu name to access dialog boxes, submenus, and commands. XTensions are also accessed via the menu bar.

4 *Application (or document) minimize button*

Click the application minimize button to shrink the application to an icon on the task bar. Click the icon on the task bar to restore the application window to its previous size.

Click the document minimize button to shrink the document to an icon at the bottom left corner of the application window. Click the icon to restore the document window to its previous size.

5 *Application (or document) maximize/ restore button*

Click the application or document restore button to restore a window to its previous size. When a window is at the restored size, the restore button turns into the maximize button. Click the maximize button to enlarge the window.

6 *Close box*

To close the application or a document, dialog box, or palette, click its close box.

7 *Tools palette*

Most of the palettes are opened from the View menu: Tools (and Web Tools), Measurements, Document Layout, Style Sheets, Colors, Trap Information, Lists, Layers, Profile Information, Hyperlinks, Index,

Sequences, and Placeholders. Library palettes are created via File > New > Library.

8 *Document title bar*

The document's title appears here. Drag the title bar to move the document within the application window (this won't work if the document window is maximized).

9 *Ruler origin box*

Drag from the ruler origin box to reposition the intersection of the horizontal and vertical rulers (the "zero point"). Click the ruler origin box again to reset the zero point to the uppermost left corner of the page.

10 *Rulers*

You can choose inches, inches decimal, picas, points, millimeters, centimeters, ciceros, or agates as the default measurement increment for rulers and entry fields. In a Web document, you can also choose pixels. Choose View > Show Rulers or Hide Rulers. Non-printing guides, which are dragged from the vertical and horizontal rulers, are used for aligning and positioning objects.

11 *Page boundary*

The edge (trim size) of the page.

12 *Pasteboard*

The pasteboard functions as a scratchboard for creating page elements or as a holding area for storing page elements for later use. Web documents don't have a pasteboard.

13 *Margin guides*

The non-printing margin guides are displayed for layout purposes only. Choose View > Show Guides or Hide Guides.

14 *View percent field*

The zoom level of a document is displayed, and can be modified, via this field.

15 *Go-to-page pop-out menu*

Display a document or master page by choosing it from this menu.

16 *Resize box*

Drag this box to resize the document window.

QuarkXPress Screen (Windows)

The Tools palette

The Tools palette contains 30 tools, and they are used for item creation and editing.

■ To **open** the Tools palette, choose View > **Show Tools** (F8).

■ **Choose** a visible tool by **clicking** on it; choose a hidden tool from a **pop-out menu**.

■ The default Tools palette is pictured at right, but it can be reconfigured. To **move** a tool from a pop-out menu to the first level of the palette, hold down **Control/Ctrl** as you choose the tool. **Control-click/Ctrl-click** a tool to **restore** it to its pop-out menu. The last-used Tools palette configuration will remain in effect when you re-launch the program.

■ Hold down **Option/Alt** and choose any item creation or linking tool to **keep it selected**. To deselect a tool, click another tool.

■ To set **preferences** for a tool, **double-click** the tool (see page 391), then click Modify.

■ To access the **Item** tool when the Content tool is chosen, hold down **Cmd/Ctrl**.

■ To restore the **default** Tools palette, choose Edit > Preferences > Preferences > Document–Tools, click **Default Tool Palette**, then click OK.

■ If **Show Tools Tips** is checked in Edit > Preferences > Preferences > Application–Interactive, you can rest the pointer on a visible tool or palette button and its name will appear on the screen.

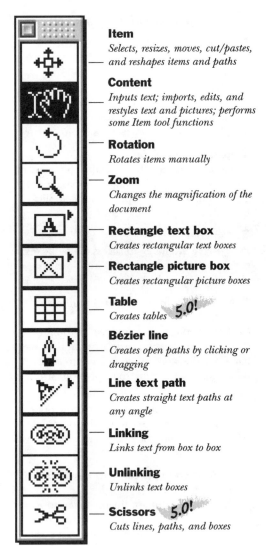

Item
Selects, resizes, moves, cut/pastes, and reshapes items and paths

Content
Inputs text; imports, edits, and restyles text and pictures; performs some Item tool functions

Rotation
Rotates items manually

Zoom
Changes the magnification of the document

Rectangle text box
Creates rectangular text boxes

Rectangle picture box
Creates rectangular picture boxes

Table
Creates tables **5.0!**

Bézier line
Creates open paths by clicking or dragging

Line text path
Creates straight text paths at any angle

Linking
Links text from box to box

Unlinking
Unlinks text boxes

Scissors **5.0!**
Cuts lines, paths, and boxes

Tools Palette

Tools on the default pop-out menus

Text box tools

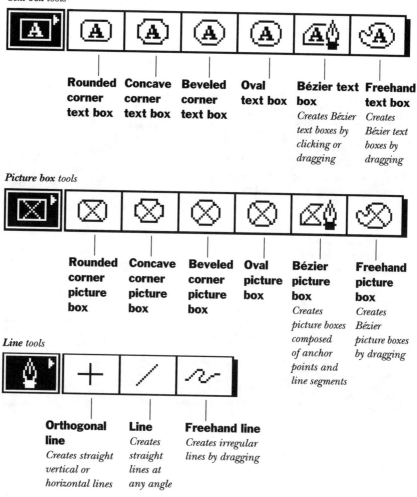

Rounded corner text box	**Concave corner text box**	**Beveled corner text box**	**Oval text box**	**Bézier text box** *Creates Bézier text boxes by clicking or dragging*	**Freehand text box** *Creates Bézier text boxes by dragging*

Picture box tools

Rounded corner picture box	**Concave corner picture box**	**Beveled corner picture box**	**Oval picture box**	**Bézier picture box** *Creates picture boxes composed of anchor points and line segments*	**Freehand picture box** *Creates Bézier picture boxes by dragging*

Line tools

Orthogonal line *Creates straight vertical or horizontal lines*	**Line** *Creates straight lines at any angle*	**Freehand line** *Creates irregular lines by dragging*

Text path tools

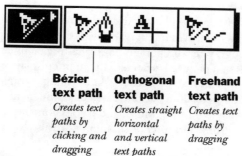

Bézier text path *Creates text paths by clicking and dragging*	**Orthogonal text path** *Creates straight horizontal and vertical text paths*	**Freehand text path** *Creates text paths by dragging*

Tools Palette

The QuarkXPress menus

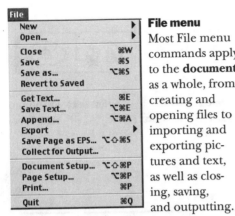

File menu

Most File menu commands apply to the **document** as a whole, from creating and opening files to importing and exporting pictures and text, as well as closing, saving, and outputting.

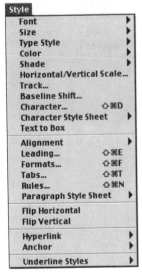

*Note: The **Jabberwocky, Guide Manager, Shape of Things, Super Step and Repeat,** and **Type Tricks** XTensions are available as free downloads from the Quark Web site (see page 26).*

Edit menu

This **workhorse** menu is used for undoing edits; selecting and copying items; replacing text or text attributes; and setting preferences. Style sheets, colors, hyphenation and justification settings, lists, and dashes & stripes are **created** via this menu. Web document commands and free XTensions are located at the bottom of the menu.

*Note: In Windows, there is a **Paste Special** command; **Delete** replaces Clear; and there are no Subscribe commands.*

Text selected

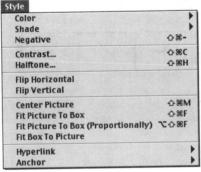

Picture selected

Line selected

Style menu

Style menu commands are used to edit the **contents** of an item. When text is selected, the menu displays typographic and paragraph formatting commands. When a picture is selected, the menu displays picture color, contrast, positioning, and scaling commands. And when a line or table is selected, the menu displays line style, width, and color commands. The Hyperlink and Anchor submenus are also found on this menu.

The Menus

Item menu

The Item menu commands—Modify, Frame, Group, Duplicate, Delete, Lock, Space/Align, etc.—modify **whole items** rather than their contents. These commands are available only when an item is selected. New 5.0 features appear in the lower portion of the menu.

Page menu

Commands on this menu add, delete, renumber, display, and change the margins and column guides for, **pages**.

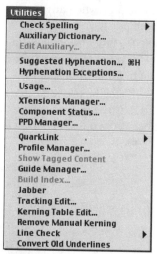

Utilities menu

Utilities menu commands include an assortment of functions, such as spell-checking, hyphenation, picture usage, font usage, tracking and kerning tables, and indexing.

View menu

View menu commands control what you **see** on screen—the zoom level of a document and the display of guides, rulers, invisibles, and palettes.

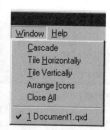

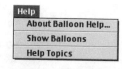

Help menu

This menu provides access to balloon help and Quark's online **help**.

Note: The User Guide is in the form of a PDF file in the Quark 5 > Documents > Guides to Quark XPress folder (not on the Help menu).

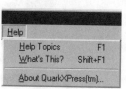

 The Scripts menu is not covered in this QuickStart Guide.

Dialog boxes

Dialog boxes are like fill-in forms with multiple choices. The various methods of indicating one's choices are shown in the illustrations on this page and the next page. Numbers can be typed into fields in any of the measurement units that are used in QuarkXPress. Click OK or press Return/Enter to exit a dialog box and implement the indicated changes.

A dialog box can be opened from a menu or via its assigned keyboard shortcut. A dialog box will open when any menu item that has an ellipsis (…) is chosen.

TIP In any dialog box, press Tab to highlight the next field or press Shift-Tab to highlight the previous field.

TIP For some dialog boxes, you can use the Cmd-Z/Ctrl-Z shortcut while the dialog box is open to restore the last-used values.

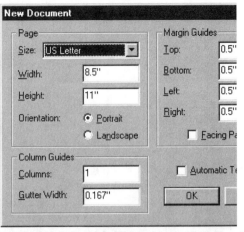

*In Windows, if you press **Alt** + the letter on the keyboard that corresponds to an **underlined letter** in a dialog box, that field will become highlighted. For example, in the dialog box illustrated above, pressing Alt+W would cause the Width field to become highlighted.*

*Double arrowheads open into a **pop-up menu**.*

*To **move** a dialog box, drag its title bar.*

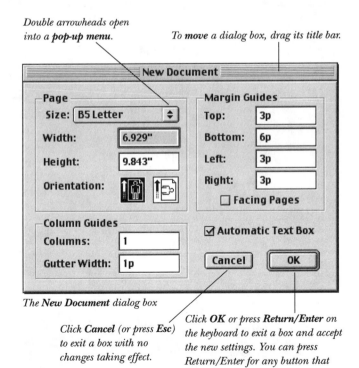

*The **New Document** dialog box*

*Click **Cancel** (or press **Esc**) to exit a box with no changes taking effect.*

*Click **OK** or press **Return/Enter** on the keyboard to exit a box and accept the new settings. You can press Return/Enter for any button that has a double border, such as Save.*

It's all a blank

If the currently selected text or items have different values, the corresponding field will be blank. For example, if highlighted text contains both 8 pt. and 12 pt. leading, the Leading field will be blank (as in the Leading field in the illustration below).

Dialog box panes

Related dialog box panes are housed under one roof. For example, if you choose Item > Modify, at the top of the dialog box you'll see tabs lined up across the top. Click a tab to display that pane. With the Modify dialog box open for a picture, you may see the Box, Picture, Frame, Runaround, Clipping, and OPI tabs. It's like one-stop shopping. Let's say a text box is selected and you choose Item > Modify. You could change the Vertical Alignment for the box in the Text pane, click the Frame tab, choose frame specifications, click the Box tab, and add a background color—all from one central hub.

Click a **tab** *to display a pane.*

A **check box** *option can be clicked on or off.*

Paragraph Attributes

Formats | Tabs | Rules

Left Indent: 2p
First Line: -2p
Right Indent: 0p
Leading:
Space Before: 0p
Space After: 0p
Alignment: Left
H&J: ✓ Standard Subheads

☑ Drop Caps
Character Count: 1
Line Count: 3

☑ Keep Lines Together
⦿ All Lines in ¶
◯ Start: 2 End: 2

☐ Keep with Next ¶
☐ Lock to Baseline Grid

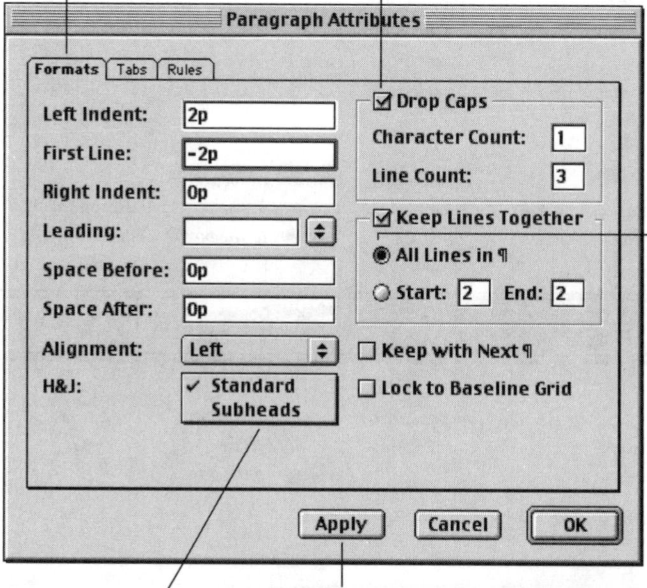

A radio **button** *can be clicked on or off. Only one button can be selected at a time in a related group.*

Apply | Cancel | OK

Press/click to choose from a **pop-up** *menu.*

Click **Apply** *(or press* **Cmd-A** *in the Mac OS) to preview modifications in the document with the dialog box open. Option-click/Alt-click Apply (or press* **Alt-A** *in Windows) to turn continuous Apply mode on or off. Press* **Tab** *to execute a change while a dialog box is open.*

The QuarkXPress palettes

The Measurements palette

The Measurements palette contains some of the same commands and options that are available under the menus. The options on the Measurements palette change depending on what kind of item and tool are selected in your document. The palette is blank when nothing is selected.

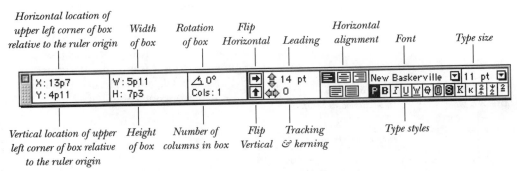

*The Measurements palette with the **Content** tool and a **text box** selected*

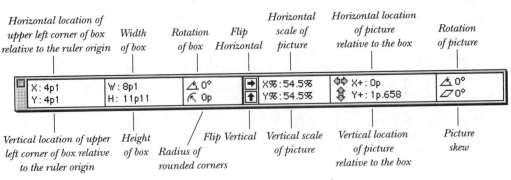

*The Measurements palette with the **Content** tool and a **picture box** selected*

Measurements palette shortcuts

Show/hide the palette	F9
Highlight the first field	Cmd-Option-M/Ctrl-Alt-M
Highlight Font field	Cmd-Option-Shift-M/Ctrl-Alt-Shift-M
Highlight next field	Tab
Highlight previous field	Shift-Tab
Exit palette without applying changes	Cmd. (period) or Esc

Measurements Palette (side tab)

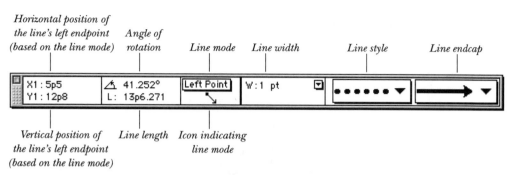

Horizontal position of the line's left endpoint (based on the line mode)

Angle of rotation

Line mode

Line width

Line style

Line endcap

Vertical position of the line's left endpoint (based on the line mode)

Line length

Icon indicating line mode

*The Measurements palette with the **Content** tool and a straight **line** selected*

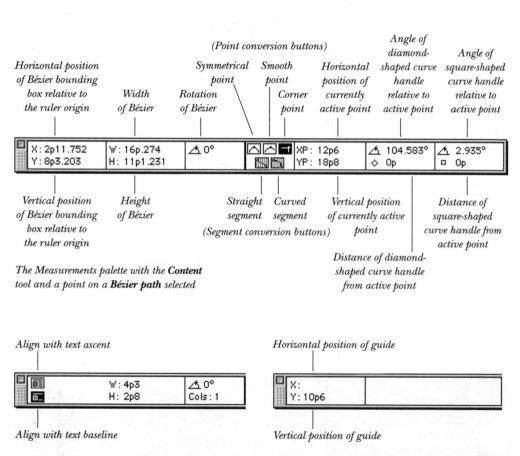

Horizontal position of Bézier bounding box relative to the ruler origin

Width of Bézier

Rotation of Bézier

(Point conversion buttons)

Symmetrical point

Smooth point

Corner point

Horizontal position of currently active point

Angle of diamond-shaped curve handle relative to active point

Angle of square-shaped curve handle relative to active point

Vertical position of Bézier bounding box relative to the ruler origin

Height of Bézier

Straight segment

Curved segment

(Segment conversion buttons)

Vertical position of currently active point

Distance of diamond-shaped curve handle from active point

Distance of square-shaped curve handle from active point

*The Measurements palette with the **Content** tool and a point on a **Bézier path** selected*

Align with text ascent

Align with text baseline

*The left side of the Measurements palette with the **Content** tool and an **anchored box** selected*

Horizontal position of guide

Vertical position of guide

*The left side of the Measurements palette while a **guide** is being dragged downward from the horizontal ruler*

Measurements Palette

The Document Layout palette

The Document Layout palette is used to rearrange, insert, and delete document pages; move through a document; and create, modify, and apply master pages.

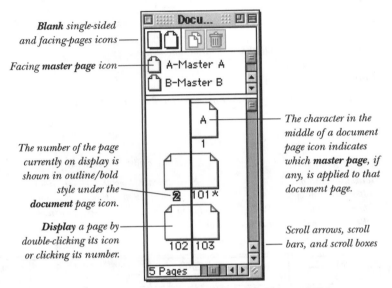

Blank *single-sided and facing-pages icons*

Facing **master page** *icon*

The number of the page currently on display is shown in outline/bold style under the **document** *page icon.*

Display *a page by double-clicking its icon or clicking its number.*

The character in the middle of a document page icon indicates which **master page**, *if any, is applied to that document page.*

Scroll arrows, scroll bars, and scroll boxes

The Style Sheets palette

The Style Sheets palette is used to apply style sheets, which are sets of character and paragraph specifications.

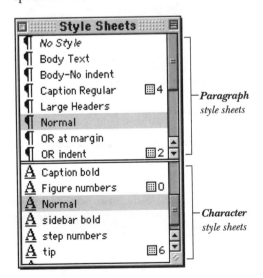

Paragraph style sheets

Character style sheets

The Colors palette

The Colors palette is used to apply process, spot, and Web-safe colors to text, pictures, boxes, lines, and tables.

Frame Text Background Tint *percentage*

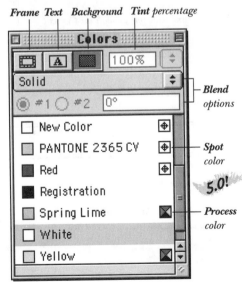

Blend *options*

Spot *color*

Process *color*

5.0!

The Trap Information palette

The Trap Information palette is used to
assign trapping specifications to individual
objects.

*Pop-up menus for
choosing the **trap
type** for each compo-
nent of the currently
selected item*

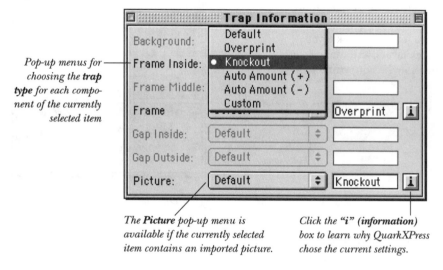

*The **Picture** pop-up menu is
available if the currently selected
item contains an imported picture.*

*Click the "i" (**information**)
box to learn why QuarkXPress
chose the current settings.*

The Lists palette

The Lists palette is used to build a table
of contents or an alphabetized list of
headings for the current document or
for multiple chapter files in a book.

*Choose to **Show
List For** a single
document (current
document) or a book.*

*The **List Name***

*Find a word in the
list scroll window.*

*The list **previews** in
the **scroll window.***

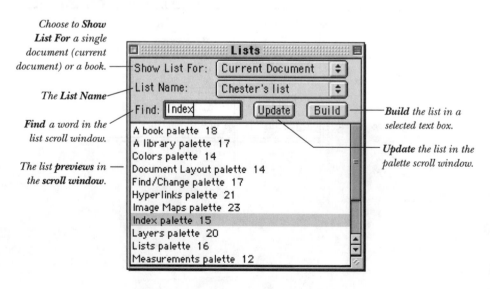

*Build the list in a
selected text box.*

*Update the list in the
palette scroll window.*

The Layers palette

The Layers palette allows you to organize objects in a document according to their front-to-back stacking order. Using this palette, you can create new layers, move an item to a different layer, merge two or more layers together, restack layers, delete layers, lock layers, and make layers temporarily invisible or nonprintable.

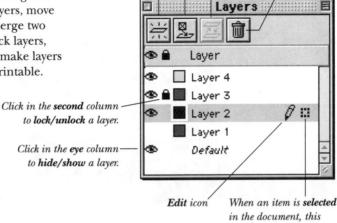

New Layer | *Move Item to Layer* | *Merge Layers* | *Delete Layer*

*Click in the **second** column to **lock/unlock** a layer.*

*Click in the **eye** column to **hide/show** a layer.*

Edit icon

*When an item is **selected** in the document, this indicator shows which layer the object is on.*

The Profile Information palette

The Profile Information palette is used to display the current characteristics of a selected picture and to change its color profile or rendering intent for color management.

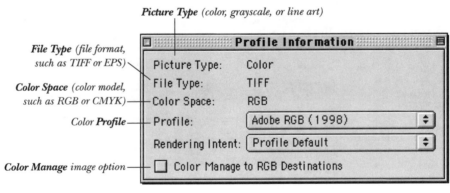

Picture Type (color, grayscale, or line art)

File Type (file format, such as TIFF or EPS)

Color Space (color model, such as RGB or CMYK)

*Color **Profile***

Color Manage image option

The Index palette

An index is constructed by marking each
individual entry for indexing in the actual
document, and then using the Index
palette to assign formatting specifications
for how each entry will appear in the index,
such as its style and level of indentation.

*The **Text** that is currently selected in the document*

*The **Sort As** field for changing an entry's alphabetical location in the index*

*The entry's **Level** (of indent)*

*The **Style** sheet for the entry's page (or "see") reference*

*The **Scope** (range) in the document within which other instances will be searched for*

Arrow designating which index entry the current entry will be indented under (for a second, third, or fourth indent level)

A page reference

A second level (indented) entry

Edit entry

Delete entry

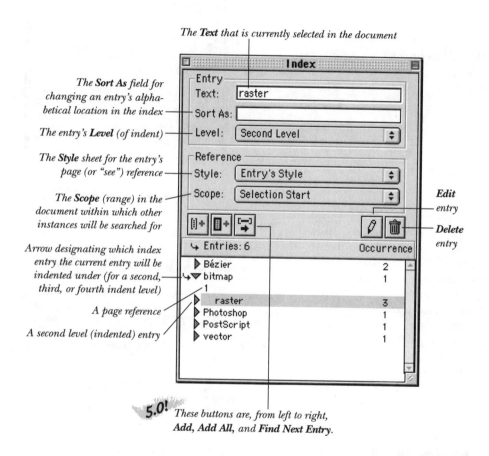

5.0! *These buttons are, from left to right,* ***Add, Add All,*** *and* ***Find Next Entry.***

The Hyperlinks palette 5.0!

Hyperlinks ("links," for short) are the graphic devices that Web designers use to help users navigate to other Web pages. Links range from simple underlined words to image maps and rollovers. In QuarkXPress, the Hyperlinks palette is used to assign a link to highlighted text, an image map area, a picture box, or other selected item. Links are only interactive when viewed in a browser. Hyperlinks can also be assigned to text in a non-Web document to be exported as a PDF file.

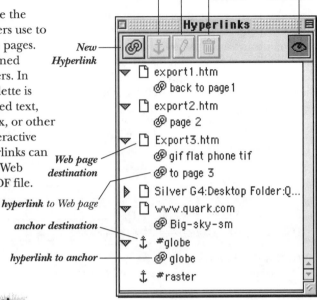

New Anchor   *Edit*   *Delete*   *Show/Hide*

New Hyperlink

Web page destination

hyperlink to Web page

anchor destination

hyperlink to anchor

The Placeholders palette 5.0!

In QuarkXPress, placeholders are used to style XML element content. To start with, a QuarkXPress template is created, and blank text boxes are created in the template. Next, an XML file is opened via the Placeholders palette; the hierarchical outline of the XML elements is displayed on the palette. Element names are then dragged from the Placeholders palette into each text box in the Quark-XPress file, and each placeholder name in the template is styled via a style sheet.

Next, an XML file with matching elements is opened using the Placeholders palette. Each XML element matches a placeholder of the same name and acquires style sheet attributes from that placeholder. To preview the XML content that will be substituted for the placeholders, the Toggle Placeholders/Content button is clicked. Finally, to style the XML file, the Convert placeholders to Text button is clicked. For more information about placeholders, see the QuarkXPress documentation.

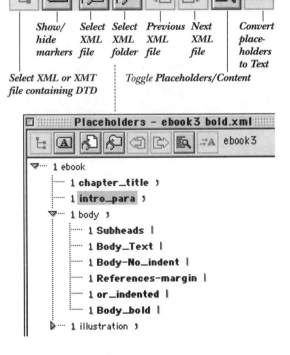

Placeholders palette buttons

Show/hide markers   *Select XML file*   *Select XML folder*   *Previous XML file*   *Next XML file*   *Convert placeholders to Text*

Select XML or XMT file containing DTD   *Toggle Placeholders/Content*

The XML Workspace palette 5.0!

XML is a system that allows text and picture content to be categorized in order to provide greater flexibility when outputting to the Web or print. First each basic element within XML (e.g., field of text or data) is assigned its own name and given a heirarchical relationship to other elements in the XML file. Then the contents (items or paragraphs) of a Quark-XPress file are tagged to various XML elements. This is done by dragging item boxes onto elements on the XML Tree on the XML Workspace palette. This palette is also used to define and view XML elements and their content, and also to preview the actual code in the XML file.

*The **XML Tree** is a list of the elements used in the current XML fle.*

XML Workspace palette buttons

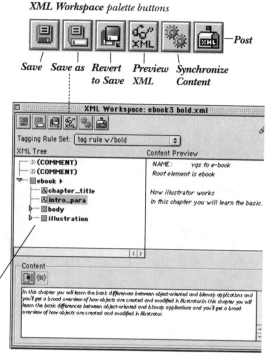

Save   Save as   Revert to Save   Preview XML   Synchronize Content   Post

The Sequences palette 5.0!

The Sequences palette is used to make a list of items in a QuarkXPress document, known as a sequence. If a sequence is dragged from the Sequence palette onto the topmost element on the XML Workspace palette, the content from those items is tagged automatically to the appropriate XML elements.

New Sequence

Sequence list

Document items

Add Item   Go To   Move Down   Synchronize Content

Edit Name   Move Up   Delete

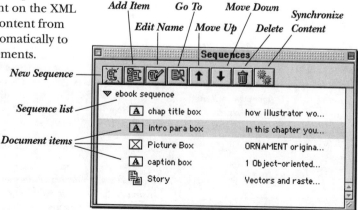

The Find/Change palette

The Find/Change palette is used to search for and replace text characters, paragraph- or character-based style sheets, fonts, point sizes, type styles, or colors.

*The text, style sheets, and attributes to be searched for are entered or chosen in the **Find What** area.*

*The text, style sheets, and attributes to be changed to are entered or chosen in the **Change To** area.*

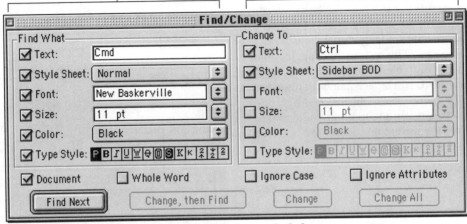

*This is the Find/Change palette when **Ignore Attributes** is **unchecked**.*

A book palette

A book is a collection of individual chapter files in which style sheets, colors, H&Js (settings for hyphenation and justification), lists, and dashes & stripes are synchronized. Each book has its own book palette that's used to add, delete, print, and change the order of chapters.

Move chapter down

Synchronize book button for synchronizing style sheets, colors, H&Js, lists, and dashes & stripes between the master file and chapter files

Print chapter

Remove chapter

Move chapter up

Add chapter

The master file from which all the style sheets, colors, etc. are derived

M	Document	Pages	Status
M	.:master vqs 2	1	**Available**
	.:toc book vqs 2	i*–iii*	Available
	.:1 How Illus Works	1*–8*	Available
	.:2 STARTUP	9–16	Open
	.:3 VIEWS	17–24	Available
	.:4 OBJECTS BASICS	25–34	Available

*The **Status** column indicates whether a chapter is **Available, Modified,** or **Missing** and also tells members on a network whether a chapter is **Open** at the current station or open on **another station**.*

A library palette

Library palettes are used to store any item or group of items: picture boxes (with or without pictures), text boxes (with or without text), lines, text paths, or tables. To add an item to a library, simply drag it into the palette. To retrieve an item (or group) from a library, drag it from the library into your document window. You can create an unlimited number of library palettes, and more than one library palette can be open at a time.

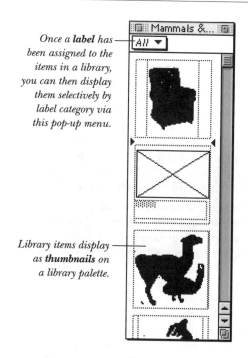

*Once a **label** has been assigned to the items in a library, you can then display them selectively by label category via this pop-up menu.*

*Library items display as **thumbnails** on a library palette.*

Your own redoing

If you're nervous about making mistakes, relax. You will never (okay, rarely) have to retrace your steps if you take advantage of all the safety mechanisms QuarkXPress has to offer. Your computer has a memory, and you can rely on it.

In most cases, the last maneuver you performed can be undone using Edit > **Undo** (Cmd-Z/Ctrl-Z). Unfortunately, QuarkXPress doesn't offer multiple undos, so you have to use the command right away. If you change your mind again, choose Edit > **Redo** (Cmd-Z/Ctrl-Z—the same shortcut).

Get in the habit of **saving** after every couple of moves (see pages 32–34). For some reason, beginning "Quarkers" are often reluctant to use this command (or are too absorbed with other tasks) and end up learning the hard way. Having learned a few hard lessons ourselves, we now save

constantly, and we make a special point of saving before we perform any complicated maneuvers. Then, if we make the inevitable multiple-step blunder, we choose File > **Revert to Saved** to get back to the last-saved version of the document.

The undo shortcut (Cmd-Z/Ctrl-Z) can also be used to **restore** the last-used settings in an open dialog box. To cancel out of a dialog box altogether without applying any values, click **Cancel** (Cmd-./Ctrl-.).

QuarkXPress has two features for backing up a whole document: **Auto Save** and **Auto Backup**. Read about these features on page 383.

And finally, if you're working on a complicated object, you can **duplicate** it (Item > Duplicate or Cmd-D/Ctrl-D) and set the copy aside for safekeeping (put it on the pasteboard). Then later you can compliment yourself on your great foresight.

XTending XPress with XTensions

What is an XTension?

QuarkXPress doesn't do everything. In fact, one of its great selling features is that third-party developers have written hundreds of add-on software modules for the program, called XTensions, that extend or enhance its features. XTensions can do everything from a simple object alignment to catalogue databasing, and they range in price from petty cash to hundreds of dollars.

XTensions are mentioned occasionally in this book, but with hundreds of choices out there, it's obviously just a small sampling (and some XTensions may not be available or may have changed after this book was printed*). Make sure the XTension you're using is optimized for QuarkXPress version 5. To get info about an XTension that is already installed, choose Utilities > XTensions Manager, click the XTension name, then click About.

Where should I install them?

In order to use an XTension, it has to be installed in the XTension folder inside the QuarkXPress application folder. Some XTensions come with an installer that will do the job for you; others must be copied manually into the XTension folder. If an installer places an XTension in the QuarkXPress folder but not in the XTension folder, make sure to drag it into the XTension folder yourself.

Once an XTension has been correctly installed on your hard drive, you can use the XTensions Manager feature within the application to enable or disable it (see pages 393–395). In order to use a newly enabled XTension, you must re-launch QuarkXPress.

In Edit > Preferences > Preferences > Application–XTensions Manager, you can specify whether or not the XTensions Manager will open each time QuarkXPress is launched (see page 384).

Shopping for XTensions

Some XTensions are sold individually, while others are sold in a bundle, such as XPert Tools and Xdream. Luckily, most XTensions are available in a demo version so you can try them out before you invest.

For a **directory** of XTensions, visit the Quark Web site: **www.quark.com**. Individual developer names and contact numbers are listed for each XTension. To see a list of distributors, including international distributors, click XTensions Catalog (on the right side of the screen, at least as of this writing), then click Resource Locator: Where to Buy. You can also download **free** XTensions from this site, such as **Shape of Things** for creating star-shaped boxes, so it's worth a visit for that alone. Other free XTensions that are available for downloading include Jabberwocky, Guide Manager, Super Step and Repeat, and Type Tricks.

If you'd rather shop from a distributor who sells XTensions from an assortment of developers, try **www.thepowerxchange.com** (click QuarkXPress at the top of their home page).

Ask whichever manufacturer or distributor you purchase your XTensions from what their upgrade policy is and what technical support they offer, if any.

And while you're at it, check out this site for tips and resources: **www.xpressobar.com** (it's not related to Quark, Inc.).

At the time of this writing, 5.0-compatible versions of the XTensions weren't yet available, so some of our information about specific XTensions may be inaccurate or out-of-date. The purpose of our mentioning individual XTensions is to give you a taste of what's available, not to make an endorsement.

XTensions

Abbreviations

Inches	in *or* "
Inches Decimal	in *or* " with a decimal
Picas	p
Points	pt *or* p followed by a number (as in "p6")
Millimeters	mm
Centimeters	cm
Ciceros	c
Agates	ag
quarter of a millimiter	q
Pixels	px

Note: Pixels cannot be chosen in a print document, but "px" can be used in entry fields in a print document.

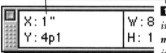

1 *Enter a number in any **measurement unit** used in QuarkXPress.*

2 *When Return/Enter is pressed, the value is converted into the currently chosen **default** measurement units.*

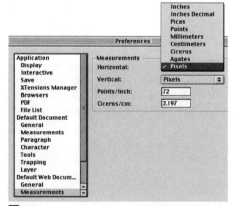

3 *Measurement units for a **Default Web Document***

Measurement units

With a few exceptions, values in palettes and dialog boxes display in the current default horizontal or vertical measurement unit. To choose new default measurement units for all future documents, make sure no documents are open; or leave a document open to change the units for that document only. Go to Edit > Preferences > Preferences, click Measurements under Document or Web Document, then under Horizontal and/or Vertical, choose **Inches, Inches Decimal, Picas, Points, Millimeters, Centimeters, Ciceros**, or **Agates** **1**–**2**. For a Web document, you can also choose **Pixels**. Web and print documents can have different default measurement units **3**.

To enter a value in a non-default measurement unit, you must use the proper abbreviation (see the sidebar at left). For example, you can use "pt" or "p" for points, but not "pts". Agates, in case you're wondering, are used to measure vertical column lengths in classified ads.

Picas and points

A pica is the standard unit of measure used in the graphic arts. Six picas equals 1 inch; 1 pica equals 12 points. Picas and points can be combined in the same entry field. For example, to indicate four picas and six points, you would enter "4p6."

Regardless of the current measurement units, points are always used to measure type sizes, leading, rule widths, frame widths, and line widths.

Using math in a field

To **add**, enter + after the current number, then the amount you want to add. To **subtract**, enter -, then the value you want to subtract. To **multiply**, enter *, then the multiplier. To **divide**, enter /, then the divider. (To divide 38 by 3, for example, you would enter "38/3".) In each case, press Return/Enter to execute the math.

Measurement Units

Preferences (a sneak preview)

Preferences are the default settings that can be chosen for an individual document or for the application as a whole. Chapter 22 is devoted entirely to the Preferences dialog boxes, and some preferences are discussed in individual chapters, where relevant. As you learn QuarkXPress, you may change a preferences setting here or there, and thus gradually familiarize yourself with them. Below is a list of some of the settings that can be changed.

TIP Turn on Runaround and/or define a frame for one of the picture box tools, and turn those settings off for a second picture box tool—then you'll have one of each. Change the Corner Radius to zero if you want to create a second rectangular box tool.

A partial listing of preferences

- Margin, ruler, or grid guide colors
- Preview resolution for imported pictures
- Scroll speed
- Smart quotes options
- Drag-and-drop text on or off
- Pasteboard width
- Auto save and auto backup options
- Auto library save on or off
- Save document position on or off
- Show XTensions Manager options
- Measurement units for rulers, dialog boxes, and Measurements palette
- Auto page insertion options
- Guides in front or behind
- Auto picture import options
- Keep or delete master page items

Other kinds of defaults

If you add, delete, or edit **style sheets** (including the Normal style sheet), **colors**, **hyphenation exceptions**, **H&Js** (settings for hyphenation and justification), or an **auxiliary dictionary** when no documents are open, those specifications will become the new defaults for any subsequently created documents.

The same holds true for any **Document Preferences** that you change while no document is open, such as Measurement units, Auto Page Insertion, or Auto Picture Import on or off. Preferences are chosen in Edit > Preferences. Take the time to set up document defaults this way—it will save you oodles of time later!

- Live Refresh on or off
- Baseline grid increment
- Hyphenation method
- Auto kerning value
- Flex space width
- Ligatures options
- Text inset, runaround, line width, etc.
- Trapping options
- Tool preferences, including style, width, color, shade, and Runaround settings for the Line or text path tools; background color, angle, frame, and Runaround settings for the picture box or Bézier tools; background color, number of columns, frame, and Runaround for the text box tools; and the Zoom percentage for each click of the Zoom tool.

Startup 2

1 *In the Mac OS: Click the QuarkXPress application icon on the Launcher...*

2 *...or double-click any QuarkXPress file icon to launch the application and open that file simultaneously.*

3 *Once QuarkXPress is launched, you can switch back to the program via a tear-away representation of the Applications menu.*

4 *Click QuarkXPress 5.0 on the Start menu...*

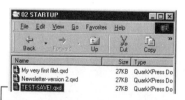

5 *...or double-click any QuarkXPress file icon to launch the application and open that file simultaneously.*

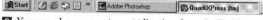

6 *You can choose any open application from the Taskbar.*

To launch QuarkXPress in the Mac OS:

Click the QuarkXPress application icon on the Launcher **1**.

or

Open the QuarkXPress folder in the Finder, then double-click the diamond-shaped QuarkXPress application icon.

or

Double-click any existing QuarkXPress file icon on the Finder desktop (the program will launch automatically) **2**.

TIP If you activate the Finder desktop by clicking on it—whether intentionally or not—and you want to get back into QuarkXPress, click in any open QuarkXPress document window; or click the application icon on the Launcher; or click the application icon on a tear-away Application menu (drag from the Application menu in the upper right-hand corner of your screen to create a tear-away menu) **3**.

To launch QuarkXPress in Windows:

In Windows 98 or 2000, click the Start button on the Taskbar **4**, choose Programs, choose QuarkXPress, then click Quark-XPress 5.0.

or

In Windows Explorer, double-click a QuarkXPress file icon. The application will launch and that file will be maximized on screen **5**.

TIP Once QuarkXPress is running, you can choose it (or any other open application) from the Taskbar at the bottom of the screen **6**.

Launch QuarkXPress

To create a new file:

1. Launch QuarkXPress (instructions on previous page).

2. Choose File > New > Document (Cmd-N/Ctrl-N). (*Don't* choose File > Open—that command opens existing, already saved files.)

Change any of the following settings (press Tab to move from one field to the next):

3. Choose a preset size from the **Size** pop-up menu (**1**, next page).
   or
   Enter numbers in the **Width** and **Height** fields to create a custom-size document. (This is the document size, not the paper size, and it can be changed later.) You can enter values in any measurement unit used in QuarkXPress.

4. *Optional:* Click the un-highlighted Orientation icon to swap the document's width and height values.

5. Change any of the **Margin Guides**. If you check **Facing Pages**, the Left and Right Margin Guides fields will convert to Inside and Outside and document pages will be stacked in pairs.

6. Change the number of **Columns**. If the number of columns is greater than 1, change the **Gutter Width**. Try 1p or 1p6.

7. *Optional:* Check **Automatic Text Box** to have a text box appear automatically within the margin guides on master page A and on every document page with which master page A is associated (see Chapter 14, *Master Pages*). This is used for multi-page files.

8. Double-check that you're satisfied with the current settings. Your choices aren't irrevocable, but it's easier to change them now than it is to fix them later. Click OK. A new, untitled document will appear on your screen.

TIP The last used settings in the New Document dialog box will reappear next time it's opened.

Pre-defined pagesets

You can avoid having to reenter New Document values using the **Xpert PageSets** XTension, which is part of Volume 2 of the XPert Tools toolkit from a lowly apprentice production, inc. Using this XTension, you create document setup styles, called pagesets, that contain page dimensions, margins, columns, and other specifications. Any pagesets you have created will appear on, and can be chosen from, a menu in the New Document dialog box.

(sidebar) Create a New File

Choose a preset **Page Size** or enter a number between 1" and 48" in the **Width** and **Height** fields. A4 Letter is 210 mm x 297 mm, B5 Letter is 182 mm x 257 mm, and Tabloid is 11" x 17". Numbers can be entered in any measurement unit used in QuarkXPress.

Margin Guides don't print, but they're useful in the layout process. The **Left** and **Right** fields convert to **Inside** and **Outside** when Facing Pages is turned on.

Click the portrait or landscape **Orientation** icon.

Enter a number between 1 and 30 in the **Columns** field.

If the number of columns is greater than 1, enter a **Gutter Width** between 3 and 288 points (4").

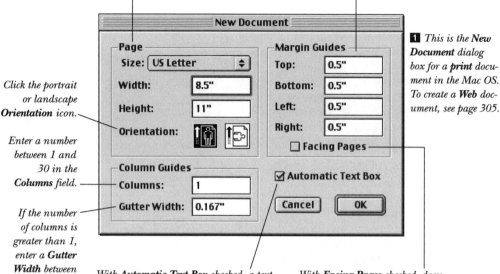

1 *This is the* **New Document** *dialog box for a* **print** *document in the Mac OS. To create a* **Web** *document, see page 305.*

With **Automatic Text Box** checked, a text box containing the number of columns and gutter width specified in the Column Guides fields will appear on the default master page A and on any document pages that are associated with that master.

With **Facing Pages** checked, document page 1 will appear by itself on the right-hand side and any additional pages will be stacked below it in pairs. The Facing Pages format is used for books and magazines.

Margin   Column   Gutter

First of all he said to himself: "That buzzing-noise means something. You don't get a buzzing-noise like that, just buzzing and buzzing, without its meaning something. If there's a buzzing-

noise, somebody's making a buzzing-noise, and the only reason for making a buzzing-noise that I know of is because you're a bee.

Then he thought another long time, and said: "And the

only reason for being a bee that I know of is making honey."

And then he got up, and said: "And the only reason for making honey is so I can eat it." So he began to climb the tree.   *A.A. Milne*

If your file has never been saved, ever, these are the instructions for you. To resave an already saved file, see page 34.

To save an unsaved file:

1. Choose File > Save (Cmd-S/Ctrl-S).

2. Type a name for the document. In the Mac OS, the "Save current document as" field will highlight automatically **1**.

3. To create a print document, in the Mac OS: Choose Type: Document. In Windows: Choose Save as type: Document (*.qxd). To create a Web document, see page 305. To create a template, see page 35.

4. Choose a location for the file:

In the Mac OS: Click Desktop, choose a drive from the scroll list, then click Open. Make sure the drive or folder into which you have chosen to save the document appears on the pop-up menu at the top of the dialog box **2**. *Optional:* To create a new folder for the document in the location you have chosen, click New, enter a name, then click Create.

1 *Type a* ***name*** *for the new file.*

Faster save 5.0!

If you tend to Save or Save As over and over to the same folder, you can make that folder appear automatically as the location for saving by choosing it in Edit menu > Preferences > **Default Path Preferences** (see page 402). You can also choose a default path for the Open, Get Text, or Get Picture dialog box. Every little bit helps.

2 *Make sure the name of the drive or* ***folder*** *into which you have chosen to save the document appears here.*

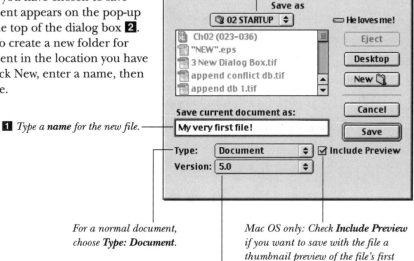

For a normal document, choose ***Type: Document***.

Leave the ***Version*** *setting on* ***5.0*** *unless you need to save to an earlier version.*

Mac OS only: Check ***Include Preview*** *if you want to save with the file a thumbnail preview of the file's first page for display in the Open dialog box.*

Save an Unsaved File

1 *Make sure the name of the drive or folder into which you have chosen to save the document is displayed in the* **Save in** *field.*

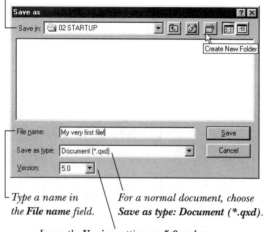

Type a name in the **File name** *field.*

For a normal document, choose **Save as type: Document (*.qxd)**.

Leave the **Version** *setting on* **5.0** *unless you need to save to an earlier version.*

2 *In the Mac OS: Check* **Preview** *to see a thumbnail of the first page of your document in the* **Open** *dialog box. In order to see a preview, a file has to be saved with* **Include Preview** *checked.*

In Windows: Use the Up One Level button and the Folder List arrow to navigate to the desired location. Make sure the drive or folder into which you have chosen to save the file appears in the Save In field **1**. *Optional:* To create a new folder for the file in the location you have chosen, click the Create New Folder button, type a name for the new folder, then double-click the new folder to open it.

5. *Optional in the Mac OS:* Check the Include Preview box to have a thumbnail of the first page of the document display when you reopen the document using File > Open (check the Preview box in the Open dialog box to display the preview) **2**. If you forget to check the Include Preview box here, you can add the preview later using Save As (see page 34).

6. Click Save (Return/Enter).

Save an Unsaved File

Save frequently! We save almost every time we make a change—it's like an automatic reflex. *Note:* In addition to manual saving, you may also want to use the Auto Save feature, too (see the sidebar).

To resave a file:

Choose File > Save (Cmd-S/Ctrl-S). The Save command will be dimmed if no modifications were made to the file since it was last saved.

The Save As command creates a copy of a document under a different name. We usually use it when we want to create a variation of an existing document. And occasionally, if we have a file that seems corrupted (e.g., it won't let us save), we'll try a Save As on it—sometimes that does the trick. This command also can be used to downsave a document to QuarkXPress version 4.0 (for print documents only).

To save a new version of a file:

1. Open the file to be duplicated.

2. Choose File > Save As (Cmd-Option-S/ Ctrl-Alt-S).

3. Change the name in the Save current document as field (Mac OS) **1**/ File name field (Win) **2**.

4. *Optional in the Mac OS:* Check Include Preview to have a thumbnail of the first page of the document display in the Open dialog box.

5. *Optional:* To downsave the document, choose Version: 4.0.

6. Choose a location in which to save the duplicate file.

7. Click Save. The **new** version of the document will remain **open**; the **original** version of the document will **close**.

TIP If you don't change the file name in the Save as dialog box, a warning prompt will appear when you click Save. Click Replace to save over the original file or click Cancel.

Auto save or auto backup?

Auto Save is like power or system failure insurance—when you reboot, you'll be able to rescue the last mini-saved version of your document. The **Auto Backup** feature creates multiple backups of a file. Both features are discusssed on page 383.

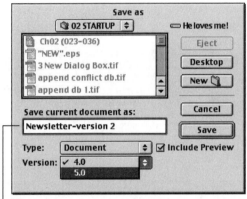

1 *In the Mac OS, enter a different **name** for the duplicate file or alter the existing name, then click **Save**.*

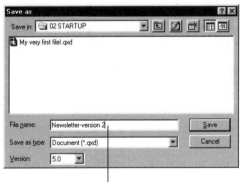

2 *In Windows, type a different **file name** for the duplicate file or modify the existing name, then click **Save**.*

Resave; Save New Version

Lock it another way

In the Mac OS, to prevent any type of file from being overwritten or renamed, highlight its icon in the Finder, choose File > **Get Info** > General Information > Cmd-I/Ctrl-I), then check **Locked**. If you check **Stationery Pad** instead, a copy of the file will open when you try to open it and the original will remain closed.

To do the same thing in Windows, select a file in Windows Explorer, Right-click its icon so the content menu appears, choose **Properties**, make sure the **Read-only** attribute is checked, then click OK to close the Properties dialog box.

1 *Mac OS: Double-click the file name you want to* **open**.

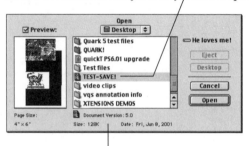

The file's QuarkXPress **version** *number,* **storage size**, *and* **date** *it was last modified.*

Click the **Details** *button to* **2** *Windows: Double-click the* *see the file type, storage size,* *file name you want to* **open**. *and date it was last modified.*

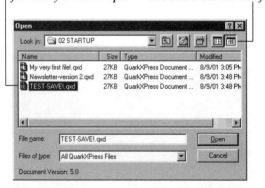

The point of creating a template is to preserve a version of a document that contains master page items, style sheets, custom colors, H&J settings, etc.—any item or any layout you'll want to reuse in subsequent versions.

To create a template:

1. Choose File > Save or Save As.

2. In the Mac OS, choose Type: Template. In Windows, choose Save as type: Template (*.qxt). For a Web document, choose Web Template/Web template (*.qwt).

3. To create a normal document from the template, open the file, choose File > Save (the Save As dialog box will open automatically), enter a name for the non-template version, then click Save.

TIP To edit the template itself, open it, edit it, choose File > Save, reenter the **exact same name** of the template, choose its **current location**, click Save, then click Replace/Yes when the prompt appears.

To open a QuarkXPress file from within the application:

1. Choose File > Open (Cmd-O/Ctrl-O).

2. Locate and double-click a file name **1**–**2**.
   or
   Click a file name once (Mac OS only: Check Preview to display a thumbnail of the first page of the document), then click Open. The number of QuarkXPress files that can be open at a time is limited only by available memory.

   Note: Be sure to read "Things that may happen when a file is opened," starting on page 37.

Template; Open a File

If you're going to reopen a recently opened and saved file, instead of going all the way back to the Open or Save dialog box, you can choose one of those files from the File menu.

To reopen a recently opened and saved file:

Choose from a list of files on the File > Open submenu or at the bottom of the File menu ■. The location of the list will depend on the current File List Preferences setting (see below). Books, templates, and XML documents will not appear on the menu or submenu.

To choose File List preferences:

1. Choose Edit > Preferences > Preferences (Cmd-Y/Ctrl-Y).

2. Click Application–File List on the list on the left side of the dialog box ■.

3. Do any of the following:

   Enter the maximum Number of Files (3–9) that you want to appear on the File menu.

   Click Append Files to File Menu to have file names appear at the bottom of the File menu or click Append Files to Open Menu Item to have file names appear on the File menu > Open submenu.

   Check Alphabetize Names to have file names appear in alphabetical order. With this option unchecked, names will appear in the order in which they were opened or saved.

   Check Show Full Paths to have the file location (disk and folder) be listed next to the file name.

4. Click OK.

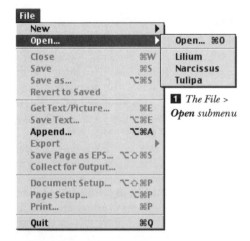

■ *The File > Open submenu*

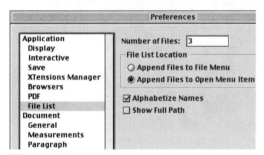

2 *In **File List** Preferences, you can specify where, in what format, and how many file names may appear on the File menu.*

Downsaving

If you downsave a QuarkXPress 5.0 file back to 4.0, some document elements that were created using 5.0 features (e.g., tables, layers, and multiple text insets) will **revert** back to their 4.0 equivalents. You won't see these changes until you close and then reopen the file.

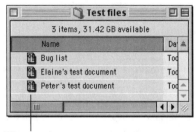

1 *Mac OS: Open a QuarkXPress file from the Finder by double-clicking its icon.*

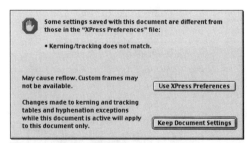

2 **Windows Explorer**: *Double-click the file you want to open.*

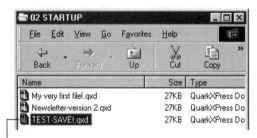

3 *The XPress Preferences prompt*

To open a QuarkXPress file from the Finder/Windows Explorer:

In the Mac OS: Double-click a file icon **1** or drag a QuarkXPress file icon over the application icon on either the Launcher or a tear-away application menu.

In Windows Explorer: Double-click a QuarkXPress file icon **2** or drag a QuarkXPress file over the program shortcut on the Desktop.

If QuarkXPress hasn't yet been launched, it will launch now.

To convert a file from a previous version of QuarkXPress to 5.0:

1. Open the file using File > Open—not by double-clicking its icon.

2. Immediately after the document opens and you've responded to the XPress Preferences prompt, choose File > Save.

3. Choose 5.0 from the Version pop-up menu, click Save, then click Replace. *Note:* If Hyphenation Method: Expanded is currently chosen in Edit > Preferences > Preferences > Document–Paragraph, the text may reflow.

Things that may happen when a file is opened

Non-matching preferences prompt

Kerning and tracking table settings, hyphenation exceptions, and custom frame data are stored in individual documents and in the QuarkXPress folder in a file called XPress Preferences. If, upon opening a file, the document settings do not match the XPress Preferences settings, a prompt will appear **3**. Click **Use XPress Preferences** (or press Cmd-./Alt-U) to apply the Preferences currently resident on that machine (the text may reflow!) or click **Keep Document Settings** (Return/Enter) to leave the document as is.

(Continued on the following page)

Open, Convert File; XPress Preferences

Fonts are missing

If you open a document that uses fonts that are not installed or currently available in your system (perhaps the font is temporarily deactivated), a prompt will appear:

1. Click List Fonts to see a list of missing fonts **1**. *Note:* If you click Continue and the missing fonts subsequently become available, they will display properly.

2. To replace a Missing Font, click a font name **2**. An asterisk in the Replacement Font column indicates that font has *not* been replaced.

3. Click Replace.

4. In the Replacement Font dialog box, choose a font from the pop-up menu **3**.

5. Click OK. *Beware!* All instances of the font will be replaced, including any use of the font in a style sheet.

6. Repeat steps 2–5 for any other missing fonts you want to replace. If you change your mind after choosing a replacement font, click the replacement font, then click Reset.

7. Click OK.

Profiles are missing

This is a giant leap ahead, but we'll be brief. "Profiles" is short for Quark Color Management System profiles, which the program uses to achieve color matching among various devices. If a profile that's been assigned to your document is missing when you try to open it (or print it), the Missing Profiles prompt will appear **4**. You can either click Continue to open the document without replacing the missing profile (the simplest solution for now) or click List Profiles to proceed ahead to the Missing Profiles dialog box (**1**, next page). Profiles are assigned to input and output devices as well as to individual pictures. Read more about profiles on pages 396–402.

Using ATM

If you're using Adobe ATM Deluxe in the Mac OS, you can check **Enable Font Substitution** in the ATM File > Preferences > General dialog box to have fonts that are missing from your system be simulated on screen. If fonts are missing when a file is opened, the missing font alert prompt may or may not appear, and if it appears, the simulated fonts won't be listed. (Restart your computer if you change this ATM preference setting.)

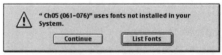

1 *If the **missing fonts** prompt appears, click **List Fonts** to open the Missing Fonts dialog box or click **Continue** to open the file without replacing the missing fonts.*

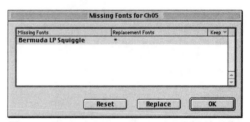

2 *In the **Missing Fonts** dialog box, click a font name, click **Replace**...*

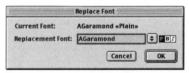

3 *...then choose a **Replacement Font** from the pop-up menu.*

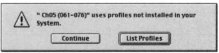

4 *If the **missing profiles** prompt appears, click **List Profiles** to substitute profiles or click **Continue** to ignore the profile.*

Have it done for you

Instead of having to open the necessary font suitcases yourself, you can use an XTension to do the job. Take a look at **Font Reserve** by Diamondsoft, **Suitcase XT** by Extensis, or **Font Fetch** by NRG Software.

1 *In the* **Missing Profiles** *dialog box, click a profile name, click* **Replace**, *choose a replacement profile, click OK, then click Done.*

2 *This prompt will appear if, when you open a document, any original picture files for the document are* missing *or were* modified.

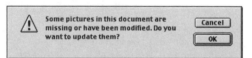

3 *In the* **Missing/Modified Pictures** *dialog box, double-click the name of a missing picture, locate and highlight the picture file name, then click Open.*

Pictures are missing

If pictures are used in the document that were moved or modified since the document was last opened and Auto Picture Import: Verify is chosen in Edit > Preferences > Preferences > Document–General (or Web Document–General), yet another prompt will appear **2**. Click OK to proceed, and then to update the picture-document link, double-click the name of a missing or modified picture **3**, locate and highlight the picture file name, then click Open (or click OK). Repeat for other missing or modified pictures. Click Done when you're done. See pages 165–166.

If a "No XTension" prompt appears, the document contains a PCX, JPEG, PhotoCD, or LZW TIFF picture for which an import XTension filter must be enabled.

Note: If additional missing pictures are located in the same folder as the first missing picture, you'll get a prompt indicating that you can update them all at once. This works only for missing pictures—not for modified pictures.

XTensions Manager opens

The XTensions Manager may open, depending on the current setting in Edit > Preferences > Preferences > Application–XTensions Manager. Click Show XTensions Manager at Startup: Always to have the XTensions Manager appear with every launch; or click "When: 'XTension' folder changes" to have the Manager open only if an XTension was added or removed from the XTension folder; or click "When: Error loading XTension occurs" (see pages 393–395).

To change a document's page size:

1. Choose File > Document Setup (Cmd-Option-Shift-P/Ctrl-Alt-Shift-P).

2. Choose a preset page Size.
   or
   Change the Width and/or Height values **1**.
   or
   Click the opposite page Orientation icon.

3. *Optional:* To convert a single-sided document into a facing-pages document, check Facing Pages (to learn more about facing pages, see page 227).

   Converting a facing-pages document into a single-sided document is more complicated, because it involves deleting master pages, which we cover in Chapter 14.

4. Click OK **2**. Any text box that fits exactly within the margin guides (such as the automatic text box) will resize automatically to fit within the new margins.

show/hide guides

Use the **F7** shortcut to show/hide guides. With guides hidden, margin guides, ruler guides, column guides, the X in empty picture boxes, and the edges of unselected boxes that don't have a frame will disappear from view. Show guides to position objects; hide them to judge the overall compositional balance of a page.

Column and margin guides are modified in the **Master Guides** dialog box, which can be opened from the Page menu only when a master page is currently displayed (see page 227).

1 *Change the* **Width** *and/or* **Height** *of a document and check or uncheck the* **Facing Pages** *option in the* **Document Setup** *dialog box.*

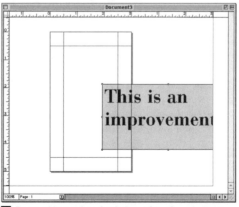

2 *Parts of items that don't fit within the new page dimensions will be temporarily hidden from view.*

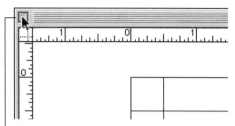

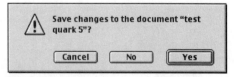
1 *Mac OS:* Click the **close** box in the upper left-hand corner of the document window to close a file.

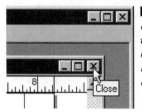
2 *Windows: If the document is **not maximized**, click the **close** box in the upper right-hand corner of the document window.*

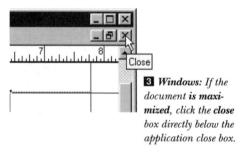
3 *Windows: If the document **is maximized**, click the **close** box directly below the application close box.*

4 *If you attempt to close a file that has **never** been **saved**, this prompt will appear.*

Save changes to the document "test quark 5"?
Cancel   No   Yes

5 *If you try to quit/exit the application and **modifications** were made to the file since it was last **saved**, this prompt will appear.*

To close one file:

Mac OS: Click the close box in the upper left corner of the document window **1**.

Windows: If the document is not maximized, click the document close box in the upper right-hand corner of the document window **2**. If the document is maximized, click the document close box directly below the application close box **3**.
or
Choose File > Close (Cmd-W/Ctrl-F4).

TIP If you try to close a file that has never been saved, a prompt will appear. You can cancel the close operation (click Cancel), discard the file altogether (click No), or save the file before it's closed (click Yes) **4**.

To close all open QuarkXPress files:

Mac OS: Option-click the close box or press Cmd-Option-W.

Windows: Choose Window > Close All.

To quit/exit the application:

Choose File > Quit/Exit (Cmd-Q/Ctrl-Q).

TIP If any open file has unsaved changes when you try to quit/exit the application, a prompt will appear for each file. You can cancel the quit/exit operation (click Cancel), close the file without saving the changes (click No), or save the changes before the file is closed (click Yes) **5**.

Close Files; Quit/Exit QuarkXPress

Using the Append dialog box, you can selectively pick and choose which individual style sheets, colors, H&Js, lists, and dashes & stripes you want to append.

To append style sheets, colors, H&Js, lists, or dashes & stripes from one file to another:

1. Open the file you want to append the style sheets, colors, H&Js, lists, or dashes & stripes to.

2. Choose File > Append (Cmd-Option-A/ Ctrl-Alt-A).
   or
   Click Append in the Style Sheets, Colors, H&Js, Lists, or Dashes & Stripes dialog box.

3. Locate and highlight the name of the file that contains the components that you want to append, then click Open. You can append from a library.

4. Click the Style Sheets, Colors, H&Js, Lists, or Dashes & Stripes tab. If a tab isn't there, it means the document you're appending from doesn't contain any custom components in that category.

5. In the Available column on the left side, click the name of the style sheet, color, H&J, list, or dashes & stripes style you want to append **1**.

   To append multiple components, click the first component in a series of consecutively-listed components, then Shift-click the last in the series. Or Cmd-click/Ctrl-click to select/deselect individual components.

6. Click the right-pointing Append Items arrow **2**.

7. Click OK. If a warning prompt appears, click OK again **3**. Check Do Not Show This Warning Again if you don't want to see it again.

8. If an appending component has the same name as a component in the file

1 *Click the name of the style sheet (or color, H&J, list, or dashes & stripes) you want to append.*

2 *Then click the right-pointing arrow to move those items to the Including/Include column.*

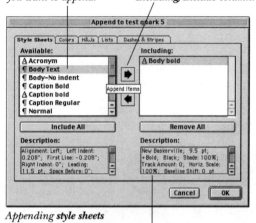

Appending style sheets

*Read the **Descriptions** to compare the two components.*

3 *Click **OK** when this warning prompt appears.*

Append

Quick-and-dirty append

If text to which a style sheet or sheets have been applied is pasted from another document using the Clipboard, drag-copied from another document, or retrieved from a library, the style sheet or sheets will be appended—barring any name conflicts. Colors and H&Js can also be appended this way.

1 *Click* **Rename** *or* **Auto-Rename** *to keep the existing item* **and** *append the new.*

2 *Or click* **Use New** *to replace the existing item with the appending item.*

3 *Or click* **Use Existing** *to prevent an item with the same name from appending.*

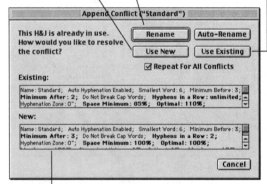

In the **Append Conflict** *dialog box, any setting in a* **New** *(appending) style sheet that doesn't exactly match an equivalent setting in an* **Existing** *style sheet of the same name in the document you're appending to will appear in* **boldface**.

you're appending to, the Append Conflict dialog box will open. Do one of the following for each conflict that arises:

Note: To have the same response be applied automatically to any remaining conflicts, check Repeat For All Conflicts before clicking Rename, Auto-Rename, Use New, or Use Existing.

To keep the existing component, append the new component, and rename an individual component yourself, click **Rename** **1**, type a new name, then click OK.

or

To have an asterisk be inserted automatically next to the name of any appending component that has a match in the open, destination document, click **Auto-Rename**.

or

To replace the existing item with the appending component, click **Use New** **2**.

or

To cancel the append of that item, click Use Existing **3**.

9. Click OK.

TIP To append all the components listed, don't highlight any of them, and click Include All. Click Remove All to delete the whole Including: list.

TIP If a style sheet that you are attempting to append has the same keyboard equivalent as a style sheet in the active file to which you are appending, the style sheet will append, but not the keyboard equivalent.

(Illustrations on the following page)

Append

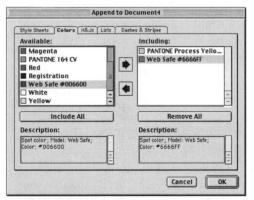

*Appending **colors***

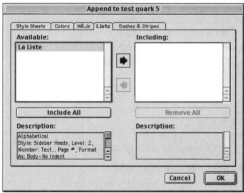

*Appending **lists***

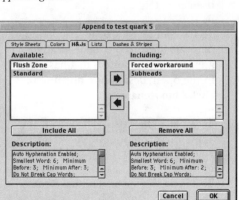

*Appending **H&Js***

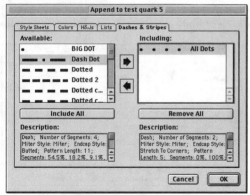

*Appending **dashes & stripes***

Revert to Saved, which restores the last-saved version of a document, is most useful if you save often. Make a point of saving before performing a complicated maneuver, such as rearranging pages, creating a book, or reshaping a Bézier item. For a cat that pays no heed to a "Get Down!" command and strolls across your keyboard, Revert to Saved can be a lifesaver (for the cat).

To revert to the last saved version:

1. Choose File > Revert to Saved.

2. When the prompt "Revert to the last version saved?" appears, click OK ∎.

TIP Choose Revert to Saved with Option/Alt held down to revert the file to its last Auto-Saved version (see page 383).

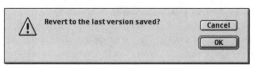

∎ *If you choose File > **Revert to Saved**, this prompt will appear. Click OK to restore the last saved version of the file.*

Get Around 3

Zoom In or Out

Zoom shortcuts

Fit in (document) Window	Cmd-0/Ctrl-0 (zero)
Actual Size	Cmd-1/Ctrl-1 (one)
Thumbnails	Shift-F6
Make all open windows Thumbnails view (print documents only)	Option-Shift choose Tile Documents from the document title bar/ Alt-Shift-choose Window menu > Tile Horizontally or Tile Vertically
Fit pasteboard in window	Cmd-Option-0/ Ctrl-Alt-0
Highlight view percent field	Control-V/ Ctrl-Alt-V
100%–200% toggle	Cmd-Option-click/ Ctrl-Alt-click

For the Zoom in and Zoom out shortcuts, see the following page.

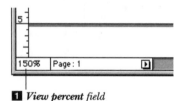

1 *View percent* field

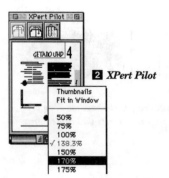

2 *XPert Pilot*

Change zoom levels

To minimize eye and neck strain, it's essential to learn how to switch zoom levels, from a magnified view to edit a small detail, back to Fit in Window or a lower zoom level to check out the overall layout, and so on. Changing the zoom level doesn't alter a document's page or print size; it only changes the way it looks on screen.

To zoom in or out using the View menu or view percent field:

Choose View > Fit in Window (Cmd-0/ Ctrl-0), 50%, 75%, Actual Size (Cmd-1/ Ctrl-1), 200%, or Thumbnails (Shift-F6).
or
Double-click the view percent field in the lower left-hand corner of the document window **1** (Control-V/Ctrl-Alt-V), type a number between 10 and 800, then press Return/Enter. You don't have to enter the % symbol. For Thumbnails view, enter "T", then press Return/Enter.

TIP Page elements cannot be modified in Thumbnails view. Pages within a file *can* be rearranged in Thumbnails view, however (see page 76), and whole pages can be drag-copied from one file to another if both documents are in Thumbnails view (see page 83).

TIP For an almost-thumbnails view in which page elements are editable, choose a very small view size, like 25%.

TIP To choose user-defined view sizes from a pop-up menu, use the XPert Pilot XTension, which is in Volume 2 of the XPert Tools toolkit by a lowly apprentice production, inc. **2**

Accessing the Zoom tool from the keyboard is much speedier than selecting and then deselecting the tool from the Tool palette.

5.0! In the Mac OS: In QuarkXPress 5.0, you have to pay attention to a new preferences setting when you access the Zoom tool using the keyboard. If you click **Control Key Activates: Contextual Menu** in Edit > Preferences > Preferences > Application–Interactive, you can use the shortcuts as listed below. If Control Key Activates: **Zoom** is chosen, on the other hand, you'll need to eliminate the Shift/Spacebar key from the shortcuts (this is how it worked in QuarkXPress 4).

To zoom in or out using a shortcut:

Control-Shift-click/Ctrl-Spacebar-click on the page to zoom in **1**.
or
Control-Option-click/Ctrl-Alt-Spacebar-click on the page to zoom out.
or
Control-Shift-drag/Ctrl-Spacebar-drag a marquee across an area on the page that you want to magnify **2**.

TIP To set the Minimum, Maximum, and Increment percentages for the Zoom tool, double-click the tool, then click Modify.

TIP Click the document window zoom box to enlarge the window to full screen size; click it again to restore the window's former size.

TIP The maximum zoom on a Windows monitor may vary depending on the current Display DPI Value (screen resolution) in Edit > Preferences > Preferences > Application–Display.

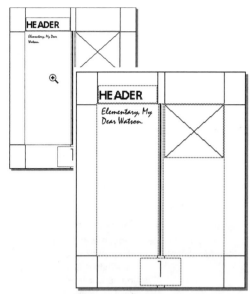

1 *Control-Shift-click/Ctrl-Spacebar-click on a page to zoom in.*

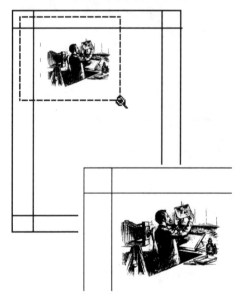

2 *Control-Shift-drag/Ctrl-Spacebar-drag over a section of a page to magnify that chosen area.*

Screen redraw shortcuts

Forced redraw   Cmd-Option-. (period)/
Ctrl-Alt-. Use this to correct
an incomplete screen redraw.

Stop redraw   Cmd-./Ctrl-. (period) *or* Esc *or*
perform another action (select
an item, choose another command, etc.)

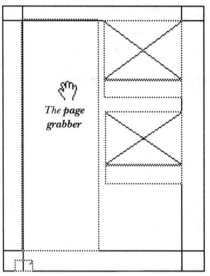

1 *Option-drag/Alt-drag* with the mouse to *move a page in the document window.*

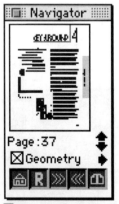

2 *The **Navigator** palette XTension*

Move around

Note: In the Mac OS, the page grabber isn't accessible while the Caps lock key is pressed down. In the Mac OS and in Windows, the page grabber isn't accessible while the Zoom tool is chosen.

To move a document in its window using the page grabber hand:

Option-drag/Alt-drag to move a page in the document window. The cursor will temporarily turn into a hand icon **1**. The document will redraw as you scroll. If Speed Scroll is turned on (Edit > Preferences > Preferences > Application–Interactive), pictures and blends may be greeked (grayed out) as you scroll.

TIP To move around your document pages using a palette XTension, explore the Navigator palette **2** in the Xdream XTension from Vision's Edge or the XPert Pilot palette in Volume 2 of the XPert Tools XTension toolkit by a lowly apprentice production, inc. ("alap," for short). On both palette XTensions you'll see a thumbnail-sized view of the currently displayed page. When you click on an area of the palette, zip— that part of the page appears on screen.

TIP The Edit > Preferences > Preferences > Application–Interactive options, including Scrolling, Speed Scroll, Live Scroll, Show Contents, and Live Refresh, are discussed on page 382.

To move a document in its window using the scroll arrows, bars, or boxes:

Click a scroll **arrow** to scroll a short distance through a document in the direction in which the arrow is pointing (print documents only) **1**.
or

Move a scroll **box** to move through a document more quickly. Note the page number in the page field in the lower left corner of the document window as you do this.
or

Click a grey scroll **bar** area to scoot through a document one full screen at a time: Click above the right scroll box to jump a full screen upward or click below it to jump a full screen downward. Click to the left of the bottom scroll box to jump a full screen to the left or click to the right of it to jump a full screen to the right.

TIP The scroll speed and other scroll preferences are set in Edit > Preferences > Preferences > Application–Interactive (see page 382).

To move through a document using the extended keyboard:

Press Page Up or Page Down to move up or down one full screen **2**–**3**.
or

Press Home/Ctrl-Home to go to the top of the first page in the document. *Note:* In Windows, the Home and End commands move the cursor.
or

Press End/Ctrl-End to go to the bottom of the last page (or the blank space to the right of the last page) in the document.
or

Press Shift-End/Ctrl-Page Down to go to the top of the last page in the document.
or

Press Shift-Page Up to go to the top of the previous page.
or

Press Shift-Page Down to go to the top of the next page.

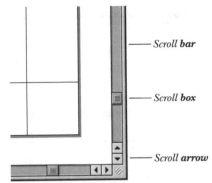

1 *The standard **Macintosh** window features: **scroll boxes, bars,** and **arrows***

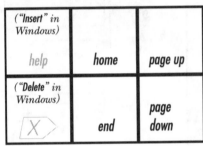

2 *A section of an extended keyboard in the Mac OS.*

3 *The page that's currently showing in the **upper left hand corner** of the document window is the page that QarkXPress considers to be displayed, even if only a small part of that page is in view.*

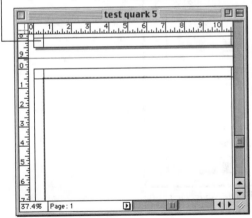

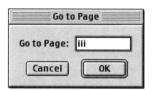

1 *Press Cmd-J/Ctrl-J to get to the* **Go to Page** *dialog box quickly.*

2 *The* **Document Layout** *palette*

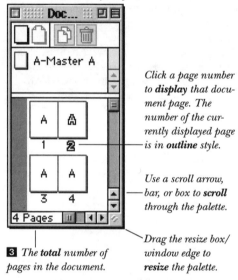

Click a page number to **display** *that document page. The number of the currently displayed page is in* **outline** *style.*

Use a scroll arrow, bar, or box to **scroll** *through the palette.*

Drag the resize box/ window edge to **resize** *the palette.*

3 *The* **total** *number of pages in the document.*

4 *To display a document page, choose from the* **pop-up** *menu at the bottom of the document window.*

5 *Or double-click the current page number,* **enter** *the desired page number, then press Return/Enter.*

To go to a page using a command:

Choose Page > Previous, Next, First, or Last.
or
Choose Page > Go to (Cmd-J/Ctrl-J), enter the desired page number in the Go to Page field, then click OK **1**.

TIP If the desired page has a prefix that was applied using the Section command, be sure to enter the prefix along with the number in the Go to Page field. Also make sure to enter the number in the correct format (e.g. lowercase Roman, numeric). To display a page based on its position in the document rather than its applied Section number, enter "+" before the number.

To go to a page using the Document Layout palette:

1. Choose View > Show Document Layout (F10/F4).

2. Click the desired page number under the document page icon **2**.
or
Double-click a document page icon. (Single-clicking will highlight the icon, but not display the page.)

TIP When a page icon is highlighted, its number displays in the lower left corner of the Document Layout palette. If a page is the start of a section, an asterisk will follow the number. If no page icon is highlighted, the total number of pages the document contains will display instead (e.g., "4 Pages") **3**.

To go to a page using the Go-to-page menu or field:

Choose a document page number from the Go-to-page pop-up menu at the bottom of the document window **4**.
or
Double-click the current page number **5**, enter the desired page number, then press Return/Enter.

Move Through Document

Stack, tile, or activate open document windows:

In the Mac OS, go to the View > Windows submenu or Shift-press an open document title bar. In Windows, go to the Window menu. Choose:

Stack Documents/Cascade to stack document windows at full size in a stair-stepped configuration **1**–**2**.

or

Tile Documents/Tile Horizontally to arrange document windows in horizontal strips **3**.

or

The name of an open document to activate it.

or

Windows only: Choose Tile Vertically to arrange document windows in columns.

TIP If more than one monitor is hooked up, the open documents will be divided among the monitors.

Freeze the frame

With **Save Document Position** checked in Edit menu > Preferences > Preferences > Application–Save, a document will reopen in the same location, display size, and window size that it was in when it was last closed. With this option unchecked, a document will reopen at full window size in Fit in Window view.

Nifty trick

In the Mac OS, **Option-Shift**-click a document title bar and choose from the top of the pop-up menu to stack or tile all open documents into **Thumbnails** view. In Windows, **Alt-Shift**-click and choose Cascade or a Tile command from the Window menu. **Control-Shift**-click/**Ctrl-Alt**-click for **Actual Size** view; **Cmd-Shift**-click/**Ctrl-Shift**-click for **Fit in Window** view.

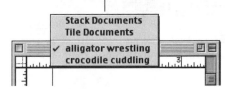

1 *Mac OS only: **Shift-press** a document title bar, then from the pop-up menu, choose a different document window configuration or activate a different open document.*

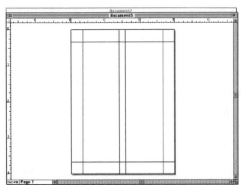

2 *This is after choosing View > Windows > **Stack Documents** in the Mac OS. In Windows, the **Cascade** command does the same thing.*

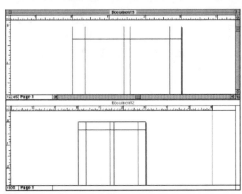

3 *This is after choosing View > Windows > **Tile Documents** in the Mac OS. In Windows, **Tile Horizontally** does the same thing.*

Text Input 4

Continuing with your studies

Once you've learned the rudiments of manipulating text from this chapter—getting it into a box, highlighting it, and rearranging it—you'll be ready to explore these other topics:

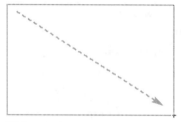

1 *Drag with a **text box** tool.*

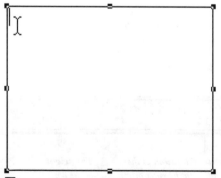

2 *A new text box is created.*

How does text get onto a page?

To input or import text in QuarkXPress, you have to first create a box to put it in or a text path to put it on. QuarkXPress has five tools that are expressly used for creating different-shaped text boxes, as well as two Bézier text box tools and four text path tools. In addition, you can convert any item into a text box or text path.

Note: If you checked Automatic Text Box in the New Document dialog box when you created your document, an automatic text box was placed on all your document pages. This box is used to flow text from page to page, and you'll learn all about it in the next chapter. For now, you can just delete the auto text box if it gets in the way (click on it, then press Cmd-K/Ctrl-K— or if you're in a lousy mood, Cmd-Option-Shift-K/Ctrl-Alt-Shift-K might cheer you up).

To create a text box:

1. Choose any text box tool except a Bézier text tool (they're covered in Chapter 18). **A** Ⓐ Ⓐ Ⓐ Ⓐ The cursor will turn into a crosshair.

2. Drag in any direction **1**. When the mouse is released, the finished box will be selected and ready for inputting **2**. When the Content tool is chosen and a text box is selected, a blinking text insertion marker appears in the box and the pointer turns into an I-beam.

TIP Remember the Undo command, which undoes most operations: Cmd-Z/Ctrl-Z.

To resize a text box manually:

1. Choose the Item or Content tool (Shift-F8).

2. Click a box.

3. Drag any handle **1**–**2**.
   or
   To resize the box and preserve its original proportions, hold down Option-Shift/Alt-Shift while dragging. (Hold down Shift without Option/Alt to turn the box into a square.) Release Shift or Option-Shift/Alt-Shift after you release the mouse.

TIP Make sure the point of the cursor arrow is directly over one of the box handles before pressing the mouse. The cursor will change into a pointing-hand icon.

TIP If Delayed Item Dragging: Live Refresh is on in Edit > Preferences > Preferences > Application–Interactive and you pause before dragging a handle of a text box, the text wrap will update continuously as you drag (the pointer will turn into a cluster of arrows) **3**. In the Delay field (0.1–5), you can specify the length of the pause required before dragging.

To resize a text box using the Measurements palette:

1. Choose the Item or Content tool.

2. Click on a box.

3. Change the W value on the Measurements palette for the width of the box, then press Return/Enter **4**. A number can be entered in any measurement unit used in QuarkXPress. Be sure to include the proper abbreviation, such as "p" or "mm," if the number is in a measurement unit other than the default (see page 27).
   and/or
   Change the H value on the Measurements palette for the height of the box, then press Return/Enter.

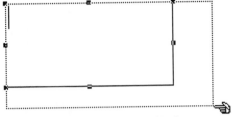

1 *Resize a box by dragging any of its four* **corner handles** *(note the hand pointer)...*

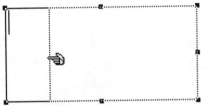

2 *...or drag any of its four* **midpoint handles**.

After a brief shower of orange juice, low clouds of sunny-side up eggs moved in followed by pieces of toast.
—*Judi Barrett*

3 *Pause-dragging with* **Live Refresh** *on*

The **horizontal location** *of the box relative to the ruler origin: This number can be replaced, or a plus or minus sign and then a specified amount can be entered to the right of the current number to add to or subtract from it.*

The **width** *of the box*

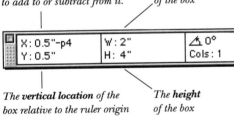

X : 0.5"-p4	W : 2"	△ 0°
Y : 0.5"	H : 4"	Cols : 1

The **vertical location** *of the box relative to the ruler origin*

The **height** *of the box*

4 *The "X" field contains two different measurement units; the value wil be converted to inches (the default unit) after Return/Enter is pressed.*

Snap to it

If View > **Snap to Guides** is turned on (Shift-F7 toggles it on and off) and you drag the handle of a box or an anchor point near a guide, the handle or point will snap to the guide with a little tug. Turn Snap to Guides off to drag items manually without the little tug.

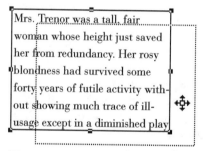

1 *Pause before dragging to see the contents of the item as you move it...*

Mrs. Trenor was a tall, fair woman whose height just saved her from redundancy. Her rosy blondness had survived some forty years of futile activity without showing much trace of ill-usage except in a diminished play

2 *... or drag **without pausing** to see only the **outline** of the box as it's moved. Use this method on a slow machine.*

```
X: 6p      W: 2"      ∠
Y: 0.5"    H: 4"      C
```

3 *To **position** an object very precisely, enter new X and/or Y values on the Measurements palette.*

```
X: 1"      W: 2"      ∠
Y: 0.5"    H: 4"      C
```

4 *After pressing Return/Enter, the X **pica** value is converted into its equivalent in the default measurement unit, which in this case is **inches**.*

To move a text box manually:

1. Choose the Item tool. Or hold down Cmd/Ctrl to temporarily use the Item tool if the Content tool is selected.

2. Press inside a text box, pause briefly for the text to redraw, then drag the item to a new location on the same page or on a different page **1**–**2** (the cursor will be a cluster of arrowheads). The X and Y position values on the Measurements palette will update as you drag. To force scrolling, knock into the edge of the document window while dragging.

TIP Hold down Shift as you drag to constrain the movement to a horizontal or vertical axis. Release the mouse before releasing Shift. To use ruler guides to position an item, see page 185.

Use the Measurements palette to move the upper left corner of an item to a precise *x/y* location, relative to the ruler origin.

To reposition a text box or any other item using the Measurements palette:

1. Choose the Item or Content tool.

2. Click on the item you want to reposition.

3. Enter a new number in the X field on the Measurements palette to change the horizontal position of the box relative to the ruler origin **3**, which, unless you change it, is located at the uppermost left corner of the document. *and/or*
Enter a new number in the Y field on the Measurements palette to change the vertical position of the box relative to the ruler origin.

4. Press Return/Enter **4**.

TIP To use arithmetic in the X or Y field, enter "+" after the current number, then the amount you want to add. To subtract, enter "-"; to multiply, enter "*", or to divide, enter "/".

Move Text Box

To input text:

1. Choose the Content tool.

2. Click in a text box (or click on a text path) to create an insertion point.

3. Start typing **1**. Press Return/Enter whenever you want to begin a new paragraph.

TIP Choose View > Show Invisibles (Cmd-I/Ctrl-I) to reveal paragraph returns, spaces, and other non-printing characters **2**.

TIP To move text inward from *all* sides of its box, choose Item > Modify, click the Text tab, then enter a Text Inset: All Edges value (click Apply to preview). To specify different values for each edge, click Text Inset: Multiple Insets, then change the Top, Left, Bottom, or Right values (see page 59). And remember, you can always move the text box downward on the page!

What is the text overflow symbol?

If a text box is too small to display all the text that it contains, a text overflow symbol appears in the lower right-hand corner of the box **3**. The text overflow symbol will disappear if the text box is enlarged enough to display all the type that it contains or if the box is linked to another box for the text to spill into.

The text overflow symbol doesn't print; it's merely an indicator that there is hidden text in the buffer. Only text that is visible in a box will print.

TIP If pages are mysteriously added to your document when a text box becomes full, it means Auto Page Insertion is turned on in Edit > Preferences > Preferences > Document–General.

Keep the case open

Lowercase characters can be converted into caps or small caps with a flick of a switch on the Measurements palette, but characters input with the **Caps Lock** key pressed can't be converted back to lowercase—so **don't** type with the Caps Lock key pressed down! (Unless you buy the Text Toolkit XTension by Visions Edge, Inc. and use its Text Conversion feature when you need it.)

As soon as they were gone, Elizabeth walked out to recover her spirits; or in other words, to dwell without interruption on those subjects that must deaden them more. Mr. Darcy's behavior astonished

1 *Text is typed into a text box with the Content tool.*

As·soon·as·they·were·gone,·Elizabeth· walked·out·to·recover·her·spirits;·or·in· other·words,·to·dwell·without·interruption· on·those·subjects·that·must·deaden·them· more.·Mr.·Darcy's·behavior·astonished· and·vexed·her.¶
"Why,·if·he·came·only·to·be·silent,·
Jane Austen

2 *Press* **Return** *to begin a new* **paragraph**. *Choose View >* **Show Invisibles** *to display paragraph returns and other non-printing characters.*

As soon as they were gone, Elizabeth walked out to recover her spirits; or in other words, to dwell without interruption on those subjects that must deaden them more. Mr. Darcy's behavior astonished ⊠

3 *The red* **text overflow symbol** *appears when a box is too small to display all the text that it contains.*

> On an exceptionally hot evening early in **July**, a young man came

1 *Double-click anywhere in the middle of a **word** to highlight it **without** including any punctuation.*

> On an exceptionally hot evening early in **July,** a young man came

2 *Double-click between a **word** and a **punctuation mark** or to the right of the punctuation mark to select both. Read more about **smart space** on page 176.*

> On an exceptionally hot evening early in
> July, a young man came out of the garret
> in which he lodged in S. Place and
> walked slowly, as though in hesitation,
> towards K. Bridge.
> **He had successfully avoided meeting**
> his landlady on the staircase. His garret
> was under the roof of a high, five-storied

3 ***Triple-click** to highlight a **line**.*

> **On an exceptionally hot evening early in**
> **July, a young man came out of the garret**
> **in which he lodged in S. Place and**
> **walked slowly, as though in hesitation,**
> **towards K. Bridge.**
> He had successfully avoided meeting
> his landlady on the staircase. His garret
> was under the roof of a high, five-storied

4 *Click **four** times to highlight a **paragraph**.*

To highlight text:

1. Choose the Content tool.

2. Drag over the text you want to highlight.
or
Use a fast-clicking method **1**–**4**:

Number of clicks	What gets highlighted
1 click	Creates an **insertion point**
2 clicks on word	A **word** (but *not* the space following it)
2 clicks between word and punctuation	A **word** *and* the punctuation following it (but *not* the space following it)
3 clicks	A **line**
4 clicks	A **paragraph**
5 clicks	A whole **story** (all the text in a box or in a series of linked boxes)

or
To highlight a **whole story**, click in a text box, then choose Edit > Select All (Cmd-A/Ctrl-A). Hidden overflow text, if any, will be included in the selection. *Note:* If the Item tool is selected when you choose Select All, all items on the currently displayed page or spread and surrounding pasteboard will become selected instead!
or
Click in a text box at the beginning of a **text string**, then Shift-click at the end of the text string. (To highlight non-contiguous text strings, you have to use an XTension, such as Text Grabber from Meadows Information.)
or
To select from the current **cursor position** to the **end of a story**: Cmd-Option-Shift-down arrow/Ctrl-Alt-Shift-down arrow. (See pages 462–463 for more shortcuts.)
or
To select a **series of words**, double-click the first word, keep the mouse button down on the second click, then drag. Or triple-click, then drag downward to highlight a **series of lines**.

To delete text:

1. Choose the Content tool.

2. Click to the right of the character to be deleted **1**, then press Delete/Backspace. (Press the left or right arrow on the keyboard to move the insertion point one character at a time.)
or
First highlight the text you want to delete **2** (see the previous page). Then in the Mac OS, press Delete or choose Edit > Clear. In Windows, press Backspace or Delete or choose Edit > Delete.

TIP To delete the character to the right of the cursor, press the del/Delete key on an extended keyboard or press Shift-Delete on a non-extended keyboard.

The Line text path tool and Orthogonal text path tool are discussed here. The Bézier text path and Freehand text path tools are discussed in Chapter 18.

To create a straight text path:

1. Choose the Orthogonal text path tool ⟂ to draw a straight horizontal or vertical text path **3**.
or
Choose the Line text path tool ✐ to draw a straight line path at any angle with no corners or bends **4**.

2. Drag to draw the path, and leave it selected.

3. Choose the Content tool.

4. Start typing. The text will march along the path.

Same ol' selection

If you deselect and then reselect a box with the Content tool, the **last** group of characters that were highlighted, if any, will re-highlight. To create a new insertion point, click once more in the text box.

1 *Pressing Delete with the cursor at this insertion point would remove the "S."*

2 *Pressing Delete with this selection highlighted would delete the "HES."*

3 *Drag vertically or horizontally with the* **Orthogonal text path** *tool.*

4 *Drag at any angle with the* **Line text path** *tool.*

Repeating yourself?

You can store and retrieve frequently used words or phrases using the **Glossary,** 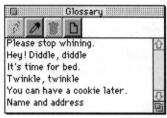 which is part of the **Xdream** XTension from Vision's Edge.

Need to **alphabetize** a series of words or phrases? Use the **Sort Paragraphs** command in the same Xdream XTension.

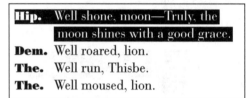

1 *The **Xdream Glossary** palette*

> **Hip.** Well shone, moon—Truly, the moon shines with a good grace.
> **Dem.** Well roared, lion.
> **The.** Well run, Thisbe.
> **The.** Well moused, lion.

2 *To move text, highlight it, then choose Edit > **Cut**.*

> **Dem.** Well roared, lion.
> **The.** Well run, Thisbe.
> **The.** Well moused, lion.

3 *Click to create a new insertion point.*

> **Dem.** Well roared, lion.
> **The.** Well run, Thisbe.
> **Hip.** Well shone, moon—Truly, the moon shines with a good grace.
> **The.** Well moused, lion.
> *William Shakespeare*

4 *Choose Edit > **Paste**.*

To delete any item:

Choose the Item or Content tool, click the item you want to delete, then choose Item > Delete (Cmd-K/Ctrl-K).
or
Choose the Item tool, and click the item you want to delete. Then in the Mac OS, press Delete or choose Edit > Clear. In Windows, press Delete or Backspace or choose Edit > Delete.

The Clipboard is a holding area that stores one cut or copied selection at a time. The current contents of the Clipboard can be retrieved an unlimited number of times via the Paste command. The current Clipboard contents will be replaced if you Copy or Cut in any application and will be deleted if you turn off your computer.

To rearrange text using the Clipboard:

1. Choose the Content tool.

2. Highlight the text you want to move **2**.

3. Choose Edit > **Cut** (Cmd-X/Ctrl-X) to place the highlighted text on the Clipboard and **remove** it from its current location.
   or
   Choose Edit > **Copy** (Cmd-C/ Ctrl-C) to place a **copy** of the highlighted text on the Clipboard and leave the highlighted text in its current location.

4. Click in a text box to create a new insertion point **3**.

5. Choose Edit > **Paste** (Cmd-V/Ctrl-V) **4**. Smart Space takes care of adding spaces where needed (see page 176).

TIP The Clipboard can also be used to cut or copy a text box, picture box, line, or group when the Item tool is selected, or a picture if the Content tool is chosen. Paste using the same tool that was used to Cut or Copy—unless you want the item to be anchored (see page 181).

The Drag and Drop Text feature is used to move or copy text quickly without having to execute the Clipboard commands. You can drag-and-drop text within the same box or between linked boxes (a story), but not between unlinked boxes. This is a very handy feature for making quick copy-edits.

Note: In order to use the drag-and-drop feature, the **Drag and Drop Text** box has to be checked in Edit > Preferences > Preferences > Application–Interactive .

In the Mac OS only, if Drag and Drop Text is unchecked, you can still use the drag-and-drop feature using these keystrokes: Cmd-Control-drag to move the text or Cmd-Control-Shift-drag to move a copy of it.

To drag-and-drop text:

1. Choose the Content tool.
2. Highlight the text you want to move or copy (see page 55) **2**.
3. Release the mouse.
4. To move the highlighted text, press on it, drag the blinking cursor to a new location in the same text box or in a box that it's linked to (a hollow box displays as you drag), then release the mouse **3**.
   or
   To move a copy of the text, hold down Shift while dragging the blinking cursor to a new location (a hollow box and a plus sign display as you drag).

TIP The drag and drop text is automatically placed on the Clipboard, but you won't be aware of it unless you use the Paste command or choose Edit > Show Clipboard.

1 *Check* **Drag and Drop Text** *in Edit > Preferences > Preferences > Application–***Interactive***.*

> If you want to get somewhere else, you must run at least twice as fast as that. Now, *here*, you see, it takes all the running *you* can do, to keep in the same place.
>
> *Lewis Carroll*

2 *To* **drag and drop** *(move) text, highlight it, release the mouse, then press on the highlighted text and drag the blinking cursor to a new position.*

> "Now, *here*, you see, it takes all the running *you* can do, to keep in the same place. If you want to get somewhere else, you must run at least twice as fast as that..."
>
> *Lewis Carroll*

3 *The sentences have been swapped.*

Drag-and-Drop Text

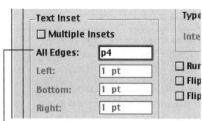

1 *To make the* **Text Inset uniform** *on all sides, leave Multiple Insets unchecked, and enter an* **All Edges** *value.*

Promote then as an object of primary importance, institutions for the general diffusion of knowledge. In proportion as the structure of a government gives force to public opinion, it is essential that public opinion be enlightened.

George Washington

2 *A text box with a* **Text Inset** *of 0 pt*

Promote then as an object of primary importance, institutions for the general diffusion of knowledge. In proportion as the structure of a government gives force to public opinion, it is essential that public opinion be enlightened.

3 *The same text box with a* **Text Inset** *of 7 pt*

---

4 *To enter separate* **Text Inset** *values for the* **Top, Left, Bottom,** *and* **Right** *edges of a text box, first check* **Multiple Insets.**

The Text Inset is the blank space between text and the four edges of the box that contains it. A Text Inset value greater than zero should be applied to any box that has a frame to create breathing space between the text and the frame.

To change the text inset:

1. Choose the Item or Content tool.
2. Click on the text box.
3. Choose Item > Modify (Cmd-M/ Ctrl-M), then click the Text tab.
4. To apply a uniform Text Inset value to all edges of the text box, leave Multiple Insets unchecked, then enter a value in the **All Edges** field (1 pt. is the default) **1**–**3**. If you're entering a value in points, you don't have to reenter the "pt."
   or
   To enter a different Text Inset value for each edge of the text box, check **Multiple Insets 4**–**5**, then enter **Top, Left, Bottom,** and **Right** values.
5. *Optional:* Click Apply to preview, then readjust the Text Inset values, if desired.
6. Click OK.

5.0!

Text Inset

Promote then as an object of primary importance, institutions for the general diffusion of knowledge. In proportion as the structure of a government gives force to public opinion, it is essential that public opinion be enlightened.

5 *The text box with a* **different Text Inset** *value on each side*

To apply a frame to a text or picture box:

1. Choose the Item or Content tool.

2. Click on a box (Bézier or standard).

3. Choose Item > Frame (Cmd-B/Ctrl-B).

4. Choose a preset Width from the pop-up menu or enter a custom Width 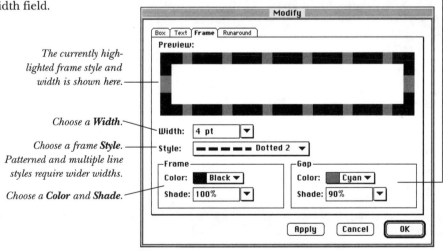.

5. Choose from the Style pop-up menu. (To create a custom dashed or multi-line (striped) frame, see pages 207–208.) *Note:* Only the Solid, Solid Shade (HR), and Solid 3-D frames are available for HTML text boxes. If you convert an HTML text box to a raster box, any frame can then be applied (check Convert to Graphic on Export at the bottom of the dialog box).

6. Choose from the Color pop-up menu.

7. Choose from the Shade pop-up menu or enter a Shade percentage.

8. *Optional:* To recolor the white areas in a multi-line or dashed style, choose from the Gap: Color and Shade pop-up menus.

9. Click Apply to preview, make any adjustments, then click OK (illustrations on the next page).

TIP To remove a frame, enter 0 in the Width field.

How to frame like a pro

- Apply a **Text Inset** greater than zero in Item > Modify (Text pane) to add breathing room between the text and the frame.

- Use narrow, **delicate** frames rather than thick, ornate ones. Gaudy frames distract from, and overwhelm, the text. Less is more.

- Unless you want the whole world to know you're new to graphic design, use frames **judiciously** in a couple of spots—not frames, frames everywhere.

You can recolor the gaps in a multi-line or dashed frame by choosing from the **Gap: Color** *and* **Shade** *pop-up menus.*

The currently high-lighted frame style and width is shown here.

Choose a **Width**.

Choose a frame **Style**. *Patterned and multiple line styles require wider widths.*

Choose a **Color** *and* **Shade**.

1 *The* **Frame** *pane of the Item >* **Modify** *dialog box.*

Frames illustrated

Speak what you think now in hard words, and to-morrow speak what to-morrow thinks in hard words again, though it contradict every thing you said to-day.—"Ah, so you shall be sure to be misunderstood."—Is it so bad, then, to be misunderstood? Pythagoras was misunderstood, and Socrates, and Jesus, and Luther, and Copernicus, and Galileo, and Newton, and every pure and wise spirit that ever took flesh. To be great is to be misunderstood.

Ralph Waldo Emerson

Fish, like guests, smell after three days.

If you have built castles in the air, your work need not be lost; that is where they should be. Now put the foundations under them.

Henry David Thoreau

*Sometimes **simplest** is best.*

DO I CONTRADICT MYSELF?

VERY WELL THEN...

I CONTRADICT MYSELF;

I AM LARGE...

I CONTAIN MULTITUDES.

Walt Whitman

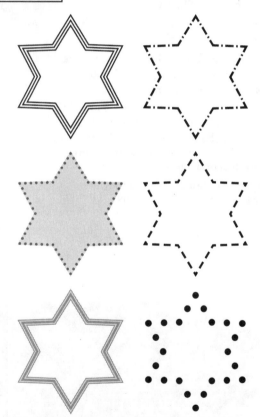

*These Bézier boxes have **dashed** or **striped** frames. The star shapes were created using the free **Shape of Things** XTension from Quark Inc.*

Frame Text or Picture Box

Text boxes can be made see-through so they can be layered on top of each other.

To make a text box transparent:

1. Choose the Item or Content tool.

2. If all the items are on the same layer, click on the text box that is to be on top. And if it's not on top, choose Item > Bring to Front (F5). If the items are on different layers, make sure the layers are in the correct stacking order (see page 262).

3. Choose Item > Runaround (Cmd-T/ Ctrl-T).

4. Choose Type: None ■, then click OK.

5. If the Colors palette isn't already open, choose View > Show Colors (F12).

6. Click the Background color icon on the Colors palette ②.

7. Click None ③–④. (Don't choose Black at a 0 shade percentage. It will look opaque white—not transparent.)

TIP To select an item that's behind another item, Cmd-Option-Shift-click/Ctrl-Alt-Shift-click. Each click will select the next item behind in succession (more about this on page 179).

TIP To group multiple items so they'll move in unison, see page 168.

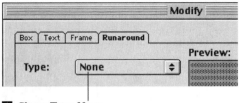

■ *Choose* **Type: None.**

② *First click the background color icon.*

③ *Then click* **None** *to make the selected box transparent.*

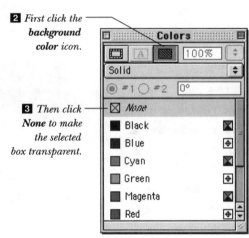

The **Colors** *palette*

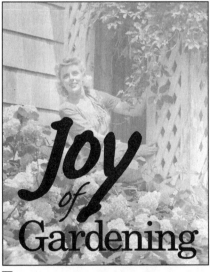

④ *Text in a* **transparent** *box on top of a picture*

Transparent Box

Get there fast

With the Item tool selected, you can double-click inside a text box to quickly open the **Modify** dialog box. Cmd/Ctrl double-click if the Content tool is selected.

Once upon a time there was a Pussy-cat called Ribby, who invited a little dog called Duchess to tea.

Once upon a time there was a Pussy-cat called Ribby, who invited a little dog called Duchess to tea.

Beatrix Potter

1 *First Baseline 0*   **2** *First Baseline 1p6*

To move text downward in its box:

To move the first line of text downward from the top of its box, select the box, choose Item > Modify (Cmd-M/Ctrl-M), click the Text tab, then enter a First Baseline: Offset value greater than 0. This value will be added to the current Text Inset value. From the Minimum pop-up menu, choose whether the first baseline will start at the largest Cap Height, Cap + Accent [mark], or Ascent (the top of the tallest character, as in an "l"or a "t") **1**–**2**.
or
Choose Item > Modify (Cmd-M/Ctrl-M), check Text Inset: Multiple Insets, then enter a higher Top value.
or
This may feel like cheating, but sometimes simplest is best: Just drag the whole box downward on the page with the Item tool. There's no law against doing that.

To skew text:

1. Choose the Item or Content tool.

2. Click on any shaped text box. You can only skew one item at a time.

3. Choose Item > Modify (Cmd-M/Ctrl-M), then click the Box tab.

4. Enter a Skew value between -75 and 75. Enter a positive number to skew to the right or a negative number to skew to the left. The higher the skew value, the more distorted—and thus the less legible—the text will be.

5. Click OK **3**. You can edit the skewed text. To undo the skew, make the Skew value 0.

Sometimes I've believed as many as six impossible things before breakfast.
~Lewis Carroll

3 *A rectangular text box **skewed** at a 40° angle*

To rotate a text box using the Measurements palette:

1. Choose the Item or Content tool.

2. Click on a text box.

3. In the rotation field on the Measurements palette, enter a positive value between 0° and 360° to rotate the box counter-clockwise 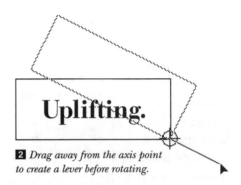 or a negative value to rotate it clockwise, then press Return/Enter. You can edit the text in its rotated position.

To rotate a text box using the Rotation tool:

1. Choose the Rotation tool. ↺

2. Click on a text box.

3. Press to create an axis point for rotation, then drag the mouse away from the axis to create a "lever" **2**. The further you drag away from the axis before rotating, the easier the rotation will be to control.

4. Drag clockwise or counterclockwise **3**. Hold down Shift while dragging to rotate at an increment of 45°.

The flip commands flip all the text in a box, but not the box itself. Text can be modified in its flipped position.

To flip text:

1. Choose the Content tool.

2. Click on a text box.

3. Choose Style > Flip Horizontal or Flip Vertical.
   or
   Click the Flip Horizontal ➡ and/or Flip Vertical ⬆ icon on the Measurements palette **4**–**5**.

1 *The **rotation angle** of a text box*

X: −0.366"	W: 2"	⟋ 30°
Y: 1.171"	H: 4"	Cols: 1

Uplifting.

2 *Drag away from the axis point to create a lever before rotating.*

3 *The box rotated -90°*

It's a poor sort of memory that only works sbɹɐwʞɔɐq

~*Lewis Carroll*

4 *The word "backwards" is in a separate text box, which is **flipped horizontally**.*

Narcissus

5 *The text box containing the gray "Narcissus" was **flipped vertically**.*

Rotate Text Box; Flip Text

Wrapping all around

Normally, text will only wrap around three sides of a box within a column. To wrap text around all sides of a box within a column, select the box that contains the text that's doing the **wrapping**, choose Item > Modify, click the Text tab, check **Run Text Around All Sides**, then click OK. See page 192.

To wrap text around another box:

1. Stack the text box that you want to wrap text around on top of another text box. To move a box to the top of its layer, select it, then choose Item > Bring to Front (F5) (read about layers in Chapter 16).

2. With the new box still selected, choose Item > Runaround (Cmd-T/Ctrl-T).

3. Choose Type: Item **1**.

4. Enter Top, Left, Bottom and Right values for the space between the text box and the type wrapping around it **2**. If you're entering a value in points, you don't have to reenter the "pt". Press Tab to move quickly from field to field.

5. Click Apply to preview, make any adjustments, then click OK **3**–**4**.

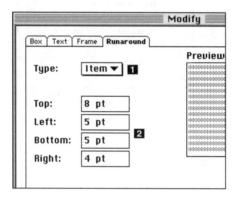

We thus learn that man is descended from a hairy, tailed quadruped, probably arboreal in its habits, and an inhabitant of the Old World. This creature, if its whole structure had been examined by a naturalist, would have been classed amongst the Quadrumana, as surely as the still more ancient progenitor of the Old and New World monkeys. The Quadrumana and all the higher mammals are probably derived from an ancient marsupial animal, and this through a long series of diversified forms, from some amphibian-like creature, and this again

> We thus learn that man is descended from a hairy, tailed quadruped, probably arboreal in its habits, and an inhabitant of the Old World.
> *Charles Darwin*

3 *Normally, text will only wrap around three sides of a box that is placed within a column (unless Run **Text Around All Sides** is turned for the text that is wrapping—see the sidebar, above).*

We thus learn that man is descended from a hairy, tailed quadruped, probably arboreal in its habits, and an inhabitant of the Old World. This creature, if its whole structure had been examined by a naturalist, would have been classed amongst the Quadrumana, as surely as the still more ancient progenitor of the Old and New World monkeys. The Quadrumana and all the higher mammals are probably derived from an ancient marsupial animal, and this through a long series of diversified forms, from some amphibian-like creature, and this again from some fish-like animal. In the dim obscurity of the past we can see that the early progenitor of all the Vertebrata must have

> We thus learn that man is descended from a hairy, tailed quadruped, probably arboreal in its habits, and an inhabitant of the Old World.
> *Charles Darwin*

4 *Text will always wrap around all four sides of a box if the topmost box **straddles** two columns.*

Wrap Text Around a Box

65

The Vertical Alignment options affect the entire text box. Leading and inter-paragraph spacing, which are paragraph formatting commands, are discussed in Chapter 6, Formats.

To change vertical alignment:

1. Choose the Item or Content tool, then click on a rectangular text box. Or choose the Item tool, then select multiple boxes (see page 167).

2. Choose Item > Modify (Cmd-M/Ctrl-M).

3. Click the Text tab.

4. From the Vertical Alignment: Type pop-up menu, choose Top, Centered, Bottom, or Justified **1**.

5. In vertically justified text with an Inter ¶ Max value of 0, space is added evenly between lines and paragraphs. An Inter ¶ Max value greater than 0 is the maximum space that can be added between paragraphs before leading is affected. Try raising this value and see what happens.

6. Click Apply to preview, then click OK **2**. *Note:* Make sure there is no return at the end of the last line in a box to which Bottom, Centered, or Justified Vertical Alignment has been applied, or the alignment will be thrown off. The Vertical Alignment options are affected by the First Baseline and text Inset: Top values.

TIP Vertical justification won't work if the justified text box is behind another box whose Runaround setting is other than None. To make justification work, change the Runaround Type to None for the top box (Item > Runaround).

TIP If you've chosen Centered alignment and your text happens not to have any descenders (characters that extend below the baseline), you may need to Baseline Shift the type downward slightly to make it look more centered.

1 *The four* **Vertical Alignment** *options*

2

Top vertical alignment

Bottom vertical alignment

Centered vertical alignment

Justified vertical alignment

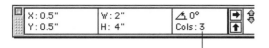

1 *The number of* **columns** *in a text box can be changed using the Measurements palette.*

There was a nice hot singey smell; and at the table, with an iron in her hand, stood a very stout short person staring anxiously at Lucie. Her print gown was tucked up, and she was wearing a large apron over her striped petti-

coat. Her little black nose went sniffle, sniffle, snuffle, and her eyes went twinkle, twinkle, twinkle; and underneath her cap—where Lucie had yellow curls—that little person had PRICKLES!

Beatrix Potter

2 *A* **two-column** *text box…*

There was a nice hot singey smell; and at the table, with an iron in her hand, stood a very stout short person staring anxiously at Lucie.

Her print gown was tucked up, and she was wearing a large apron over her striped petti-coat. Her little black nose went sniffle, snuffle,

and her eyes went twinkle, twinkle, twinkle; and underneath her cap—where Lucie had yellow curls—that little person had PRICKLES!

3 *…is converted into a* **three-column** *text box.*

Follow either set of instructions on this page to change the number of columns and/or the gutter width in an individual box. To change the non-printing margin and column guides or to change the number of columns in a box originating from a master page, follow the instructions on page 227.

To change the number of columns using the Measurements palette:

1. Choose the Item or Content tool.
2. Select a text box.
3. Enter a number in the "Cols" field on the Measurements palette **1**.
4. Press Return/Enter **2**–**3**.

To change columns and/or gutter width using a dialog box:

1. Choose the Item or Content tool.
2. Select a text box.
3. Choose Item > Modify (Cmd-M/ Ctrl-M), then click the Text tab.
4. Change the number in the Columns field (1–30) **4**.
   and/or
   Change the Gutter Width value for the blank space between the columns.
5. Click OK.

Change Columns, Gutter

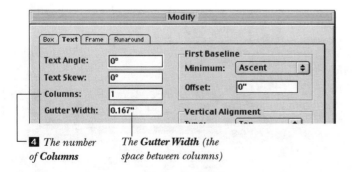

4 *The number of* **Columns**   *The* **Gutter Width** *(the space between columns)*

You can save a copy of text from a QuarkXPress file in the ASCII format, the XPress Tags format, or any of a number of different word processing file formats. If you apply style sheets to text in QuarkXPress and then export the text in the Microsoft Word format, the style sheets will save with the file and will be usable in Word. You can save all the text in a story, or just a highlighted portion.

To save text as a word processing file:

1. Choose the Content tool.

2. Highlight the text to be saved.
or
Click in a story.

3. Choose File > Save Text (Cmd-Option-E/Ctrl-Alt-E).
or
Control-click/Right-click and choose Save Text from the context menu.

4. Type a name for the text file in the Save text as/File name field **1**–**2**.

5. If text is highlighted in the document, you can click Entire Story or Selected Text. If you clicked in a story but didn't highlight any text, only the Entire Story option will be available.

6. Choose a file format from the Format pop-up menu. The import/export filter for a file format must be enabled in order for it to appear on the list. Use the XTensions Manager to turn a filter on or off (see page 393).

7. *Optional in Windows:* If you're saving in the ASCII format and you check Mac OS Line Endings, the standard Windows line break that is represented by a return and line feed character will be replaced by just a return character, which is standard in the Mac OS.

8. Choose a location in which to save the text file.

9. Click Save (Return/Enter).

What might get stripped out

Text saved in the ASCII format will be stripped of all formatting. Text saved in a word processing application format may be stripped of some formatting. Text saved in the XPress Tags format will retain all formatting, but it will display the special codes that are used for formatting when viewed in a word processing application. To learn more about XPress Tags, see the QuarkXPress documentation or David Blatner's *Real World QuarkXPress 5* (Peachpit Press).

1 *Type a name in the* **Save text as/File name** *field.*

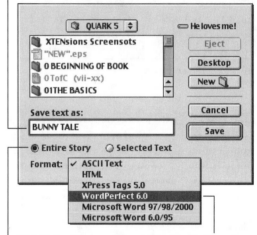

Click **Entire Story** *or click* **Selected Text** *(if available).*   *Choose a file* **Format**. *This is the Save Text dialog box in the* **Mac OS**.

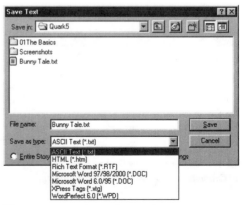

2 *The* **Save Text** *dialog box in* **Windows**

(sidebar) Save Text as Word Processing File

5.0!

Text Flow **5**

What if

If you didn't turn on **Automatic Text Box** in the New Document dialog box but later on you decide you need an auto text box, you can add it manually. See the instructions on page 238.

1 *In Edit > Preferences > Preferences > Document–General, choose* **Auto Page Insertion: End of Story, End of Section,** *or* **End of Document.**

In the previous chapter, you learned how to get text into a box. The next step is to learn how to route overflow text from box to box and from page to page. If the Auto Page Insertion option is on in Edit > Preferences > Preferences > Document–General, and your document contains an automatic text box, and then text is imported or input into an automatic text box, new pages will be added, if necessary, to contain any overflow text and text boxes will be linked from page to page. Auto page insertion is appropriate for documents in which a story flows consecutively from one page to the next, as in a book or booklet. A document can contain up to 2,000 pages. *Note:* For documents that contain multiple stories that may flow onto non-consecutive pages, as in a newsletter, manual linking is a better choice (see page 77).

To turn on auto page insertion:

1. Choose File > New (Cmd-N/Ctrl-N) to create a new print document.

2. Check Automatic Text Box to have an automatic text box appear on every document page.

3. Define the Page Size, Orientation, Margin Guides, and Column Guides, then click OK.

4. Choose Edit > Preferences > Preferences (Cmd-Y/Ctrl-Y), then click Document–General on the left side.

5. Choose Auto Page Insertion: End of Story, End of Section, or End of Document **1** (the location where you want new pages to be added).

6. Click OK.

A text file created in a word processing or spreadsheet program can be imported into a text box or boxes in QuarkXPress, provided its import/export filter is installed and enabled (see page 393). Formats that can be imported include word processing files (such as WordPerfect and MS-Word), HTML files, XPress Tags, and ASCII text with or without XPress Tags.

To import text:

1. *Optional:* Turn on Auto Page Insertion (see steps 4–6 on the previous page).

2. Choose the Content tool.

3. Click in a text box. Click in an automatic text box for auto page insertion. (If Auto Page Insertion is off, the imported text will flow into a box or a series of linked boxes, but new pages won't be added.)

4. Choose File > Get Text (Cmd-E/Ctrl-E).

5. Make sure Convert Quotes is checked ■.

6. *Optional:* Check Include Style Sheets if the file contains style sheets that you want to import.

7. Highlight a text file, then click Open. In Windows, you can use the "Files of type" drop-down menu to narrow or widen the selection.
or
Double-click a text file (■–■, next page).

*In the Mac OS, the **Type** (format) and **Size** of the currently highlighted file are shown here. In Windows, the **Name, Format, File Size,** and **Date** of the currently highlighted file are shown.*

■ *Check **Convert Quotes** to convert foot and inch marks into quotation marks (see page 118) and to convert double hyphens into em dashes.*

Word styles

■ To import style sheets applied to text in Microsoft Word, check **Include Style Sheets** in the Get Text dialog box. If any style sheet names in the Word document match style sheet names in the QuarkXPress document, an alert dialog box will appear. To learn about the options in that dialog box, see page 43 (the same dialog box appears if a conflict crops up while appending style sheets). Also check Include Style Sheets to import ASCII text with XPress tags as styled text (typographic and formatting attributes are included).

■ The **XPress Tags** filter must be enabled for the Include Style Sheets box to be available. Use the XTensions Manager to enable/disable this import/export filter.

*Click the **text file** to be imported.*

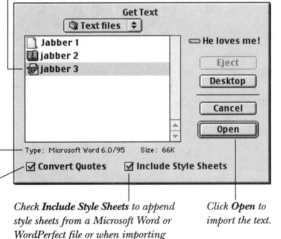

*Check **Include Style Sheets** to append style sheets from a Microsoft Word or WordPerfect file or when importing an ASCII file with XPress Tags codes.*

*Click **Open** to import the text.*

Import Text

Auto Page Insertion on

1 *Auto Page Insertion is on, an automatic text box is selected, and then a text file is imported.*

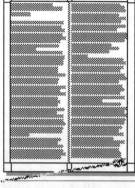

2 *New pages are created automatically to accommodate the imported text, and the text is linked in a continuous flow.*

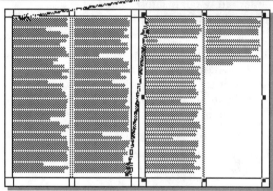

Auto Page Insertion off

3 *Auto Page Insertion is off, a non-automatic text box is selected, and then a text file is imported.*

4 *The box can't accommodate all the text, so the **text overflow** symbol appears in the lower right-hand corner.*

New pages can be added to a document using either the Insert Pages dialog box or the Document Layout palette. We usually use the Document Layout palette to add single pages and the dialog box to add multiple pages.

To insert pages using a dialog box:

1. *Optional:* We take a methodical approach to adding pages, since it can have a domino effect on the existing pages in a document. Our first step is to save our document, so we can use Revert to Saved if we need to. Our second step is to choose Page > Go to (Cmd-J/Ctrl-J), enter the number of the page we want pages inserted before or after, and then click OK.

2. If you want to link the new pages to an existing text chain, choose the Item or Content tool, then click a box in the chain.

3. Choose Page > Insert.

4. In the Insert field, enter the number of pages to be inserted (1–1999!) **3**.

5. Click **before page**, **after page**, or **at end of document**, and make sure the correct page number appears in the field. The number of the currently displayed document page will appear there, but you can enter a different number. If the page has a prefix or Roman style that was assigned via the Section command, type it in that manner.

6. Choose Master Page: Blank Single, Blank Facing Page, or a master page.

   If you want to link the new pages using an automatic text box, choose a Master Page that contains an automatic text box on which to base the new page(s), and check Link to Current Text Chain. (Linking is covered on pages 77–79 in this chapter, and Chapter 14 is devoted entirely to master pages.)

7. Click OK.

How many?

Need to know the total number of pages in a document? Make sure no page icons are highlighted on the Document Layout palette, then look at the total page count readout in the **lower left-hand corner** of the palette **1**.

Need more detailed information? Use an XTension. The **Text Toolkit** from Vision's Edge, Inc., for example, includes a **Document Statistics** dialog box and a **Count Story** dialog box, both of which list the number of words, characters, lines, and other data in a file **2**.

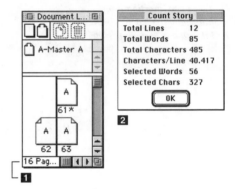

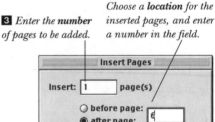

*Choose a **location** for the inserted pages, and enter a number in the field.*

3 *Enter the **number** of pages to be added.*

*Check **Link to Current Text Chain** to have the new pages linked to the end of the currently selected text chain.*

*Choose whether the inserted pages will be based on an existing **master** page or a **blank** master page.*

Master pages

Master pages are used to add repetitively used items to document pages, and you'll learn all about them in Chapter 14. For now, keep in mind that if you add an uneven number of pages to a facing-pages document (unless you drag it manually to a spread by itself with the Force Down pointer), the left and right master pages will reapply automatically from the inserted pages forward. Master pages won't reapply if you add an even number of pages to this type of document.

Single-sided blank   Facing-pages blank

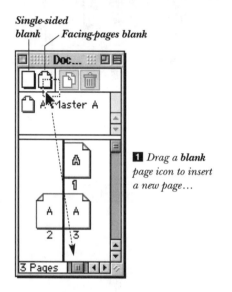

1 *Drag a **blank** page icon to insert a new page...*

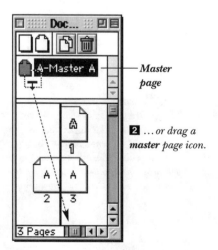

2 *...or drag a **master** page icon.*

Master page

If you check the Facing Pages box in the New Document dialog box for a print document, all pages after the first page will be stacked in pairs along a central spine. This format is used for book and magazine layouts. Facing document page icons have a turned-down (dog-eared) corner.

If you uncheck Facing Pages in the New Document dialog box, pages will be stacked singly. Single-sided page icons have square (not dog-eared) corners. To create a spread in a single-sided document, you can arrange document page icons side by side (see the following page). To convert a document from single-sided to facing-pages, or vice versa, see page 227.

Beware! Changes made using the Document Layout palette, such as adding, deleting, or rearranging pages, can't be undone with the Undo command, so be sure to save your document before performing any of those operations. Then, if something goes awry, you can resort to File > Revert to Saved to rescue your document.

To insert pages using the Document Layout palette:

1. Choose View > Show Document Layout (F10).

2. Drag a blank or master page icon into the document icon area (**1**–**2**, this page and **1**–**4**, next page). A blank page will not be associated with a master page and will not have an automatic text box, but a master page can be applied to it later (see page 231).

TIP You can't insert a page to the left of the first page in a facing-pages document, unless the document begins with an even section number (see page 84).

TIP If you Option-drag/Alt-drag a blank or master page, the Insert pages dialog box will open.

(Continued on the following page)

Insert Pages Manually

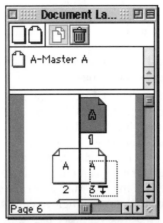

1 *To insert a page between spreads in a facing-pages document, release the mouse when the* **Force Down** *pointer is displayed.*

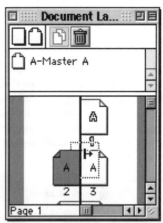

2 *In a facing-pages document, if you release the mouse when the* **Force Right** *pointer is displayed, subsequent pages may reshuffle. Pages won't reshuffle in a single-sided document.*

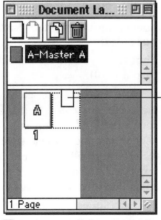

If you see this **non-force** *pointer (no arrow) when you release the mouse,* **no page reshuffling** *will occur.*

3 *To create a* **spread** *in a single-sided document (print documents only), drag a new page next to an existing page. Choose a very small view size for your document so you can see how the new arrangement looks.*

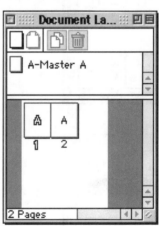

4 *With the page icons in this arrangement, pages 1 and 2 display side-by-side in the document window. The maximum overall width is 48". Pages will print one at a time unless Spreads is checked in File > Print > Document.*

Pages keep coming back

If, when you delete document pages from a print document, **Auto Page Insertion** is on (Edit > Preferences > Preferences > Document–General), the master page has an intact (not broken) chain icon (which means an automatic text box is present), and the text in a linked chain doesn't fit completely on the pages that remain, new pages will be added automatically to accommodate the overflow text. If this makes you feel like the sorcerer's apprentice, turn Auto Page Insertion off—the overflow symbol will appear, and no new pages will be added. In both scenarios, the overflow text is preserved.

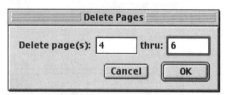

1 *Enter starting and ending page numbers if you want to delete a series of pages.*

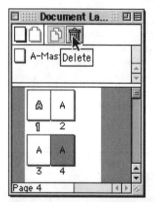

2 *To delete a page, click its icon, then click the **Delete** button.*

3 *Click OK when this prompt appears.*

Both methods on this page work equally well for deleting pages. It all comes down to personal preference—whether you're a dialog box kind of person or a palette kind of person.

To delete pages using a dialog box:

1. Choose Page > Delete.

2. Enter a number in the first field to delete one page.
or
Enter numbers in both fields to delete a range of pages **1**. If a page has a prefix or Roman style that was assigned via the Section command, type it in that manner. You can enter "end" in the second field to delete pages from the starting number through the end of the document.

3. Click OK.

To delete pages using the Document Layout palette:

1. On the Document Layout palette:
Click a document page icon **2**.
or
Click the icon of the first page in a series of pages to be deleted, then Shift-click the icon of the last page in the series.
or
Cmd-click/Ctrl-click non-consecutive page icons. (Cmd-click/Ctrl-click a selected page icon if you need to deselect it.)

2. Click the Delete button on the palette.

3. When the prompt "Are you sure you want to remove this page [or these pages]?" appears, click OK **3**.

TIP Option-click/Alt-click the Delete button on the palette (step 2, above) to bypass the prompt.

Delete Pages

If you rearrange pages in thumbnails view, you will be less likely to move the wrong ones, because you'll be able to see which ones you're moving.

To rearrange pages in Thumbnails view:

1. Choose View > Thumbnails (Shift-F6).
   or
   Press Control-V/Ctrl-Alt-V, press "t", then press Return/Enter.

2. Drag a page icon to a new location in the document window . If automatic page numbering was applied to the document, the numbers will update to reflect their new position.

3. Choose a different display size for the document.

TIP To move more than one page at a time, click the first page in a series of consecutive pages, Shift-click the last page in the series, then drag. Or Cmd-click/Ctrl-click to select non-consecutive pages, then drag.

TIP You can also rearrange pages using the Page > Move dialog box.

To rearrange pages using the Document Layout palette:

1. Choose View > Show Document Layout (F10).

2. Drag a document page icon to a new location 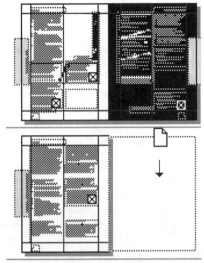–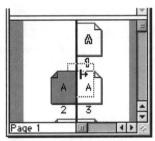.
   or
   Click the icon of the first page in a series of pages to be moved, Shift-click the icon of last page in the series, release Shift, then drag the pages to a new location. Or Cmd-click/Ctrl-click to select non-consecutive pages, then drag. (See also the figures on page 74.)

■ *A page being dragged to a new location*

2 *If you force a page between two* **pages** *in a facing-pages document, the remaining pages may reshuffle. Note the* **Force Right** *pointer.*

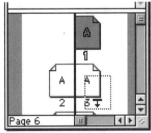

3 *If you force a page between two* **spreads** *in any kind of document, the remaining pages won't reshuffle. Note the* **Force Down** *pointer.*

Rearrange Pages

Keep on linkin'

Option-click/Alt-click the Linking tool to keep it selected so as to link multiple boxes. Click another tool when you're done linking. This works with the Unlinking tool, too.

Restoring deleted links 5.0!

In previous versions of QuarkXPress, if you deleted multiple text boxes that were linked to other text boxes that you didn't delete, you couldn't use Undo to restore the deleted boxes. Well, now you can.

Text that flows from box to box in a series of manually or automatically linked boxes is called a story. Manual linking can be used in addition, or as an alternative, to automatic page insertion. In a print document, you can use it to flow text between non-consecutive pages, as in a newsletter or magazine, or from one box to another on the same page. In a Web document, you can use it to link boxes on the same page.

To link text boxes or paths manually:

1. Choose the Linking tool. ⊛

2. Click on a text box or text path. It can contain text or it can be empty. A "marching ants" marquee will appear **1**.

3. Click on an **empty** text box or path. An arrow will appear briefly, showing the new link **2**–**3**. A new box can be added at any juncture in an existing chain.

TIP If you click the wrong box with the Linking tool, to stop the box from flashing, choose a different tool or click outside the box.

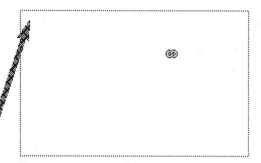

Again I see you're about to pounce,
alas, my poor computer mouse.

And losing this page I cannot afford,
but there you march across the keyboard.

You can't be hungry again so fast
Why the time's just barely passed.

Oh maybe I'll give you just a nibble,
just so you'll stay out of trib'l.

1 *Click a text box (or text path)…*

2 *…then click on an **empty** text box.*

Again I see you're about to pounce,
alas, my poor computer mouse.

And losing this page I cannot afford,
but there you march across the keyboard.

You can't be hungry again so fast
Why the time's just barely passed.

Oh maybe I'll give you just a nibble,
just so you'll stay out of trib'l.

I know it's warmer than my lap,
but the printer's not the place to nap.

And I don't need your claws to catch,
the printer's pages as they hatch.

To keep you from my papers chew'n
I guess I shouldn't leave them strew'n.

I just wish you wouldn't eat'm
before I've had a chance to read'm.

3 *The boxes are now **linked**.*

Link Text Boxes or Text Paths

To unlink text boxes or paths:

1. Choose the Unlinking tool. 🔧

2. Click one of the text boxes in the chain that you want to unlink.

3. Click the head or tail of the link arrow **1**. Links preceding the break will remain intact; the link to succeeding boxes or paths will be broken **2**. (You can't undo this, but you can relink.)

TIP If you are unable to unlink with the Unlinking tool, make sure there are no other items obstructing the one that you're trying to click on.

TIP If you click in a linked box with the Content tool, you can use the up or down arrow on the keyboard to jump from the first line in the box to the last line of the previous box in the chain or from the last line in the box to the first line in the next box in the chain.

TIP If you rearrange pages in a text chain, the links will stay intact.

Find the links

To see where the links are in a document, choose a small display size (around 30%), then click one of the boxes in the link chain with the Unlinking tool. Choose a different tool when you're finished.

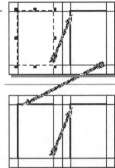

Ah, what can ever be more stately and admirable to me than mast-hemm'd Manhattan?

River and sunset and scallop-edg'd waves of flood-tide?

The sea-gulls oscillating their bodies, the hay-boat in the twilight, and the belated lighter?

What gods can exceed these that clasp me by the hand, and with voices I love call me promptly and loudly by my nighest name as I approach?

What is more subtle than this which ties me to the woman or man that looks in my face?

Which fuses me into you now, and pours my meaning into you?

Walt Whitman

1 *With the Unlinking tool, click a text box, then click the **head** or **tail** of the **arrow** that connects it to another box.*

Ah, what can ever be more stately and admirable to me than mast-hemm'd Manhattan?

River and sunset and scallop-edg'd waves of flood-tide?

The sea-gulls oscillating their bodies, the hay-boat in the twilight, and the belated lighter?

2 *The link is **broken**.*

Unlink Text Boxes or Text Paths

Oronte. Do you find anything to object to in my sonnet?

Alceste. I do not say that. But, to keep him from writing, I set before his eyes how, in our days, that desire had spoiled a great many very worthy people.

Oronte. Do I write badly? Am I like them in any way?

Alceste. I do not say that. But, in short, I said to him: What pressing need is there for you to rhyme, and what the deuce drives you into print? If we can pardon the sending into the world of a

badly-written book, it will only be in those unfortunate men who write for their livelihood. Believe me, resist your temptations, keep these effusions from the public, and do not, how much soever you may be asked, forfeit the reputation which you enjoy...

Molière

1 *Choose the **Unlinking** tool, then **Shift-click** inside the box to be unlinked from the chain.*

Copy, paste, duplicate linked boxes

You can copy, paste, or duplicate a linked text box or boxes. You can also drag-copy a linked box between documents or into a library. Text preceding the box in the chain, if any, won't copy; overflow text will copy, but it will be hidden. To copy an entire story, be sure to copy the **first** box in the chain.

To delete a box or a path from a text chain and preserve the chain:

1. Choose the Item or Content tool.

2. Select the box or path to be deleted.

3. Choose Item menu > Delete (Cmd-K/ Ctrl-K). Simple! The text will be rerouted to the next box in the chain.

To unlink a text box or path from a chain and preserve the box and chain:

1. Choose the Unlinking tool. 🔗

2. Shift-click **inside** the text box to be removed from the chain **1**–**2**.

TIP Using the Text Toolkit XTension from Vision's Edge, Inc., you can perform magic tricks, like unlinking a chain but leaving the text exactly where it is.

Oronte. Do you find anything to object to in my sonnet?

Alceste. I do not say that. But, to keep him from writing, I set before his eyes how, in our days, that desire had spoiled a great many very worthy people.

Oronte. Do I write badly? Am I like them in any way?

Alceste. I do not say that. But, in short, I said to him: What pressing need is there for you to rhyme, and what the deuce drives you into print? If we can pardon the sending into the

2 *The middle box has been **unlinked** from the chain.*

Unlink Text Boxes or Text Paths

Let's say you're doing a rough layout and you need some mock text to fill in some boxes on your page. The free, downloadable Jabberwocky XTension supplies you with a choice of five default "languages," in prose or verse. Actually, it's a bunch of mindless babble written by overworked Quark programmers. If you're ambitious or have a light schedule, you can create and edit your own jabber text.

Jabberwocky, if you don't happen to know, is the name of a wonderful poem in the book *Through the Looking Glass* by Lewis Carroll ("Twas brillig, and the slithy toves did gyre and gimble in the wabe..."). Love that book.

To fill text boxes with dummy text:

1. *Optional:* To specify the text to be used, choose Edit > Preferences > Preferences–Jabberwocky, choose English, Esperanto, Klingon, Latinesque, Politics Speak, or a custom language from the "When Jabbering, use" pop-up menu **1**, choose Prose or Verse from the "Jabber in" pop-up menu, then click OK.

2. To fill a text box/path or a series of linked boxes/paths with dummy text based on the parameters chosen in Jabberwocky Preferences, choose the Content tool, click in a text box or path, then choose Utilities > Jabber **2**–**3**.

   Note: If you used Jabber to fill a chain of boxes or paths, there won't be any hidden overflow text. The text will stop at the end of the last box or path in the chain.

You can invent your own Jabberwocky language or edit an existing language.

To create or edit a Jabberwocky set:

1. Choose Edit > Jabberwocky sets.

2. Click an existing set, then click Edit **4**.
   or
   Click New, then enter a name in the Set name field.

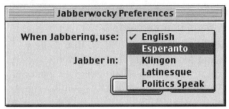

1 *Choose a "language" in the **Jabberwocky Preferences** dialog box.*

> Qo'noS Qagh reH
> 'ach wa' verengan jon vatlh Qav DenIbya' Qatlhs
> Ach QI'tomer ah po' tlb tera'.
> Wa' pov Quch HIv vatlh QaQ meHloDnI'S
> Joq vagh QIp 'ejyo'S reH chop Qo'noS.
> Vatlh DIvI'S tlha' wa' ych

2 *Klingon verse*

> Two irascible lampstands laughed, and one sheep grew up, even though two pawnbrokers ran away almost drunkenly, and five wart hogs telephoned botulisms, although Batman bought Minnesota, and five aardvarks towed Quark. One bourgeois trailer quickly fights two fountains. One mat ran

3 *The point of using dummy text is to create a text "texture." If you find any of the jabber languages distracting or idiotic, by all means don't use them. This is QuarkXPress' **English** prose jabber language.*

4 *You can create, edit, duplicate, or delete a jabberwocky set using the **Edit Jabberwocky Sets** dialog box.*

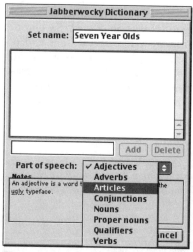

1 Use the **Jabberwocky Dictionary** dialog box to add or delete words from a Jabberwocky set.

Simoneyeh logega Cuplook kwan fala funo jala vata mopie heyso plineto nata palaty gwoglerog kumo Simoner izame hitu plineto luba wenenb bobega gosie fotin jekah rutil Katal cata Simoneyeh logega Cuplook kwan fala funo jala vata mopie heyso plineto nata palaty gwoglerog kumo Simoner izame hitu

2 *Alicia's invented words*

Waper Watershlash pladerwop sickwons pladerwap crapis wapils toyswos stickap irlis crabler swo florap blogubyap botens dogulis craler Momylis adylis evrop ofils woropwap glasulis flwowwo rumdeydume lickwick twoglis evroslis swols swigis eywoshlis cinbwlis irpulis swundedome crocklis ircks flopis

3 *Simona's invented words*

3. Here's where the fun starts. Choose a Part of speech from the pop-up menu, type a real or made-up word in the field, then click Add **1**. (To delete a word, click on it, then click Delete.)

4. Click Save **2**–**3**. The new set will appear on the first pop-up menu in the Jabberwocky Preferences dialog box.

The Line Check command, which is part of the free TypeTricks XTension, can be used to find out how many overflow text boxes are present in a document, along with other typesetting data, and it can get your cursor to each and every one, if you want to go there.

To use the Line Check command:

1. Choose Utilities > Line Check > Search Criteria.

2. Check Text Box Overflow, and check or uncheck any other boxes to include/exclude those criteria from the search **4**.

3. Click Count, if desired, and note the figures. Then click OK.

4. To start the search, click in a text box, then choose Utilities > Line Check > First Line. The first instance will be highlighted in the document.

5. To jump from one instance to the next, press Cmd-;/Ctrl-;.

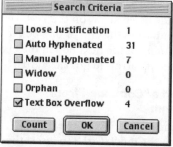

4 *In the **Search Criteria** dialog box, choose what you want QuarkXPress to search for.*

Line Check

When text is linked between non-consecutive pages, as in a newsletter or magazine, there is usually an indicator to guide the reader to the continuation of a story or article. These "Continued on" and "Continued from" indicators are called "jump lines." When the Next Box Page Number command is inserted, like magic, it instantly converts into the page number of the next linked box in the chain. If that text is re-linked or moved to a different page, the page number will update automatically.

To insert a "Continued on" command:

1. Choose the Rectangle text box tool. Or if you want to get fancy, choose a Bézier text box or text path tool.

2. Create a separate, small box or path that overlaps the main text box of the story, and keep it selected.

3. Choose Item > Runaround (Cmd-T/ Ctrl-T).

4. Choose Type: Item.

5. Click OK.

6. Choose the Content tool.

7. Type any desired text into the small box, such as "Continued on page," or use a graphic symbol, such as an arrow. The keystrokes for entering Zapf Dingbat characters are in Appendix A.

8. Press Cmd-4/Ctrl-4 to insert the Next Box Page Number command **1**–**3**. Don't enter the actual page number! It will appear automatically.

TIP Use the down arrow on the keyboard to jump from the end of one box to the beginning of the next box in the chain (or the up arrow to go backwards).

To insert a "Continued from" command:

Follow the instructions above, but for step 8, press Cmd-2/Ctrl-2 to insert the Previous Box Page Number command **4**.

Elizabeth here felt herself called on to say something in vindication of his behaviour to Wickham; and therefore gave them to understand, in as guarded a manner as she could, that by what she had heard from his relations in Kent, his actions were capable of a very different construction; and that his

Continued on page 3

1 *A text box containing the **Next Box Page Number** command is positioned so that it overlaps the main text box.*

Continued from page <None>

2 *If the characters <**None**> appear instead of a page number, either the text box or path containing the Previous or Next Box Page Number command is not overlapping a linked text box, or the text box it overlaps is not linked to a box on another page.*

Continued on page 3

3 *You can create a jump line on a text path.*

4 *The **Previous Box Page Number** command is inserted here.*

Continued from page 1

character was by no means so faulty, nor Wickham's so amiable, as they had been considered in Hertfordshire. In confirmation of this, she related the particulars of all the pecuniary transactions in which they had been connected, without actually naming her authority, but stating it to be such as might be relied on.

Jane Austen

Rescuing an unsaveable file

If you get an error message that says your file can't be saved, **DON'T CLOSE IT**! Take a deep breath, chant a mantra, create a new document or open a template that has the same dimensions, use the method on this page to drag pages from the old document to the new (saving the new file periodically), then trash the corrupted file. If that doesn't work, the Markz Tools XTension by Markzware Software has a salvage feature for opening and salvaging damaged files.

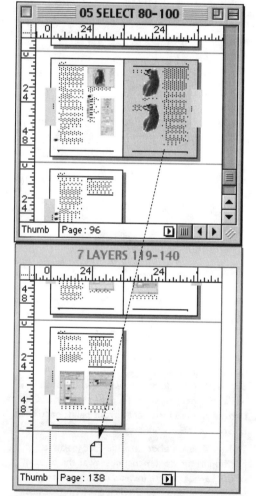

1 *Drag-copying pages* in *Thumbnails* view from one document to another

Notes: You can't copy a page to a document that has a smaller page size. A page to which a facing-pages master has been applied can't be copied to a single-sided document. Any style sheets, colors, dashes and stripes, lists, H&Js, or master pages on the appending pages will be added to the target document. And finally, if your document contains multiple layers, please read the sidebar on page 261!

To drag-copy pages from one document to another:

1. Open the document you want to copy from and the one you want to copy to.

2. In the Mac OS: Option-Shift-press the title bar of either document and choose Tile Documents. In Windows: Choose Window > Tile Vertically, then choose View > Thumbnails.

   TIP To make room for new pages at the end of a document, drag the resize box on the target document window upward, click the down scroll arrow to scoot the document pages upward, then drag the resize box to lengthen the document window again (see the bottom window in the illustration at left).

3. Drag a page icon from one document window into the other. A copy of the page will appear in the target document. Pages will reshuffle depending on where you release the mouse (watch for the Force Right, Force Left, Force Down, or non-force pointer).
   or
   To drag multiple pages, click the first page in a series of consecutive pages, Shift-click the last page in the series **1**, then drag (or Cmd-click/Ctrl-click non-consecutive pages). If the pages to be drag-copied contain linked text, copy all the linked pages at once. Otherwise, the text from the linked boxes will copy, but the links will be broken.

Drag-Copy Pages Between Documents

The Section command renumbers all or some of the pages in a document with a user-specified starting number. This is useful for publications like books that are composed of multiple files. You can choose a different page numbering format for each section. For example, in this book, the lowercase Roman format is used for the Table of Contents and the numeric format is used for the main body of the book. *Note:* To make the page numbers actually appear on your document pages, follow the instructions on page 228.

To number a multi-file document automatically, you can use the Book feature (see Chapter 21).

To number a section of a file:

1. Display the page where the new section is to begin by double-clicking its icon on the Document Layout palette.
   or
   Choose Page > Go to (Cmd-J/Ctrl-J), enter the number of the page that is to begin the new section, then click OK.

2. Click the page number in the lower left corner of the Document Layout palette.
   or
   Choose Page > Section.

3. Check Section Start **1**.

4. Enter the desired starting Number for the section.

5. *Optional:* Enter a maximum of four characters in the Prefix field (e.g., "Page").

6. *Optional:* Choose a different numbering Format.

7. Click OK.

TIP If you section-number a facing-pages document starting with an even number, the first page will become a left-hand page. The remaining pages won't necessarily follow suit and switch their right or left-hand positions, though.

1 *Check Section Start, enter a Prefix (if you need one), enter the starting Number, and choose a numbering Format.*

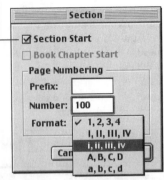

(The Book Chapter Start box is available only when a chapter is opened independently of its book.)

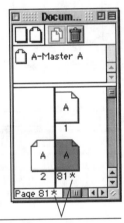

Why the asterisk?

An asterisk below a page icon on the Document Layout palette signifies that a **section** starts on that page. If the first page in a section is currently displayed in the document window, an asterisk will also appear next to the page number at the bottom of the Document Layout palette and the bottom of the document window.

To have a page's **absolute** number (relative position in the document) display at the bottom of the Layout palette instead of its number in a section, Option-click/Alt-click the icon (see also the first tip on page 49).

Number a Section

Using the Next Box and Next Column characters

The Next Box character pushes text to the next box in a linked chain. The Next Column character pushes text to the next column within the same box (or in some cases, the next text box in the chain).

I come from haunts of coot and hern,
I make a sudden sally,
And sparkle out among the fern,
To bicker down a valley.

By thirty hills I hurry down,
Or slip between the ridges,
By twenty thorps, a little town,
And half a hundred bridges.

Till last by Philip's farm I flow
to join the brimming river,
For men may come and men may go,
But I go on for ever.

I chatter over stony ways,
In little sharps and trebles,
I bubble into eddying bays,
I babble on the pebbles.

With many a curve my banks I fret
By many a field and fallow,
And many fair foreland set
With willow-weed and mallow.

I chatter, chatter, as I flow
To join the brimming river,
For men may come and men may go,
But I go on for ever.

—*Alfred Tennyson*

The original text boxes

I come from haunts of coot and hern,
I make a sudden sally,
And sparkle out among the fern,
To bicker down a valley.

By thirty hills I hurry down,
Or slip between the ridges,
By twenty thorps, a little town,
And half a hundred bridges.

Till last by Philip's farm I flow
to join the brimming river,
For men may come and men may go,
But I go on for ever.
⤋

I chatter over stony ways,
In little sharps and trebles,
I bubble into eddying bays,
I babble on the pebbles.

With many a curve my banks I fret
By many a field and fallow,
And many fair foreland set
With willow-weed and mallow.

I chatter, chatter, as I flow
To join the brimming river,
For men may come and men may go,
But I go on for ever.

—*Alfred Tennyson*

*Instead of shortening the text box to push the text to the next box, a **Next Box** character (**Shift-Enter***) is inserted. Remove a Next Box character as you would any text character: Click to the right of it with the Content tool, then press Delete/Backspace.*

*Use the numeric keypad.

*The **Next Box** character (Shift-Enter*)(turn on View > **Show Invisibles** to see it)*

I come from haunts of coot and hern,
I make a sudden sally,
And sparkle out among the fern,
To bicker down a valley.

By thirty hills I hurry down,
Or slip between the ridges,
By twenty thorps, a little town,
And half a hundred bridges. ↓

Till last by Philip's farm I flow
to join the brimming river,
For men may come and men may go,
But I go on for ever.

I chatter over stony ways,
In little sharps and trebles,
I bubble into eddying bays,
I babble on the pebbles.

*The **Next Column** character (**Enter***)*

Placing one header over two columns

Ruler guide

The Night in Isla Negra

The ancient night and the unruly salt
beat at the walls of my house;
lonely is the shadow, the sky
by now is a beat of the ocean,
and sky and shadow explode
in the fray of unequal combat;
all night long they struggle,
nobody knows the weight

of the harsh clarity that will go on opening
like a languid fruit;
thus is born on the coast,
out of the turbulent shadow, the hard dawn,
nibbled by the salt in movement,
swept up by the weight of night,
bloodstained in its marine crater.

Pablo Neruda

*You can align text baseline-to-baseline in **separate** boxes using a **ruler guide**. Make sure the leading is the same in both boxes.*

TIP *Choose the Item tool and press the up or down arrow key to nudge the box upward or downward one point at a time; press Option-arrow/Alt-arrow to nudge it in $\frac{1}{10}$-point increments.*

The Night in Isla Negra

The ancient night and the unruly salt
beat at the walls of my house;
lonely is the shadow, the sky
by now is a beat of the ocean,
and sky and shadow explode
in the fray of unequal combat;
all night long they struggle,
nobody knows the weight

of the harsh clarity that will go on opening
like a languid fruit;
thus is born on the coast,
out of the turbulent shadow, the hard dawn,
nibbled by the salt in movement,
swept up by the weight of night,
bloodstained in its marine crater.

Pablo Neruda

*Or place the header in a separate box and put the main text in a **two-column** box below it.*

Formats **6**

Do it with style!

Once you learn the basics of paragraph formatting, by all means learn how to apply all the same attributes via **style sheets**. Believe us, you'll save yourself a lot of monotonous work.

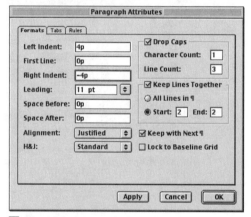

1 *Most of the commands that affect whole paragraphs are found in the Formats, Tabs, and Rules panes of the Paragraph Attributes dialog box.*

Paragraph formats

Well, you've managed to get some text onto your page, but it's just sitting there in a big clump and it's hard to read. By adding space between lines and paragraphs and applying other formats where appropriate, not only will your type look more elegant and professional, it will also be easier to read.

All the formatting commands described in this chapter affect entire paragraphs rather than individual characters. These commands, which are accessed via the **Style** menu when text is highlighted, include horizontal alignment, hyphenation and justification, indents, leading, space before/after, keeping lines together, rules, tabs, and paragraph style sheets **1**. In the next chapter, you'll learn the ins and outs of typography (styling characters in different fonts, point sizes, and so on).

A paragraph consists of one or more characters or words, followed by an invisible **Return** character. A Return looks like this when View > Show Invisibles is on: ¶. Paragraph formats can be applied manually—or even better, using a style sheet (see Chapter 13).

The following features are *not* available for HTML text boxes: Force and Justified alignment; H&Js; Lock to Baseline Grid; Tabs; First Baseline; and Inter-Paragraph Max. Those features are available for an HTML text box that has been converted to a raster text box (Item > Modify > Convert to Graphic on Export). Raster boxes increase file size and download time, however, so this option should be used judiciously (see Chapter 19.)

To indent a whole paragraph:

1. Choose the Content tool.

2. Click in a paragraph or drag downward through a series of paragraphs **1**.

3. Choose Style > Formats (Cmd-Shift-F/Ctrl-Shift-F).

4. Enter a Left Indent and/or Right Indent value in any measurement system used in QuarkXPress **2**.

5. Click Apply to preview (Cmd-A in the Mac OS) **3**–**4**. Or Option-click/Alt-click Apply to turn on continuous apply (Alt-A in Windows). Click in, or Tab to, another field to activate it.

6. Click OK.

TIP Individual format dialog boxes can be accessed from the bottom of the Style menu or by clicking the Formats, Tabs, or Rules tab in the Paragraph Attributes dialog box.

THE MAIN CONCLUSION ARRIVED AT IN THIS WORK, NAMELY, THAT MAN IS DESCENDED FROM SOME LOWLY ORGANISED FORM, WILL, I REGRET TO THINK, BE HIGHLY DISTASTEFUL TO MANY. BUT THERE CAN HARDLY BE A DOUBT THAT WE ARE DESCENDED FROM BARBARIANS.

1 *A paragraph with 0 indents*

2 *Enter **Left Indent** and/or **Right Indent** values.*

THE MAIN CONCLUSION ARRIVED AT IN THIS WORK, NAMELY, THAT MAN IS DESCENDED FROM SOME LOWLY ORGANISED FORM, WILL, I REGRET TO THINK, BE HIGHLY DISTASTEFUL TO MANY. BUT THERE CAN HARDLY BE A DOUBT THAT WE ARE DESCENDED FROM BARBARIANS.

3 *A paragraph with a **left indent** of 2p (called a "block" indent)*

THE MAIN CONCLUSION ARRIVED AT IN THIS WORK, NAMELY, THAT MAN IS DESCENDED FROM SOME LOWLY ORGANISED FORM, WILL, I REGRET TO THINK, BE HIGHLY DISTASTEFUL TO MANY. BUT THERE CAN HARDLY BE A DOUBT THAT WE ARE DESCENDED FROM BARBARIANS.

Charles Darwin

4 *A paragraph with a **right indent** of 2p*

Paragraph Indents

1 *The **First Line** indent field in the Paragraph Attributes (Formats) dialog box*

Paragraph Attributes

| Formats | Tabs | Rules |

Left Indent: 4p

First Line: p10

Right Indent: 0p

Leading: 14 pt

Space Before: 0p

☐ Drop

Charact

Line Co

☐ Keep

○ All Li

> Oronte. [To Alceste] But for you, you know our agreement. Speak to me, I pray, in all sincerity.
>
> Alceste. These matters, sir, are always more or less delicate, and every one is fond of being praised for his wit.
>
> But I was saying one day to a certain person, who shall be nameless, when he showed me some of his verses, that a gentleman ought at all times to exercise a great control over that itch for writing which sometimes attacks us, and should keep a tight rein over the strong propensity which one has to display such amusements; and that, in the frequent anxiety to show their productions, people are frequently exposed to act a very foolish part.
>
> *Molière*

2 *A **first line indent** enhances readability.*

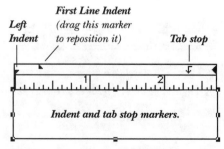

First Line Indent
(drag this marker to reposition it)

Left Indent

Tab stop

Indent and tab stop markers.

3 *The width of the Paragraph **Formats** ruler matches the width of the currently selected text box.*

If you need to indent type in QuarkXPress, you should use the Indent fields in the Format dialog box. You shouldn't use spaces (Spacebar) to indent text. If you do, the lines won't line up properly because typeset characters are not equal in width, as they are on a typewriter.

To indent the first line of a paragraph:

1. Choose the Content tool.

2. Click in a paragraph or drag downward through a series of paragraphs.

3. Choose Style > Formats (Cmd-Shift-F/ Ctrl-Shift-F).

4. Enter a First Line value **1**. If you're not sure what value to use, start with the point size of the text you're indenting.

5. Click Apply to preview (Cmd-A/Alt-A).

6. Click OK **2**.

TIP When the Paragraph Formats dialog box is open, a ruler displays over the currently selected text box. Indents and tab stops can be adjusted by dragging the indent and tab stop markers in the ruler **3**. To insert a new tab stop, click in the ruler. (Read more about tabs in Chapter 8.)

TIP The first paragraph in a story, especially the paragraph that follows a headline or subhead, looks better flush left than indented.

TIP Paragraph indent values will be added to any Text Inset value applied to the text box (see page 59).

Leading (line spacing) is the distance from baseline to baseline between lines of type, and it's measured in points. Three types of leading are used in QuarkXPress:

Absolute leading is an amount that remains fixed regardless of the point size of the type to which it is applied **1**.

We use Absolute leading because we like to specify fixed leading values, but there is an alternative, called **Auto** leading, that you may as well know about. Auto leading is calculated for each line of text based on the point size of the largest character in that line **2**. The percentage used for that calculation is specified in the Auto Leading field in Edit > Preferences > Preferences > Document–Paragraph, and it applies to the entire document. If 20% were the current percentage and the largest character in a line of text is 10 pt., the leading for that line would be 12 pt. You won't see a percentage in the Leading field; you'll just see the word "auto." Alternatively, you can enter an incremental value, such as +2 or -2, in the Auto Leading field. In this case the leading is calculated based on the point size of the largest character in each line, plus or minus that increment; the increment will appear in the Leading field on the Measurements palette.

To change paragraph leading using the Measurements palette:

1. Choose the Content tool.

2. Click in a paragraph or drag downward through a series of paragraphs.

3. Enter a number in the Leading field on the Measurements palette **3**.
or
Click the up arrow on the Measurements palette to increase the leading or the down arrow to reduce the leading in 1-point increments. Option-click/Alt-click an arrow to increase or reduce the leading in .1-point increments.

But the moment that she moved again he recognized her. The effect upon her old lover was electric, far stronger than the effect of his presence upon her. His fire, the tumultuous ring of his eloquence, seemed to go out of him. His lip struggled and trembled under the words that lay upon it; but deliver them it could not as long as she faced him. His eyes, after their first glance...

1 *A paragraph with 11 pt. **absolute** leading: The leading is consistent throughout, despite the fact that two different point sizes are applied to the type in the first line of the paragraph.*

But the moment that she moved again he recognized her. The effect upon her old lover was electric, far stronger than the effect of his presence upon her.

2 *The same paragraph with **auto** leading: The large initial cap is throwing the whole thing off, and it ain't pretty.*

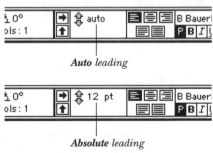

Auto leading

Absolute leading

3 *The **leading** area on the **Measurements** palette*

He put some sticking plaster on his fingers, and his friends both came to dinner. He could not offer them fish, but he had something else in his larder.

Sir Isaac Newton wore his black and gold waistcoat. And Mr. Alderman Ptolemy Tortoise brought a salad with him in a string bag.

And instead of a nice dish of minnows they had a roasted grasshopper with lady-bird sauce, which frogs consider a beautiful treat; but I think it must have been nasty!   *Beatrix Potter*

*Use **spacious leading** to enhance readability if your text is set in a **wide column**, in a **sans serif** or **bold** font, or in a font that has a **large x-height**, **tall ascenders**, or **tall descenders**. This is 8 pt. Gill Sans Regular with roomy 11 pt. leading.*

He put some sticking plaster on his fingers, and his friends both came to dinner. He could not offer them fish, but he had something else in his larder.

Sir Isaac Newton wore his black and gold waist-coat.

And Mr. Alderman Ptolemy Tortoise brought a salad with him in a string bag.

And instead of a nice dish of minnows they had a roasted grasshopper with lady-bird sauce, which frogs consider a beautiful treat; but I think it must have been nasty!

*You can use **tighter leading** for **serif** body text or **multiple-line headlines** or **subheads**. This is 8 pt. Bauer Bodoni with 10 pt. leading.*

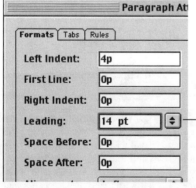

1 *The **Leading** area in the Paragraph Attributes (Formats) dialog box*

To change paragraph leading using the keyboard:

1. Choose the Content tool.

2. Click in a paragraph or drag downward through a series of paragraphs.

3. Hold down Cmd/Ctrl and Shift and press ' to increase leading or ; to decrease leading in 1-point increments. When the leading is on auto, it switches to absolute when you use this shortcut.

TIP Add Option/Alt to the keystroke above to modify leading in .1 increments.

TIP The traditional way to notate point size and leading is to divide the two values by a slash. For example, "8/11" represents 8-point type with 11-point leading.

To change paragraph leading using a dialog box:

1. Choose the Content tool.

2. Click in a paragraph or drag downward through a series of paragraphs.

3. Choose Style > Leading (Cmd-Shift-E/Ctrl-Shift-E).

4. The Leading field will highlight automatically. Type an amount in an increment as small as .001 **1**. You don't need to enter the "pt".

5. Click OK.

TIP Leading has no affect on the position of the first line of text in a box. To lower text from the top of its box, select the box, choose Item > Modify, click the Text tab, click Text Inset: Multiple Insets, then enter a Top value.

Leading

To change horizontal alignment:

1. Choose the Content tool.

2. Click in a paragraph or drag downward through a series of paragraphs.

3. Click one of the five horizontal alignment icons on the Measurements palette **1**. The Justified and Force Justified options are not available for HTML text boxes.

   Note: Forced Justified alignment justifies all the lines in a paragraph—including the last line. For this option, make sure the paragraph has a Return character (¶) at the end.

TIP Only one alignment option can be applied per paragraph.

TIP Horizontal alignment can also be changed using the shortcuts listed at right; the Style > Alignment submenu; or the Alignment pop-up menu in the Style > Formats dialog box.

TIP Hyphenation should be turned on for justified text to help reduce gaps between words (see pages 103–105).

Horizontal alignment shortcuts

Flush left, ragged right	Cmd-Shift-L/Ctrl-Shift-L
Centered	Cmd-Shift-C/Ctrl-Shift-C
Flush right, ragged left	Cmd-Shift-R/Ctrl-Shift-R
Justified	Cmd-Shift-J/Ctrl-Shift-J
Forced Justified	Cmd-Option-Shift-J/ Ctrl-Alt-Shift-J

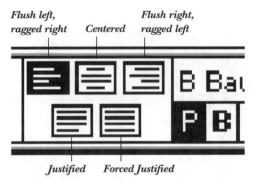

1 *The five* **horizontal alignment** *icons on the Measurements palette*

So we was all right now, as to the shirt and the sheet and the spoon and the candles, by the help of the calf and rats and the mixed-up counting; and as to the candlestick, it warn't no consequence, it would blow over by and by....
Mark Twain

Flush left, ragged right

So we was all right now, as to the shirt and the sheet and the spoon and the candles, by the help of the calf and rats and the mixed-up counting; and as to the candlestick, it warn't no consequence, it would blow over by and by....

Centered

So we was all right now, as to the shirt and the sheet and the spoon and the candles, by the help of the calf and rats and the mixed-up counting; and as to the candlestick, it warn't no consequence, it would blow over by and by....

The more **varied** *the line lengths are in* **centered** *text, the better it looks.*

So we was all right now, as to the shirt and the sheet and the spoon and the candles, by the help of the calf and rats and the mixed-up counting; and as to the candlestick, it warn't noconsequence, it would blow over by and by....

Flush right, ragged left

So we was all right now, as to the shirt and the sheet and the spoon and the candles, by the help of the calf and rats and the mixed-up counting; and as to the candlestick, it warn't no consequence, it would blow over by and by....

Justified

So we was all right now, as to the shirt and the sheet and the spoon and the candles, by the help of the calf and rats and the mixed-up counting; and as to the candlestick, it warn't no consequence, it would blow   over   by   and   by.

Forced Justifed

Use this method to adjust a headline or fix an awkward break in ragged left or ragged right copy. We have to admit, QuarkXPress does a poor job of wrapping and hyphenating text, and we often have to fiddle with our paragraphs manually to make them look better. Sigh. (Quark 6?)

To break a line without creating a new paragraph:

1. Choose the Content tool.

2. Click just to the left of a word that you want to bring down to the next line.

3. If it's a hyphenated word, hold down Cmd/Ctrl and press "-" (hyphen) to insert a discretionary hyphen. (To remove a discretionary hyphen, click at the beginning of the next line, then press Delete/Backspace.
or
If the word isn't hyphenated, press Shift-Return/Shift-Enter **1**–**3**.

1 *This is an awkward break.*

The night so luminous on the spar-deck, but otherwise on the cavernous ones below—levels so very like the tiered|galleries in a coal-mine—the luminous night passed away. Like the prophet in the chariot disappearing in heaven and dropping his mantle to Elisha, the withdrawing night transferred its pale robe to the peeping day.

The night so luminous on the spar-deck, but otherwise on the cavernous ones below—levels so very like the tiered¶

galleries in a coal-mine—the luminous night passed away. Like the prophet in the chariot disappearing in heaven and dropping his mantle to Elisha, the withdrawing night transferred its pale robe to the peeping day.

2 *A paragraph **Return** creates a new **paragraph**— no good.*

The night so luminous on the spar-deck, but otherwise on the cavernous ones below—levels so very like the tiered galleries in a coal-mine—the luminous night passed away. Like the prophet in the chariot disappearing in heaven and dropping his mantle to Elisha, the withdrawing night transferred its pale robe to the peeping day.
Herman Melville

3 *Pressing **Shift-Return/Shift-Enter** creates a line break within the same paragraph—much better.*

Line Break

Note: The numbers entered in the Space Before and Space After fields are added together, so try to be consistent and use one most of the time and the other for special circumstances. For example, we use Space After for body text and use Space Before to add extra space above our subheads.

To add space between paragraphs:

1. Choose the Content tool.
2. Click in a paragraph or drag downward through a series of paragraphs.
3. Choose Style > Formats (Cmd-Shift-F/ Ctrl-Shift-F).
4. Enter a Space Before or Space After value **1**.
5. Click Apply to preview (Cmd-A/Alt-A).
6. Click OK **2**.

TIP The Space Before command has no effect on the first line of text in a box. To move text downward on a page, the simplest thing is to move the box itself—an obvious solution that's easy to forget! If you don't want to move the box, use First Baseline (see page 63) or Text Inset (see page 59).

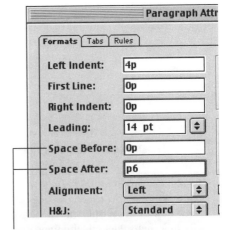

1 *The Space Before and Space After fields in Paragraph Attributes > Formats*

O to be a Virginian where I grew up! O to be a Carolinian! O longings irrepressible! O I will go back to old Tennessee and never wander more.

Mannahatta

I was asking for something specific and perfect for my city, Whereupon lo! upsprang the aboriginal name.

Now I see what there is in a name, a word, liquid, sane, unruly, musical, self-sufficient, I see that the word of my city is that word from of old, Because I see that word nested in nests of water-bays, superb…

～ *Walt Whitman*

2 *If you want to fine-tune the spacing between paragraphs, use the Space Before or Space After field. Don't insert extra returns—it's so-o-o unprofessional.*

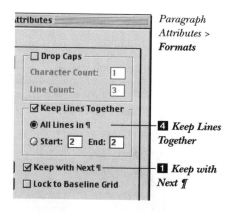

Paragraph Attributes > Formats

4 *Keep Lines Together*

1 *Keep with Next ¶*

Apply the Keep with Next ¶ command to a subhead to ensure that it always remains attached to the paragraph that follows it. Like all paragraph formats, Keep with Next ¶ can be applied manually or via a style sheet. Don't apply it to body text.

To keep paragraphs together:

1. Choose the Content tool.

2. Click in a paragraph.

3. Choose Style > Formats (Cmd-Shift-F/ Ctrl-Shift-F).

4. Check Keep with Next ¶ **1**.

5. Click OK.

As QuarkXPress defines it, a widow is the last line of a paragraph that's stranded at the top of a column **2**. An orphan is the first line of paragraph that's stranded at the bottom of a column **3**. Both are type-setting no-no's. The Keep Lines Together command can be used to prevent orphan and widow lines. It can also be used to keep *all* the lines in a paragraph—such as a subhead—together.

To prevent orphan and widow lines:

1. Choose the Content tool.

2. Click in a paragraph.

3. Choose Style > Formats (Cmd-Shift-F/ Ctrl-Shift-F).

4. Check Keep Lines Together **4**.

5. Click All Lines in ¶ to keep all the lines of a paragraph together. Use this for subheads or any other paragraphs that mustn't be broken at all.
or
Click Start to turn on orphan and widow control, then enter "2" (or even "3") in the Start and End fields to ensure that no less than two lines of a paragraph are stranded at the bottom or top of a column, respectively.

6. Click OK.

2 *An unsightly widow*

"I am dreadfully afraid it *will* be mouse!" said Duchess to herself— "I really couldn't, *couldn't* eat mouse pie. And I shall have to eat it, because it is a party. And *my* pie was going to be veal and ham. A pink and white pie-dish! and so is mine; just like Ribby's dishes; they were both bought at Tabitha Twitchit's." Duchess went into her larder and took the pie off a shelf and looked at it. "Oh what a good idea! Why shouldn't I rush along and put my pie into Ribby's oven when Ribby isn't there?"

Beatrix Potter

"I am dreadfully afraid it *will* be mouse!" said Duchess to herself— "I really couldn't, *couldn't* eat mouse pie. And I shall have to eat it, because it is a party. And *my* pie was going to be veal and ham. A pink and white pie-dish! and so is mine; just like Ribby's dishes; they were both bought at Tabitha Twitchit's." Duchess went into her larder and took the pie off a shelf and looked at it. "Oh what a good idea! Why shouldn't I rush along and put my pie into Ribby's oven when Ribby isn't there?"

3 *An unsightly orphan*

Keep Lines Together

95

A format in which the first line of a paragraph is aligned flush left and the remaining lines are indented is called a hanging indent. Hanging indents can be used to make subheads, bullets, or other special text more prominent or to hang punctuation (see page 120). A hanging indent that's created using the Formats dialog box can be applied via a style sheet.

To create a hanging indent using the Formats dialog box:

1. Choose the Content tool.

2. Click in a paragraph or drag downward through a series of paragraphs.

3. Choose Style > Formats (Cmd-Shift-F/ Ctrl-Shift-F).

4. Enter a Left Indent value—1 or 2 picas to start with **1**.

5. Enter a First Line value that is equal to or less than the number you entered in the previous step, preceded by a minus (-) sign.

6. Click Apply to preview (Cmd-A/Alt-A), make any adjustments, then click OK **2**–**3**.

1 *Enter a positive Left Indent…*

…and a negative First Line.

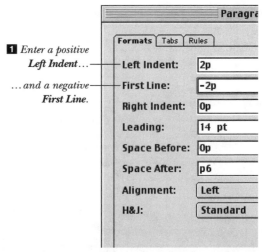

*The Paragraph Attributes > **Formats** pane*

*A **tab** stop is created automatically at the location of the indent. (To style this text, we used a character style sheet. A character style sheet could also be used to style bullets or dingbats/wingdings in a bulleted list.)*

I mean in singing; but in loving—Leander the good swimmer, Troilus the first employer of panders, and a whole book full of these quondam carpet-mongers, whose names yet run smoothly in the even road of a blank verse, why, they were never so truly turned over and over as my poor self in love.

Marry, I cannot show it in rhyme; I have tried; I can find out no rhyme to lady but baby—an innocent rhyme;

William Shakespeare

2 *In this example, a **positive Left Indent** and a **negative First Line** creates a hanging indent formation in each paragraph.*

D. Pedro. He is in earnest.

Claud. In most profound earnest; and I'll warrant you for the love of Beatrice.

D. Pedro. And hath challenged thee?

Claud. Most sincerely.

D. Pedro. What a pretty thing man is when he goes in his doublet and hose, and leaves off his wit!

Claud. He is then a giant to an ape: but then is an ape a doctor to such a man?

William Shakespeare

3 *In this example, after the hanging indents were created via a positive Left Indent and a negative First Line, a **tab** character was also inserted manually following the bold text in each paragraph to align the text to the tab stop that QuarkXPress inserted automatically.*

THESEUS. |Now, fair Hippolyta, our nuptial hour draws on apace; four happy days bring in another moon: but, oh, methinks, how slow this old moon wanes! She lingers my desires, like to a step-dame or a dowager, long withering out a young man's revenue.

William Shakespeare

1 *To insert the* **Indent Here** *character, click in the text, then press* **Cmd-\/Ctrl-\.**

THESEUS. Now, fair Hippolyta, our nuptial hour draws on apace; four happy days bring in another moon: but, oh, methinks, how slow this old moon wanes! She lingers my desires, like to a step-dame or a dowager, long withering out a young man's revenue.

2 *A hanging indent is created.*

3 *The* **Indent Here** *character displays as a vertical dotted line when View > Show Invisibles is turned on. Choose a large view size to see it.*

THESEUS. |Now, fair Hippol hour draws on days bring in oh, methinks,

On the positive side, the Indent Here character instantly creates a hanging indent wherever your cursor happens to be positioned. On the minus side, the Indent Here character has to be inserted manually into each paragraph, it can't be incorporated into a style sheet, and it can't be added or removed using Find/Change. It's very handy for quickly formatting a unique paragraph here or there. To create a hanging indent in multiple paragraphs, though, follow the instructions on the previous page instead.

To create a hanging indent using the Indent Here character:

1. Choose the Content tool.

2. Click in a paragraph where the indent is to be inserted **1**.

3. Press Cmd-\(backslash)/Ctrl-\ **2**.

To remove an Indent Here character:

1. Choose the Content tool.

2. Choose View > Show Invisibles (Cmd-I/Ctrl-I), if invisibles aren't currently showing.

3. Click just to the right of the Indent Here character **3**. If you're having trouble locating the correct spot, you can use the left or right arrow key on your keyboard to move the text cursor one character at a time.

4. Press Delete/Backspace. Choose View > Show Invisibles again, if desired, if you perfer to have this feature off.

Indent Here Character

An interesting drop cap (or caps) can add pizazz to a page and spark your reader's interest. *Caution:* Because they're so easy to create, it's tempting to use drop caps here, there, and everywhere. Don't succumb— like hot chilis, they're best used sparingly.

To insert an automatic drop cap:

1. Choose the Content tool.
2. Click in a paragraph.
3. Choose Style > Formats (Cmd-Shift-F/ Ctrl-Shift-F).
4. Check Drop Caps **1**.
5. Click Apply to preview (Cmd-A/Alt-A), and move the dialog box out of the way, if necessary.
6. *Optional:* To "drop cap" more than one character, enter that number in the Character Count field (1–127).
7. *Optional:* To adjust the height of the drop cap, change the Line Count (2–16). The drop cap will adjust automatically to fit the line count.
8. Click Apply to preview again (Cmd-A/ Alt-A), then click OK **2**–**3**.
9. *Optional:* Highlight the drop cap and change its color, shade, or font (see the next chaper). Be bold and imaginative!

TIP To anchor a picture box or text box as a drop cap or a large initial cap, see page 181.

Line Count: The number of vertical lines of text the drop cap will adjust to fit into

1 *Check **Drop Caps** in Paragraph Attributes > Formats.*

Character Count: The number of characters to be "dropped"

Paragraph Attributes

☑ **Drop Caps**

Character Count: `1`

Line Count: `5`

☐ **Keep Lines Together**

Not only was her first-floor flat invaded at all hours by throngs of singular and often undesirable characters but her remarkable lodger showed an eccentricity and irregularity in his life which must have sorely tried her patience. His incredible untidiness, his addiction to music at strange hours, his occasional revolver practice within doors, his weird and often malodorous scientific experiments, and the atmosphere of violence and danger which hung around him made him the very worst tenant in London. On the other hand, his payments were princely...

Sir Arthur Conan Doyle

2 *A **drop cap** with a **character count** of 1 and a line count of 5*

NOT only was her first-floor flat invaded at all hours by throngs of singular and often undesirable characters but her remarkable lodger showed an eccentricity and irregularity in his life which must have sorely tried her patience. His incredible untidiness, his addiction to music at strange hours, his occasional revolver practice within doors, his weird and often malodorous scientific experiments, and the atmosphere of violence and danger which hung around him made him the very worst tenant in London. On the other hand, his payments were princely...

3 *A **drop cap** with a **character count** of 3 and a line count of 2*

An anomaly which often struck me in the character of my friend Sherlock Holmes was that, although in his methods of thought he was the neatest and most methodical of mankind, and although also he affected a certain quiet primness of dress, he was none the less in his personal habits one of the most untidy

Sir Arthur Conan Doyle

1 *A drop cap is highlighted.*

An anomaly which often struck me in the character of my friend Sherlock Holmes was that, although in his methods of thought he was the neatest and most methodical of mankind, and although also he affected a certain quiet primness of dress, he was none the less in his per-

2 *The drop cap is enlarged to 125%.*

For those who like this sort of thing, this is the sort of thing they like.

Abraham Lincoln

3 *The cursor correctly positioned for kerning next to a drop cap.*

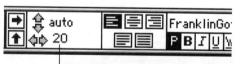

4 *The tracking/kerning section of the Measurements palette*

To resize an automatic drop cap manually:

1. Choose the Content tool.

2. Highlight the drop cap character or characters **1**.

3. Change the size percentage (16.7%–400%) in the upper right corner of the Measurements palette **2**.

or

Choose Style > Character (Cmd-Shift-D/Ctrl-Shift-D), then change the Size percentage.

To kern next to a drop cap:

1. Choose the Content tool.

2. Click in the first line of the paragraph between the drop cap and the character to the right of it. A long blinking insertion cursor will appear when the cursor has been inserted correctly **3**.

3. In the tracking/kerning section of the Measurements palette, click the left arrow to delete space or the right arrow to add space **4**. Option-click/Alt-click the left or right arrow to kern in finer increments.

or

To kern using the keyboard, use the Cmd-Shift-[/Ctrl-Shift-[or Cmd-Shift-]/Ctrl-Shift-] shortcut. Include Option/Alt in the shortcut to kern in finer increments.

To remove an automatic drop cap, just back out the same way you came in.

To remove an automatic drop cap:

1. Choose the Content tool.

2. Click in the paragraph that contains the drop cap.

3. Choose Style > Formats (Cmd-Shift-F/Ctrl-Shift-F).

4. Uncheck Drop Caps.

5. Click OK.

Automatic Drop Cap

Paragraph Rules

There are many reasons to use a paragraph rule. First, a paragraph rule stays anchored to its paragraph even if the paragraph is moved or reflows (a line created with a line tool would stay put). Second, a paragraph rule can be applied using a style sheet. And finally, unlike the Underline type style, a paragraph rule can be modified in its appearance and position. Paragraph rules are horizontal; they can't be made vertical.

To insert a paragraph rule:

1. Choose the Content tool.

2. Click in a paragraph or drag downward through a series of paragraphs.

3. Choose Style > Rules (Cmd-Shift-N/Ctrl-Shift-N).

4. Check Rule Above and/or Rule Below **1**.

5. Choose or enter a **Width 2**. Click Apply to preview (Cmd-A/Alt-A).

6. Choose **Indents** or **Text** from the **Length** pop-up menu. If you choose

Becoming unruly

To remove a paragraph rule, reopen the Rules dialog box (Cmd-Shift-N/Ctrl-Shift-N), then **uncheck Rule Above** and/or **Rule Below**. To remove a rule from a style sheet, click Rules in the Edit Style Sheet dialog box, then uncheck Rule Above and/or Rule Below.

3 *Choose **Length:** **Indents** or **Text**.*

4 *Choose a **Style**. To create a custom style, use the Dashes & Stripes feature.*

*The amount a rule is indented is equal to the **From Left** and/or **From Right** values—plus any existing paragraph indents and text inset values.*

1 *Check **Rule Below** (or **Rule Above**) to add a rule; **uncheck** the box to **remove** it.*

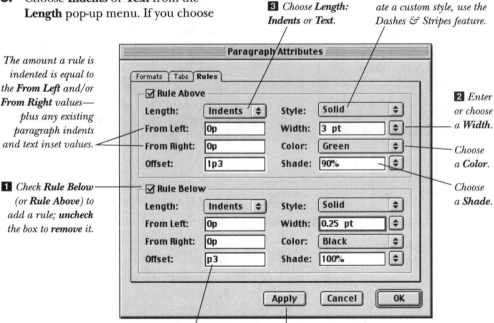

2 *Enter or choose a **Width**.*

*Choose a **Color**.*

*Choose a **Shade**.*

*Enter a number to **Offset** a **Rule Above** upward from the baseline of the **first** line of the paragraph or to Offset a **Rule Below** downward from the baseline of the **last** line of the paragraph.*

*Click **Apply** to preview.*

Hey! diddle, diddle,
The cat and the fiddle,

1 *In this example, the first line of the paragraph is **indented**, which causes the rule to indent as well.*

Hey! diddle, diddle,
The cat and the fiddle,

2 *To align the rule with the left edge of the rest of the paragraph, as in this example, in the From Left field we entered the same value as the paragraph's left indent, except with a minus sign in front of it: –1p.*

Hey! diddle, diddle,
The cat and the fiddle,
The cow jumped over the moon;
The little dog laugh'd
To see such sport,
And the dish ran away with the spoon.

3 *A 2-pt Rule Above, Length: **Indents**, Offset p10*

Hey! diddle, diddle,
The cat and the fiddle,
The cow jumped over the moon;
The little dog laugh'd
To see such sport,
And the dish ran away with the spoon.

4 *A 2-pt Rule Above, Length: **Text**, Offset p10*

H*ey! diddle, diddle,*
The cat and the fiddle,
The cow jumped over the moon;
The little dog laugh'd
To see such sport,
And the dish ran away with the spoon.

5 *A 2-pt Rule Above, Length: Text, **From Left** 1p10, Offset p10*

(For more illustrations, see the next page.)

Text, the rule will be the width of the first line of text in the paragraph for a Rule Above or the width of the last line of text in the paragraph for a Rule Below (**3**, previous page). If you choose Indents, the rule will be the width of the paragraph, unless you enter a number other than 0 in the From Left and/or From Right field (see step 8). *Note:* The rule will also be shortened by the Indent values in the Formats dialog box and the Text Inset values in the Modify dialog box (**2**, this page).

7. Highlight the entire **Offset** field, and enter the fixed distance (in any measurement unit) that you want to offset the bottom of the Rule Above upward from the baseline of the first line of the paragraph or offset the top of the Rule Below downward from the baseline of the last line of the paragraph. For a Rule Above, enter an Offset that is at least as large as the point size of the type.
or
Enter a percentage Offset (0–100%). A Rule Below with a 20% Offset, for example, would position the rule closer to the bottom of the currently selected paragraph than would an 80% offset. If this method is used and the spacing between the paragraphs is altered, the rule position will adjust automatically. We're not big fans of this option.

8. *Optional:* Change the From Left and/or From Right values to indent, and thus shorten, the rule.

9. Choose a style from the Style pop-up menu (**4**, previous page). To create a custom style, see pages 207–208.

10. Choose a color from the Color pop-up menu.

11. Choose or enter a Shade percentage.

12. Click Apply to preview, then click OK **1**–**5**.

ETHAN FROME

By Edith Wharton

I had the story, bit by bit, from various people, and, as generally happens in such cases, each time it was a different story.

If you know Starkfield, Massachusetts, you know the post-office. If you know the post-office you must have seen Ethan Frome drive up to it, drop the reins on his hollow-backed bay

Rules can be used to jazz up subheads

Rules can be used to jazz up subheads

*Rules of varying **lengths** and **weights***

Going in reverse

To create a **reverse rule**, color the text white, and use a negative Offset and a wide width (the point size of the type plus a few points) for the rule. A negative value of up to half the width of the rule can be used. This is a 16-point black Rule Above, Length: Indents, Left and Right Indents: 0, and Offset: -p4. The headline text is 9 pt.

Cumin
Cayenne
Coriander
Chervil
Cinnamon

*To add alternating **tints** behind text, use a wide Rule Above with a negative Offset. Apply it via a style sheet!*

*Need to fill up a page with horizontal **lines**? Apply a paragraph rule, then keep hitting Return/Enter.*

Norton Thorpe clapped the young Frenchman on the shoulder and, with a hearty smile, shook his hand. "My dear chap! How could I possibly object to my daughter becoming not only the new Countess d'Auvergne but also the wife of an up-and-coming electronics genius!" Lisa, her eyes moist with tears of joy, not

*Here paragraph rules are used to **separate** a pull quote from the main body text.*

"How could I possibly object to my daughter becoming not only the new Countess d'Auvergne but also the wife of an up-and-coming electronics genius..."

only because of her future marriage but also because of her restored relationship with her father, threw her arms around Nancy in a warm embrace exclaiming: "Oh, Nancy, none of this could ever have happened if you hadn't worked so hard to solve

Carolyn Keene

*Rules can be used as **decorative** elements or for **emphasis**. In this example, a Return was inserted after every line, making every line a separate paragraph.*

ALL

THE

REALLY GOOD

IDEAS

I EVER HAD

CAME

TO ME

WHILE I WAS

MILKING

A COW.

Grant Wood

Appending an H&J

To append an H&J from one document to another, choose File > **Append** or click Append in the H&J dialog box (you'll get to the same place). An H&J that is created when no documents are open will appear on the H&J pop-up menu in all subsequently created documents.

1 *Click New. Or choose an existing H&J and click Edit. Click Append to append an H&J from another document.*

2 *Choose hyphenation settings in the Edit Hyphenation & Justification dialog box.*

Auto Hyphenation lessens gaps between words in justified type and smoothes ragged edges in non-justified type. A set of hyphenation and justification settings is called an "H&J," and a document can contain up to 1,000 of them. (Manual hyphenation (discussed in the sidebar on page 106) should only be used to correct awkward breaks here and there.

Note: To **apply** an H&J to individual paragraphs, you have to choose it from the H&J pop-up menu in Style > Formats. You can also apply an H&J via a paragraph style sheet (click Formats in the Edit Paragraph Style Sheet dialog box). H&Js are not available for HTML text boxes.

To create or edit an H&J:

1. Choose Edit > H&Js (Cmd-Option-H/Ctrl-Alt-H).

2. To create a new H&J, click New **1**, then enter a name.
   or
   Click an existing H&J, then click Edit. The Standard H&J can be modified.

3. Check Auto Hyphenation **2**.

4. Change any of the hyphenation settings:

   In the **Smallest Word** field, the minimum number of characters a word must contain to be hyphenated. We use 5 or 6.

   In the **Minimum Before** field, the minimum number (1–6) of a word's characters that must precede a hyphen.

   In the **Minimum After** field, the minimum number (2–8) of characters that can follow a hyphen. For the sake of readability, we use 3 rather than the default 2.

   Check or uncheck **Break Capitalized Words** for words that begin with an uppercase character.

(Continued on the following page)

Create or Edit an H&J

In the **Hyphens in a Row** field, the number of consecutive lines that can end with a hyphen. More than two hyphens in a row can impair readability.

Enter a **Hyphenation Zone** value above zero to create a more ragged edge (less hyphenation).

5. To tighten word spacing in justified paragraphs, enter lower **Space: Min./Minimum** and **Space: Max./Maximum** values **1**. The subheads and thumb tabs in this book have slightly tightened word spacing. Headlines also tend to look better with tighter-than-normal word (and character) spacing. To loosen word spacing, enter higher values.

To tighten the character spacing in justified paragraphs, enter lower **Char: Min./Minimum** and **Char: Max./Maximum** values. To loosen character spacing, enter higher values. Experiment, and make your final judgment from a printout. The effect may vary depending on the font.

To change the word or character spacing in justified and non-justified paragraphs, change either or both of the **Opt./Optimum** values.

6. *Optional:* The Flush Zone, which is the span within which the last word in a justified paragraph must fall in order to be justitifed, can be widened. Single Word Justify forces any single word on a line by itself to justify (this usually occurs at the end of a paragraph). *Note:* The Forced Justify alignment option justifies single words automatically. In fact, Forced Justify nullifies both the Flush Zone and Single Word Justify setttings.

7. Click OK.

8. Click Save. To apply an H&J, follow the instructions on the next page.

TIP To delete an H&J, click its name, then click Delete. If the H&J is currently applied to text in your document, you'll be prompted to choose a replacement H&J for the deleted one.

1 *The* **Space** *values affect inter-word spacing; the* **Char.** *values affect character (letter) spacing.*

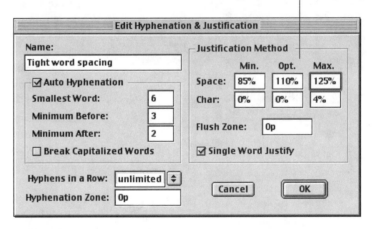

**SEASONINGS FOR WHITE SAUCE, FRICAS-
SEES, AND RAGOUTS**
White pepper, nutmeg, mace and
lemon-peel, pounded together.

CATSUPS
Mushroom is most esteemed; but the
difficulty in our country of obtaining
the right kind of plant (some are
poisonous), renders a recipe of little
consequence. It is better to buy this
catsup at the shops.   *Sara Josepha Hale*

*In this illustration, **hyphenation** is turned
on for the **subheads** (a no-no!) and turned
off for the **justified body** text (another no-no,
because it creates ugly rivers of white space).*

**SEASONINGS FOR WHITE SAUCE,
FRICASSEES, AND RAGOUTS**
White pepper, nutmeg, mace and
lemon-peel, pounded together.

CATSUPS
Mushroom is most esteemed; but the
difficulty in our country of obtaining
the right kind of plant (some are poisonous), renders a recipe of little consequence. It is better to buy this
catsup at the shops.

*Here **hyphenation** is turned **off** for the **subheads** and turned **on** for the **justified body**
text. An improvement, don't you think?*

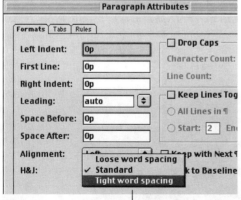

1 *To apply an H&J to highlighted text or to make it
part of a style sheet, choose from the **H&J** pop-up menu
in Paragraph Attributes (**Formats** pane).*

H&Js are applied to individual paragraphs
using the Paragraph Formats dialog box.
If you're using more than one H&J setting
in a document, the most efficient way to
apply them to your text is via a style sheet
(see Chapter 13). The Normal style sheet
will have the Standard H&J associated with
it unless a different H&J is chosen for it.

To apply an H&J:

1. Choose the Content tool.

2. Click in a paragraph or drag downward
   through a series of paragraphs.

3. Choose Style > Formats (Cmd-Shift-F/
   Ctrl-Shift-F).

4. Choose from the H&J pop-up menu **1**.

5. Click Apply, if desired (Cmd-A/Alt-A),
   then click OK.

TIP The Expanded Hyphenation Method,
which uses a built-in hyphenation
dictionary, creates better word breaks
than the other methods. Choose Edit >
Preferences > Preferences (Cmd-Y/
Ctrl-Y), click Document–Paragraph,
then choose Hyphenation Method:
Expanded. The Standard and
Enhanced methods are from earlier
versions of QuarkXPress. To tell you
the truth, we find even the Expanded
Hyphenation Method to be lacking,
compared with other applications.
Dear Quark: Please try harder.

TIP Use a non-breaking (permanent)
hyphen if you want a word to *always*
hyphenate but never break at the
end of a line (a compound word like
"e-mail" or "on-screen," for example).
Here's how to insert it: Cmd-=/Ctrl-=.

The hyphenation dialog box is used not only to enter words you don't want hyphenated, but also to specify how specific words are to be hyphenated.

To enter Hyphenation Exceptions:

1. Choose Utilities > Hyphenation Exceptions.

2. Type a word that you **don't** want hyphenated 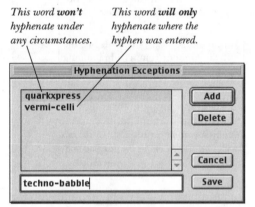. You can't type spaces or punctuation marks. And don't bother typing upper and lower case—all the characters will be added as lowercase anyway.
    or
    Specify how a word **will** be hyphenated by typing it with a hyphen.

3. Click Add (Return/Enter).

4. *Optional:* To edit an entry, click on it, edit it in the field, then click Replace.

5. Repeat steps 2–3 or 4 for any other words. Be sure to add any variations of a word, such as its plural form.

6. Click Save. Hyphenation exceptions are saved in the XPress Preferences file.

TIP To prevent a compound word from hyphenating, add each part of the word separately as a Hyphenation Exception.

TIP You can use the Line Check feature to search for manually and/or automatically hyphenated words (see page 81).

Hyphenating manually

Have you ever noticed, in your reading, a hyphen in the middle of a line that wasn't supposed to be there? Don't let this happen to you. If for some reason you want to hyphenate a word manually, don't use a regular hyphen, because it will stay in your text if the text reflows. Instead, use a **discretionary** hyphen (Cmd-hyphen/Ctrl-hyphen), which will disappear if the text reflows (though the invisible marker for it will remain).

If you're not sure how to hyphenate a particular word, choose the Content tool, click in the word, then choose Utilities > **Suggested Hyphenation** (Cmd-H/Ctrl-H). If no hyphens display in the dialog box, it means that word isn't supposed to be hyphenated, period.

*This word **won't** hyphenate under any circumstances.*   *This word **will** only hyphenate where the hyphen was entered.*

1 *Using the **Hyphenation Exceptions** dialog box, you can specify how a word **is** to be hyphenated and also specify which words you **don't** want hyphenated.*

Hyphenation Exceptions

Do it without the grid

To align text without using the Lock to Baseline Grid feature, make sure the sum of the space before and after any subheads or between paragraphs is a multiple of the **leading** value. For example, if your body text has 14 pt. leading, add eight points before each subhead and six points after. Use style sheets to ensure that your body text leading is uniform.

There are several methods of making coffee, each highly recommended—I cannot decide which is best, but the following way is a good one:—

To make Coffee.— Take fresh-roasted coffee (a quarter of a pound for three persons is the rule, but *less* will do;) allow two tablespoonfuls for each person, grind it just before making, put it in a basin and break into it an egg, yolk, white, shell and all. Mix it up with the spoon to the consistence of mortar, put in a warm not *boiling* water in the coffee pot; let it boil up and *break* three times; then stand a few minutes, and it will be as clear as amber, and the egg will give it a rich taste.

Another Way to make Coffee.—Pour hot water into your coffee pot, and then stir in your coffee, a spoonful at a time, allowing three to every pint of water; this makes *strong* coffee. Stir it to prevent the mixture from boiling over, as the coffee swells, and to force it to combine with the water. This will be done after it has boiled gently a few minutes. Then let it stand and boil slowly for half an hour; remove it from the fire, and pour in a tea-cup of cold water, and set it in the corner to settle. As soon a it becomes clear, it is to be poured, gently, into a clean coffee pot for the table.

Made in this manner it may be kept two or three days in summer, and a week in winter; you need only heat it over when wanted.

Sara Josepha Hale from *The Good Housekeeper*, 1841

1 *Text aligned across columns using* **Lock to Baseline Grid**

The Lock to Baseline Grid command is used to precisely align text across columns (for an alternate method, see the sidebar). This command is not available for HTML text boxes.

To align text to a grid:

1. Take note of what the current leading for your body text is. Also, go to Item menu > Modify, click the Text tab, then jot down the current First Baseline: Offset value on a scrap of paper (paperless office? Ha!).

2. *Optional:* To display the non-printing gridlines, choose View > Show Baseline Grid (Option-F7/Ctrl-F7). *Note:* If the Option-F7 shortcut doesn't work in Mac OS 9x, go to Control Panels > Keyboard, click Function Keys, uncheck the box under Hot Function Key Settings, click OK, then close the Keyboard dialog box.

3. Choose Edit > Preferences > Preferences, then click Document–Paragraph.

4. Enter as the Start value the vertical (y) position of the First Baseline of the text (from Item > Modify).

5. Enter as the Baseline Grid: Increment the current leading value or a multiple of the leading value.

6. Click OK.

7. To snap text to the grid lines, select the paragraphs you want to lock (or better yet, use a style sheet), choose Style > Formats, check Lock to Baseline Grid, then click OK **1**. *Note:* If vertical justification is on, only the first and last lines in the column will lock to the grid.

Note: Also see the information about Maintain Leading on page 389.

TIP You might not want to lock subheads to the grid.

You can use this trick to copy paragraph formats within the **same** text box or between **linked** text boxes, but not between unlinked boxes. Both paragraph style sheet and local formatting specifications will copy; character attributes (font, size, color, etc.) won't copy.

To copy formats in the same story:

1. Click in a paragraph **1** or drag downward through a series of paragraphs that you want to reformat.

2. Option-Shift-click/Alt-Shift-click the paragraph whose formats you want to copy **2**.

> **Then there was nothing but the air and the swiftness of the little cloud that bore me and those two men still leading up to where white clouds were piled like mountains on a wide blue plain, and in them thunder beings lived and leaped and flashed.**
>
> *Now suddenly there was nothing but a world of cloud, and we three were there alone in the middle of a great white plain with snowy hills and mountains staring at us; and it was very still; but there were whispers…*
>
> *John G. Neihardt, from Black Elk Speaks*

1 *Click in a paragraph (or highlight a series of paragraphs) to be **reformatted**.*

> **Then there was nothing but the air and the swiftness of the little cloud that bore me and those two men still leading up to where white clouds were piled like mountains on a wide blue plain, and in them thunder beings lived and leaped and flashed.**
> *Now suddenly there was nothing but a world of cloud, and we three were there alone in the middle of a great white plain with snowy hills and mountains staring at us; and it was very still; but there were whispers…*
>
> *John G. Neihardt, from Black Elk Speaks*

2 *Then **Option-Shift-click/Alt-Shift-click** the paragraph whose **formats** you want to **copy**. The top paragraph is reformatted (the Left Indent, Space After, Alignment, and Space After values are changed). The font remains the same, though, since the font is a character attribute—not a paragraph attribute.*

Copy Formats

Typography 7

Reformat type the fast way

Once you've mastered the typographic basics, we urge you to read Chapter 13, **Style Sheets!**

Choose a preset point size
from the **Size** pop-up menu.

Or enter a point size between
2 and 720 in the **Size** field.

7 pt	
9 pt	
10 pt	
✓ 12 pt	
14 pt	
18 pt	
24 pt	
36 pt	

1 *The right-hand side of
the Measurements palette*

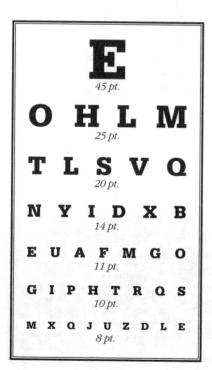

E
45 pt.

O H L M
25 pt.

T L S V Q
20 pt.

N Y I D X B
14 pt.

E U A F M G O
11 pt.

G I P H T R Q S
10 pt.

M X Q J U Z D L E
8 pt.

Tired of 12 pt. Helvetica? Now you'll have some fun. In this chapter, not only will you learn how to change basic type attributes (point size, font, etc.), you'll also learn how to add professional touches, like smart quotation marks.

To resize type using the Measurements palette:

1. Choose the Content tool.
2. Highlight the text to be resized.
3. Choose a preset size from the Size pop-up menu on the right side of the Measurements palette **1**.
   or
   Double-click the Size field on the Measurements palette, enter a point size (2–720) in an increment as small as .001 point, then press Return/Enter. You don't have to enter the "pt." (Only full sizes are permitted for HTML text.)

TIP To open the Character Attributes dialog box and highlight the Size field in one keystroke: Cmd-Shift-\Ctrl-Shift-\ .

Use this method to resize type if your highlighted text contains more than one point size—all the type will resize at once. (To scale type and its box, see page 116.)

To resize type using the keyboard:

1. Choose the Content tool.
2. Highlight the text to be resized.
3. Press Cmd-Shift-</Ctrl-Shift-< to reduce the text in preset sizes. Use ">" to enlarge the text. Or press Cmd-Option-Shift-</Ctrl-Alt-Shift-< to reduce the text in 1-point increments or > to enlarge the text.

If you're new to typography, read our "Type for print" on page 123. For further reading on this topic, explore one of Robin Williams' terrific books, such as *The Non-Designer's Type Book* (Peachpit Press).

To change a font:

1. Choose the Content tool.

2. Highlight the text to be modified.

3. Choose a font from the Font pop-up menu on the Measurements palette 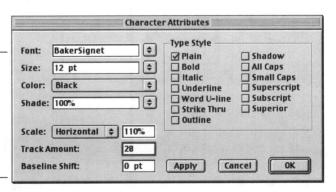.
or
On the Measurements palette, click in the Font field to the left of the current font name, type the first few characters of the desired font name, then press Return/Enter 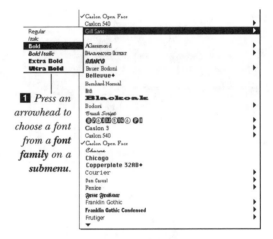.
or
Choose a font from the Style > Font submenu. In the Mac OS, fonts that were previously chosen during the same work session are listed at the top of the Font menu.

TIP To recolor type, see page 248.

Font shortcuts

Highlight font field on the Measurements palette	Cmd-Option-Shift-M/ Ctrl-Alt-Shift-M
Apply next font on font menu	Option-F9*/ Ctrl-F9
Apply previous font on font menu	Option-Shift-F9*/ Ctrl-Shift-F9

Note: The Option-F key shortcuts don't work in Mac OS 9x because of a conflict with the System Keyboard Control panel.

1 *Press an arrowhead to choose a font from a **font family** on a submenu.*

*Click just to the left of the current font name, then start **typing** a new font name…*

*…or press this arrowhead to choose from the **Font pop-up** menu.*

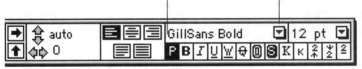

2 *The **Font** area is on the right side of the Measurements palette.*

One-stop styling

If you'd like to make all your Font, Size, Color, Shade, Scale, Track Amount, Baseline Shift, and Type Style choices from one dialog box, choose Style > **Character** (Cmd-Shift-D/ Ctrl-Shift-D). Don't forget to click Apply to preview!

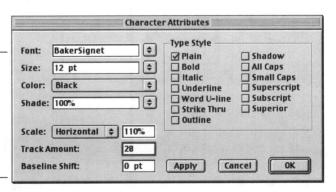

Type style shortcuts

First highlight the type, then hold down **Cmd-Shift/Ctrl-Shift** and press one of the following keys (use the shortcut again to remove that style):

Plain	**P**
Bold	**B**
Italic	**I**
Underline	**U**
Word Underline	**W**
Outline	**O**
Shadow	**S**
All Caps	**K**
Small Caps	**H**
Superscript	**+**
Subscript	**-**
Superior	**V**

Note: The outline, shadow, small caps, superior, and word underline styles are not available for HTML text boxes.

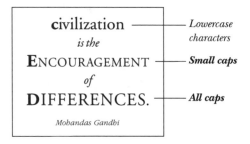

civilization ——— *Lowercase characters*
is the
Encouragement ——— ***Small caps***
of
DIFFERENCES. ——— ***All caps***
Mohandas Gandhi

Note: Looking for boldface or italics? Choose the actual bold or italic font from the Font menu—it's less likely to cause a printing error.

To style type:

1. Choose the Content tool.
2. Highlight the text to be styled.
3. Click one or more of the style buttons on the Measurements palette ∎.

TIP To remove *all* styling from highlighted type, click the "P" on the Measurements palette. To remove one style at a time, click any already highlighted style button. If a style is grayed out, it means not all the currently highlighted type has that style.

TIP Don't input text with the Caps lock key down; lowercase characters can easily be converted into caps or small caps, but characters input with Caps lock down can't be converted back to lowercase (unless you use a third-party case-conversion XTension). When the small caps style is applied, uppercase characters remain uppercase and lowercase characters turn into small caps.

TIP Superscript type sits above the baseline (as in ®). Subscript type sits below the baseline (as in ₉). Superior type aligns with the cap height of the type and is reduced in point size (as in 18th). Adjust the proportions of these styles in Edit > Preferences > Preferences > Document–Character (try reducing the Scale).

Style Type

∎ *The **style** buttons on the Measurements palette*

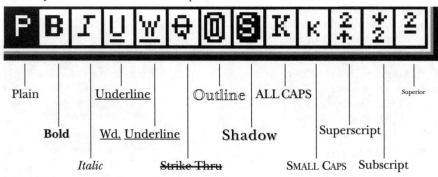

Plain		Underline		Outline	ALL CAPS			Superior
Bold		Wd. Underline			Shadow		Superscript	
	Italic			Strike Thru		Small Caps	Subscript	

Kerning is the manual adjustment of space between a pair of characters when the cursor is inserted between them. Tracking is the adjustment of the space to the right of one or more highlighted characters; it can be used to create a variety of typographic effects. The same section of the Measurements palette is used for tracking as for kerning. Neither feature is available for HTML text boxes. *Note:* Before kerning manually, go to Edit > Preferences > Preferences > Document–Character and make sure Auto Kern Above is turned on at or below your type size.

To kern or track type manually using the Measurements palette:

1. Choose the Content tool, and zoom in on the type you're going to kern or track.

2. For kerning, click between two characters **1**.
   or
   For tracking, highlight any number of characters.

3. Click the right Tracking & Kerning arrow to add space or the left arrow to remove space **2**–**5**. To track or kern in finer increments, Option-click/Alt-click the right or left arrow.
   or
   Enter a number between -500% and 500% in an increment as small as .001 in the Tracking & Kerning field.

TIP To restore normal tracking to highlighted text or to restore normal kerning at a text insertion point, enter 0 in the Tracking & Kerning field or click the left or right arrow until 0 appears in the field.

TIP To apply tracking or kerning values via a dialog box, choose Style > Track or Kern. The Track Amount or Kern Amount field will highlight automatically. To change letterspacing for long passages of text, use an H&J (see page 103).

Kern or Track

You can't kern/track HTML text

And that's not all you **can't** do! For a list, see page 124.

Tomorrow

1 *Click **between** two characters to **kern** them.*

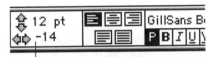

2 *The **Tracking & Kerning** arrows and field on the Measurements palette*

Tomorrow

3 *Now the "T" and the "o" are **closer** together.*

C I V I L I Z A T I O N
is the
E N C O U R A G E M E N T
of
D I F F E R E N C E S.
Mohandas Gandhi

4 *A phrase with positive **tracking** values*

Nothing great was ever achieved without enthusiasm.
Emerson

5 *A phrase with a **negative tracking** value of -6.*

To Tr Ta Yo Ya Wo Wa We Va Vo

1 *These are a few of the character pairs that often need **extra kerning**, particularly if they're set in a large point size.*

THE TALE OF MRS. TIGGY-WINKLE
THE TALE OF MRS. TIGGY-WINKLE

---

2 *Wide letterspacing is popular nowadays, especially since it's so easy to do. But it should be used only for **small** bits of type, as it can be tiring to read in large quantities. Small caps, as in this illustration, look nice "tracked out." Type that is very chunky or very thin (e.g., a condensed font) may also look good with extra letterspacing.*

Style is self-plagiarism.

3 *This phrase has **normal word spacing**.*

Style is self-plagiarism.

Alfred Hitchcock

4 *Here the same phrase has a **word space tracking** value of -10. Negative word space tracking can improve the appearance of headlines and other large-sized text.*

This is the quickest method—and our favorite.

To kern or track using the keyboard:

1. Choose the Content tool.
2. Click between two characters or highlight any number of characters.
3. Press Cmd-Shift-[/Ctrl-Shift-[(left bracket) to remove space, or "]" (right bracket) to add space **1**–**2**. To kern or track in finer increments, include the Option/Alt key in the shortcut.

Use the Word Space Tracking shortcut described in the following instructions to adjust inter-word spacing in an isolated phrase, like a large headline. This command and the Remove Manual Kerning command, discussed next, are included in the free TypeTricks XTension.

Note: To adjust inter-word spacing in repetitive text, like subheads, or in a larger body of text, create an H&J with tighter word spacing and apply it via a style sheet. The word spacing of the subheads in this book (e.g., "To adjust inter-word spacing:" below) was ever-so-slightly tightened that way.

To adjust inter-word spacing:

1. Choose the Content tool.
2. Highlight one or more words.
3. In the Mac OS, press Cmd-Control-Shift-[(left bracket) to remove space or "]" (right bracket) to add space **3**–**4**. For finer word space adjustments, include the Option key. In Windows, press Ctrl-Shift-1 or Ctrl-Shift-2.

To remove kerning and word space tracking:

1. Choose the Content tool.
2. Highlight the kerned text.
3. Choose Utilities > Remove Manual Kerning. This command has no effect on tracking values.

Some character pairs, because of their shape and how they fit side by side, have noticeable gaps between them. To ameliorate this problem, fonts have hundreds of built-in kerning pairs—character duos that are nudged together slightly. To turn this pair kerning on, check **Auto Kern Above** in Edit > Preferences > Preferences > Document–Character.

If you're unhappy with the default spacing in a particular kerning pair or pairs that appear repetitively in your documents, you can use the kerning editor to specify your own kerning values. Your goal as a typesetter should be to correct any particularly large, toothy gaps so they don't stand out in the crowd—not to equalize every single space between every single character. Gaps tend to be more noticeable in large type. To adjust overall letterspacing, use an H&J (see page 103). Adjust headlines manually.

To use the Kerning Table Editor:

1. Choose Utilities > Kerning Edit. If it's unavailable, enable the Kern-Track Editor via Utilities > XTensions Manager.

2. Start typing or click the name of the font that you want to edit 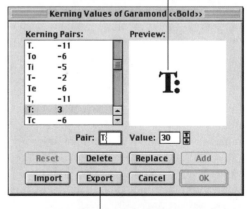, then click Edit.
or
Double-click the name of the font that you want to edit.

3. Click a kerning pair on the list.
or
In the Pair field, type a kerning pair.

4. Enter a new kerning Value or click the up or down arrow (use a negative value to bring characters closer together). Option-click/Alt-click to kern in a finer increment.

5. When you're satisfied with the new kerning value, as shown in the Preview window **2**, click Replace to replace the existing pair or click Add to add it as a new pair.

6. Click OK, then click Save.

Kerning Table Editor

Keep document settings

Kerning table changes are made on a font-by-font basis, but they apply to the whole application. Click Keep Document Settings when you open a document if you don't want it to be affected by new kerning table values. To restore a font's original, manufacturer-defined kerning values for all pairs, click **Reset** in the Kerning Values of... dialog box. QuarkXPress' kerning values don't affect font usage in other applications.

1 *Click the font whose kerning you want to edit, then click* ***Edit***.

2 *Note the* ***Preview*** *as you change a kerning pair's* ***Value***. *The most accurate preview, of course, is high-resolution output.*

To save the kerning pairs you've adjusted for one font to reuse with another font, click ***Export***, *then Save. Choose another font, then click* ***Import*** *to import those values.*

Alligator

1 *Futura Regular,* **normal scale**

Alligator

2 *Fudging a condensed font:*
Futura Regular, **condensed 30%**

Alligator

3 *Futura Condensed Regular,*
*normal scale—***a true condensed**
font*—has more balanced proportions.*

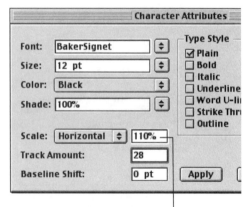

4 *The* **Scale: Horizontal** *field in the Character*
Attributes dialog box

Whale

Extended type

Giraffe

Condensed type

5 **Horizontal scaling** *is used for* **stylizing** *type.*

Normal text has a horizontal scale value of 100%. Horizontal scaling is the extending (widening) or condensing (narrowing) of type. Horizontal scaling only affects a character's width; vertical scaling only affects a character's height.

Note: Since the Scale command affects only the vertical parts of letters—not the horizontals (or vice versa)—it distorts letter shapes. For narrow characters, it's better to use a Condensed typeface than it is to create a "fudged" version of a condensed typeface by horizontally scaling a Regular one **1**–**3**. The true condensed font looks more elegant and balanced.

The same holds true for an extended typeface. To enlarge characters without distorting them, change their point size. Another option is to create custom weights for an Adobe Multiple Masters font. That being said, we still use these features occasionally.

To scale type using a dialog box:

1. Choose the Content tool.
2. Highlight the text to be scaled.
3. Choose Style > Horizontal/Vertical Scale. The Scale field will highlight automatically.
4. For horizontal scaling, choose Scale: Horizontal, then enter a percentage between 25 and 99 to condense the type (make it narrower than normal) or a percentage between 101 and 400 to expand the type (make it wider than normal) **4**. A Horizontal Scale percentage of 60%, for example, will condense type 40%. A Horizontal Scale percentage of 125% will expand type 25%.
or
Choose Scale: Vertical, then enter the desired percentage.

   Note: You can scale type in one direction —horizontally or vertically (not both).
5. Click Apply (Cmd-A/Alt-A), make any adjustments, then click OK **5**.

To scale type horizontally or vertically using the keyboard:

1. Choose the Content tool.

2. Highlight the text to be scaled (not HTML text).

3. Hold down Cmd/Ctrl and press left bracket "[" to condense or shorten in 5% increments, or right bracket "]" to expand or lengthen **1**–**4**. Include the Option/Alt key to scale in 1% increments. Scaling will be horizontal or vertical depending on which option is currently selected in the Character Attributes dialog box.

This method for scaling type interactively rather than by specifying an exact point size is appropriate when you're working visually—trying to make a headline or a logo look just so.

To scale type interactively:

1. Choose the Item or Content tool.

2. To scale type while preserving the proportions of the type and the box or path, Cmd-Option-Shift-drag/Ctrl-Alt-Shift-drag a handle **5**–**6**. The leading will readjust proportionately. You can't scale a box or path that is linked to another box or path. *Note:* To scale type on a path, make sure Item > Edit > Shape is off (Shift-F4/F10 toggles it on and off). You should see the handles of the bounding box when the path is selected, not the anchor points.
or
To scale type and its box (or path) without preserving their proportions, Cmd-drag/Ctrl-drag a side midpoint handle to scale horizontally or a top or bottom midpoint handle to scale vertically. The type will condense or expand to fit the shape of the box or path.

TIP To restore normal scaling to type, highlight it, choose Style > Horizontal/Vertical Scale, then enter 100 in the Scale field.

"It was much pleasanter at home," thought poor Alice, "when one wasn't always growing larger and smaller, and being ordered about by mice and rabbits."

1 *Normal (100%) horizontal and vertical scale*

"It was much pleasanter at home," thought poor Alice, "when one wasn't always growing larger and smaller, and being ordered about by mice and rabbits."

2 *75% vertical scale*

"It was much pleasanter at home," thought poor Alice, "when one wasn't always growing larger and smaller, and being ordered about by mice and rabbits."
Lewis Carroll

3 *80% horizontal scale*

"It was much pleasanter at home," thought poor Alice, "when one wasn't always growing larger and smaller, and being ordered about by mice and rabbits."

4 *110% horizontal scale*

"Oh, I'm not particular as to size," Alice hastily replied; "only one doesn't like changing so often, you know."

5 *The original text*

"Oh, I'm not particular as to size," Alice hastily replied; "only one doesn't like changing so often, you know."

6 *The text and box are scaled interactively, and their proportions are preserved.*

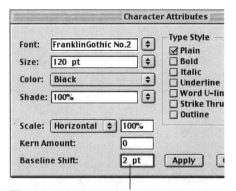

1 *A positive **Baseline Shift** value shifts characters above the baseline; a negative Baseline Shift shifts characters below the baseline.*

2 *The "C" was baseline shifted downward. Baseline Shift is handy for creating signs, company logos, and the like.*

Using the Baseline Shift command, one or more characters can be raised above or lowered below the baseline. Don't use this command to shift a whole paragraph— that's the job of leading. Use Baseline Shift only to fiddle with a little bit of type— to nudge a bullet, a dash, or an anchored item slightly upward or downward, for example, or to shift the position of text on a Bézier path. A Baseline Shift value can be incorporated into a paragraph or character style sheet. Baseline Shift is not available for HTML text boxes.

To vertically shift type using a dialog box:

1. Choose the Content tool.
2. Highlight the characters to be shifted.
3. Choose Style > Baseline Shift. The Baseline Shift field will highlight automatically.
4. Enter a number up to three times the point size of the type to be shifted. Enter a minus sign (-) before the number to shift the type below the baseline **1**–**2**.
5. Click OK.

TIP If you change the point size of type that has a Baseline Shift value other than zero, the Baseline Shift value will adjust accordingly.

To vertically shift type using the keyboard:

1. Choose the Content tool.
2. Highlight the characters to be shifted.
3. In the Mac OS, press Cmd-Option-Shift-hyphen "-" to lower the type below the baseline in 1-point increments or plus sign "+" to raise the type above the baseline.

   In Windows, press Ctrl-Alt-Shift-close paren ")" or open paren "(".

Baseline Shift

It's easy to input the curly, smart quotation marks that professional typesetters use or foreign language quotation marks, like guillemets (« »). With the Smart Quotes feature on, press ' to produce a single quotation mark in the style currently specified in the Interactive Preferences dialog box (' for English) or press Shift-' (") to produce a double quotation mark (").

To turn on Smart Quotes:

1. Choose Edit > Preferences > Preferences > (Cmd-Option-Shift-Y/ Ctrl-Alt-Shift-Y).

2. Click Application–Interactive.

3. Check Smart Quotes.

4. Choose a style for the quotes from the Quotes: Format pop-up menu **1**.

5. Click OK **2**.

TIP Uncheck Smart Quotes to produce foot and inch marks when you type ' and ", respectively. To produce a single smart quote when Smart Quotes is unchecked or to produce a foot mark when Smart Quotes is checked, press Control-'/ Ctrl-'. To produce a double smart quote when Smart Quotes is unchecked or to produce an inch mark when Smart Quotes is checked, press Control-Shift-'/Ctrl-Alt-'.

TIP If you import text with Convert Quotes checked in the Get Text dialog box, smart quotes will be substituted for straight quotes.

TIP It's a little counter-intuitive, but sometimes a quotation mark should curve in the opposite direction from the way Smart Quotes would insert it. A date, for example, should not be written like this: '94. Instead, the quote should curve toward the absent character: '94. To enter quotation marks manually in the Mac OS, press Option-Shift-] or [or Option-] or [. In Windows, it's Alt-Shift-] or [and Alt-] or [. Here's another example: Sugar 'n' spice.

Smart Quotes

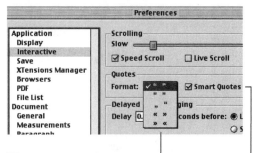

1 *In Preferences > Application–Interactive, check* **Smart Quotes** *and choose a quotes* **Format**.

"HATE THE SIN
and
LOVE THE SINNER"

Mohandas Gandhi

2 *Use* **Smart Quotes** *for* **quotation** *and* **apostrophe marks**.

Prime time

Please—we beg of you—use straight quotes *only* for foot and inch marks **3** (not for quotation marks). Or better yet, use oblique foot and inch marks, called **prime marks**. To produce a **foot** mark in the Mac OS, choose the **Symbol** font (Cmd-Shift-Q), then press **Option-4 4**; to produce an **inch** mark, press **Option- ,** (comma). In Windows, choose the **ZappedPiFH** font for a foot mark, then press **Shift-M**; for an **inch** mark, press **Shift-N**. If the Symbol/ZappedPiFH font isn't available or you don't like the way it looks, use the italic inch or foot mark in your current font instead.

> The woman is 5'6" tall.

3 *Use* **straight quotes** *only for* **foot** *and* **inch** *marks or* **minute** *and* **second** *marks.*

> The woman is 5'6″ tall.

4 *Or better yet, in the Mac OS, use the* **Symbol** *font:* **Option-4** *for a* **foot** *mark,* **Option-,** *(comma) for an* **inch** *mark. In Windows, use the* **ZappedPiFH** *font:* **Shift-M** *for a* **foot** *mark,* **Shift-N** *for an* **inch** *mark.*

A few special characters

©   Option-G/Alt-Shift-C

®   Option-R/Alt-Shift-R

™   Option-2/Alt-Shift-2

é   Option-e, then e again/Alt+0233*

¢   Option-4/Alt+0162*

¶   Option-7/Alt-Shift-7

°   Option-Shift-8/Alt+0176*

*On the numeric keypad

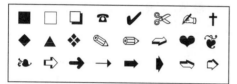

1 A few **Zapf Dingbats** *characters*

Sir Isaac Newton wore his black and gold waistcoat. And Mr. Alderman Ptolemy Tortoise brought a salad with him in a string bag. And instead of a nice dish of minnows they had a roasted grasshopper with lady-bird sauce, which frogs consider a beautiful treat; but I think it must have been nasty!

Beatrix Potter

2 *You can use a symbol to separate sentences or paragraphs or to mark the end of a story or article. But don't limit yourself to the Zapf Dingbat and Symbol fonts—other symbol fonts are available. These symbols are from the Adobe* **Minion Ornaments** *font.*

3 *The* **PopChar Pro** *palette inserts special characters in your text in the current font.*

Note: To insert dingbats repetitively, as in a bulleted list, use a character style sheet.

To insert one Zapf Dingbat or Symbol character:

1. Choose the Content tool, then click in your text to create an insertion point.

2. For a Zapf Dingbat character, press Cmd-Shift-Z/Ctrl-Shift–Z. For a Symbol character, press Cmd-Shift-Q/Ctrl-Shift-Q.

3. Press any key or keyboard combination to produce the desired Zapf Dingbat character **1**–**2**. If you continue to type, the original, non-Dingbat typeface will reappear automatically.

TIP Design idea: Make the Zapf dingbat, or any other dingbat, slightly smaller than the surrounding text, or make it huge, so it serves as a graphic.

Special characters in other fonts

To insert special characters, first you need to know which keystroke to use. **Appendix A** is a chart of Zapf Dingbat, Symbol, and other special characters. To find other characters, in the Mac OS, you can use Apple 🍎 > **Key Caps**. Choose from the Font menu, then study the keyboard map. Press Option, Shift, or Option-Shift to display other characters. Type the keystroke to confirm it, Copy it (Cmd-C), then choose Paste (Cmd-V) in your document.

A faster approach is to buy the inexpensive Apple menu utility **PopChar Pro 3** from Unisoftwareplus.com. To use PopChar Pro, click in a text box with the Content tool to create an insertion point, then click the desired character on the PopChar palette—the character will appear at your insertion point in the current font.

In Windows, you can use the **Character Map** to insert special characters, but a faster and easier method is to use the **Fontasy** palette in the Windows TeXT ColleXTion XTension from Vision's Edge.

Special Characters

Hanging punctuation

If you're setting text that starts or ends with punctuation and that is larger or more noticeable than standard body text (a pull quote in an article, for example, or a quotation on a book jacket), the paragraph alignment will be more pleasing if the punctuation hangs outside the main body of the text.

How to do it. Unfortunately, it's not a flick-of-the-switch operation, like a drop cap. Here are a couple of methods: Create a **hanging indent** using either positive or negative indents (see page 96), or use the **Indent Here** character (see page 97) **1**–**3**. (You could also use either technique to hang a large initial cap.)

Here's one more way to hang punctuation: Type a space before the punctuation mark **4**, then apply **negative kerning** **5**. If the box has a low Text Inset value, the first character may be partially or completely hidden, but it will still print.

Copyfitting

If you need to squeeze text into a tight space or bring up a stubborn orphan word or hyphenated word (horrors!) from the end of a paragraph, use whichever of these techniques you think your readers are least likely to notice:

- Use Auto Hyphenation (see page 103).
- Turn on Auto Kern Above for the smallest type size you're using in Edit > Preferences > Preferences > Document–Character.
- Apply -.5, -1 or -2 tracking (not more!).
- Rewrite the copy—delete, add, rearrange, or substitute words (only if you have permission to do so or it's your writing!)
- Widen the column.
- Apply 99% scaling.
- Apply slightly tighter word spacing using an H&J.
- Switch to a condensed font.

Breaking a rule

Draw lines using the Orthogonal Line tool, then use Item > Step & Repeat (Cmd-Option-D/Ctrl-Alt-D) to duplicate them horizontally (0 Vertical Offset).

Early American Cookery

"There is no such thing as a non-working mother."

1 *Non-hanging punctuation*

"There is no such thing as a non-working mother."

2 *Hanging punctuation, created using a **hanging indent**: The left alignment of the paragraph is cleaner.*

"There is no such thing as a non-working mother."

3 *Even better: Here the second line is aligned with the stem of the "T."*

"There is no such thing ↵ as a non-working mother."

4 *To create hanging punctuation using kerning, insert a space to the left of the first character in the paragraph...*

"There is no such thing as a non-working mother."

Hester Mundis

5 *...and then apply **negative kerning**. It may look peculiar on screen, but it will print just fine.*

How to get attention

- Make the text you want to stand out larger.

- Use **boldface** or *italics* in the same font family as the body text.

- Choose a **contrasting** font or color.

Don't use the <u>underline</u> or ALL CAPS style to get attention. Those styles actually make type look more uniform, and thus harder to read.

A few embellishments

> **PUMPKIN PIE** Stew the pumpkin dry, and make it like squash pie, only season rather higher. In the country, where this *real yankee pie* is prepared in perfection, ginger is almost always used with other spices.

*To create **side-by-side paragraphs**, anchor a text box on the left side (Align with Text: Ascent) and create a hanging indent in the main paragraph (see page 96). Baseline Shift the anchored box upward, if necessary. This could also be done in a **table**.*

Pumpkin pie
Stew the pumpkin dry, and make it like squash pie, only season rather higher. In the country, where this *real yankee pie* is prepared in perfection, ginger is almost always used with other spices.

*Here an anchored box with a 10% black background is used as a **drop cap**.*

Stew the pumpkin dry, and make it like squash pie, only season rather higher. In the country, where this *real yankee pie* is prepared in perfection, ginger is almost always used with other spices.

Sara Josepha Hale

*Ultra simple, but oh so elegant: We chose a different font for the first character (Bodoni Highlight), and enlarged it. This is called a **raised initial cap**.*

Type in reverse

There's no one-step method for creating reversed type. You have to change the type color to white (see page 248) and change the background of the text box to black (see page 249). To create reversed type in subheads or other repetitive text, use a very legible typeface and a black or colored paragraph rule (see pages 100–101).

Get your dashes straight

When to use a regular hyphen: To write a compound word, as in "three-year-old."

When to use an **en dash** (Option-hyphen/ Ctrl-Alt-Shift-hyphen): Between a range of numbers, as in "Figures 4–6," a time frame, as in "4–6 weeks," or a distance, as in "4–6 miles."

When to use an **em dash** (Option-Shift-hyphen/Ctrl-Shift-=): To break up a sentence, as in "Bunny rabbit—excuse me— stay here." Don't add a whole space around an em dash — it will be too noticeable (as in this sentence). Instead, you can add a little bit of space by kerning—as in this sentence—or use a narrow flex space (Option-Shift-Spacebar/Ctrl-Shift-5 inserts a breaking flex space). Specify a Flex Space Width percentage in Edit > Preferences > Preferences > Document–Character (see page 390). Or use an em dash with built-in thin spaces around it from an expert font set.

To create a **non-breaking standard hyphen** (as in "write-off"), press Cmd-=/Ctrl- =.

Dot, dot, dot

To produce an **ellipses** character (…), press Option-;/Alt-0133. If those dots are too close together for your comfort, you can type periods instead and then track them out a little bit (. . .).

Or you can alternately type period (.), then non-breaking flex-space (Cmd-Option-Shift-Space bar/Ctrl-Alt-Shift-5), then period (. . .), then flex-space, and so on.

Fractions

There are several ways to produce fractions in QuarkXPress:

- In Windows, for ¼, press Alt + 0188; for ½, press Alt + 0189; and for ¾, press Alt + 0190.

- Use an expert character set, like Adobe Garamond Expert. It looks like this: ¾. Or use a math font.

- Type the numerator, a slash, and the denominator, highlight all the characters, then choose Style > Type Style > Make Fraction. The fraction will look like this: ¾. You can kern between the characters in this type of fraction. Choose Fraction/Price preferences in Edit menu > Preferences > Fraction/ Price **1**. Fraction/Price is also part of the free TypeTricks XTension.

- And lastly, you can build a fraction by hand, but it's a cumbersome process. Type the numerator, type a virgule (Option-Shift-1/Alt + 0218), type the denominator, apply the Superior style to the numerator, and finally, divide the point size of the denominator in half. This is what you get: ¾. You can adjust the Superior style Offset, VScale, and HScale in Edit > Preferences > Preferences > Document–Character.

TIP Speaking of preferences, to choose default Character settings (e.g., Ligatures, Auto Kern Above, Subscript and Superior style) for all future documents, close all QuarkXPress documents, then go to Edit > Preferences > Preferences > Document–Character.

Fractions (side tab)

Non-printing characters

The character		The keystroke
Tab	→	Tab
Word space	.	Spacebar
New paragraph	¶	Return/Enter
New line	↵	Shift-Return/ Shift-Enter
Next column	↓	Enter
Next box	⇙	Shift-Enter (on the keypad)
Indent here	⁝	Cmd-\/Ctrl-\

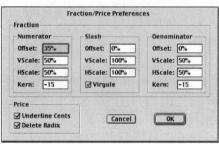

1 The **Fraction/Price Preferences** dialog box

Old style numerals have graceful descenders, as in 3, 4, 5, 7, and 9. You can find them in the Adobe Expert and other special font sets. These numerals have variable widths, though, unlike modern numbers, so they shouldn't be used for tables. Use them only in documents where their decorative value can be appreciated.

Make your rags look pretty

When all the copy is in place and ready for imagesetting, stop for a moment to fine-tune the right edge of your left-aligned paragraphs. Try to make the second-to-last line longer than the third-to-the-last line:

Every child is an artist.
The problem is how to remain
an artist once he grows up.

Or make the last line the longer than the second-to-last line:

Every child is an artist. The
problem is how to remain
an artist once he grows up. Pablo Picasso

But don't let the whole thing cave inward:

Every child is an artist. The problem
is how to remain an artist once
he grows up.

Typography terms

Sans serif *font*

Baseline

Serif *font*

Type for print

Our philosophy about choosing fonts for print output is similar to our philosophy about friendship: Pick a few sturdy, dependable **serif** font families to use for body text that you really like and get to know them well. Serif fonts are the least tiring to read. A few of our current favorites in this category include New Baskerville (which you're reading now), Sabon, and Caslon. Garamond and Goudy are other good classics. Use fonts from the **same family**—not from different families: Regular for the main text, bold and/or italics for emphasis.

For subheads, headers, and the like, pick a strong, contrasting **sans serif** face, such as Frutiger, Futura, Gills Sans, or Franklin Gothic.

Then, just as there are acquaintances that you enjoy seeing once in a while but would tire of if you saw every day, there are special fonts that you should choose only for special occasions. Fonts that fall into this category include script faces and other **decorative** faces, such as Caflisch Script Bold, which you see in the sidebar headers in this book. They're great for party invitations, drop caps, headlines and the like, but would be tiring to read in long passages. We have a "Weird fonts" folder that we dig into once in a while when we're looking for something unusual. Just as it's good to stand by your old, reliable friends, it's also good to be open to meeting new "faces."

The best way to learn more about typography is to study typography in the **real world** around you and try to identify which fonts are being used. Whether it's a poster, year-end report, newspaper, newsletter, brochure, book, book cover, magazine, food label, cosmetics label, menu, matchbook cover, shopping bag, or even the credits at the next movie you see, wherever you see words (unless it's written by hand), it's printed in a particular font.

Type for the Web

Unfortunately, the tried-and-true rules that designers are accustomed to following for print documents don't always apply to Web documents. When you choose a typeface for a print document, for example, you can depend on your final output being crisp— and in the typeface you chose. A Web page, on the other hand, can (and probably will) look different on different monitors or in different operating systems. That's due to differing monitor **resolutions** and the fact that the **fonts** you chose may not be available on a user's station and thus font substitution may occur. Your job as a Web designer is to keep the strengths and pitfalls of your output medium in mind as you create your page. And at the present time, text on a Web page can be unreliable.

One solution to the font substitution dilemma is to **convert** text into graphics (raster text boxes), but this isn't universally useful, as it increases the download time for the page. Luckily, you can perform such a conversion on some text boxes and not others. It's a good solution for headlines, logos, and other text blocks that you would want users to see in the original font. Then, for your body text, choose a font that is readily available on most users' systems (e.g., Times, Courier, or Helvetica).

Whereas as a print designer you won't see how your final work looks until it's printed, as a Web designer you can see your page in the actual environment in which it will be viewed—and the more **variables** you test, the better. View it on various browsers and operating systems so you'll know whether its download time is acceptable at various modem speeds and whether the layout works on different-sized screens. This way, you'll know whether you need to change a font here or there or convert text to graphics to improve the appearance and delivery of the page.

What you can't do

The following features are **not** available for **HTML** text boxes:

Typography
- Fractional point sizes (e.g., 12.5 pt)
- Outline, shadow, small caps, superior, and word underline type styles
- Kerning
- Tracking
- Baseline shift
- Indent here, discretionary hyphen, nonbreaking hyphen, discretionary new line
- Nonbreaking spaces; en, em, and flex spaces; and punctuation spaces and tabs are converted to standard spaces on export

Formats
- Tabs
- Lock to baseline grid
- H&Js
- Force and justified alignment

Box controls
- Flip horizontal, flip vertical
- First baseline
- Inter-paragraph max
- Box rotation
- Disproportionate interactive resizing
- Text box linking from page to page (you can link within the same page)
- Skewing
- Text paths and non-rectangular boxes are converted to raster boxes
- Columns are converted to an HTML table on export

Tables and Tabs 8

What's a table?

A **table**, according to *The Oxford Modern English Dictionary* (Oxford University Press), is "a set of facts or figures systematically displayed, esp. in columns." In QuarkXPress, a table can contain text and/or numerals, pictures, or a combination thereof.

Shade plants

Genus	Hardiness zone	Height	Bloom time
Astilbe	4–8	24–36"	June-July
Dicentra	3–8	10–15"	May–Oct
Hosta	3–8	6–48"	Jul-Sep
Lamium	3–8	12"	Jun–Jul

1 An **table** containing **text**

*Each block in a table is called a **cell**.*

Perennials

GENUS		HARDINESS ZONE	HEIGHT	BLOOM TIME
Dianthus		3–8	6"	June-Oct
Hemerocallis		3–8	18–48"	June-Oct
Monarda		4–8	36–48"	July-Aug
Rudbeckia		4–8	30–40"	July–Oct

2 A **table** containing **pictures** and **text**

Tables and tabs

If you've ever tried to build a chart in previous versions of QuarkXPress, you'll appreciate the new **table** features that are built into QuarkXPress 5. Not only can you stack columns of **text** and/or **numerals** **1**, you can also create a table of **pictures** or even combine text and picture cells in the same table **2**. Best of all, the features are simple to use.

You can create a table first using the **Tables tool** and then put text and pictures into it or you can convert existing text to a table. You can't convert existing pictures into a table, but you can cut and paste or import pictures into a table. A table contains blocks, called **cells**, that you type or import text into or import a picture into. As you type into a text cell, the type wraps automatically.

Once a table is created, you can change the information or pictures that it contains; you can change the overall shape of the table itself; you can change the way the cells are configured by adding or removing **rows** or **columns**; and you can change the table's appearance by recoloring or restyling its outer frame or interior **gridlines**.

Note: If you need to line up numerals on the decimal point or align page numbers with a dot leader for a table of contents, you'll need to use **tabs**, which we start discussing on page 143. Tables will work for most of your chart-making needs, though. In fact, you can insert tabs into text inside a table cell!

Tables Introduced

Creating tables

As we said on the previous page, you can create a table either of two ways: Either create the table and then enter type into it or convert existing text into a table. First, we'll show you how to do the former.

To create an empty text table:

1. Choose the Tables tool. ⊞

2. Drag a box in the document window (Shift-drag to make a square.)

3. Enter the desired number of Rows and Columns **1**.
   and
   Click Text Cells. The cell size will be calculated automatically to fit within the overall table.

   The overall table dimensions, as well as the individual row and column sizes, can be changed later.

4. Click OK.

5. Choose the Content tool.

6. Enter text into the cells **2**.
   or
   Click in a cell and import text into it using File > Get Text. The text will flow into that cell only, as one story (some of it will probably be hidden as overflow text).

   You can apply all the standard style and paragraph formatting attributes to table text, either manually (see Chapters 6 and 7) or via paragraph and/or character style sheets (see Chapter 13). Style sheets can be applied to more than one cell at a time. To select multiple cells, see the sidebar on page 129.

TIP To reconfigure the table (e.g., change the number of rows or columns), see page 134.

TIP The maximum number of rows and columns depends on the size of the overall table. A table with many cells (say, more than 1,000) may redraw slowly.

Jumping around

Jump one cell to the **right** or from the end of a **row** to the beginning of the next row — Control-Tab/Ctrl-Tab

Jump back to **previous** cell — Control-Shift-Tab/ Ctrl-Shift-Tab

Jump one **character** at a time within a cell or from the end of one cell to the beginning of the next cell — Right arrow

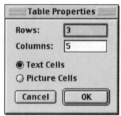

1 *Choose table parameters in the **Table Properties** dialog box.*

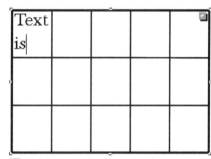

2 *Text is entered in the **new table**.*

New, Empty Table

Dianthus,3–8,6",June-
Oct ¶
Hemerocallis,3–8,18–
48",June–Oct¶
Monarda,4–8,36–48",J
uly-Aug¶
Rudbeckia,4–8,30–40"
,July–Oct

1 *Select the text you want to appear in the table. Note that there are* **no** *spaces after the commas.*

Convert Text to Table

Separate Rows With:	Paragraphs ⬍
Separate Columns With:	Commas ⬍
Rows:	4
Columns:	4
Cell Fill Order:	Z ▾

Canc

✓Z Left to Right, Top Down
Ƨ Right to Left, Top Down
И Top Down, Left to Right
И Top Down, Right to Left

2 *Use the* **Convert Text to Table** *dialog box to control how the existing text is to be separated into cells.*

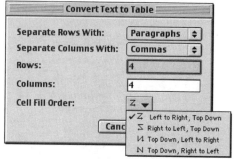

3 *The table that resulted*

Dianthus	3–8	6"	June-Oct
Hemerocallis	3–8	18–48"	June–Oct
Monarda	4–8	36–48"	July-Aug
Rudbeckia	4–8	30–40"	July–Oct

4 *After* **resizing** *the table*

To create a table from existing text:

1. Decide which characters in the original text—returns, tabs, spaces, or commas—will be used to separate it into cells in the table (see steps 5 and 6). Add or delete those characters now, if necessary.

2. Choose View > Show Invisibles, if Invisibles is currently off.

3. Choose the Content tool, then select only the text that you want to appear in the table **1**. (The text will be copied automatically into the table cells.)

4. Choose Item > (or Control-click/Right-click) Convert Text to Table.

5. Rows in the table will be set up according to the characters currently in the highlighted text, as reflected on the Separate Rows With pop-up menu **2**. You can change this setting, if necessary, to Paragraphs [Returns], Tabs, Space, or Commas. The default cell size will be .25" high and 1" wide, but you can resize the cells later (see page 130).

6. Columns in the table will be set up according to the characters currently in the highlighted text, as reflected on the Separate Columns With pop-up menu. You can change this setting, too.

7. Leave the Rows and Columns values as is, unless you want to add a blank row or column.

8. From the Cell Fill Order pop-up menu, choose the direction in which you want the existing text to flow into the new table. Each new paragraph will start at the next cell in the Cell Fill Order.

9. Click OK **3**. If there is any text left over that doesn't fit within a cell, the overflow symbol will appear in the lower right corner of that cell.

TIP To resize the table **4** (e.g., make it wider or narrower) or reconfigure the table (e.g., change the number of rows or columns), see page 134.

Table from Text

We've devoted the whole next chapter to pictures, and Chapter 11 to combining pictures and text. You should learn the picture basics before you learn how to make picture tables.

To create a picture table:

1. Choose the Tables tool. ⊞

2. Draw a rectangle in the document window. The box shape and size can be changed later.

3. Enter the desired number of Rows and Columns **1**.
and
Click Picture Cells.

4. Click OK.

5. Choose the Content tool, click a cell, then use File > Get Picture to import a picture **2**.
or
Copy and paste pictures that have already been imported from a normal picture box into any picture cell.

Resize or move the pictures inside the cells as you would in a normal picture box.

TIP To reshape a column or row, see page 130. To reshape the overall table, see page 133. Or to convert any of the cells to text cells, see page 132.

It always runs around

Most of the Item > **Modify** controls that are available for a standard picture or text box are also available for individual cells in a table, such as Text Inset, Vertical Alignment, and Text Angle.

Runaround (the feature that causes text to wrap around an obstructing item) is a different story. With the Item tool chosen and a table selected, you can go to Item > **Runaround** and specify a Runaround value for the whole table (Type > **Item**), but that's the extent of it. You can't choose any other Type of Runaround.

1 *Choose* **Row** *and* **Columns** *values and click* **Picture Cells***.*

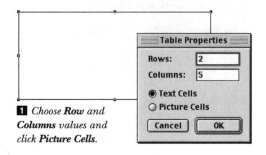

2 *After importing pictures into some of the cells*

Picture Table

Selecting table cells and their contents

Choose the **Content** tool, click the table, then:

Select the content of a **cell**	Cmd-A/Ctrl-A
Select all the cells in a **row**	Click just outside the left or right edge of the table (➡ pointer)
Select all the cells in a **column**	Click just outside the top or bottom edge of the table (⬇ pointer)
Select all the cells in a **series** of **rows** or **columns**	Drag along, and just outside of, any edge of the table
Select **adjacent** or **non-adjacent** cells	Shift-click cells

1 *Click at the top or bottom of a column to select it.*

2 *Click at the beginning or end of a row to select it.*

3 *Or Shift-click individual cells.*

To edit the contents of a table cell:

1. Choose the Content tool.
2. Click the cell whose attributes you want to change.
   or
   To select multiple cells using one of the selection methods listed in the sidebar on this page **1**–**3**
3. Do any of the following:

   Each text cell is really a text box. Some of the options that you find in Item > Modify for standard text boxes are also available for text cells.

   To edit the typographic attributes of text in a table cell, use the standard methods (that is, Style > Character, the Measurements palette, or style sheets).

   To edit the paragraph attributes of text in a table cell, use Style > Formats or use style sheets.

   To move text from one cell to another, highlight it, then use the Cut (Cmd-X/Ctrl-X) and Paste commands (Cmd-V/Ctrl-V).

   To modify a cell's attributes, such as its width, background color or shade, or Text Inset, use Item > Modify (Cmd-M/Ctrl-M). You can even rotate or skew text within its cell. The Cols and Gutter options are not available for table cells.

   To modify picture cells, use the Cell or Picture pane in Item > Modify.

   To recolor the table border segments or gridlines, see page 253.

   To convert text cells to picture cells, or vice versa, see page 132.

To resize a column or row by dragging:

1. Choose the Item tool, then double-click the table.

2. In the Modify dialog box:

Check Maintain Geometry if you want the overall size of the table to remain fixed as you resize columns or rows. Other columns and rows will resize automatically to compensate.

or

Uncheck Maintain Geometry if you want to resize only one column or row at a time. The table will become larger or smaller to accommodate the new column or row size.

Note: The current Maintain Geometry setting will remain in effect; you don't have to re-choose it every time you resize a column or row.

Click OK.

3. Choose the Content tool.

4. Drag the vertical or horizontal gridline that separates two columns or rows (the pointer will become a double-headed arrow ↔) **1**–**3**.

If the column or row contains text, the text may re-wrap inside each cell. If the row or column contains a picture or pictures, more of the pictures will become exposed or cropped as a result.

TIP To resize the overall table, see page 133.

1 *Move a gridline to* **resize** *a* **column** *or* **row**.

2 *The column is* **enlarged** *with* **Maintain Geometry checked**. *The overall table size remains the same.*

2 *The column is* **enlarged** *with* **Maintain Geometry unchecked**. *The overall table enlarges automatically to accommodate the larger column.*

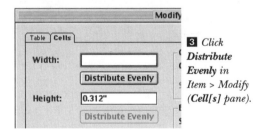

1 *In Item > Modify (Cell[s] pane), enter new **Width** and/or **Height** values for a selected **row** or **column**.*

GENUS		HARDINESS ZONE	HEIGHT	BLOOM TIME
Dianthus		3–8	6"	June–Oct
Hemerocallis		3–8	18–48"	June–Oct
Monarda		4–8	36–48"	July–Aug
Rudbeckia		4–8	30–40"	July–Oct

2 *Five columns of uneven **width** are selected.*

Modify

Table | **Cells**

Width: [ ]

[Distribute Evenly]

Height: [0.312"]

[Distribute Evenly]

3 *Click **Distribute Evenly** in Item > Modify (Cell[s] pane).*

GENUS		HARDINESS ZONE	HEIGHT	BLOOM TIME
Dianthus		3–8	6"	June–Oct
Hemerocallis		3–8	18–48"	June–Oct
Monarda		4–8	36–48"	July–Aug
Rudbeckia		4–8	30–40"	July–Oct

4 *After clicking **Width: Distribute Evenly**, all the columns are now the **same** width. The text rewrapped automatically in the first column.*

To resize a column or row by entering values:

1. Choose the Content tool.

2. Select the column(s) or row(s) you want to reshape or resize (see the sidebar on page 129).

3. Control-click/Right-click and choose Modify (Cmd-M/Ctrl-M).

4. In the Table pane, check Maintain Geometry if you want the overall size of the table to remain fixed as you resize columns or rows. Other columns and rows will resize automatically.
   or
   Uncheck Maintain Geometry if you want to resize only one column or row at a time. The table will become larger or smaller to accommodate the new column or row size.

   Note: The current Maintain Geometry setting will remain in effect; you don't have to re-choose it every time you resize a column or row.

5. Click the Cell[s] tab, then enter the desired Width or Height **1**.

6. Click Apply (Cmd-A/Alt-A), make any adjustments, then click OK.

Let's say you've ended up with columns and rows of non-uniform sizes, but now you want to make them all the same size again.

To make columns and/or rows uniform in scale:

1. Choose the Content tool.

2. Select the rows or columns you want to make uniform **2** (see the sidebar on page 129).

3. Control-click/Right-click and choose Modify, then click the Cell[s] tab.

4. Click Distribute Evenly under Width and/or Height **3**–**4**. A value will be entered in the field automatically. This option will be grayed out if the selected columns or rows are already uniform.

5. Click OK.

A table can contain text cells, picture cells, contentless cells, or a combination thereof. Follow these instructions to change the content of existing cells.

Beware! If a cell already contains a picture or text, that picture or text will be **deleted** when you change its content. You'll get a warning prompt, so you'll have a chance to change your mind at the last minute.

To change the content of a cell (picture, text, or none):

1. Choose the Content tool.

2. Select the cell or cells you want to convert (use one of the selection methods listed in the sidebar page 129 to select multiple cells) **1**.

3. Choose Item (or Control-click/Right-click) > Content > Picture, Text, or None. If you choose None, you will be able to recolor the background of the cell or apply a blend to it—period. You can't put text or a picture inside it.

4. Respond in the alert dialog box, if one appears **2**–**3**.

1 *A column of cells is* **selected***.*

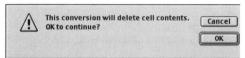

2 *Item >* **Content** *>* **Picture** *is chosen. Since the cells already contain text, this alert dialog box appears.*

3 *Clicking OK in the alert dialog box causes the text to be* **deleted***. The cells in the third column are now empty picture cells.*

Change Cell Content

Modifier keys for resizing a table

Drag a **handle** of the table with the following keys held down:

Resize table, rows, and columns (not content) non-proportionally	No modifier keys
Resize table, rows, and columns (not content) proportionally	Option-Shift/ Alt-Shift
Resize table to a square; content doesn't resize	Shift/Shift
Resize table, rows, columns, and content non-proportionally	Cmd/Ctrl
Resize table, rows, columns, and content proportionally	Cmd-Option-Shift/ Ctrl-Alt-Shift

To resize a whole table:

1. Choose the Item tool, then click the table.

2. Using one of the shortcuts listed in the sidebar, drag any of the table's eight handles **1**–**2**. The cells will reshape to fit the new table dimensions.
or
Change the W [width] or H [height] value on the Measurements palette.
or
Choose Item > Modify (Cmd-M/ Ctrl-M), click the Table tab, enter new Width and/or Height values, click Apply to preview, if desired, then click OK.

TIP To place a table in a precise location on your page, enter Origin Across and Origin Down values in Item > Modify (Table pane) or change the X and Y values on the left side of Measurements palette.

Dianthus			6"	June–Oct
Hemerocallis			18–48"	June–Oct
Monarda			36–48"	July–Aug
Rudbeckia			30–40"	July–Oct

1 *A corner handle is dragged with **Option-Shift/ Alt-Shift** held down.*

Dianthus			6"	June–Oct
Hemerocallis			18–48"	June–Oct
Monarda			36–48"	July–Aug
Rudbeckia			30–40"	July–Oct

2 *The table's dimensions are enlarged **proportionally**, but not its content.*

To add columns or rows to a table:

1. Choose the Content tool.

2. Before you add columns or rows, you need to decide whether to permit the overall width and height of the table to change as a result. Click the table, choose Item > Modify (Cmd-M/Ctrl-M), then click the Table tab. With Maintain Geometry checked, the overall dimensions of the table will be preserved as columns or rows are added, but existing cells will become smaller in order to accommodate the new ones. With Maintain Geometry unchecked, the cell sizes won't change, but the overall table dimensions will increase.

3. Click OK, then click the row or column next to which you want the new row or column to be inserted **1**.

4. Choose Item menu (or Control-click/Right-click) > Table > Insert Rows or Insert Columns.

5. Enter the desired Number of Rows or Columns **2**–**3**, then click where you want the new rows or columns to be inserted.

6. Click OK **4**.

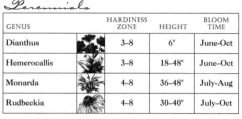

1 *The original table*

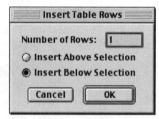

2 *In the **Insert Table Rows** dialog box, enter the Number of **Rows** you want to add, and choose a location.*

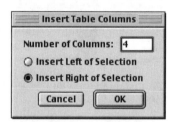

3 *Or in the **Insert Table Columns** dialog box, enter the Number of **Columns** you want to add, and choose a location.*

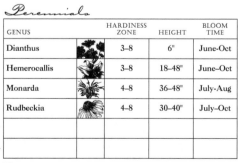

4 *In this case, we added two new **rows** to the **bottom** of the table.*

To delete a row or column from a table:

1. Choose the Content tool.

2. Before you delete a row or column, you need to decide whether to permit the overall width and height of the table to change. Click the table, choose Item > Modify (Cmd-M/Ctrl-M), then click the Table tab. With Maintain Geometry checked, the overall dimensions of the table will be preserved as columns or rows are deleted, but existing cells will be enlarged in order to fill the gap. With Maintain Geometry unchecked, the cell sizes won't change, but the overall table dimensions will decrease.

3. Click OK, then click just outside the edge of the table to select the whole row or column you want to delete **1**.

4. Choose Item > Table > Delete Rows or Delete Columns (or move the pointer over one of the selected cells, Control-click/Right-click, then choose Table > Delete Rows or Delete Columns) **2**.

Perennials

GENUS		HARDINESS ZONE	HEIGHT	BLOOM TIME
Dianthus		3–8	6"	June-Oct
Hemerocallis		3–8	18–48"	June-Oct
Monarda		4–8	36–48"	July-Aug
Rudbeckia		4–8	30–40"	July-Oct

1 *A row is selected.*

Perennials

GENUS		HARDINESS ZONE	HEIGHT	BLOOM TIME
Dianthus		3–8	6"	June-Oct
Monarda		4–8	36–48"	July-Aug
Rudbeckia		4–8	30–40"	July–Oct

2 *After choosing Item > Table > **Delete Rows***

There are many reasons why you might want to unite (combine) two or more cells into one. Maybe you want a header to span across the whole top of your table. Or perhaps you want to display a picture more prominently in a larger portion of the table.

To combine cells:

1. *Beware!* The text or picture in the topmost left selected cell will be preserved when you combine other cells with it, but any text or pictures in other selected cells will be **discarded** (you'll get a warning prompt). To preserve text or a picture for later use, take a moment now to copy and paste it either into a separate box outside the table or into a cell that you're not combining.

2. Choose the Content tool.

3. Shift-click a cell, then Shift-click the other cells you want to combine with it **1**.

4. Choose Item (or Control-click/Right-click) > Table > Combine Cells. If the cells currently contain text and/or pictures, an alert dialog box will appear **2**. Click "Do not show this warning again," if desired, then click OK **3**.

   The selected cells will be combined into one. If the topmost left selected cell contained text, that text will now spread across or downward to fill the now larger cell size. If that cell contained a picture, the picture either will now fill, or can be scaled to fill, the whole combined cell.

To un-combine cells:

1. Choose the Content tool.

2. Click the cell you want to split up.

3. Choose Item menu (or Control-click/Right-click) > Table > Split Cell. The content of the cell will be placed inside the first of the newly-divided cells.

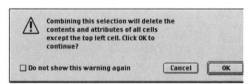

1 *Three cells in the top row are selected.*

2 *This **alert** dialog box will appear if the cells you are combining contain text or pictures.*

Perennials for fall planting			
Dianthus		3–8	6"
Hemerocallis		3–8	18–48"
Monarda		4–8	36–48"
Rudbeckia		4–8	30–40"

3 *After choosing Item > Table > **Combine Cells**, the top three cells are combined into one, preserving only the text from the first of the selected cells, and the text rewraps. We applied a blend to the combined cell (via Item > Modify, Cell pane) to prove our point.*

Perennials for fall planting			
Dianthus		3–8	6"
Hemerocallis		3–8	18–48"
Monarda		4–8	36–48"
Rudbeckia		4–8	30–40"

1 *The original table*

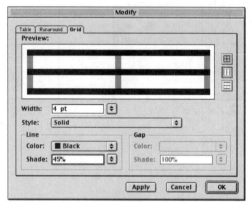

2 *Choose* **Width, Style, Color,** *and* **Shade** *options for gridlines in Item > Modify (* **Grid** *pane).*

Perennials for fall planting			
Dianthus		3–8	6"
Hemerocallis		3–8	18–48"
Monarda		4–8	36–48"
Rudbeckia		4–8	30–40"

3 *This is after checking Maintain Geometry in the Table pane of Item > Modify, and then in the* **Grid** *pane, clicking the* **Vertical gridlines only** *button and changing the Width and Shade (to 45% black).*

You can dramatically change the appearance of a table by changing the Line Style, Width, Color, or Shade of its gridlines or border, and this can be done using a dialog box (instructions on this page) or using submenus (see next page). The default border and gridlines are black, and 1 pt. in width.

To restyle the border and gridlines using a dialog box:

1. Choose the Item tool, then double-click the table **1**.

2. If you're going to change the width of the border/gridlines, you need to decide whether or not to permit the overall width and height of the table to change. Start by clicking the Table tab. If you check Maintain Geometry, the overall dimensions of the table will be preserved, but existing cells will resize automatically in order to fill the gap. If you uncheck Maintain Geometry, the cell sizes won't change, but the overall table dimensions will change.

3. Click the Grid tab.

4. Click one of the three icons at the right side of the dialog box for the gridlines and borders you want to restyle: Horizontal and Vertical ⊞, Horizontal only ⊟, or Vertical only ⊞ **2**.

5. Choose a gridline Width, Style, Line Color, and Shade, and also choose a Gap Color and Shade if the line style contains gaps. The horizontal gridlines will print over the vertical gridlines.

6. Click Apply. At this point you can click another icon and apply different settings, if you like. Adjust any of the settings, then click OK **3**.

TIP To make a gridline disappear, apply the same color to it as the color of the background of the table. As of this writing, you can't apply a color of None or a width of 0 to a gridline—arghh!

Following these instructions, you can restyle all or a select few gridlines—picking and choosing which ones you want to change. You can also restyle the border segments separately.

To restyle the border or gridlines via submenus:

1. Choose the Content tool.

2. Shift-click a gridline, then Shift-click additional gridlines, if desired. You can select both horizontal and vertical gridlines, if desired. You can also Shift-click individual border (outer) segments. If the gridline is narrow, it may be hard to tell if it's selected.
   or
   Control-click/Right-click and choose Gridlines > Select Horizontal, Select Vertical, Select Borders **1** [the outer frame of the table], or Select All [all gridlines and borders].

3. Choose attributes via the Style > Line Style [dash or stripe style], Width, Color, or Shade submenu **2**–**4** Or Control-click/Right-click and choose any of those commands from the context menu.

TIP You can also change the gridline color (but not the gap color) (see page 253).

TIP You can use the Measurements palette to change the line width or style one gridline or border segment at a time.

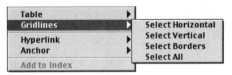

1 *You can use the Gridlines submenu to select multiple gridlines, borders, or both.*

Perennials for fall planting			
Dianthus		3–8	6"
Hemerocallis		3–8	18–48"
Monarda		4–8	36–48"
Rudbeckia		4–8	30–40"

2 *The original table*

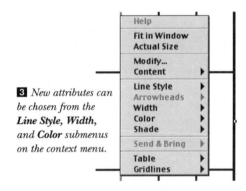

3 *New attributes can be chosen from the Line Style, Width, and Color submenus on the context menu.*

Perennials for fall planting			
Dianthus		3–8	6"
Hemerocallis		3–8	18–48"
Monarda		4–8	36–48"
Rudbeckia		4–8	30–40"

4 *This is after restyling the outer border segments and the first horizontal gridline with different line styles and widths and changing the first vertical gridline (between the plant name cells and the picture cells) to white.*

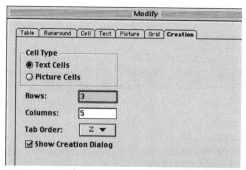

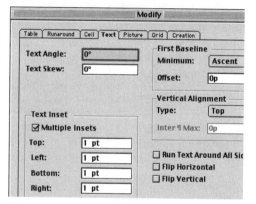

1 *Choose preference settings for newly-created tables in the **Creation** pane of the **Modify** dialog box.*

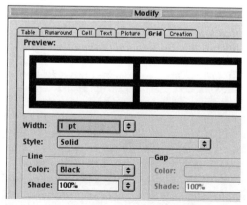

2 *Choose text preferences for newly-created tables in the **Text** pane.*

If you create tables frequently and you tend to choose the same parameters over and over for them, it's worth your while to take a moment to set a few preferences. These Creation preferences affect future tables that you create using the Tables tool, but not tables created using the Convert Text to Table command.

To choose Table tool preferences:

1. Double-click the Tables tool ▦.
   or
   Or choose Edit > Preferences > Preferences > Document–Tools, then click the Tables tool icon.

2. Click Modify, then click the Creation tab.

3. Choose whether you want newly created tables to contain text or picture cells, and make default Rows, Columns, and Tab Order choices **1**.

4. *Optional:* To prevent the Table Properties dialog box from opening each time you use the Tables tool, uncheck Show Creating Dialog. With this option checked, the Table Properties dialog box will open each time you use the Tables tool, displaying your preferences.

5. Click the Runaround, Cell, Text **2**, Picture, or Grid **3** tab, and change any of the available options in those panes, if desired.

6. Click OK twice.

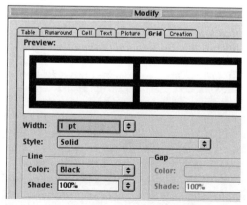

3 *Choose Width, Style, Color, and Shade preferences for gridlines in newly created tables in the **Grid** pane.*

Table Tool Preferences

When the Convert Table to Text command is applied to a table, a new text box is created, and it is filled with a copy of the text from the table. You can choose in what order the text blocks from the table cells will flow into the new box, and whether they will be separated by Returns, Tabs, Commas, or Spaces. You can also choose whether you want the original table to be preserved (the default setting) or deleted.

Note: If the table contains pictures, those pictures will become anchored picture boxes within the new text box.

To convert a table to conventional text:

1. Choose the Item or Content tool.

2. Click the table you want to convert ▉.

3. Choose Item menu (or Control-click/Right-click) > Table > Convert Table to Text.

4. From the Separate Rows With pop-up menu ▉, choose which character you want to have inserted at the end of each row (the default is paragraph Returns).

5. From the Separate Columns With pop-up menu, choose which character you want to have inserted between each column (the default is Tabs).

6. Choose an option from the Text Extraction Order pop-up menu for the order in which text is to be extracted from the table (the default is ⤢, which is left to right, top to bottom).

7. Check Delete Table if you want the table to be deleted. Whether this box is checked or not, the converted text will appear in a new, separate box after you click OK.

8. Click OK ▉. This conversion command can't be undone. To redo it, delete the new text box and start over from the beginning.

Dianthus	3–8	6"	June-Oct
Hemerocallis	3–8	18–48"	June–Oct
Iris	3–9	24–50"	June
Malva	4–7	36–48"	July–Oct
Monarda	4–8	36–48"	July-Aug
Rudbeckia	4–8	30–40"	July–Oct

▉ *The original table*

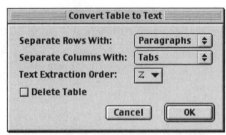

▉ *Choose settings for the extracted text in the* **Convert Table to Text** *dialog box.*

Dianthus 3–8 6"
June-Oct
Hemerocallis 3–8 18–48"
June–Oct
Iris 3–9 24–50"
June
Malva 4–7 36–48"
July–Oct
Monarda 4–8 36–48"
July-Aug
Rudbeckia 4–8 30–40"
July–Oct

▉ *After choosing Item > Table >* **Convert Table to Text***: In this case, the columns are separated by tabs and the rows are separated by paragraph returns.*

Modify

Table | Frame | Runaround | Grid | Export

Origin Across: `170 px`

Origin Down: `104 px`

Width: `225 px`

Height: `115 px`

☐ Maintain Geometry

☑ Convert Table to Graphic on Export

[Apply]

1 *Check **Convert Table to Graphic on Export** in Item > Modify (Table pane).*

On this page and the next, we'll discuss tables in Web documents. You can export a table as an image to preserve any Quark-XPress formatting that isn't supported by HTML. The border of tables created in a Web document look three-dimensional.

To specify that a whole table be exported as an image:

1. With a QuarkXPress Web document active, choose the Item tool, then click the table.

2. Choose Item > Modify (Cmd-M/ Ctrl-M), then click the Table tab.

3. Check Convert Table to Graphic on Export **1** at the bottom of the dialog box. This option converts the whole table into a bitmap image; the cells will no longer be individually editable. If this option is not checked, the table will be converted to HTML.

Note: Each table has its own Convert Table to Graphic on Export setting, which means you have to remember to check it for each table you want rasterized. To read about the Export options, see pages 308–312.

Convert Table to Graphic

If an entire table is exported as an image, all its cells will be included in the image; you won't be able to export individual cells as HTML content. If a table is not set to rasterize on export, you can still choose to rasterize the contents of individual cells, as per these instructions.

To have cell contents rasterize at export:

1. In a Web document in QuarkXPress, choose the Content tool, then select the cell[s] you want rasterized.

2. Choose Item > Modify.

3. Uncheck Convert Table to Graphic on Export.

4. Click the Cell[s] tab.

5. Check Convert Cell to Graphic on Export. The table layout will be converted to an HTML table, and the converted boxes will be rasterized as pictures.

   Picture cells and cells with a content of None are automatically exported as images; the Convert Cell to Graphic on Export option is not available for them. To choose export options for picture cells or cells with a content of None, use the Export pane of Item > Modify.

TIP In the Text pane of Item > Modify, uncheck Convert Table to Graphic on Export to see what formatting options are HTML-compatible (only those options will be available). With this option checked, all formatting options are available because the cell contents will be rasterized on export.

You can't have everything

For table **cells** that **won't** be converted to a graphic on export, these options are **not** available:

■ Dashes and stripes on table gridlines. Borders and gridlines have to be solid.

■ Varying widths for table gridlines. Gridlines must have a uniform width. That width will become the cell spacing in the HTML export.

And for **text** in a table cell that **won't** be converted to a graphic on export, these options are **not** available:

■ First Baseline, Minimum, Offset, and Inter-Paragraph Max values.

■ The Flip Horizontal/Flip Vertical command for text.

■ Rotated or skewed text.

■ Run Text Around All Sides option.

Rasterize Cell Contents

On the right

Press **Option-Tab/Alt-Tab** to set a **right indent tab** that stays flush with the current right indent of the box. If you resize the text box or table by dragging the right handle, the tab will still hug the right edge of the box. You won't see a marker on the Tabs ruler for this kind of tab.

A **decimal-aligned** tab with a dot leader

Cafe L'argent

Palourdes	10.00
Vin	40.00
Salade	7.00
Poitrine de Poulet	24.95
Café	3.00
Kir à la Framboise	6.75
Digestif	10.75
Sub-Total	102.45
Tax	8.45
Total	$110.90

Thank you!

1

A **left-aligned** tab   An **outrageous** tab

Setting tabs

Tabs are invisible commands that tell blocks of text where to line up (don't use spaces to create columns; the columns will be uneven due to variable character widths) **1**–**2**. If no custom tabs are set and you press Tab, text will jump to the nearest default tab stop. The default tab stops are ½ inch apart. Before you can set custom tab stops (next two pages), you must insert invisible tab characters → into your text.

You can set up columns of text and/or numerals using just the tables feature, without tabs. Tabs are handy, though, for inserting dot leaders or aligning numbers on the decimal. Tabs can be added to text in a table, but not to HTML text.

To insert tabs into text:

1. Choose the Content tool, then click in a text box.
2. Press Tab as you input copy before typing each new column. The cursor will jump to the next default tab stop. Don't keep pressing the Tab key to move the type over. If you're not happy with the location of the default stops (we rarely are), set custom stops (see next page). *or*

   To add a tab to already inputted text, click to the left of the text that is to start each new column and press Tab.

Insert Tabs into Text

Endangered vs. Non-Endangered Bears			
	1930	**1992**	**2000** (Projected)
Pandas	1 million	4 thousand	0
Koalas	6 million	3 thousand	7
Poohs	1 million	2 billion	3 billion

2 *Use tabs to align columns of text.*

Endangered·vs.··Non-Endangered·Bears¶			
→	**1930** →	**1992** →	**2000**·(Projected)

Choose View > Show Invisibles to reveal tab symbols and other non-printing characters.

You can set a virtually unlimited number of custom stops per paragraph (one tab per point).

To set custom tab stops:

1. Choose the Content tool.

2. Zoom in on your document to make it easier to see the tab ruler increments, but make sure you can still see the full width of the text column.

3. Select **all** the paragraphs for which the tab stops are to be set.

4. Choose Style > Tabs (Cmd-Shift-T/ Ctrl-Shift-T), and move the dialog box if it's in the way. Also, we like to turn on continuous Apply so we can preview our changes immediately (Option-click/ Alt-click the Apply button).

5. Click the Left, Center, Right, Decimal, or Comma, or Align On icon (**1**, next page). To align numerals, choose Decimal or Comma. To align to a character of your choosing, click Align On, then enter the character.

6. *Optional:* To create a leader, type one or two characters in the Fill Characters field (**1**–**4** on this page and **2** on the next page). Type a period (.) to create a dot leader.

7. Click in the tabs ruler to insert a tab stop (**3**, next page). To move a marker, drag it to the left or the right. *or* Enter a position number (location on the ruler) in the Position field using any measurement system, then click Set (**4**, next page).

8. *Optional:* Repeat steps 5–7 to create additional tab stops.

9. Click OK.

TIP To set a series of tabs by specifying the distance between them, enter "+" and then the gap length in the Position field (e.g., "p10+p12"). If the list gets too long, click the last tab marker on the ruler, then continue on your way.

Work smart

Tabs, like all paragraph formats, can be applied via a **style sheet**. We usually create a style sheet based on a paragraph that already contains custom tabs where we need them.

If you edit the tabs for the Normal style sheet or any other style sheet when no documents are open, you will in effect be creating your own default tabs.

```
Steamed vegetable dumplings . . . . . . . . . 3.50
Shrimp rolls . . . . . . . . . . . . . . . . . . . 4.00
```

1 *To create a dot leader with extra space between the dots, enter a **period** and a **space** in the Fill Characters field.*

```
Steamed vegetable dumplings - - - - - - - - 3.50
Shrimp rolls - - - - - - - - - - - - - - - - - 4.00
```

2 *To create a dashed line with extra space between the dashes, enter a **hyphen** and a **space** in the Fill Characters field.*

```
Steamed vegetable dumplings _ _ _ _ _ 3.50
Shrimp rolls _ _ _ _ _ _ _ _ _ _ 4.00
```

3 *To change the point size, tracking, color, or other attributes of a tab leader, you must do it manually (you can use Find/Change). The tab leader in this example is tracked out, horizontally scaled, and baseline shifted downward.*

TIP *You can **copy-and-paste** a tab from one line of text to another. If you double-click the tab character, the whole leader will select along with it.*

```
Steamed vegetable dumplings  ≈  ≈  ≈  ≈ 3.50
Shrimp rolls  ≈  ≈  ≈  ≈  ≈  ≈  ≈  ≈ 4.00
```

4 *You can use **any character** as a fill character. Be creative! Mac OS: This is Option-X and a space. Windows: This is Alt + 0187 in the Symbol font and a space. The font has to be changed manually.*

Set Custom Tab Stops

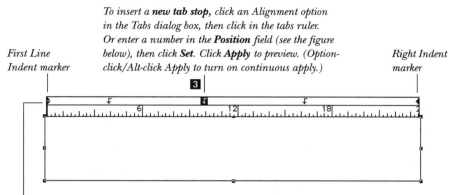

To insert a **new tab stop,** *click an Alignment option in the Tabs dialog box, then click in the tabs ruler. Or enter a number in the* **Position** *field (see the figure below), then click* **Set.** *Click* **Apply** *to preview. (Option-click/Alt-click Apply to turn on continuous apply.)*

First Line Indent marker

Right Indent marker

3

Left Indent marker

TIP *You can move the indent markers to change the paragraph indents. To enter indents numerically, use Style > Paragraph Attributes > Formats (see pages 88–89).*

To align columns to a specific character, click the **Align On** *alignment icon, then type a character in the* **Align On** *field.*

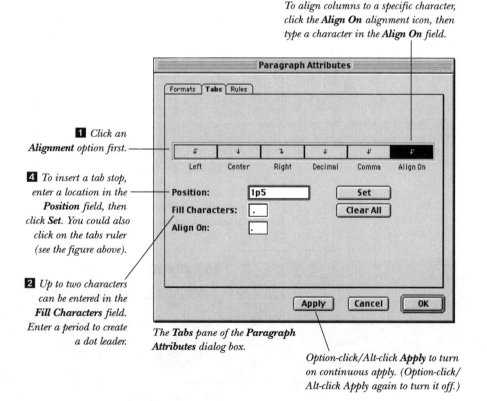

1 *Click an* **Alignment** *option first.*

4 *To insert a tab stop, enter a location in the* **Position** *field, then click* **Set.** *You could also click on the tabs ruler (see the figure above).*

2 *Up to two characters can be entered in the* **Fill Characters** *field. Enter a period to create a dot leader.*

The **Tabs** *pane of the* **Paragraph Attributes** *dialog box.*

Option-click/Alt-click **Apply** *to turn on continuous apply. (Option-click/ Alt-click Apply again to turn it off.)*

To edit or remove custom tab stops:

1. Choose the Content tool.

2. Select **all** the paragraphs that contain the stops you want to change or from which you want to remove tab stops.

3. Choose Style > Tabs (Cmd-Shift-T/ Ctrl-Shift-T).

4. Do any of the following:

   To change the alignment of a stop, click its marker, then choose a different Alignment option.

   or

   To change a Fill character, click the marker, then change the character.

   or

   To move a tab stop, drag it manually. Or click on it, change the Position value, then click Set (Cmd-S/Alt-S).

   or

   To remove one tab stop, drag its marker upward or downward out of the ruler 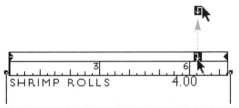.

   or

   To remove *all* the tab stops, click Clear All (Alt-C in Windows) **2** or Option-click/Alt-click the ruler.

5. Click Apply to preview (Cmd-A/Ctrl-A), readjust the settings, if desired, then click OK.

Blank ruler?

If the paragraphs you highlight before choosing Style > Tabs contain more than one set of tab stops, only the tab stops for the first paragraph will display on the tabs ruler, but any new tab settings will affect **all** the currently highlighted text.

1 *Drag a tab stop marker out of the ruler to* **remove** *it.*

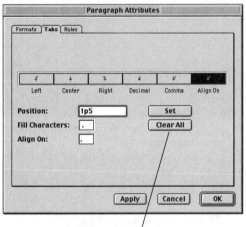

2 *Click* **Clear All** *to remove* **all** *tab stops from the currently highlighted text. The* **default** *tab stops will be restored to the text.*

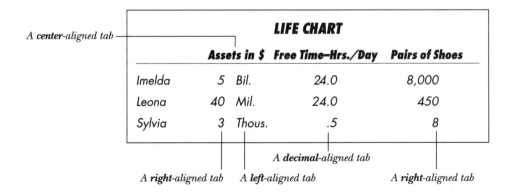

A *center*-aligned tab

LIFE CHART

	Assets in $	Free Time–Hrs./Day	Pairs of Shoes
Imelda	5 Bil.	24.0	8,000
Leona	40 Mil.	24.0	450
Sylvia	3 Thous.	.5	8

A *decimal*-aligned tab

A *right*-aligned tab   A *left*-aligned tab   A *right*-aligned tab

Edit Custom Tab Stops

Pictures 9

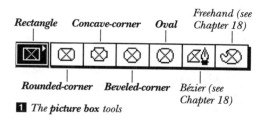

Rectangle Concave-corner Oval *Freehand (see Chapter 18)*

Rounded-corner *Beveled-corner* *Bézier (see Chapter 18)*

1 *The **picture box** tools*

2 *Drag to create a **picture box**.*

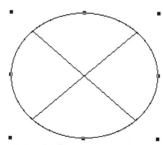

3 *An empty picture box has an "x" through its center.*

In QuarkXPress, a picture can be imported into a variety of different-shaped picture boxes. First you create a box using one of the picture box tools (Bézier or non-Bézier), then you import a picture into it.

File formats that can be imported include TIFF, PAINT, PICT, EPS, JPEG, DCS, PCX, PDF, PNG, OS/2 bitmap, Windows Metafile (WMF), and Bitmap (BMP). If the PhotoCD Import XTension is enabled (use Utilities > XTensions Manager), you can also import a Kodak PhotoCD picture from a PhotoCD.

Note: Most of the commands that are discussed in this chapter can be applied to a Bézier picture box, in addition to a standard picture box. Béziers are covered in Chapter 18.

To create a picture box:

1. Choose any picture box tool **1** except the Bézier or Freehand picture box tool. The cursor will temporarily turn into a crosshair icon.

2. Drag in any direction **2**–**3**.

TIP Shift-drag a handle to turn a rectangular picture box into a square or an oval picture box into a circle. This also works with a text box.

TIP To apply a frame to a picture box, use Item > Frame (Cmd-B/Ctrl-B).

TIP Need more than one? Use the Item > Duplicate, Step and Repeat, or Super Step and Repeat command to create multiples of any item.

When a picture is imported into a picture box, a screen preview version of it is saved with the QuarkXPress file for display purposes. Also saved with the QuarkXPress file is information about changes made to the picture within the document, such as cropping or scaling. The original picture file is not modified by such changes. Instead, a link is created to the original picture file, which the QuarkXPress file accesses when the document is printed. If the link to the original picture file is broken (the original picture is moved) or the picture itself is modified, you must update the link or it won't output properly (see pages 165–166).

To import a picture:

1. Choose the Item or Content tool, then click a picture box.
   or
   Choose the Content tool, then click a box in a group or a picture cell in a table **1**.

2. Choose File > Get Picture (Cmd-E/ Ctrl-E). Or Right-click/Control-click the box or cell, then choose Get Picture from the context menu. **5.0!**

3. *Optional:* Check Preview to display a thumbnail of the picture (the picture has to have been saved with a preview).

4. Click a picture file name **4** (and **1**, next page) then click Open, or just double-click the file name **2**–**3**.

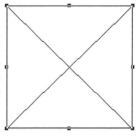

1 *Click a picture box. Note: If the box already contains a picture, the picture you import will replace the existing one.*

2 *The picture is imported using File > Get Picture—but where is it? If it has a large white background, it may be off to the side.*

3 *Ctrl-click/Right-click and choose Fit Box to Picture to make the box fit the picture, or drag the picture using the Content (hand) tool.*

4 *Click a picture file name (or type the first character or two of the name).*

With Preview checked, a thumbnail preview of the currently selected file will display.

The picture's Color (bit) Depth, Dimensions, Resolution, Type (file format), File Size (storage size), and Date it was last modified

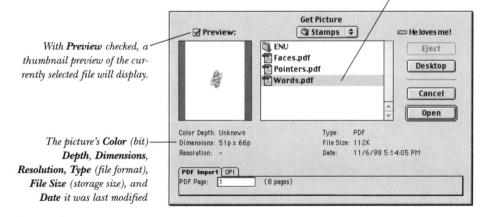

Faster navigating 5.0!

If you tend to import pictures over and over from the same folder, you can make that folder appear automatically in the Open dialog box by choosing it in Edit > Preferences > **Default Path Preferences** (see page 402).

1 *Click a* **picture** *file* **name** *(or type the first character or two of the name in the* **File name** *field).*

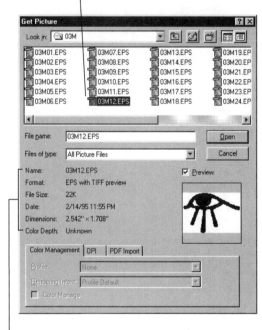

The picture's **Name,** *file* **Format, File Size** *(storage size),* **Date** *it was last modified,* **Dimensions,** *and* **Color** *(bit)* **Depth, Resolution.**

Formats you can import

You can import a TIFF, EPS, JPEG, DCS, GIF, PDF, PNG, PICT, OS/2 bitmap, PCX, PhotoCD, or Windows Bitmap picture into a QuarkXPress picture box. (In the Mac OS, a Windows Metafile will translate into a PICT when it's imported.) QuarkXPress can color separate an RGB or CMYK TIFF.

To import a picture in the JPEG, PDF, PCX, BMP, PhotoCD, or LZW TIFF format, make sure that format's import filter is enabled. If the required filter is disabled, you will get an error message that reads "This file requires XTensions software to be read properly." Use the Utilities > XTensions Manager to enable/disable filters.

If the Quark CMS, OPI, or PDF Filter QuarkXTensions software module is installed and enabled, a pane for that topic will be available at the bottom of the Get Picture dialog box. To read about Quark CMS, see page 396. To read about OPI, see the QuarkXPress CD-ROM. For a PDF, enter the number of the page you want to import in the Page field.

Pictures come in two basic flavors

A picture that is created in a bitmap program (e.g., Photoshop or Painter), or that is scanned, is actually composed of tiny pixels. You'll only see the individual pixels if you zoom way in on the image. The important thing to remember about a bitmap image is that enlarging it above 100% in QuarkXPress will diminish its resolution and output quality, whereas shrinking it will actually increase its resolution and output quality. If you're preparing an image in a bitmap program or scanning it for output from QuarkXPress, you should plan ahead and be sure to save it at the appropriate resolution, orientation, and size. You're also better off making color adjustments to a picture in a bitmap program rather than in QuarkXPress.

(Continued on the following page)

A picture that is created in a drawing program, like Illustrator or FreeHand, is actually composed of mathematically-defined objects. This type of picture is called "vector," or "object-oriented." A vector picture can be moved, scaled, recolored, and yes, enlarged, without affecting its output quality at all. It will be crisp at 20% and crisp at 120% (though enlarging it much beyond 100% may lengthen its print time). The higher the resolution of the output device, the sharper a vector picture will print. A vector picture can't be edited in QuarkXPress, however. It can be scaled, rotated, or skewed, but not recolored.

TIP Rotate, crop, or scale your picture in its native application rather than in QuarkXPress—it will redraw and print more quickly.

Choosing the right resolution for a bitmap picture

For online display, you merely need to match the resolution of the most common monitor that your viewers will use, which in most cases is 72 ppi. For print output, choose one-and-a-half to two times the lpi (lines per inch) your commercial printer plans to use. For example, let's say your printer says they're going to use a 133 line-screen. A color picture should be saved at twice the line screen. 133 times two equals 266, so you should save the picture in its original application at 266 ppi. For a grayscale picture, one-and-a-half times the line screen is sufficient (200 ppi, in our example).

Every rule has its exceptions, however. A bitmap image that contains sharp linear elements will require a higher resolution (600 ppi or higher). For a very painterly picture that contains amorphous shapes, on the other hand, a resolution value that is less than twice the output line screen may suffice.

Keeping the layers

Can you import a Photoshop image with layers into QuarkXPress? The answer is, only with a third-party XTension. Both **ImagePort** from alap inc. and **Photoshop Import XT** from Techno Design make it possible to import a Photoshop image with layers.

Here, spot

If you import an EPS picture into a QuarkXPress document, spot colors that were assigned to the picture will automatically append to the QuarkXPress document's Colors palette.

TIP To *prevent* applied colors from importing with an EPS picture, hold down Cmd/Ctrl as you click Open in the Get Picture dialog box.

A vector-based picture from a drawing application is resolution independent, which means it will print at the resolution of the output device. Just make sure it's saved in a file format that QuarkXPress can read.

TIP A picture's file size, dimensions, color depth, and other information are listed in the Get Picture dialog box. For information about an already imported picture, click on it, choose Utilities > Usage > Pictures, and check More Information.

Enlarge or shrink?

Scaling a bitmap picture in QuarkXPress affects its output resolution. If you shrink a bitmap picture in QuarkXPress, its output resolution will increase; if you enlarge a bitmap picture, its output resolution will decrease. Here's an example: Take a 150 ppi image and shrink it by half. Its ppi will increase to 300. Why should you bother to pay attention to this? Because enlarging a bitmapped picture above 100% in QuarkXPress will diminish its print quality. A vector-based image (e.g. an Illustrator EPS) won't degrade in quality if it's enlarged in QuarkXPress, but it may take longer to print. And if you shrink a picture down significantly, its file storage size will be much larger than required and it will also take longer to print. So the moral of the story is... plan ahead.

Picture preview options

Every EPS picture has a PICT or TIFF preview built into it (unless it's specifically saved without one) so you can see it on screen or print it on a non-PostScript printer. The higher a picture preview's bit depth, the longer it may take to render on screen and the larger will be the file storage size of the document into which it's imported. Choose display options for imported TIFF pictures in Edit >

(Continued on the following page)

Scaling; Picture Previews

Preferences > Preferences > Application–Display (see page 381). In some applications (e.g., Photoshop, Illustrator) you can choose a bit depth for the preview. When you save an image for export to QuarkXPress, save it with a preview, if that option is available. An EPS picture that doesn't have a built-in preview will appear as a gray box in QuarkXPress, but it will print normally.

Saving a picture for QuarkXPress

Illustrator	Illustrator EPS with a preview
FreeHand	EPS with a preview
Photoshop	TIFF (RGB or CMYK), DCS, or EPS (ask your printer)
Scanner	TIFF
PhotoCD	Open in QuarkXPress using the PhotoCD XTension

For on-screen display (not color separation), leave the image in RGB color mode and at resolution of 72 ppi.

To color-separate a bitmap picture from QuarkXPress, one option is to convert it to CMYK Color mode and save it in the EPS, DCS 2.0, or TIFF format in Photoshop. (A DCS picture is pre-separated.) Another option is to have QuarkXPress separate an RGB TIFF into CMYK. You need to decide (or ask your print shop!) whether you want Photoshop or QuarkXPress to do the conversion. Whichever program you choose, you'll need to become familiar with its color management features.

TIP The Enhance Preview XTension from Koyosha Graphics of America improves (raises the resolution of) image previews in QuarkXPress, allowing you to see sharper details.

Looks like Greek to you

To speed up screen redraw, check **Greek Pictures** in Edit > Preferences > Preferences > Document–General (Cmd-Y/Ctrl-Y). Greeked pictures look solid gray on screen at some view sizes, but they print normally. To display a greeked picture, just click on it.

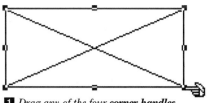

1 *Drag any of the four **corner handles** of a box...*

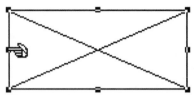

2 *...or drag any of the four **midpoint handles** of a box.*

*The **Width** field with two inches being added to the existing four-pica width of a box*

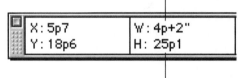

X: 5p7　　W: 4p+2"
Y: 18p6　　H: 25p1

*The **Height** of a box*

3 *You can enter a value in the **Width** and **Height** field (or in any other field) in any measurement unit used in QuarkXPress.*

To scale a picture box manually:

1. Choose the Item or Content tool.

2. Click on a picture box. For a Bézier picture box, turn off Item > Edit > Shape (Shift-F4/F10 toggles this command on and off).

3. Drag any handle **1**–**2**. Hold down Option-Shift/Alt -Shift while dragging to preserve the original proportions of the box.

To scale a picture box using the Measurements palette:

1. Choose the Item or Content tool.

2. Click on a picture box.

3. Double-click the W field on the Measurements palette, enter a number in an increment as small as .001 to modify the width of the box **3**, then press Return/Enter.
and/or
Double-click the H field on the Measurements palette, enter a number to modify the height of the box, then press Return/Enter.

TIP To enlarge or reduce the dimensions of a box by a specified amount, insert the cursor after the current value in the W or H field, enter a plus (+) or minus (-) sign, then enter the amount you want to add or subtract in any measurement unit used in QuarkXPress. You can also use / (backslash) to divide the current value or * (asterisk) to multiply it.

Scale Picture Box

To delete a picture box:

1. Choose the Item or Content tool.

2. Click on a picture box.

3. Choose Item > Delete (Cmd-K/Ctrl-K).

TIP A picture box that is selected with the Item tool can also be deleted by pressing Delete/Backspace on the keyboard or by choosing Edit > Clear.

To move a picture box manually:

1. Choose the Item tool or hold down Cmd/Ctrl if the Content tool is currently chosen.

2. With the pointer inside the picture box, drag in any direction. Pause before dragging to display the picture as it's moved (if Live Refresh is chosen in Edit > Preferences > Preferences > Application–Interactive, the four-headed arrow cursor will change into a cluster of arrows) **1**. Or drag without pausing to display only the outline of the box as it's moved **2**.

TIP You can drag a picture box or any other item from one page to another. As you drag, you can knock into the edge of the document window to force scrolling to help you reach the desired page.

Take your pick

With **Delayed Item Dragging: Show Contents** chosen in Edit > Preferences > Preferences > Application–Interactive, if you move or rotate an item that's behind other items, its full contents will be visible as you move it. If **Live Refresh** is chosen instead, the item will stay as it actually looks in its layer as you move it, complete with text wrap—whether it's obscured or not.

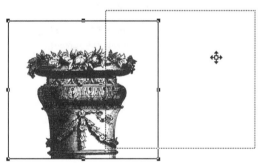

1 *To move a box, drag inside it with the **Item** tool. Pause before dragging to see the **picture** as you move it...*

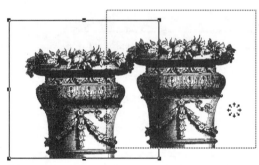

2 *...or drag without pausing to see only the **outline** of the box as it's moved.*

Delete, Move Picture Box

*The **horizontal** location of the upper left corner of a picture box relative to the ruler origin*

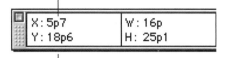

*The **vertical** location of the upper left corner of a picture box relative to the ruler origin*

1 *The Measurements palette*

2 *Add a positive or negative number to the right of the current value in the X or Y field, then press Return/Enter.*

| X: 5p7+3p | W: 16p |
| Y: 18p6 | H: 25p1 |

| X: 8p7 | W: 16p |
| Y: 18p6 | H: 25p1 |

3 *The two numbers are added together and the box is repositioned.*

4 *These items are positioned for a bleed.*

To reposition a picture box using the Measurements palette:

1. Choose the Item or Content tool.

2. Click on a picture box.

3. To change the horizontal position of the box relative to the ruler origin, which is normally located in the upper left corner of the document, change the X value on the Measurements palette **1**.

and/or

To change the vertical position of the box, change the Y value on the Measurements palette.

TIP To move a box a specified horizontal or vertical distance, insert the cursor to the right of the current X or Y value, type a plus (+) or minus (-) sign, and then enter a value in any measurement unit used in QuarkXPress **2**–**3**.

TIP To nudge a picture box or any other item one point at a time, select it with the Item tool, then press any of the four arrow keys on the keyboard. Or Option-press/Alt-press an arrow key to move an item in .1-point increments.

A bleed is any item that runs off the edge of the page. The overhanging portion will be trimmed by the print shop after the page is printed.

To create a bleed:

To create a bleed, position any item so that part of the item is on the page and part of it extends onto the pasteboard **4**. Items that are completely on the pasteboard won't print.

When you're ready to print your document, enter the width of the bleed area that you want to print and choose other print options in the Bleed pane in File > Print (see pages 404–405).

Reposition Picture Box; Bleed

To scale a picture:

1. Choose the Item or Content tool.

2. Click on a picture.

3. Hold down Cmd-Option-Shift/
Ctrl-Alt-Shift and press the ">" key to
enlarge the picture 5% at a time or the
"<" key to shrink the picture.
or
On the Measurements palette, enter
new X% and/or Y% (picture size)
values **1**–**5**.

TIP Press Tab to move from field to field
on the Measurements palette (press
Shift-Tab to reverse your steps).

TIP You can copy values from one field
on the Measurements palette and
paste them into another field, such as
from the X% field into the Y% field,
or vice versa.

Horizontal scale of picture   *Horizontal location of
picture relative to upper
left corner of picture box*

X%: 50%	X+: 0p
Y%: 100%	Y+: 0p

Vertical scale of picture   *Vertical location of picture relative to upper
left corner of picture box*

1 *When the X and Y scale percentages differ from
each other, it means the picture's proportions no
longer match that of the original.*

X%: 75%	X+: 0p
Y%: 75%	Y+: 0p

2 *When the X and Y scale percentages match, it
means the picture's proportions are the same as that
of the original.*

3 *A picture with an X coordinate of
55% and a Y coordinate of 55%*

4 *A picture with an X
coordinate of 40% and a Y
coordinate of 60%*

5 *A picture with an X coordinate of 60%
and a Y coordinate of 40%*

To fit a picture to its box:

1. Choose the Item or Content tool.

2. Click on a picture.

3. To scale the picture to fit the vertical dimension of the box while maintaining its original proportions (aspect ratio), press Cmd-Option-Shift-F/Ctrl-Alt-Shift-F **1**–**2**.
or
To fit the picture into the box, but with its proportions altered relative to the original, press Cmd-Shift-F/Ctrl-Shift-F or Control-click/Right-click the picture and choose Fit Picture to Box **3**.

5.0!

1 *A picture before being resized*

2 *After applying the **Cmd-Option-Shift-F/Ctrl-Alt-Shift-F** keystroke, the picture fits into the vertical dimension of the box and its proportions are maintained.*

3 *The original image after pressing **Cmd-Shift-F/Ctrl-Shift-F**: The image stretches to fit the box.*

4 *Cmd-Option-Shift-drag/ Ctrl-Alt-Shift-drag a handle to resize a picture and its box simultaneously— and proportionally.*

Follow these instructions if the picture fits nicely in its box, but you want to scale the whole shebang.

To scale a picture and its box:

1. Choose the Item or Content tool.

2. For a Bézier picture box, turn off Item > Edit > Shape (Shift-F4/F10).

3. Hold down Cmd-Option-Shift/Ctrl-Alt-Shift, press a handle, pause briefly for the picture to redraw, then drag **4**.

Scale Picture

Along with resizing, cropping a picture can dramatically alter its impact on a page. Don't be afraid to crop drastically. Sometimes less is more. One caveat, though: If you're going to substantially crop a bitmapped picture, do it in the picture's original application. This will reduce the picture's file size and make it print faster.

To crop a picture by moving it within its box:

1. Choose the Content tool.

2. Press on a picture, pause briefly until the hand icon appears, then drag **1**.

TIP Click on a picture and press an arrow key to nudge a picture 1 point at a time. Option-press/Alt-press an arrow key to nudge a picture .1 point at a time.

TIP You can also use a clipping path to prevent part of a picture from printing (see Chapter 11).

To crop a picture by resizing its box:

1. Choose the Item or Content tool, then click on a picture box.

2. Drag any handle of the box **2**–**3**. For a Bézier box, turn off Item > Shape > Edit (Shift-F4/F10) first.

TIP To crop a picture by reshaping its box, read Chapter 13, Béziers.

To fit a box to a picture:

1. Choose the Item or Content tool, then click on a picture box.

2. Control-click/Right-click and choose Fit Box To Picture.

To delete a picture (and keep the box):

1. Choose the Content tool, then click on a picture box.

2. Press Delete/Backspace.

1 *A picture being **moved** within its box*

2 *Drag any handle to **crop** a picture.*

3 *After cropping*

*The **picture and box angle***

X: 6p7	W: 23p1	△ 0°
Y: 4p3	H: 8p10	⚓ 0p

1 *The left side of the Measurements palette*

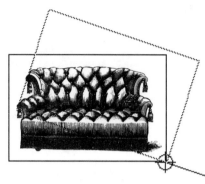

2 *If you **drag** away from the axis point before rotating, you will create a **lever**, and the rotation will be easier to control. If you don't pause before dragging, only the outline of the box will be displayed as you rotate it.*

3 *A **picture** and its **box** being **rotated** together*

Note: Whenever possible, rotate, crop, or scale a picture in its original application rather than in QuarkXPress—it will redraw, process, and print more quickly.

To rotate a picture and its box using the Measurements palette:

1. Choose the Item or Content tool.

2. Click on a picture box.

3. In the picture and box angle field on the left side of the Measurements palette, enter a positive number between 0° and 360° to rotate the picture and box counterclockwise or enter a negative number to rotate them clockwise **1**.

TIP To flip a picture, select it, then click the Flip Horizontal and/or Flip Vertical button on the Measurements palette.

To rotate a picture and its box using the Rotation tool:

1. Choose the Rotation tool. ↺

2. Click on a picture box.

3. Press to create an axis point, pause briefly for the picture to redraw (if desired), drag to reposition the cursor away from the axis point to create a lever **2**–**3**, then drag the lever clockwise or counterclockwise.

TIP Hold down Shift while dragging with the Rotation tool to rotate an item at an increment of 45°.

TIP With Delayed Item Dragging: Show Contents chosen in Edit > Preferences > Preferences > Application–Interactive, if you move or rotate an item that's behind other items, its full contents will be visible as you move it. If Live Refresh is chosen instead, you'll see the item as it actually looks (or is hidden, as the case may be) in its layer as you move it. You won't see a lever as you rotate an object in Live Refresh mode, but it works just the same.

Rotate Picture

To rotate a picture (and not its box):

1. Choose the Item or Content tool.

2. Click on a picture.

3. In the picture angle field on the right side of the Measurements palette, enter a positive value to rotate the picture counterclockwise or a negative value to rotate it clockwise **1**–**5**.

TIP To rotate the picture box and *not* the picture, first rotate the box and picture together, then rotate just the picture (not the box) by the negative value. For example, if the picture with its box is rotated 20°, rotate the picture back –20°.

1 *The picture angle*

X : 5p5	W : 13p5	⊿ 0°	→ X% : 100%	⬦⬦ X+ : 0p	⊿ 20°
Y : 8p2	H : 11p1	⋔ 0p	↑ Y% : 100%	⬍ Y+ : 0p	⬦ 0°

2 *0° rotation*

4 *90° rotation*

3 *40° rotation*

5 *180° rotation*

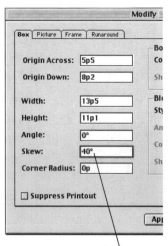

1 *To skew a picture (or text) box, choose Item > Modify, click the Box tab, then enter a **Skew** value.*

To skew a picture and its box:

1. Choose the Item or Content tool.

2. Click a picture box of any shape. Only one item can be skewed at a time.

3. Choose Item > Modify (Cmd-M/ Ctrl-M), then click the Box tab.

4. Enter a Skew value between -75 and 75 **1**. Enter a positive value to skew it to the right or a negative value to skew to the left.

5. Click OK **2**–**4**. You can edit a picture (or text) after it's skewed.

TIP To skew a picture and not its box, select it using the Content tool, then enter a Skew value between -75 and 75 on the Measurements palette (it's in the lower right corner).

2 *A picture box.*

3 *The same box **skewed** 35%.*

4 *The Box Skew feature was used to produce the top and side portions of this cube.*

The Contrast dialog box is used to perform color and tonal adjustments. These adjustments don't affect the actual picture file—they only affect how the picture displays and prints. (To be frank, we strongly prefer to use Photoshop for our color and tonal adjustments, but there's certainly no harm in exploring this feature.) To colorize a picture, see page 250.

To apply a custom contrast setting to a picture:

1. Choose the Item or Content tool.

2. Click a color bitmap picture or a color or grayscale TIFF, JPEG, PICT, Windows bitmap (BMP), PCX, GIF, PNG, or PhotoCD picture.

You can't adjust the contrast of an EPS, a WMF, a 1-bit (black-and-white) picture, or a color TIFF imported with the 16-bit/8-bit or 32-bit/24-bit Color TIFFs setting in Edit > Preferences > Preferences > Application–Display. (If you've imported the picture already using that setting, choose 8-bit Color TIFFs, then reimport the picture).

3. Choose Style > Contrast (Cmd-Shift-C/ Ctrl-Shift-C). The availability of contrast options will vary depending on the picture file type.

4. Option-click/Alt-click the Apply button to turn on continuous Apply.

5. For a color picture, choose a color Model (HSB, RGB, CMY, or CMYK). Uncheck any individual box for a Color if you don't want it to be modified.

6. Make any of the following adjustments:

To posterize the picture, click the second-to-last icon on the left side of the dialog box **1**–**2**.
or
To adjust the contrast manually, click the hand icon, then drag the entire contrast curve toward the upper left

1 *Normal Contrast*

2 *Posterization* reduces the number of grays in a picture to black, white, and four gray levels in between.

1 *A picture with the contrast curve shown in the next figure*

or lower right corner **1**–**2**. To restore the picture's original contrast values, click the sixth (normal contrast) icon.

or

Choose the pencil tool, and draw a custom curve.

or

Check Negative to create a negative of the picture.

or

Try using any of the tools pictured in **3**, below.

7. Click OK.

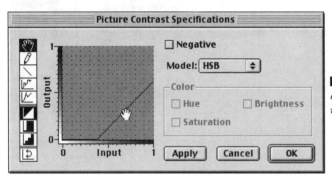

2 *The contrast curve being moved with the hand tool*

Hand: *Moves the entire curve*

Pencil: *Draws a new curve*

Line: *Adjusts the curve*

Posterizer: *Adds handles between 10% increments*

Spike: *Adds handles at 10% horizontal increments*

Normal contrast: *Resets to default*

High contrast

Posterized

Inversion: *Flips the contrast curve*

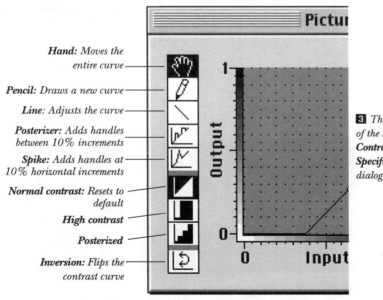

3 *The left side of the **Picture Contrast Specifications** dialog box*

Note: As with cropping and rotating, it's better to flip a picture in its original application than in QuarkXPress—it will print and redraw more quickly. The flip commands flip the contents of a box. A picture can be modified in its flipped position. (To flip a Bézier box, and not its contents, see page 302.)

To flip a picture:

1. Choose the Content tool.
2. Click on a picture box.
3. Choose Style > Flip Horizontal or Flip Vertical.
   or
   Click the Flip Horizontal and/or Flip Vertical icon on the Measurements palette 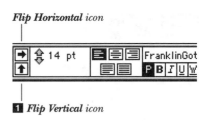–**2**.
TIP To undo a flip, choose the command again or click the icon again on the Measurements palette.

Flip Horizontal icon

1 *Flip Vertical icon*

2 *A copy of a picture flipped horizontally*

Cast a shadow

To create a soft drop shadow for any item, use the **ShadowCaster** XTension from a lowly apprentice production, inc. or **I Shadow** from Vision's Edge. Both XTensions create a shadow in a separate picture box and save it as a TIFF file.

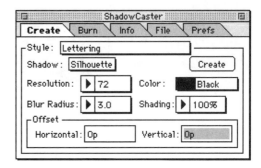

Status is everything

Modified The picture was modified in another application (but not moved).

Missing The picture was moved or renamed.

Wrong Type The picture's file format was changed. (Or the picture was compressed using a utility; you can't update this type.)

No XTension The import filter for the picture's file format is disabled.

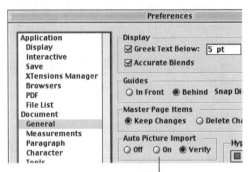

1 *In Edit > Preferences > Preferences > Document–General, click Auto Picture Import: Off, On, or Verify.*

2 *Click a picture file name, then click Update.*

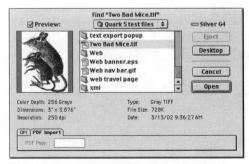

3 *Highlight the picture file name, then click Open.*

When a picture is imported into a QuarkXPress file, the original picture file name and location is stored in the QuarkXPress file. If the original picture is then renamed or moved, its path to the QuarkXPress file must be reestablished in order for it to print properly. On the other hand, if the original picture is modified, it will print, but its on-screen preview will be inaccurate. Thankfully, when a picture is updated, its scale and offset values are preserved.

To update the path to a picture upon opening a file:

In the **Auto Picture Import** area of Edit > Preferences > Preferences > Document–General, you can choose whether you want modified and missing picture files to be updated automatically when a document is opened **1**. If you open a document that was last saved with Auto Picture Import **Off**, the path to a missing or modified picture will not be updated. With Auto Picture Import **On**, the path will be updated automatically. If the setting is **Verify** and a prompt appears, do as follows:

1. Click OK.

2. Click a picture name in the Missing/Modified Pictures dialog box **2**, and note its current Status (see the sidebar).

3. *Optional:* Click Show/Show Me to see the picture selected in the document.

4. Click Update.

5. For a Modified or Wrong Type picture, click OK when the prompt appears.
or
For a Missing picture, locate and choose the picture in the Find "[ ]" dialog box, then click Open **3**.

6. Repeat for any other pictures, then click Done/Close.

TIP On Mac OS, a dagger symbol **†** next to a page number in the Missing/Modified Pictures dialog box means the picture is on the Pasteboard. In Windows, you'll see the letters "PB" instead.

The path to a picture file can be updated at any time using Utilities > Usage (Pictures pane). If a picture is updated using Auto Picture Import or the Usage dialog box, the scale, rotation, color, and other attributes that were previously applied to the picture are retained.

To update the path to a picture using Picture Usage:

1. *Optional:* Choose the Content tool, then, in the document window, click the picture you want to update.

2. Choose Utilities > Usage (F13 in the Mac OS).

3. Click the Pictures tab.

4. Click any file name whose Status is listed as Missing or Modified. If you clicked on a picture for step 1, its name will highlight automatically. *Optional:* Click Show to see the picture selected in the document window ∎.

5 Click Update ∎.

6. For a **missing** picture, click the picture file name in the Find "[   ]" dialog box, ∎ then click Open.

Note: If you update a picture using Utilities > Usage (Pictures pane) or by responding to an Auto Picture Import prompt, and other missing pictures are located in the same folder, a prompt will appear. Click OK to update all the missing pictures in that folder at once. This doesn't work for modified pictures.

For a **modified** picture, click OK.

7. Click Done.

What's-its-name?

Mac OS: If you need to know a picture's name, double-click it with the **Content** tool. The Publish and Subscribe dialog box will open, and the name of the picture will appear at the top of the dialog box. Click Cancel to close the dialog box. (Publish and Subscribe can be used to update a modified EPS, PICT, or TIFF.)

Or in the Mac OS or Windows: Click the picture, choose Utilities > **Usage**, then click the **Pictures** tab. The name of the picture will be highlighted. Click Done to exit the dialog box.

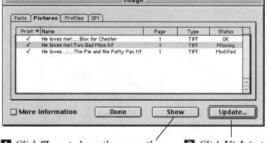

1 *Click **Show** to have the currently highlighted picture become selected in the document.*

2 *Click **Update** to search for a missing picture file.*

3 *Click the name of the **missing** picture...*

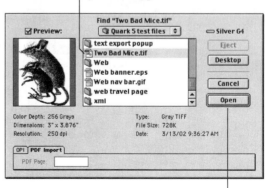

*...then click **Open**.*

(Picture Usage — side tab)

Multiple Items

Moving multiple items

Constraining the movement of a multiple-item selection to the horizontal or vertical axis is a little tricky. Once all the items are selected, start dragging the selection, then hold down Shift and continue dragging. Release the mouse, then release Shift.

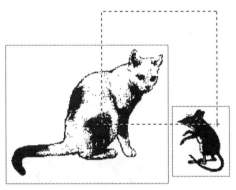

1 *Drag a marquee over multiple items with the* **Item** *tool.*

2 *Both picture boxes are* **selected***, and the handles on both boxes are visible.*

It's one thing to create individual items, and quite another thing to arrange them into a complex composition. In this chapter you'll learn many layout skills, including how to group, lock, duplicate, rotate, scale, restack, anchor, and align multiple items.

The position, size, angle of rotation, background color, and other specifications can be modified for a multiple-item selection. Modification options will vary depending on whether the items are all text boxes, picture boxes, lines, text paths, or a combination thereof.

To select multiple items:

1. Choose the Item or Content tool.

2. Shift-click each item to be selected. (Shift-click any selected item again to deselect it.)
or
Position the cursor outside all the items to be selected, then drag a marquee around at least a portion of each item **1**–**2**.

To deselect all items:

Choose the Item tool, then press Tab.
or
Choose the Item or Content tool, then click a blank area in your document.

To select all the items on a page or spread:

1. Choose the Item tool, and make sure the desired page is displayed (note the page number in the lower left-hand corner of the document window).

2. Choose Edit > Select All (Cmd-A/ Ctrl-A).

Select Multiple Items

Grouped items remain associated and move as a unit unless they're ungrouped. In this book, each picture is grouped with its accompanying caption, and in some cases multiple picture/caption groups are themselves grouped together (nested) to form a larger group. Individual items in a group always remain editable.

To group items:

1. Choose the Item or Content tool.

2. Shift-click each item to be grouped (any item type except a table). (Shift-click any selected item to deselect it.)
or
Position the cursor outside all the items to be included in the group, then drag a marquee around them. You only need to drag over a portion of all the items—just make sure to grab at least one handle on each item.

3. Choose Item > Group (Cmd-G/ Ctrl-G) **1**.

Note: Use the Content tool to modify the size or contents of an item in a group. If the group is already selected, deselect it by clicking outside it, then click the item you want to edit with the Content tool.

To move an item in a group:

1. Choose the Item or Content tool.

2. Hold down Cmd/Ctrl, press on the item to be moved, pause briefly for the item to redraw, then drag **2**.

This method for removing an item from a group deletes the item from the document altogether. To take an item out of a group without deleting it, see the sidebar.

To delete an item from a group:

1. Choose the Content tool.

2. Click the item to be deleted.

3. Choose Item > Delete (Cmd-K/Ctrl-K). This command *can* be undone.

Take it out and keep it

To take an item out of a group without deleting it, **ungroup** the group, **Shift-click** the item you want to take out of the group (the remaining items will remain selected), then choose the **Group** command again.

1 A dotted **bounding box** *surrounds a group when it's selected with the Item tool.*

2 *To move an item in a group,* **Cmd-drag/ Ctrl-drag** *the item with the Content tool.*

1 *If you resize a group while holding down **Cmd-Option-Shift/ Ctrl-Alt-Shift**...*

2 *...the items and their contents will **resize proportionately**.*

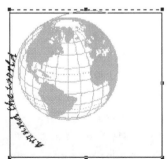

3 *If you resize a group with **no** keys held down, the **items** (box or path) will reshape, but not their contents (text or picture).*

Not only can you resize a whole group, you can also move, cut, copy, duplicate, anchor, rotate, and recolor a group. To change a group's overall dimensions, angle, background color, or shade, or to apply a blend across a whole group, use Item > Modify > Group (Cmd-M/Ctrl-M). Runaround options must be chosen individually for each item in a group.

This method for resizing multiple items is a great timesaver. Frame widths and line weights won't change.

To resize a whole group:

1. Choose the Item tool.

2. Click on the group.

3. To resize the grouped items and their contents (text or picture) proportionally, Cmd-Option-Shift/Ctrl-Alt-Shift drag a handle **1**–**2**.
   or
   To change the shape of the grouped items, but not their contents, drag a handle with no modifier keys held down **3**. You *can* undo this!

To ungroup items:

1. Choose the Item tool.

2. Click on the group you want to ungroup.

3. Choose Item > Ungroup (Cmd-U/ Ctrl-U).

Resize Whole Group; Ungroup

Locking is a safety command that can be applied to any item to prevent it from being moved, resized, reshaped, or rotated **manually**. We lock items on our master pages (e.g., headers, footers) so they can't be moved manually.

Beware! Locking does not prevent the contents of a locked text box, picture box, or table, or the attributes of a line, such as its style and width, from being edited. And a locked item can be moved or resized using the Measurements palette or a dialog box, such as Space/Align. Oh, and one further warning: A locked item can be deleted!

To lock an item:

1. Choose the Item or Content tool.
2. Select the item to be locked (or select multiple items to be locked).
3. Choose Item > Lock (F6) . Choose the same command again to unlock the item.

To duplicate an item:

1. Choose the Item or Content tool.
2. Select the item or group you want to duplicate 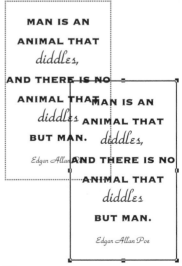.
3. Choose Item > Duplicate (Cmd-D/ Ctrl-D) . The default Duplicate offset values are 1p6 to the right and 1p6 downward. However, if the Step and Repeat dialog box has been used in the same work session, then the last-used offsets from that dialog box will be used instead of the defaults (see the next page).

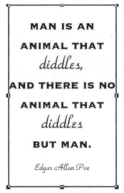

1 *The padlock icon displays if a **locked** item is selected with the **Item** tool.*

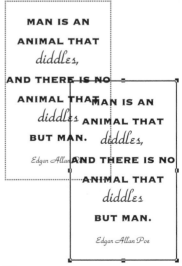

2 *Select the item to be duplicated, then choose Item > **Duplicate**.*

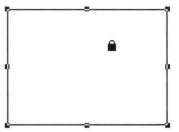

3 *A duplicate is made.*

1 *Select an item.*

2 *The **Step and Repeat** dialog box*

3 *This item was **duplicated** using these values: Repeat Count 3, Horizontal Offset 0, and Vertical Offset 5p5.*

Using the Step and Repeat command, multiple duplicates can be made at one time and you can specify how far apart the duplicates will be from one another. The offset distance is calculated from the upper left corner of each item (or the bounding box, in the case of a Bézier box, line, or text path). You can use this command to reproduce any kind of item or group (e.g., you could generate multiple picture and caption groups in neat horizontal or vertical rows).

To step and repeat an item:

1. Choose the Item or Content tool.

2. Select an item or a group of items **1**.

3. Choose Item > Step and Repeat (Cmd-Option-D/Ctrl-Alt-D).

4. Enter the number of duplicates to be made in the Repeat Count field (1–99) **2**.

5. Enter a Horizontal Offset value. Enter a minus sign before the value to step and repeat items to the left of the original. Enter 0 in this field if you want the duplicates to align along their left edges, but not move horizontally.
   and
   Enter a Vertical Offset value. Enter a minus sign before the value to step and repeat items above the original. Enter 0 in this field if you want the duplicates to align along their top edges, but not move vertically.

   Enter positive values (or negative values) in both Offset fields to produce a stair-step arrangement.

6. Click OK **3**.

TIP If an alert prompt appears, reduce the Repeat Count and/or Offset values so the duplicate items will fit within the confines of the pasteboard.

Step and Repeat

Super Step and Repeat, a free downloadable XTension, works like the Step and
Repeat command, except it can also be
used to rotate, scale, or skew the duplicates.

To rotate, scale, or skew copies of an item using Super Step and Repeat:

1. Choose the Item tool.

2. Select one text box, picture box, text
   path, or line 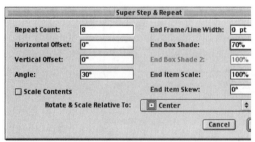 (Not a group—sorry!
   Maybe someday.) To transform from a
   point on a Bézier, select that point now.

3. Choose Item > Super Step and Repeat.

4. In the **Repeat Count** field, enter or
   choose the number of duplicates you
   want created 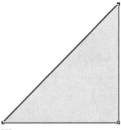.

5. In the **Horizontal Offset** field, enter
   the distance you want each copy to be
   placed on the horizontal axis *(x)* relative to the original. A positive value
   positions the copies to the right of the
   original; a negative value positions the
   copies to the left.
   and
   In the **Vertical Offset** field, enter the
   distance you want the each copy to be
   placed on the vertical axis *(y)* relative to
   the original. A positive value positions
   the copies above the original; a negative value positions the copies below
   the original. The duplicates must be
   able to fit within the pasteboard.

6. Intermediate duplicates, if any, will be
   assigned incremental angles, frame
   widths, line widths, shades, scale values,
   or skew values, depending on values
   entered in the dialog box. Change any
   of the following:

   The **Angle**, to have each duplicate
   be rotated counterclockwise by that
   amount, relative to the original or the
   previous duplicate .

   The **End Frame/Line Width** or **End
   Line Width** for the final duplicate item.
   Each duplicate will be successively

1 *Select an item.*

2 *Use the **Super Step & Repeat** dialog box for single or multiple **transformations**.*

3 *After using **Super Step & Repeat** to **rotate** copies of the item using the settings shown in the previous figure.*

Super Step and Repeat

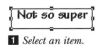

1 *Select an item.*

Super Step & Repeat	
Repeat Count: 5	End Frame/Line Width:
Horizontal Offset: 4p	End Box Shade:
Vertical Offset: 1p5	*End Box Shade 2:*
Angle: 0°	☐ Top-Left
	☐ Top-Center
☑ Scale Contents	☐ Top-Right
Rotate & Scale Relative To:	✓ Center-Left
	☑ Center
	☐ Center-Right
	☐ Bottom-Left
	☐ Bottom-Center
	☐ Bottom-Right
	◇ Selected Point

2 *From the **Rotate & Scale Relative To** pop-up menu, choose the point around or from which the item will be rotated or scaled.*

3 *This is after using the **Super Step & Repeat** settings shown in the previous figure to create incrementally **larger** copies of the item. Unfortunately, only absolute Offset values can be entered—not a percentage—so the items are equidistant from each other, and thus piled on top of each other.*

larger/smaller than the last, until the end width is reached. You can't use a value that won't fit on the final item. The current width of the selected line or frame will be entered automatically.

The **End Box Shade** or **End Line Shade** (0%–100%) for the final duplicate box or line. Intermediate duplicates will be assigned incremental shades between the original and final shades. 100% is the default.

If your box contains a blend, the **End Box Shade 2** (0%–100%) for the background shade in the final box.

For a text path or line whose line style has multiple dashes or stripes, the **End Gap Shade** (0%–100%) for the gap color in the final line. Intermediate gaps will be assigned incremental shades.

The **End Item Scale** or **End Line Scale** (1%-1000%) for the final duplicate **1**–**3**. (To scale a frame on a duplicate box or boxes, enter a final size in the End Frame/Line Width field.)

The **End Item Skew** (-75° to 75°) for the skew angle of the final duplicate. Both the box and its contents will be skewed. This works for boxes only, not for paths or lines.

7. To scale the contents of the item (text or picture) in addition to the box or path itself, check **Scale Contents**.

8. From the **Rotate & Scale Relative To** pop-up menu, choose the point around which the item will be rotated or scaled. If a point is chosen on a Bézier item, the Selected Point option will be available.

9. Click OK. Unfortunately, there is no Apply button. If you don't like the results, choose Undo or press Cmd-K/Ctrl-K—only the duplicates will disappear, not the original object.

(More illustrations on the following page)

Super Step and Repeat

1 *The original item*

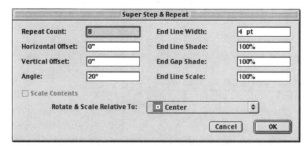

2 *The settings used to produce the next figure*

3 *The final items*

4 *The original item*

5 *The settings used to produce the next figure*

6 *The final items*

 Vortex

7 *The original item*

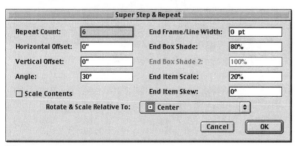

8 *The settings used to produce the next figure*

9 *The final items*

Super Step and Repeat

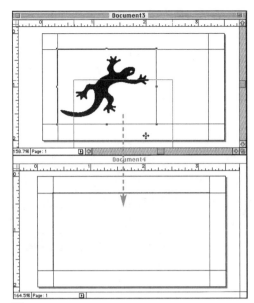

1 *Open two files, choose the **Item** tool, then drag an item from one document window into the other.*

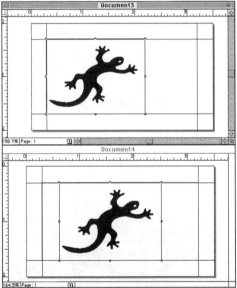

2 *A **duplicate** is made automatically as the item is dragged; the original item is unchanged.*

This method for copying items between documents doesn't use the Clipboard.

To drag-copy an item between documents:

1. Open two QuarkXPress files, and resize or move both document windows, if necessary, so they don't completely overlap each other. In the Mac OS, if you like, you can hold down Shift, press on the document title bar, and choose Tiled Documents. In Windows, choose Window > Tile Horizontally or Tile Vertically.

2. Choose the Item tool, or hold down Cmd/Ctrl if the Content tool is chosen.

3. Drag an item or group from one document window (the "source" document) into the other (the "target" document). A duplicate will be created automatically **1**–**2**. Any style sheets, H&Js, or custom colors that were applied to the item in the source document will be added to the target document.

   If the item was on a layer in the source document, the item's layer will come along with it, but not any other items on that layer.

TIP If you drag-copy a box containing linked text, the text in that box will duplicate, along with any hidden overflow text from that point to the end of the story. If your document contains multiple layers, see page 261!

TIP Individual items cannot be copied between documents in Thumbnails view, but entire pages can (see page 83).

TIP If you copy-and-paste or drag-copy text or a text box between documents, any style sheets that are applied to that item will also copy, with one exception: If the name of a style sheet from the source document matches the name of a style sheet in the target document, that style sheet won't append.

Drag-Copy Item Between Documents

5.0!

In these instructions, you will use the Clipboard to copy items from one page to another within the same document or from one document to another, and you don't have to bother tiling document windows to do it. It's an efficient method if you use the shortcuts.

To copy an item between pages or documents:

1. Choose the Item tool.

2. Click the item or group you want to copy.

3. Choose Edit > Copy (Cmd-C/Ctrl-C).

4. Click in the target document or page. In the Mac OS, to quickly choose from a menu of open documents, press on a document title bar with Shift held down.

5. Make sure the Item tool is still selected, then choose Edit > Paste (Cmd-V/Ctrl-V). (If you copy an item with the Item tool and paste it into a selected text box with the Content tool, the item will be anchored—not copied!)

TIP To store an item for reuse, put it in a library, and then retrieve it from the library whenever you need it. You'll save time in the long run. See Chapter 20.

To cut or copy contents (picture or text) between pages or documents:

1. Choose the Content tool.

2. Click the picture or highlight the text you want to copy or cut.

3. Choose Edit > Copy (Cmd-C/Ctrl-C) or Cut (Cmd-X/Ctrl-X).

4. Go to a different page in the same document or activate another document.

5. Make sure the Content tool is still selected.

6. Click the picture box, text box, or text path that you want to paste into.

7. Choose Edit > Paste (Cmd-V/Ctrl-V).

Paste in the same spot

Normally, an item will paste into the center of the document window. If you want to paste an item or group into the exact spot from which it was copied—except on a different page—use the **Xpert Paste** XTension, which is in Volume 1 of the XPert Tools toolkit from a lowly apprentice production, inc. You can set a preference so that Xpert Paste is always on or you can enable XPert Paste manually via a keyboard shortcut.

What smart space is

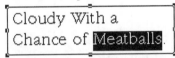

*If you double-click **inside** a word (or double-click, then drag), only that word (or words) will become selected, not any adjacent spaces or punctuation.*

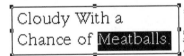

*If you double-click **between** a word and punctuation, both will become selected. If you copy and **paste** text, an **extra space** will be added, **if needed**.*

What smart space isn't

It isn't perfect.

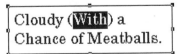

*If you cut text, the extra space left behind will be deleted, **except** if the gap occurs between a word and punctuation.*

Cloudy (With) a Chance of Meatballs.

If you double-click a word that has opening and closing punctuation (e.g. parentheses or quotation marks), only the word will become selected. To select the word and punctuation, select by dragging.

Who's afraid of Space/Align?

We were, until we got the hang of it. Now we use it all the time. This might help: When you choose between the Vertical and Horizontal options, think of the direction in which the items will move. If you want to align objects from left to right along their topmost edges for example, check the Vertical box, click Space, leave the Space value at 0, and choose Between: Top Edges. Or to align objects along their left edges, check the Horizontal box and choose Between: Left Edges. Try it.

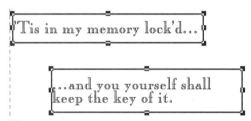

1 *Select* **two or more** *items.*

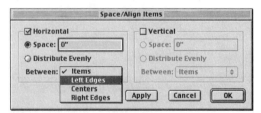

2 *Choose options in the* **Space/Align Items** *dialog box.*

'Tis in my memory lock'd...

...and you yourself shall keep the key of it.

3 *Horizontal, Space: 0, Between: Left Edges is chosen. In this case the bottom box moves horizontally to the left to align with the leftmost box.*

4 *The original items on the left; aligned* **Horizontal** *and* **Vertical: Space 0, Between: Centers** *on the right*

Note: The Space/Align feature aligns items according to the position of the leftmost or topmost of the currently selected items, depending on which option you choose from the Between pop-up menu. The results may be contrary to what you'd expect if you choose Between: Bottom Edges for the Vertical option. Items will align to the bottom of the topmost item— not to the bottom of the bottommost item.

To align items:

1. Choose the Item or Content tool.

2. Shift-click each of the items that are to be aligned **1**.
or
Position the cursor outside the items to be aligned, then drag a marquee around them. The Space/Align command *will* move a locked item.

3. Choose Item > Space/Align (Cmd-,/ Ctrl-,).

4. Check Horizontal and/or Vertical **2**.

5. Click the Space button.

6. In the Space field, enter a positive or negative number between 0" and 10" in any measurement system in an increment as small as .001 to stair-step the items to the left or the right if Horizontal is checked, or upward or downward if Vertical is checked. Think of the Space field as an offset field.
or
Enter 0 to align the items along their edges or centers.

7. Choose from either or both Between pop-up menus.

8. Click Apply to preview.

9. Click OK **3**–**4**.

TIP If you align a picture and an accompanying caption, remember to account for any Text Inset value above zero, which positions the text slightly inward from the left edge of its box.

Align Items

If items are Space/Aligned horizontally using the Distribute Evenly option, the leftmost and rightmost of the selected items will remain stationary and the remaining selected items will be evenly dispersed between them. If you choose the Vertical and Distribute Evenly options, on the other hand, the topmost and bottommost items will remain stationary.

To distribute items:

1. Select three or more items or groups  (if you don't know how to do this, follow steps 1 and 2 on the previous page).

2. Choose Item > Space/Align (Cmd-,/Ctrl-,).

3. Check Horizontal and/or Vertical 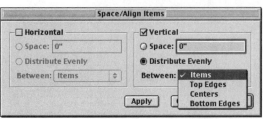.

4. Click Distribute Evenly under Horizontal and/or Vertical.

5. Choose an option from either or both Between pop-up menus.

6. Click Apply to preview. *Note:* If you change the settings and then click Apply again, the new settings will be added to the previously applied settings.

7. Click OK .

1 *Select three or more items.*

2 *The Space/Align Items dialog box*

3 *After clicking Vertical, Distribute Evenly, Between: Items*

Distribute Items

1 *The first click selects the text box, which is in front.*

2 *A second click selects the black cat. A third click would select the gray cat in the back.*

3 *The light gray cat is the backmost object.*

4 *The backmost object is **moved** in its layer.*

The most recently created item is automatically placed in front of all the other items in your document (or all the other items on the currently active layer, if your document contains more than one layer). On this page, you'll learn how to dig through stacking levels.

On the next page, you'll learn a simple way to restack objects within a layer. To learn how to move an object to a different layer, see Chapter 16.

To select an item that is behind another item:

1. Choose the Item or the Content tool—whichever tool you're going to use to edit the item you want to select. If you're going to move the item, choose the Item tool; if you're going to edit its contents, choose the Content tool.

2. Cmd-Option-Shift-click/Ctrl-Alt-Shift-click an item **1**. Repeat to select each item behind it in succession **2**. After the backmost item under the pointer is selected, the next click will reselect the topmost item in that spot.

To move an item that's behind other items:

1. Choose the Item tool.

2. Keep clicking with Cmd-Option-Shift/Ctrl-Alt-Shift held down. When you reach the item you want to move, don't release the mouse—drag **3**–**4**. This little maneuver takes a bit of practice.

TIP To see an item as it looks in its layer as you drag it, including any text wrap, turn on Live Refresh in Edit > Preferences > Preferences > Application–Interactive, and pause before dragging.

Select, Move Obscured Items

You can use the Send to Back, Send Backward, Bring to Front, or Bring Forward command to change the stacking position of any item within its layer. Sent to Back and Bring to Front move the selected item all the way to the front or back of the layer, whereas Send Backward and Bring Forward move an item backward or forward one step at a time within its layer.

To move an item forward or backward:

1. Choose the Item or Content tool.
2. Select an item 1.
3. Choose Item > Send to Back (Shift-F5) or Bring to Front (F-5) 2.
   or
   In the Mac OS, hold down Option and choose Item > Send Backward or Bring Forward.
   or
   In the Mac OS, if Control Key Activates: Contextual Menu is chosen in Edit > Preferences > Preferences > Application–Interactive, Control-click the item and choose Send & Bring > Bring To Front, Bring Forward, Send To Back, or Send Backward. If Zoom is chosen as the Control Key preference, Control-Shift-click.
   In Windows, Right-click and choose Send & Bring > Send Backward, Send To Back, Bring Forward, or Bring To Front.

5.0!

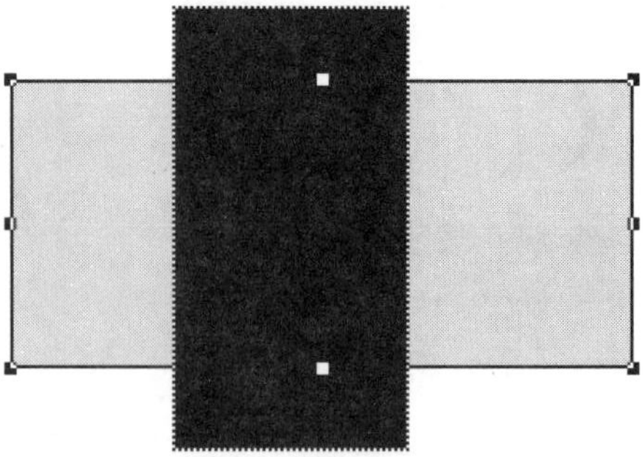

1 *A gray box (in* ***back*** *of a black box) is selected, as indicated by the eight handles, then Item >* ***Bring to Front*** *is chosen.*

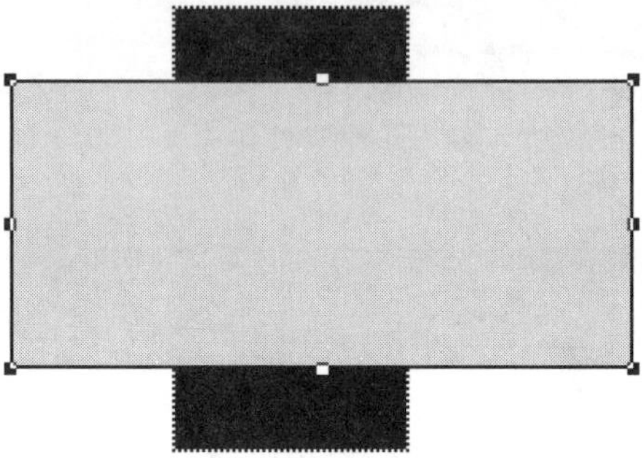

2 *The gray box is now* ***in front*** *of the black box.*

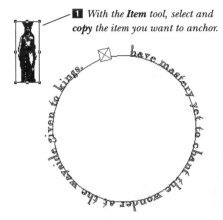

1 *With the **Item** tool, select and copy the item you want to anchor.*

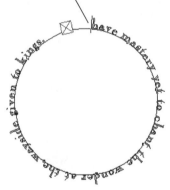

2 *Choose the **Content** tool, then click in the text to create an insertion point.*

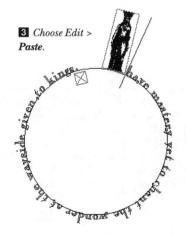

3 *Choose Edit > Paste.*

You can paste a line, picture box, or text box of any shape into a text box or onto a text path as an inline graphic. In Quark-XPress version 5.0 or later, you can also anchor a text path, table, or group! An anchored item functions like a character in that it remains anchored to the text if the text reflows, and yet it remains fully editable.

Note: Be sure to choose the right tools for these instructions!

To anchor an item into text:

1. Choose the Item tool.
2. Select the item to be anchored **1** (e.g., a table, a line, or perhaps an interesting graphic that you want to use as a drop cap).
3. Choose Edit > Copy (Cmd-C/Ctrl-C) or Cut (Cmd-X/Ctrl-X).
4. Choose the Content tool.
5. Click in a text box or on a text path to create an insertion point **2**.
6. Choose Edit > Paste (Cmd-V/Ctrl-V) **3**. You can do almost anything to an anchored item: Reshape it, rotate it, recolor it, scale it, add a frame to it, change its content (picture, text or none), convert its shape, or apply a Runaround value to it (even a negative Runaround value!). Read more about anchored items on the next two pages.

Anchor Item into Text

To realign an anchored item:

1. Choose the Item tool.

2. Click an anchored picture box, text box, or table. Then, on the Measurements palette, click the **Align with Text: Ascent** button to align the top of the anchored item with the ascent of the adjacent character to its right 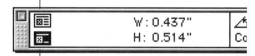–**2**. Or click the Align with Text: **Baseline** button to align the bottom of the anchored item with the baseline of the line of text in which it is anchored **3**.

   To realign an anchored line (standard or Bézier) or text path, click on it, then choose Item > Modify (Line pane), then click Align with Text: Ascent or Baseline.

TIP To vertically Offset a baseline-aligned anchored item, see the next page.

TIP Choose absolute—not auto—leading for text that contains an anchored box.

TIP You can change the Runaround for an item after it's anchored. Click on it, then choose Item > Runaround (Cmd-T/Ctrl-T).

TIP To **move** an anchored item to a new location, highlight it, cut it, and then paste it using the Content tool. To **highlight** an anchored item, click just to the left of the anchored item, then press Shift-right arrow (or to the right, then press Shift-left arrow). If you're moving the anchored item within the same text box, you can drag-and-drop it from one location to the next.

TIP You can use a hanging indent (Style > Formats) or the indent here command (Cmd-\/Ctrl-\) to make an anchored item hang outside the paragraph **4**.

The Align with Text: Ascent

1 *The Align with Text: Baseline*

have mastery yet to chant the wonder at the wayside given to kings. Still by God's grace there surges within me singing magic grown to my life and power, how the wild bird portent hurled forth the Achaeans' twin-stemmed power single hearted, lords of the youth of Hellas, with spear and hand of strength to the land of Teucrus.   *Aeschylus*

2 *An anchored picture box, **Ascent** aligned*

3 *An anchored picture box, **Baseline** aligned*

4 *An **Indent here** command is used to make the anchored item **hang** outside the paragraph.*

have mastery yet to chant the wonder at the wayside given to kings. Still by God's grace there surges within me singing magic grown to my life and power, how the wild bird portent hurled forth the Achaeans' twin-stemmed power single hearted, lords of the youth of Hellas, with

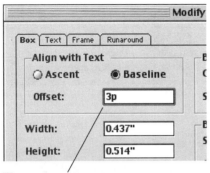

1 *Enter a number in this field to* **Offset** *an anchored item that's* **baseline-aligned**.

have mastery yet to chant the wonder at the wayside given to kings. Still by God's grace there surges within me singing magic grown to my life and power, how the wild bird portent hurled forth the Achaeans' twin-stemmed power single hearted, lords of the youth of Hellas, with spear and hand of strength to the land of Teucrus.

Aeschylus

2 *Resizing* an anchored picture box

have mastery yet to chant the wonder at the wayside given to kings. Still by God's grace there surges within me singing magic grown to my life and power, how the wild bird portent hurled forth the Achaeans' twin-stemmed power single hearted, lords of the youth of Hellas, with spear and hand of strength to the land of Teucrus.

Aeschylus

3 *The anchored box enlarged*

The Offset option is only available for an anchored item that's baseline aligned—not an item that's ascent aligned.

To offset an anchored item that's baseline-aligned:

1. Choose the Item or Content tool.
2. Click an anchored item (not a table).
3. Choose Item > Modify (Cmd-M/Ctrl-M), then click the Box or Line tab.
4. Enter a positive Align with Text: Offset value to shift the anchored item upward **1**.
5. Click OK.

To resize an anchored item:

1. Choose the Item or Content tool. If the anchored item is a Bézier, turn off Item > Edit > Shape (Shift-F4).
2. Click the anchored item.
3. Cmd-Option-Shift/Ctrl-Alt-Shift drag a handle (or drag an endpoint, if it's a line) **2**–**3**.

TIP To reshape an anchored Bézier item, turn on Item > Edit > Shape (Shift-F4/F10), then edit the shape as usual.

To delete an anchored item:

1. Choose the Content tool.
2. Click just to the right of the anchored item (we use the left or right arrow key to position the cursor).
3. Press Delete/Backspace.

To create an un-anchored copy of an anchored item:

Choose the Content tool, select the anchored item, then choose Item > Duplicate (Cmd-D/Ctrl-D).
or
Choose the Item tool, select the anchored item, choose Edit > Copy, click elsewhere, then choose Edit > Paste.

Drop anchor

To anchor highlighted text at its current location and convert it into a picture box at the same time, hold down Option/Alt as you choose Style > Text to Box **1**–**3** (also see page 296).

1 *Standard text characters are highlighted.*

2 *After choosing Style > **Text to Box** with **Option/Alt** held down, the text is simultaneously converted into a picture box and anchored at its current location.*

3 *The **anchored picture box** is filled with a picture.*

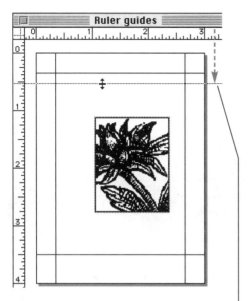

1 *Drag from a ruler to place a* **guide** *on a document or master page.*

Getting snappy

If you drag an item to a guide, the item will snap to the guide if View > **Snap to Guides** is on **2**. Choose a **Snap Distance** in Edit > Preferences > Preferences > Document–General (6 pixels is the default).

2 *An item will* **snap** *to a guide if it's dragged within the specified* **Snap Distance** *of the guide.*

To position items precisely, use ruler guides (this page) or use the X and Y fields on the Measurements palette. To align items to each other, use Space/Align (see page 177).

To create a ruler guide manually:

1. If the rulers aren't visible, choose View > Show Rulers (Cmd-R/Ctrl-R). If the margin guides aren't visible, choose View > Show Guides (F7).

2. Drag a guide from the horizontal or vertical ruler onto a document or master page **1**. As you drag, the position of the guide will be indicated in the X or Y field on the Measurements palette and by a marker on the ruler. If you release the mouse over the pasteboard as you drag a guide, the guide will extend across facing pages and onto the pasteboard.

TIP Ruler guides will display in front of or behind page elements depending on whether Guides: In Front or Behind is chosen in Edit > Preferences > Preferences > Document–General.

TIP To make a ruler guide visible only at or above a certain zoom percentage, choose that percentage, then hold down Shift as you create the guide.

To remove manual ruler guides:

To **remove one** ruler guide, choose the Item tool (or hold down Cmd/Ctrl with the Content tool if the guide is over an item), then drag the guide back onto either ruler (the pointer will be a double-arrowhead). This only works if Guides: In Front is chosen in Preferences > Document–General. Use the same technique to **move** a guide.
or
To **remove all** horizontal or all vertical guides, make sure no pasteboard is visible between the edge of the page and the corresponding ruler, then Option-click/Alt-click the horizontal ruler to remove all horizontal guides or the vertical ruler to remove all vertical guides.

Manual Ruler Guides

5.0!

The Guide Manager, yet another free downloadable XTension, is used to create a custom grid of non-printing margin guides. You can control how many guides are created as well as their placement.

To create guides using the Guide Manager:

1. If you only want the guides to appear on one page, go to that page now. Guides can't be placed on a master page.

2. Choose Utilities > Guide Manager, then click the Add Guides tab **1**.

3. From the **Direction** pop-up menu in the Guide Placement area, choose Horizontal, Vertical, or Both as the orientation for the guides.

4. *Optional:* Check **Locked Guides** to lock the new guides. They can be unlocked later.

5. From the **Where** pop-up menu, choose the location for the guides: Current Page, Current Spread, All Pages, or All Spreads.

6. Do one or more of the following:

   To specify the intervals between guides, check **Spacing**, then enter the desired interval in the Horizontal and Vertical fields. If no Spacing value is specified, the spacing will be calculated based on the Number of Guides.

   If you don't want QuarkXPress to figure out how many guides to create, check **Number of Guides**, then enter Horizontal and Vertical values.

   From the **Origin/Boundaries** pop-up menu, choose the starting point for the grid: Choose **Inset** to position guides from the edges of the page/spread at the inset values you specify; or choose **Absolute Position**, then specify a starting location for the guides; or choose **Entire Page/Spread** to have the grid start from the topmost left corner of the page or spread.

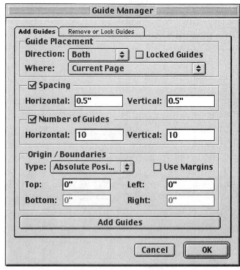

1 *The* **Add Guides** *options in the* **Guide Manager** *dialog box*

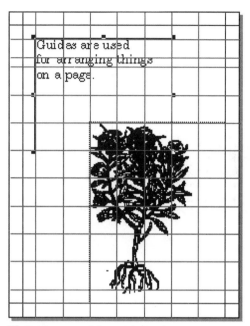

1 *Guides* are used for positioning items.

2 *The Remove or Lock Guides options are in a separate pane in the Guide Manager dialog box.*

7. *Optional:* If Where: Current Page or All Pages is chosen, you can check **Use Margins** to have the grid be contained within the current margin guides.

8. Click Add Guides **1**.

9. Click OK. You can run the Guide Manager again to add more guides.

TIP The margin, ruler, and guide colors can be changed in Edit > Preferences > Preferences > Application–Display.

To remove and/or lock/unlock Guide Manager guides:

1. Choose Utilities > Guide Manager.

2. Click the "Remove or Lock Guides" tab.

3. In the **Remove Guides** area **2**, from the **Where** pop-up menu, choose which pages you want guides to be removed from: Current Page, Current Spread, All Pages, All Spreads, or All Pages & Spreads.
   and
   From the **Direction** pop-up menu, Choose Horizontal, Vertical, or Both.
   and
   From the **Locked** pop-up menu, choose whether you want Locked, Unlocked, or Both [locked and unlocked] guides to be removed.
   then
   Click **Remove Guides**. All Guide Manager guides will be removed—as well as any guides that you dragged onto the page manually!

4. In the **Lock Guides** area, from the **Where** pop-up menu, choose which pages you want guides to be locked or unlocked on: Current Page, Current Spread, All Pages, All Spreads, or All Pages & Spreads.
   and
   From the **Direction** pop-up menu, Choose Horizontal, Vertical, or Both.
   then
   Click **Lock Guides** or **Unlock Guides**.

5. Click OK.

Guide Manager

You can do more than convert a picture from one shape to another using the Shape submenu—you can also convert a standard picture or text box into a Bézier box or convert any kind of picture box into a line. A table can't be converted into anything.

Note: If you convert a picture box that contains a picture into a line (any of the last three icons on the Shape submenu), the picture will be deleted. If you convert a text box into a line, it will become a text path.

To convert an item's shape:

1. Choose the Item or Content tool.
2. Click on an item (not multiple items).
3. Choose a shape from the Item > Shape submenu **1**–**5**.

TIP To make the corners of any of the first four shapes found under the Shape submenu more or less convex, choose Item > Modify (Cmd-M/Ctrl-M), click the Box tab, then change the Corner Radius value. 2" is the maximum.

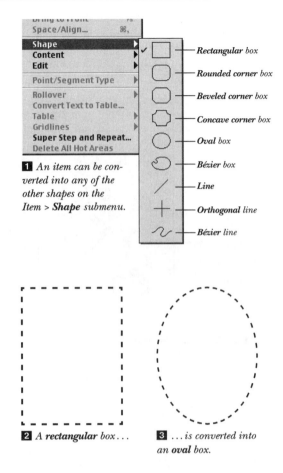

1 *An item can be converted into any of the other shapes on the Item > **Shape** submenu.*

- *Rectangular box*
- *Rounded corner box*
- *Beveled corner box*
- *Concave corner box*
- *Oval box*
- *Bézier box*
- *Line*
- *Orthogonal line*
- *Bézier line*

2 *A **rectangular** box...*

3 *...is converted into an **oval** box.*

Dinner one night consisted of lamb chops, becoming heavy at times, with occasional ketchup. Periods of peas and baked potatoes were followed by gradual clearing, with a wonderful Jell-O setting in the west.

—*Judi Barrett*

4 *A **text box**...*

5 *...is converted into a **text path** by choosing the Line icon.*

Send to Back	⇧F5
Bring to Front	F5
Space/Align...	⌘,
Shape	▶
Content	▶
Edit	▶
Point/Segment Type	▶

Picture
✓ Text
None

1 *Choose **Picture, Text,** or **None** from the Item > **Content** submenu.*

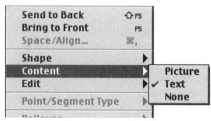

2 *A **picture box**...*

Suddenly from somewhere far away comes the sound of a fish jumping, and the moon's reflection ripples across the lake.

—Tejima

3 *...is converted into a **text** box (and text is entered).*

You can make a box or text path content-less; or change a box from a picture box to a text box, or vice versa; or change a line into a text path. Any text or picture the item originally contained will be removed; a frame will remain. A content conversion can be undone, but the original contents won't be restored. A Bézier line or text path can't be converted to a picture box; a table can't be converted at all.

You can apply a solid color, blend, or frame to a contentless box, but you can't fill it with text or a picture. Contentless boxes function strictly as decorative elements.

To convert an item's contents:

1. Choose the Item or Content tool.

2. Click a text box, picture box, line, or text path.

3. Choose Picture, Text, or None from the Item > Content submenu **1**–**4**.
   or
   Control-click/Right-click and choose Content > Picture, Text, or None. **5.0!**

4. Click OK if a warning prompt appears.

4 *A **contentless** box can contain a **frame** and a **solid color** or a **blend**—period.*

Convert Item Contents

Layout tips for Web and print

Just as a composer creates a musical score or an artist paints a picture, all the elements on your page have to be arranged so the message is understood clearly by your audience. If the writing is poor, your copywriter has more work to do, but your readers will become weary of even the best writing if the layout and typography are poor. Your audience doesn't have to be spellbound, but you do want to capture their attention long enough to get the message across. Here are a few suggestions:

- Let in some air. Leave a little **white space** around your text and pictures. How you do this depends on your subject matter. Use Text Inset values to add some air between a picture and its frame. Use ample gutters between columns (add delicate vertical rules for definition). Or gather elements up at the top of the page and leave the bottom of the page blank. Peaceful passages provide an important counterpoint to louder passages, and confident composers know how to play them off each other to their advantage.

- Use a **grid** as an underlying structure to organize elements. Whether the grid is obvious to your readers or not, it still makes for a more pleasing and orderly page, and it makes it easier to make decisions right off the bat as you lay out and edit your page. In fact, many designers still use pencil and paper to sketch out broad design ideas before they create a layout on the computer.

- **Break out** of the grid in select areas to add some punch. As an example, you could put thin rules around most of your pictures, then use a different type of picture with an irregular edge to add a more interesting, non-rectangular shape to the page.

- Just as composers juxtapose opposing forces to create what we call "**good tension**"—slow versus fast, complex versus simple, loud versus soft, percussive versus melodic, and so on—there are many ways to create good tension in a layout. For example, instead of plopping two medium-sized pictures smack in the middle of the page, put one large picture off to the side (let it bleed off) and a small picture in the opposing corner. Don't automatically stick everything in the center.

Elements that can be used to create pleasing tension include **scale** (large vs. small), **shape** (regular vs. irregular), **placement** (diagonal, vertical, and horizontal), **color** (raucus vs. subtle), and **shade** (light vs. dark).

- When you arrange multiples of a similar object (e.g., pictures and their accompanying captions), the result doesn't have to be static. Use **repetition** to your advantage to create **texture** or **rhythm**. But do align the objects carefully—misalignments are distracting (use Super Step and Repeat to make copies of an object or group or use Space/Align to align existing objects). Keep in mind the **overall** shape multiple items will form when they're grouped together (e.g., the whole navigation bar, if you're designing a Web page). A good formation will have solidity and order. To see how the whole page looks, choose a small view size and turn guides off (it's the equivalent of squinting).

- And last but not least, don't forget to set type like a professional (Chapter 7 is chock full of tips for setting professional-looking type). The **details** matter as much as the broad strokes.

Layout Tips

Pictures and Text

1 *Click the text box that you want to be in front.*

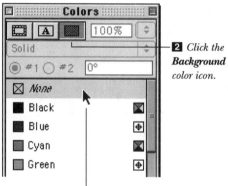

2 *Click the **Background** color icon.*

3 *Then click **None** to make the background of the top box transparent.*

4 *Now the text box is **transparent**.*

Pictures and text

There are many ways to combine text and pictures in QuarkXPress. For example, a picture can be placed behind a text box that has a transparent background. Or you can have text wrap around the perimeter of a picture box, or wrap partially or completely around the irregular contours of the picture itself.

QuarkXPress not only gives you control over how text wraps around a picture, the program can also create editable clipping paths that control how much of a picture prints. If you have a picture with a white background, for example, you can tell the program not to print the background. A clipping path can even be created from an embedded path or alpha channel that was saved with a picture in another application.

You can layer a text box over a picture box (or layer picture boxes or text boxes).

To make a text box see-through:

1. Choose the Item or Content tool.

2. Click the box that is to be in front. If it's not yet in front, choose Item > Bring to Front **1** or move the item to a higher layer (see page 260).

3. Choose View > Show Colors (F12).

4. Click the Background color icon on the Colors palette **2**, then click None at the top of the list of colors **3**–**4**. Don't select Black with a shade of 0%—you won't achieve transparency.

TIP If the item below the text is so dark that the text is unreadable, switch gears and make the text white (see page 248).

To wrap text around an item:

1. The item the text is to wrap around must be on top of the text. It can be any kind of item (picture box, text box, text path, Bézier shape, or table). To bring it forward, select it, then choose Bring To Front from the Send & Bring submenu on the context menu.

2. Choose the Item or Content tool.

3. Select the picture box.

4. Choose Item > Runaround (Cmd-T/Ctrl-T).

5. Choose Type: Item **1**.

6. To adjust the space between each side of a rectangular picture box and the text that's wrapping around it, enter Top, Left, Bottom, and Right values. If any other picture box shape is chosen, enter an Outset value.

7. Click Apply to preview the text wrap in the document window, then click OK **2**. *Note:* If the item straddles two columns, text will wrap around all its sides; if it's within a column, text will wrap around three of its sides. For a complete wrap, in the latter case, click the text box, choose Item > Modify, click the Text tab, then check Run Text Around All Sides.

TIP To choose default Runaround settings for any item creation tool, double-click the tool, click Modify, click Runaround, then choose settings.

TIP The Runaround value around a text path is calculated based on the path itself, not the text.

TIP If Maintain Leading is checked in Edit > Preferences > Preferences > Document–Paragraph and an item is positioned within a column of text, the first line of text that is forced below the item will snap to the nearest leading increment. With Maintain Leading off, the text will touch the bottom of the item, offset only by that item's current Runaround value.

Wrap Text Around an Item

The color code

The **Margin** color (the default is blue) is also used to represent an item's bounding box in the Runaround and Clipping dialog boxes. Similarly, the current **Ruler** color (the default is green) is used to represent the clipping path, and the current **Grid** color (the default is magenta) is used to represent the Runaround border. To change any of these colors, go to Edit > Preferences > Preferences > Application–Display (Cmd-Option-Shift-Y/Ctrl-Alt-Shift-Y).

1 *Choose Type:* **Item** *in the Modify >* **Runaround.**

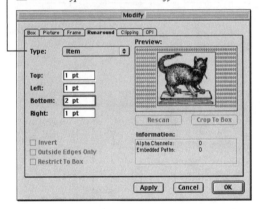

With my aversion to this cat, however, its partiality for myself seemed to increase. It followed my footsteps with a pertinacity which it would be difficult to make the reader comprehend. Whenever I sat, it would crouch beneath my chair, or spring upon my knees, covering me with its loathsome caresses. If I arose to walk it would get between my feet and thus nearly throw me down, or, fastening its long and sharp claws in my dress, clamber, in this manner to, to my breast. At such times, although I longed to destroy it with a blow, I was yet withheld from so doing, partly by a memory of my former crime, but chiefly—let me confess it at once—by absolutely *dread* of the beast...

This dread was not exactly a dread of physical evil—and yet... *Edgar Allan Poe*

2 *The* **text wraps** *around the* **picture box.**

Do you think it is said Pooh, "because ks. It is either Two night be, Wizzle, or zles and one, if so it ue to follow them." just a little anxious e animals in front of them were of Hostile Intent. And Piglet wished very much that his grandfather T.W.

1 *Before a clipping path is created, the white area around the photo **prints**.*

"Po⸱ ᴵet. "Do you think it is aˀ " said Pooh, "because ks. It is either Two night be, Wizzle, or zles and one, if so it ue to follow them." ⸱ just a little anxious now, three animals in front of them were of Hostile Intent. And Piglet wished very much that his grandfather T.W.

2 *A QuarkXPress **clipping path** is used to **prevent** the white area from printing. The text is still running behind the photo, though—it's not wrapping around it.*

"Pooh!" cried Piglet. "Do you think it is another Woozle?" "No," said Pooh, "because it makes different marks. It is either Two Woozles and one, as it might be, Wizzle, or Two, as it might be, Wizzles and one, if so it is, Woozle. Let us continue to fol-

3 *Finally, **Runaround** is turned on with the Type: Same As Clipping option for the photo to force the text to wrap around the **image**.*

What is a clipping path?

A clipping path is a mechanism that controls which parts of a picture are going to print **1**–**3**. Areas of the picture within the clipping path will be visible and will print; areas outside the clipping path will be **transparent** and won't print. You may already know how to create a clipping path in another application, like Photoshop. In that type of clipping path, the clipping information is saved in the picture itself. In QuarkXPresss, when you use a clipping path that was saved with the original picture in another application, it is called an **embedded path**.

Clipping paths in QuarkXPress work a little bit differently. While they are also used to control which parts of an image will print, they don't permanently clip areas of the image that extend outside it. Clipping path information in QuarkXPress is saved with the **document**, not the image itself. This means that you can create a different clipping path for each instance in which you use an image. If you *want* to reuse a picture and its clipping path, on the other hand, simply drag-and-drop the picture box from one document to another; a copy will appear in the target document.

Another compelling reason to use a QuarkXPress clipping path is that as you reshape it or choose different settings for it, you can see immediately how it looks within your overall layout. What's more, you can adjust the shape of a clipping path to your heart's delight using any technique you'd use to adjust a Bézier path.

You can have QuarkXPress create a clipping path based on the shape or silhouette of a picture or you can create a custom path. QuarkXPress can also generate a new, editable clipping path based on any alpha channel (saved selection) or embedded path, provided such channel or path is saved with the picture file in its original application (e.g., Adobe Photoshop).

Runaround vs. clipping, in a nutshell

A clipping path controls which parts of a picture will **display** and **print**. Runaround controls how **text wraps** around a picture. The runaround text wrap or clipping path can be controlled by any of the following parameters **1**–**2**:

Item: The edge of the picture box.

Picture Bounds: The picture's rectangular bounding box (not the QuarkXPress picture box).

Non-White Areas: The non-white edge of a picture. The path will follow the silhouette of an image if it has a white background.

Embedded Path or **Alpha Channel**: An embedded alpha channel or path that was created and saved with the picture in a graphics application. You can use an embedded path in an imported picture if it was saved in any of these formats: TIFF, EPS, BMP, JPEG, PCX, and PICT. You can also use an alpha channel in a TIFF.

To make matters even more confusing, for each Type there are additional options for controlling the placement of the clipping path or the runaround text wrap.

And there's one more Runaround option: **Auto Image**. With Auto Image chosen, text will wrap around the edge of the image (not its bounding box). The runaround is created from the original, high-resolution image (not the preview) using Bézier curves, and works effectively on an image that has a clearly defined border and a flat, light background. A combined, uneditable clipping and runaround path is created in one step (the edit clipping and runaround functions are nullified).

Choose Type: **None** in the Runaround folder tab to turn off runaround altogether.

Though they may at first seem confusing, the runaround and clipping path options offer a lot of control and flexibility, so they're worth spending some time to learn.

It's better! 5.0!

Quark's runaround and clipping path features work more smoothly now, and the redraw bugs have been eliminated.

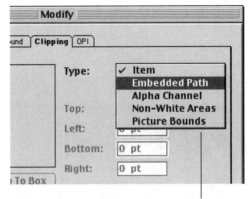

1 *The **Type** options in the **Clipping** pane of the **Modify** dialog box*

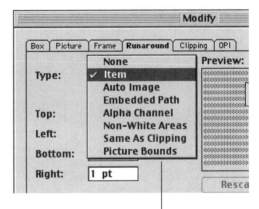

2 *The **Type** options in the **Runaround** pane of the **Modify** dialog box*

Clipping Paths

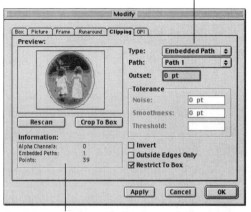

*The **Information** area displays the number of **Alpha Channels** and **Embedded Paths** in the picture file, and the number of **Points** that will be created for the QuarkXPress clipping path.*

▮a *Clipping Type: **Item**—the clipping path conforms to the box.*

▮b *Clipping Type: **Picture Bounds**—the clipping path conforms to the outer perimeter of the image (its bounding box).*

To create a clipping path:

1. Import an EPS, TIFF, BMP, PCX, or PICT file into a rectangular picture box. For this first attempt, we suggest you use an image that's silhouetted on a white background.

2. To layer a picture, make sure its box has a background of None. (Select the box, click the background icon ▦ on the Colors palette, then click None.)

3. Choose Item > Clipping (Cmd-Option-T/Ctrl-Alt-T).

4. Note the green line around the image in the preview window, which denotes the clipping path, as you choose from the **Type** pop-up menu ▮:

   (Choose **Item** to turn off the clipping path function ▮a. The picture will only be cropped by the picture box. To turn off Runaround, see page 194.)

   Choose **Picture Bounds** to have the path conform to the rectangular outer boundary of the picture (its bounding box) ▮b. If Restrict to Box is unchecked, any areas of the picture that the picture box is cropping will become visible, and may obscure items below it.

   Choose **Embedded Path** to create a clipping path based on a clipping path that was saved with the picture in another application (▮c, next page). Choose Alpha Channel to create a clipping path based on the non-black parts of an alpha channel that was saved with the picture in an image-editing program. *Note:* If the picture was saved with more than one alpha channel or path, choose the desired channel or path name from the **Alpha** or **Path** pop-up menu.

   Print documents only: Choose **Non-White Areas** to create a clipping path that follows the contours of the actual image and ignores non-white areas of the picture. The white areas have to be either close to white (e.g., very light gray) or absolute white for this to work.

   (Continued on the following page)

195

5. As you choose any of these *optional* settings, click **Apply** at any time to preview the current settings in the document:

Click **Crop To Box**, if available, to have the clipping path stop at the edge of the box.

Click **Rescan** to restore the original path.

Check **Invert** to switch the cropped and visible areas **3**a. This option isn't available when the Item or Picture Bounds Type is chosen.

Check **Outside Edges Only** for an Alpha Channel, Embedded Path, or Non-White Areas (not Item or Picture Bounds) clipping path if the picture contains a blank hole or holes where the background white shows through, and you don't want the clipping path to include them. With Outside Edges Only unchecked, an additional clipping path will be created for each hole **3**b.

Check **Restrict To Box** to have only areas of the picture inside the picture box display and print (**3**c–d, next page). Uncheck to let the entire picture display and print.

With any Type option except Item chosen, you can further expand or contract the clipping path to print more or less of the picture by entering a positive or negative value, respectively, in the **Outset** field. For the Picture Bounds Type, enter Top, Left, Bottom, or Right values. For an Embedded Path or Alpha Channel Type, the Outset value will expand or contract the entire clipping path relative to the original path or alpha channel. For the Non-White Areas type of clipping path, the Outset value will expand or contract the entire clipping path relative to the original non-white areas (**4**a–b, page 198).

6. Choose Tolerance settings for an Embedded Path, Alpha Channel, or Non-White Areas type of clipping path:

2c *Clipping Type:* ***Embedded Path***—*the clipping path conforms to a path that was saved with the image in its original application.*

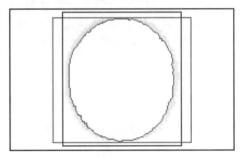

3a *Clipping Type:* ***Non-White Areas*** *with the* ***Invert*** *option* ***on***—*only pixels in the outer fringe will print.*

3b *Clipping Type:* ***Non-White Areas*** *with* ***Outside Edges*** *turned* ***off***—*the clipping path or paths surround any non-white areas in the image.*

3c *Clipping Type:* **Picture Bounds** *with* **Restrict to Box** *turned on—only areas of the picture that are inside the picture box will print.*

He trotted along happily, and by-and-by he crossed the stream and came to the place where his friends-and-relations lived. There seemed to be even more of them about than usual this morning, and having nodded to a hedgehog or two, with whom he was too busy to shake hands, and having said, "Good morning, good morning," importantly to some of the others, and "Ah, there you are," kindly, to the smaller ones, he waved a paw at them over his shoulder, and was gone; leaving such an air of excitement and I-don't-know-what behind him, that several members

3d *Clipping Type:* **Picture Bounds** *with* **Restrict to Box** *turned off—areas outside the picture box will print, even if they overlap the text.*

He trotted along happily, and by-and-by he crossed the stream and came to the place where tions lived. There seemed to be more of them about than usual morning, and having nodded hedgehog or two, with whom he was busy to shake hands, and having "Good morning, good morning," im tantly to some of the others, and there you are," kindly, to the sm ones, he waved a paw at them ove shoulder, and was gone; leaving such an air of excitement and I-don't-know-what behind him, that several members

For an alpha channel clipping path, the **Noise** value (0–288 pt.) is the minimum size an area near the border of an alpha channel must be to be included in the clipping path (**5a–b**, next page). Adjust the Noise value to exclude tiny, extraneous blobs in the background from the clipping path.

Smoothness (0–100) makes the clipping path more or less smooth by adding or decreasing points (**6a–b**, next page). The lower the Smoothness setting, the more points the clipping path will contain; the higher the Smoothness, the fewer points the path will contain and the more precisely its shape will match that of the image. A low Smoothness could cause output problems, but the program can adjust this setting automatically during printing, if need be. You may need to play with this to get the optimal setting.

Threshold works with an Alpha Channel or Non-White Areas clipping path (**7a–b**, page 199). It controls what percentages of gray on the alpha channel will be treated as white (and not mask the picture) and what percentages will be treated as black (and mask parts of the picture). At a Threshold setting of 10%, for example, gray values from 0–10% will be treated as white; gray values between 11% and 100% will be treated as black and will act as a mask. At a Threshold setting of 40%, more gray values will be treated as white, and less of the picture will be masked. For the Non-White Areas type of clipping path, the opposite is true: The Threshold is the percentage a color can be darker than white before it will be left outside the clipping path and won't print.

7. Click Apply, then click OK. If you'd like to reshape the clipping path, follow the instructions on the page 201.

(Illustrations on the following two pages)

Create a Clipping Path

197

4a *Clipping Type:* **Non-White Areas, Outset -15**—
the clipping path shrinks slightly inward.

4b *Clipping Type:* **Non-White Areas, Outset 15**—
the clipping path expands slightly outward.

5a *Clipping Type:* **Non-White Areas** *at the
default* **Noise** *setting of* **2 pt.**—*the clipping path
includes extraneous pixels outside the oval.*

5b *Clipping Type:* **Non-White Areas, Noise 30 pt.**
—*the extraneous blobs aren't included in the
clipping path.*

6a *Clipping Type:* **Non-White Areas** *at the default*
Smoothness *setting of* **2 pt.**—*the clipping path
has many points, and hugs the image precisely.*

6b *Clipping Type:* **Non-White Areas,
Smoothness 75 pt.**—*here the clipping
path is smoother, but it's less accurate.*

7a *Clipping Type: Non-White Areas, Threshold 2 —the clipping path includes the gray background.*

7b *Clipping Type: Non-White Areas, Threshold 10 —the clipping path ignores the gray background.*

Runaround and clipping: How they work together

If different runaround and clipping Type options are chosen for the same picture, the text wrap won't be at the edge of the picture. For example, if Picture Bounds is chosen as the Runaround type, and the picture's alpha channel or embedded path is chosen as the clipping type (and assuming the channel or path is smaller than the picture bounds), there will be a buffer area between the clipped picture and the text wrap.

If the Non-White Areas option is chosen for a picture in both the Runaround and the Clipping panes, text will wrap to the edge of a silhouetted picture, plus or minus the Outset width that you specify.

TIP To force text to flow into any hole or holes in a picture where the white background shows through, uncheck the Outside Edges Only option in both the Clipping and Runaround panes.

TIP Don't wrap text *inside* a clipping path unless the text or picture's contrast has been carefully adjusted to make the type readable.

Runaround and Clipping

To wrap text around a picture:

1. Choose the Item or Content tool.

2. Select a picture box, and make sure it's on top of the text box. If it's not, Control-click/Right-click and choose Send & Bring > Bring To Front.

3. Choose Item > Runaround (Cmd-T/Ctrl-T).

4. Choose Type: Non-White Areas.

5. Enter an **Outset** value in points to adjust the space between the picture and its surrounding text (-288 to 288). Try between 5 and 10 pt. Click Apply to preview.

   or

   Check **Same As Clipping** to have the text runaround conform to a Quark-XPress clipping path and utilize all the options that were chosen for that clipping path. To edit this type of wrap, edit the clipping path.

6. Click Apply to preview again.

7. Click OK.

8. Press Cmd-Option-.(period)/Shift-Esc, if necessary, to force the screen to redraw.

   Note: Normally, text will wrap around three sides of an obstruction (e.g., picture, picture box, text box) if the obstruction is placed within a column. To wrap text completely around an item, select the text box in the back, go to Item > Modify (Cmd-M/Ctrl-M), click the Text tab, check Run Text Around All Sides, then click OK **1**–**2**.

TIP *Beware!* If you choose Picture Bounds as the Clipping path type and choose Non-White Areas as the Runaround type, the text will wrap to the edge of the image, but it will be obscured by the opaque background of the picture. The edge of a picture box usually doesn't match up with the picture's bounding box.

Then, pray tell me what it is that you can infer from this hat?" He picked it up and gazed at it in the peculiar introspective fashion which was characteristic of him. "It is perhaps less suggestive than it might have been," he remarked, "and yet there are a few inferences which are very distinct, and a few others which repre-sent at least a strong bal-ance of proba-bility. That the man was highly intellectual is of course obvious upon the face of it, and to-do within the last three years, although he has now fallen upon evil days. He had foresight, but has less now than for-merly, pointing to a moral retrogres-sion, which, when taken with the decline of his fortunes, seems to indicate some evil influence, probably drink, at work upon him. This may account also for the obvious fact that his wife has ceased to love him..."

—*Sir Arthur Conan Doyle*

1 *You can make text run* **completely** *around a picture within the same column, but the text will be tiring to read, so don't use this option if you need to convey important information.*

Then, pray tell me what it is that you can infer from this hat?" He picked it up and gazed at it in the peculiar introspective fashion which was characteristic of him. "It is perhaps less suggestive than it might have been," he remarked, "and yet there are a few infer-ences which are very distinct, and a few others which represent at least a strong balance of prob-ability. That the man was highly intellectual is of course obvious upon the face of it, and also that he was fairly well-to-do within the last three years, although he has now fallen upon evil days. He had fore-sight, but has less now than formerly, pointing to a moral retrogression, which, when taken with the decline of his for-tunes, seems to indicate some evil influ-ence, probably drink, at work upon him. This may account also for the obvious fact that his wife has ceased to love him..."

2 *To run text inside the holes of a picture, choose* **Non-White Areas** *for the runaround type and* **uncheck** **Outside Edges Only**.

*Reshape a **clipping** path to change which parts of a picture will **print**.*

1 *Option-click/Alt-click a line segment to add an anchor point.*

*Hold down **Spacebar** to suspend redraw and rewrap as you reshape a runaround or clipping path.*

2 *Option-click/Alt-click an anchor point to delete it.*

"Pooh!" cried Piglet. "Do you think it i
er Woozle?" "No," said Pooh, "because
different marks. It is either Two Woo
one, as it might be, W
Two, as it might be,
and one, if so it is,
et us continue to
them." So they w
feeling just a little
now, in the case the tl

*Reshape a **runaround** path to change how **text wraps** around the picture.*

3 *Dragging a segment*

"Pooh!" cried Piglet. "Do you think it i
er Woozle?" "No," said Pooh, "because i
different marks. It is either Two Woo
one, as it mi
Wizzle, or Tv
might be, Wizz
one, if so it is,
Let us continue to
them." So they went
ing just a little anxio

4 *The text re-wraps.*

Note: QuarkXPress generates a clipping path based on the original, high-resolution picture file. But when you manually edit a clipping path (unless you use a preview-enhancing XTension), you'll be working off the low-resolution screen preview, so your adjustments may not be very precise.

To reshape a runaround or clipping path:

1. Choose the Item or Content tool.

2. Click on a picture that has a clipping path. You can edit the runaround for any of these Types: Embedded Path, Alpha Channel, Non-White Areas, or Picture Bounds.

3. Choose Item > Edit > Runaround (Option-F4/Ctrl-F10).
or
Choose Item > Edit > Clipping Path (Option-Shift-F4/Ctrl-Shift-F10).

4. Use any of the techniques that you'd normally use to reshape a Bézier path (see pages 286–293) **1**–**4**. You can add or delete an anchor point, drag a point, segment, or control handle, or convert an anchor point from corner to curved (or vice versa).

Beware! If you edit a clipping path and then reopen the Clipping pane, the clipping path Type will be listed as User Edited Path. If you choose a different Type at this point and click OK, you'll **lose** your custom path edits!

5. When you're done editing a runaround path, re-choose Item > Edit > Runaround (Option-F4/Ctrl-F10). For a clipping path, re-choose Item > Edit > Clipping Path (Option-Shift-F4/Ctrl-Shift-F10).

TIP To force the screen to redraw, press (Cmd-Option-. (period)/Shift-Esc). To have the text wrap update as you move a picture, click Live Refresh in Edit > Preferences > Preferences > Application–Interactive.

Reshape Runaround or Clipping Path

To wrap text inside a hidden picture:

1. Choose the Item or Content tool, then click a silhouetted image on a solid white or off-white background **1**.

2. Make sure the picture box is in front of the text box. If necessary, Control-click/Right-click and choose Send & Bring > Bring To Front. Also make sure the picture box completely covers the text box, otherwise the text will be visible within the picture's clipping path and around the edge of the picture box.

3. Choose Item > Modify (Cmd-M/Ctrl-M).

4. Click the Clipping tab, and choose Type: Non-White Areas.

5. Check Invert.

6. Click the Runaround tab.

7. Choose Type: Same As Clipping.

8. Click OK.

9. Press Cmd-Option-**.** (period)/Shift-Esc, if necessary, to force the screen to redraw **2**. Try using a small size for the type, and apply justified horizontal alignment.

Note: If the edge of the picture is showing (as in **2**), but you don't want it to print, click the picture, choose Item > Modify (Cmd-M/Ctrl-M), click the Box tab, then check Suppress Printout.

1 *Click on a picture that has a white background.*

> brain *n.*
> **1** an organ of soft nervous tissue contained in the skull of vertebrates, functioning as the coordinating centre of sensation, and of intellectual and nervous activity. **2** (usu. in *pl.*; prec. by *the) colloq.* **a** the cleverest person in a group. **b** a person who originates a complex plan or idea.
> brain *n.* **1** an organ of soft nervous tissue contained in the skull of vertebrates, functioning as the coordinating centre of sensation, and of intellectual and nervous activity. **2** (usu. in *pl.*; prec. by

2 *The text is wrapping inside the clipping path instead of outside it.*

Lines 12

Need more than one of an item?

- Use the **Duplicate** shortcut (Cmd-D/Ctrl-D). Or if you want to control where the duplicates land, use Item > **Step & Repeat**.

- After you draw a line with a line tool, the tool automatically deselects. To keep a line tool selected so as to draw multiple lines, **Option-click/Alt-click** the tool on the Tool palette. When you're finished using it, choose a different tool.

1 *Choose the Orthogonal Line tool, then drag.*

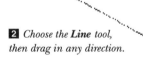

2 *Choose the Line tool, then drag in any direction.*

The line creation tools produce horizontal, vertical, and diagonal straight lines and arrows to which a variety of styles, endcaps, and colors can be applied. Using the Dashes & Stripes command, which is covered in this chapter, you can create custom line styles for use with the line tools, the Frame command, or the paragraph Rules command.

Note: To place rules under type, use the paragraph Rules feature (see pages 100–102). To anchor a line, see page 181. The Bézier line, Freehand line, Line text path, and other Bézier tools are discussed in Chapter 18.

To draw a straight horizontal or vertical line:

1. Choose the Orthogonal line tool.＋
2. Drag the crosshair icon horizontally or vertically **1**.

TIP To convert an orthogonal line into a Bézier line, select it, then choose the wiggly line icon from the Item > Shape submenu.

To draw a straight line at any angle:

1. Choose the Line tool. ／
2. Drag the crosshair icon in any direction **2**.

TIP Hold down Shift while drawing a line to constrain the line to an increment of 45°.

TIP To choose preferences for a line tool, double-click the tool, then click Modify.

203

To change the width of a line using the keyboard:

1. Choose the Item or Content tool.
2. Click on a line (Bézier or standard).
3. Press Cmd-Option-Shift->/Ctrl-Alt-Shift-> to widen the line or the < key to reduce the line width in 1-point increments. (Omit the Option/Alt key to change the line width to preset increments (Hairline, 1, 2, 4, 6, 8, or 12 pt).
   or
   In the Mac OS, press Cmd-\. The Line Width field in Item > Modify (Line pane) will highlight automatically. Enter the desired width (you don't have to type the "pt"), then click OK.

To restyle a line using the Measurements palette:

1. Choose the Item or Content tool.
2. Click on a line (Bézier or standard).
3. On the Measurements palette:
   Enter a Width value (.001–864 pt.) or choose a preset width from the pop-up menu **1**–**3**.
   and/or
   Choose from the style pop-up menu. (To create custom line styles, see pages 207–208.)
   and/or
   Choose an arrowhead from the rightmost pop-up menu **4**.

TIP You could Control-click/Right-click a line and choose from the Line Style, Arrowheads, Width, Color or Shade submenu. These submenus are also found on the Style menu. Instructions for recoloring a line are on page 250.

5.0!

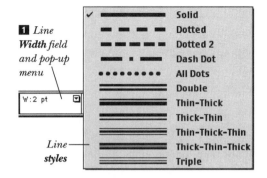

1 *Line Width field and pop-up menu*

Line styles

Arrowhead styles

2 *A line is selected.*

*Its **width** is increased.*

*A new **style** is applied.*

*An **arrowhead** is added.*

Hairline

.5 pt

1 pt

2 pt

4 pt

6 pt

3 *These are a few sample **line widths**. A Hairline prints as .125 pt. on a PostScript imagesetter.*

4 *A Bézier line with an arrow end-cap and a Gap Color of 10% black*

Hidden force

You can use a **non-printing line** to create an offbeat text shape 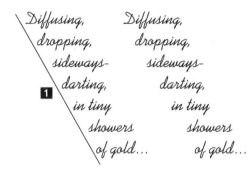. Click a line, bring it to the front, choose Item > Modify, click the Line tab, check Suppress Printout, click the Runaround tab, choose Type: Item, then specify an Outset value.

1

2 *Drag an* **endpoint** *to resize a line.*

To shorten or lengthen a line manually:

1. Choose the Item or Content tool.
2. Select a line.
3. Drag an endpoint to lengthen or shorten the line **2**. Option-Shift-drag/ Alt-Shift-drag to preserve the line's angle as you change its length.

To shorten or lengthen a line using the Measurements palette:

1. Choose the Item or Content tool.
2. Select a line.
3. Choose Left Point (the beginning of the line), Midpoint, or Right Point from the mode pop-up menu on the Measurements palette **3**. The line will be measured from this chosen point.
4. In the Length (L) field **4**, enter the desired length.

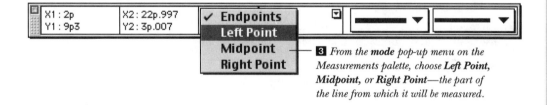

3 *From the mode pop-up menu on the Measurements palette, choose* **Left Point,** **Midpoint,** *or* **Right Point**—*the part of the line from which it will be measured.*

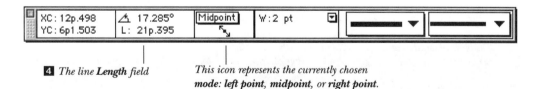

4 *The line* **Length** *field*

This icon represents the currently chosen mode: left point, midpoint, or right point.

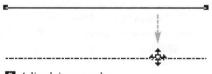

5 *A line being moved*

To move a line manually:

1. Choose the Item or Content tool.
2. Drag any part of a line other than an endpoint **5**.

To change the angle of a line:

1. Choose the Item or Content tool, then click a line.

2. To snap the line to an increment of 45° from the original angle, Shift-drag a handle **1** (this can't be done with an orthogonal line).
   or
   From the Measurements palette, choose Left Point, Midpoint, or Right Point (not Endpoints), then change the angle value **2**.
   or
   Choose the Rotate tool, ↻ press to establish an axis point, drag away from the line to create a lever, then rotate the line.

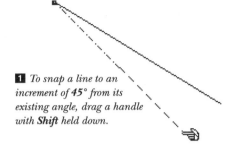

1 *To snap a line to an increment of **45°** from its existing angle, drag a handle with **Shift** held down.*

To reposition a line using the Measurements palette:

1. Choose the Item or Content tool, then click a line.

2. Choose from the mode pop-up menu on the Measurements palette—the part of the line from which its position will be measured **3**–**4**.

3. Change the X and/or Y values. You can use math (add or subtract) in any field.

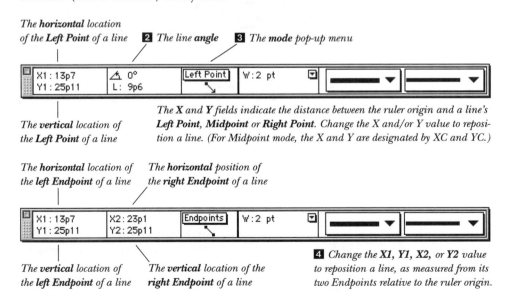

*The **horizontal** location of the **Left Point** of a line* | **2** *The line **angle*** | **3** *The **mode** pop-up menu*

*The **vertical** location of the **Left Point** of a line*

*The **X** and **Y** fields indicate the distance between the ruler origin and a line's **Left Point**, **Midpoint** or **Right Point**. Change the X and/or Y value to reposition a line. (For Midpoint mode, the X and Y are designated by XC and YC.)*

*The **horizontal** location of the **left Endpoint** of a line*   *The **horizontal** position of the **right Endpoint** of a line*

*The **vertical** location of the **left Endpoint** of a line*   *The **vertical** location of the **right Endpoint** of a line*

4 *Change the **X1, Y1, X2,** or **Y2** value to reposition a line, as measured from its two Endpoints relative to the ruler origin.*

How to apply dashes/stripes

Once a dash or stripe style is saved, it will appear in your document's Frame dialog box when a **box** is selected; on the Measurements palette style pop-up menu, on the Style > Line Style submenu, and in Item menu > Modify (Line pane) if a **line** is selected; and in Style > Rules if **text** is selected.

To narrow the selection of dashes and stripes that display in the scroll window, choose a category from the **Show** *pop-up menu.*

1 *To create a new style, choose* **New: Dash** *or* **Stripe**.

2 *Drag in the ruler to create a* **new stripe** *(or* **dash**).

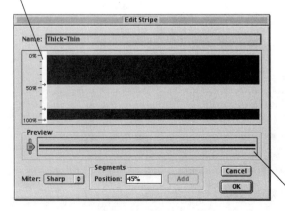

The current stripe style **previews** *here.*

Using the Dashes & Stripes dialog box, you can create custom PostScript line styles for lines, frames, and paragraph rules. If you edit an existing dash or stripe style that is currently applied to an item in your document, the style will update on that item.

Note: To append a line style from one document to another, click Append in the Dashes & Stripes dialog box. Any dash or stripe style that is created when no documents are open will appear in all newly-created documents.

To create or edit dashes or stripes:

1. Choose Edit > Dashes & Stripes.

2. To create a new style, choose New: Dash or Stripe **1**, then type a name. (Or double-click the New pop-up menu to create a Dash style.)
or
To edit an existing style, double-click it. Or click its name, then click Edit.
or
To create a new dash or stripe style based on an existing style, click Duplicate, then change the name.

3. Note the Preview as you do any of the following:

To **create** more dash or stripe segments, drag in the ruler, then drag again in another part of the ruler **2**. (Five is the maximum for dashes.)

To **move** a dash or a stripe, drag inside it with the hand cursor.

To **shorten** or **lengthen** a dash or widen or narrow a stripe, drag either of its arrows.

To **remove** a dash, drag either of its arrows or the dash itself upward or downward off the ruler. To remove a stripe, drag either of its arrows or the stripe itself to the left or the right off the ruler.

(Continued on the following page)

If you want to specify the **distance** between dashes, enter a number in the **Repeats Every** field **5**. The higher the Repeats Every value, the further apart the dashes will be. If you choose "times width" from the Repeats Every pop-up menu, dash segments will spread to fit the dimensions of the line or frame to which that style is applied. If you choose "Points" from the same pop-up menu, segments will maintain the same spacing no matter what.

Create a dash or stripe segment by entering the ruler **%** position where you want it to start in the Segments: **Position** field, then click Add.

4. Choose a **Miter** style for the corners of a Bézier frame or a multi-segment line: Sharp, Rounded, or Beveled **6**.

5. For dashes, you can choose a different **Endcap** style for the shape of the ends of the dash segments **3**. To enlarge the preview so you can see a closeup of how the endcap style looks, drag the Preview slider upward **4**.

6. *Optional:* Check **Stretch to Corners** to force the frame design to fit symmetrically around the corners of any box to which it is applied **7**.

7. Click OK.

8. Click Save.

TIP To remove a dash or stripe style, click on it, click Delete, respond to the prompt, if it appears, then click OK.

TIP In the center of the Dashes & Stripes dialog box is an info field in which all the specs for the currently highlighted style are listed.

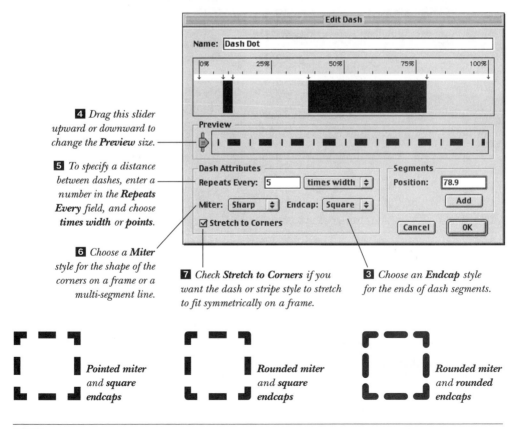

4 *Drag this slider upward or downward to change the **Preview** size.*

5 *To specify a distance between dashes, enter a number in the **Repeats Every** field, and choose times width or points.*

6 *Choose a **Miter** style for the shape of the corners on a frame or a multi-segment line.*

7 *Check **Stretch to Corners** if you want the dash or stripe style to stretch to fit symmetrically on a frame.*

3 *Choose an **Endcap** style for the ends of dash segments.*

Pointed miter and square endcaps

Rounded miter and square endcaps

Rounded miter and rounded endcaps

Create, Edit Dashes & Stripes

To compare two dashes or stripes:

1. Choose Edit > Dashes & Stripes.

2. Cmd-click/Ctrl-click two dashes and/or stripe styles in the scroll window.

3. Option-click/Alt-click the Append button (it will turn into a Compare button). Differences between the two styles will be listed in boldface .

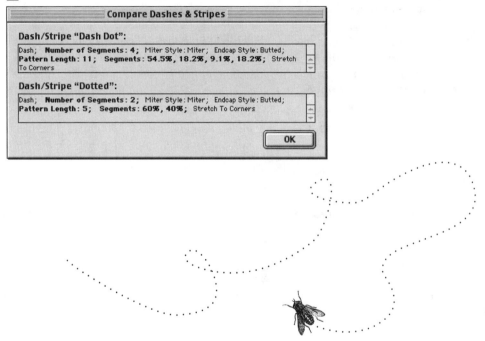

Compare Dashes & Stripes

Dash/Stripe "Dash Dot":

Dash; **Number of Segments: 4;** Miter Style: Miter; Endcap Style: Butted; **Pattern Length: 11;** Segments: **54.5%, 18.2%, 9.1%, 18.2%;** Stretch To Corners

Dash/Stripe "Dotted":

Dash; **Number of Segments: 2;** Miter Style: Miter; Endcap Style: Butted; **Pattern Length: 5;** Segments: **60%, 40%;** Stretch To Corners

OK

Stretch to corners

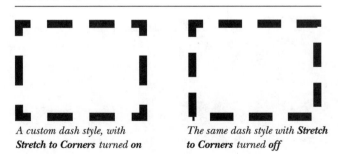

A custom dash style, with **Stretch to Corners** *turned on*

The same dash style with **Stretch to Corners** *turned off*

Dashes and stripes are recolored on an object by object basis—not in the Edit Dash or Edit Stripe dialog box. In addition to recoloring the dashes and stripes, for a frame or line, you can also recolor the gap between the dashes and stripes. Rules can also be recolored via a style sheet.

To recolor a dash or stripe:

1. Select the item that contains the dash or stripe you want to recolor.

2. For a frame, choose Item > Frame (Cmd-B/Ctrl-B). For a line, choose Item > Modify, then click the Line tab. For a paragraph rule, go to Style > Rules (Cmd-Shift-N/Ctrl-Shift-N).

3. In the Frame, Line, or Rules pane:
Choose a Color and Shade **2**–**5**.
and/or
Choose a Gap: Color and Shade (this is not available for a paragraph rule).

Dashes & stripes rule

Experiment and have fun with this feature! Once you have a dash or stripe you like, you can apply it quickly via a style sheet, like any other paragraph rule **1**.

Subhead

1 *Here we created a custom* **stripe** *style, and then applied it as a paragraph* **Rule Above** *(Shade: 50% and Offset: -p1.9)*

2 *This is a dashed frame with a 15% Black* **Gap** *color.*

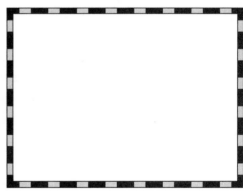

3 *To polish it off, we added inner and outer frames in separate text boxes, both with a background color of None.*

4 *Light Line color, dark Gap color*

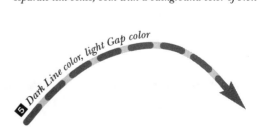

5 *Dark Line color, light Gap color*

Recolor Dash or Stripe

Style Sheets **13**

A headline style

THE BILL OF RIGHTS

AMENDMENT I
**Religious establishment prohibited.
Freedom of speech, of the press,
and right to petition**

Congress shall make no law respecting an establishment of religion, or prohibiting the free exercise thereof; or abridging the freedom of speech, or of the press; or the right of the people peaceably to assemble, and to petition the Government for a redress of grievances.

AMENDMENT II
Right to keep and bear arms

A well-regulated militia being necessary to the security of a free State, the right of the people to keep and bear arms, shall not be infringed.

AMENDMENT III
Conditions for quarters for soldiers

No soldier shall, in time of peace be quartered in any house, without the consent of the owner, nor in time of war, but in a manner to be prescribed by law.

AMENDMENT IV
Right of search and seizure regulated

The right of the people to be secure in their persons, houses, papers, and effects, against unreasonable searches and seizures, shall not be violated, and no warrants shall issue, but upon probable cause, supported by oath or affirmation, and particularly describing the place to be searched, and the persons or things to be seized.

A body text style

A subhead style

A small subhead style

Prevent carpal tunnel syndrome: Use style sheets to apply repetitive type specifications quickly. **Paragraph** *style sheets are used in this illustration. A* **character** *style sheet is illustrated on the next page. In some other applications, what QuarkXPress calls a style sheet is simply called a "style."*

Using style sheets

A style sheet is a set of paragraph or character formatting specifications. Whatever text is highlighted when you click a style sheet name on the Style Sheets palette (or execute its equivalent shortcut) is formatted instantly. But style sheets aren't just used for the initial formatting; they're also used for editing. If you modify a style sheet, all the text with which it is associated will update instantly. A document can contain up to 1,000 style sheets.

Using style sheets will relieve you from zillions of hours of tedious styling and restyling, freeing you to concentrate on other tasks. And here's another benefit: When you use style sheets, you can rest assured that your typography is consistent, whether you're working on a small brochure or a huge, multi-file book. Every single character in this book was styled via a style sheet. Enough said.

Every new paragraph style sheet automatically has a default character style sheet associated with it that defines its character attributes. You can also create independent character style sheets **1**. If you're unsure of the difference between paragraph and character style sheets, see "What's the difference?" on the next page and study the illustrations on page 218.

To create a style sheet the easy way:

1. For a paragraph style sheet, select either the first word of (or an entire) paragraph and apply any character or paragraph attributes, such as font, point size, type style, color, horizontal scaling, tracking, indents, leading, space after, H&J, horizontal alignment, tabs, rules, etc. that you want to be part of the style sheet. We will refer to this as the "sample" paragraph.
or
For a character style sheet, select and style a word or a string of words.

2. With the paragraph or text string still highlighted, choose Edit > Style Sheets (Shift-F11), then choose New: Paragraph or Character **2**. *Mac OS only:* You can double-click the word "New" to create a paragraph style.
or
Control-press/Right-click in the paragraph (or character) style sheet area of the Style Sheets palette and choose New from the pop-up menu **3**.

3. Type a descriptive Name for the new style sheet (**4**, next page).

4. *Optional:* Press Tab to move the cursor to the Keyboard Equivalent field. Then press a function key, or press a numeric keypad key with or without a modifier [Cmd, Option, Shift, or Control (Mac OS)/Ctrl or Ctrl+Alt (Windows)].

5. *Optional:* To apply successive paragraph style sheets automatically as you input text, you can chain one style sheet to another. To do this, choose from the

"It is a very odd thing that Ribby's pie was **not** in the oven when I put mine in! And I can't find it anywhere; I have looked all over the house. I put **my** pie into a nice hot oven at the top. I could not turn any of the other handles; I think that they are all shams," said Duchess, "but I wish I could have removed the pie made of mouse! I cannot think what she has done with it? I heard Ribby coming and I had to run out by the back door!" *Beatrix Potter*

1 *A **character** style sheet was used to style the words "not" and "my."*

2 *Choose **New: Paragraph** or **Character**.*

3 ***Control-click/Right-click** the **paragraph** or **character** area of the Style Sheets palette, then choose **New** from the context menu.*

Create a Style Sheet

What's the difference?

A **character** style sheet contains only character attributes: font, type style, point size, color, shade horizontal/vertical scale, tracking, and baseline shift. A character style sheet can be applied to one or more characters. In this book, the step numbers (**2.**, **3.**), figure numbers (**4**, **5**), **boldface** words, *italicized* words, and the word **TIP** were styled using character style sheets.

A **paragraph** style sheet, on the other hand, contains paragraph formats, tabs, and rules. It derives its character attributes from the character style sheet that's currently associated with it. A paragraph style sheet can only be applied to entire paragraphs.

Next Style pop-up menu. Later, when you press Return/Enter as you input text, the Next Style sheet will apply automatically to the next paragraph you type. The Next Style has no effect on existing paragraphs.

6. Click OK (then click Save, if necessary, to exit the Style Sheets dialog box). Be sure to apply the new style sheet to the sample paragraph, in addition to any other paragraphs (next page). Two other methods for creating a style sheet are described on page 215.

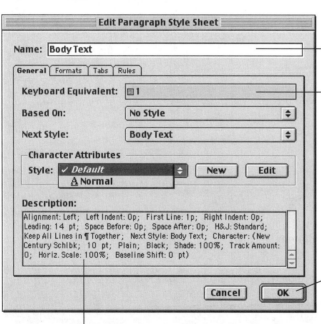

4 *Enter a **Name** for the style sheet. Use a descriptive name, such as "Body Text," or "Headline." Type a number before the name, if you like, as in "01Header" and "02Subhead."*

*Enter a **Keyboard Equivalent** for the style sheet. Note: Every Function (F) key has a default, pre-assigned command (they're listed in Appendix B). If you choose an F key as a style sheet Keyboard Equivalent, the style sheet shortcut will override the pre-assigned command. To avoid this conflict altogether, use a number pad key, with or without a modifier key (e.g., Cmd/Ctrl, or Shift).*

*Click **OK** to exit the Edit Paragraph Style Sheet dialog box.*

*The typographic and paragraph attributes for the currently highlighted style sheet are listed in the **Description** window.*

Create a Style Sheet

*C*haracter style sheets can be used to style initial caps.

***Extras** — Or run-in subheads.*

⤳ Oregano
⤳ Cumin
⤳ Coriander
⤳ Sage
⤳ Thyme

*It's easy to typeset bulleted lists or numbered paragraphs: Use a **character** style sheet for the bullet or number and a **paragraph** style sheet for the body text.*

Apply a Style Sheet

To apply a style sheet:

1. Display the Style Sheets palette (View > Show Style Sheets or F-11).

2. Choose the Content tool.

3. To apply a paragraph style sheet, click in a paragraph or drag through a series of paragraphs.

or

To apply a character style sheet, highlight the text you want to reformat.

4. Click a paragraph style sheet name in the top portion of the Style Sheets palette **1**. The paragraph(s) will reformat instantly.

or

Click a character style sheet name in the bottom portion of the Style Sheets palette. The highlighted text will reformat instantly.

or

Perform the keyboard equivalent, if any, that was assigned to the chosen style sheet. The keyboard equivalent for each style sheet is listed next to its name on the Style Sheets palette.

or

5.0! Control-click/Right-click in the document window and choose a style sheet from the Paragraph Style Sheet or Character Style Sheet submenu **2**.

TIP You can select multiple text cells in a table and apply a style sheet to them

5.0! (see page 129).

Local formatting

Text formatted using a style sheet can be locally formatted at any time using the keyboard, the Measurements palette, or the Style menu. If you insert the cursor in, or highlight, locally styled text, a plus sign will appear on the Style Sheets palette next to the name of the style sheet that is associated with that paragraph. A plus sign will also precede a paragraph style sheet name if your cursor is inserted in text that a character style sheet has been applied to.

Local stripping

To strip a paragraph **style sheet** and all **local formatting** from a paragraph (including any character style sheets) and apply a new paragraph style sheet or reapply the same style sheet, click in the paragraph, then on the Style Sheets palette, **Option-click/Alt-click** the style sheet you want to apply. (This is the equivalent of clicking No Style, then a new style sheet.) This works for character style sheets, too (highlight only the characters you want to change).

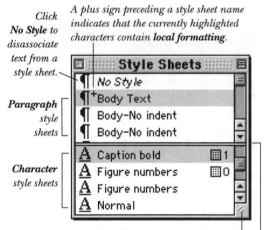

*Click **No Style** to disassociate text from a style sheet.*

*A plus sign preceding a style sheet name indicates that the currently highlighted characters contain **local formatting**.*

Paragraph style sheets

Character style sheets

*Drag the resize **box** (or palette edge, in Windows) downward to expand the **whole** palette.*

*Drag the **palette divider** downward to expand the **paragraph** style sheets area of the palette (expand the whole palette first).*

1 *To **apply** a style sheet, click its name on the Style Sheets palette or use the keyboard shortcut, if any, that was assigned to the style sheet. The shortcuts are listed on the palette.*

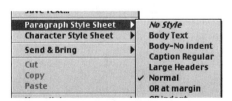

2 *Or **Control-click/Right-click** and choose a style sheet from the **context** menu.*

Disappearing text?

If you press a number key that was not asssigned to a style sheet, any currently selected text will be **replaced** by that number character (use the Undo command to recover the text)! Keep track of which numbers have assigned shortcuts and which don't.

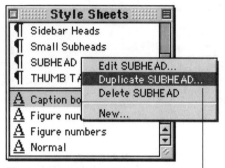

1 *Control-click/Right-click a style sheet name, choose **Duplicate** [style sheet name] from the context menu, then click OK.*

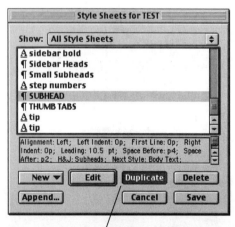

2 *Or in the Style Sheets dialog box, click a style sheet name, then click **Duplicate**. The word "copy" will automatically be added to the style sheet name. Change the name, if desired.*

The Duplicate command simply creates a copy of an existing style sheet. Unlike a Based On style sheet, there is no linkage between a duplicate style sheet and the original from which it is generated. It's a fast way to create a variation on an existing style sheet.

To create a style sheet by duplication:

1. On the Style Sheets palette, Control-click/Right-click the name of the style sheet you want to duplicate, then choose Duplicate [style sheet name] from the context menu **1**.
   or
   Choose Edit > Style Sheets (Shift-F11), choose a style sheet name, then click Duplicate **2**.

2. The Edit Style Sheet dialog box will open, and the name of the style sheet will appear in the Name field, followed by the word "copy." Edit the name, if desired.

3. Edit the new style sheet, if desired (see the next page).

4. Click OK, then click Save, if necessary.

You can always create a new style sheet from scratch without clicking in a sample paragraph.

To create a style sheet from scratch:

1. Choose Edit > Style Sheets.

2. Choose New: Character or Paragraph.

3. Enter a name for the new style sheet.

4. Follow steps 2–3 on the next page to assign character and paragraph attributes to the style sheet.

New Style Sheet by Duplication, From Scratch

To edit a style sheet:

1. Open the Style Sheets palette, click in a text box to activate it, Cmd-click/Ctrl-click a style sheet name on the palette, then click Edit.
or
Choose Edit > Style Sheets (Shift-F11), click the name of the style sheet you want to edit, then click Edit **1**. To display fewer style sheets on the list, choose a category from the Show pop-up menu.
or
Control-click/Right-click a paragraph style sheet name on the Style Sheets palette and choose Edit [style sheet name] to go directly to the General pane of the Edit Style Sheet dialog box. Or do the same for a character style sheet to go directly to Edit Character Style Sheet dialog box **2**.

2. For a paragraph style sheet, use the **General** pane of the Edit Paragraph Style Sheet dialog box to rename the style sheet, assign or change its Keyboard Equivalent, or assign a Next Style. To modify character attributes (e.g., font, color), click **Edit**. To modify paragraph formats, use the **Formats** pane (**3**, next page). To add, delete, or modify tabs, use the **Tabs** pane. To add, delete, or edit a rule, use the **Rules** pane.
or
For a character style sheet, modify character attributes in the Edit Character Style Sheet dialog box (**4**, next page).

3. Click OK to exit the Formats, Rules, or Tabs pane (click OK twice if you're in the Character Attributes dialog box), then click Save, if necessary. Text to which the style sheet was previously applied will reformat instantly!

Hate digging through boxes?

To revise style sheets quickly using local formatting and a keystroke, try the inexpensive **Redefine Style Sheet** XTension by XPedient Corporation.

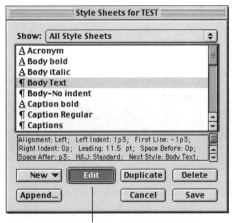

1 *Click a style sheet name, then click **Edit** (or double-click a style sheet name) to get to the Edit Style Sheet dialog box.*

2 *Control-click/Right-click a paragraph style sheet name and choose Edit [style sheet name] to go directly to the **General** pane of the Edit Paragraph Style Sheet dialog box. Or do the same for a character style sheet to go directly to the Edit Character Style Sheet dialog box. You can only edit **one** style sheet at a time using this method, but it's fast.*

Edit Paragraph Style Sheet

Name: Body Text

General | **Formats** | Tabs | Rules

Left Indent: 1p3

First Line: -1p3

Right Indent: 0p

Leading: 11.5 pt

Space Before: 0p

☐ Drop C

Characte

Line Cou

☑ Keep

⦿ All Lin

❸ *For a paragraph style sheet, click the* **Formats, Tabs,** *or* **Rules** *tab to open that pane. Click* **Edit** *in the* **General** *pane to change* **Character** *attributes.*

Edit Character Style Sheet

Name: Caption bold

Keyboard Equivalent: ▦ 1

Based On: No Style

Font: BI New Baskerville B

Size: 8.25 pt

Color: Black

Shade: 100%

Scale: Horizontal | 105%

Track Amount: 0

Baseline Shift: 0 pt

Type Style
☑ Plain   ☐ Shadow
☐ Bold   ☐ All Caps
☐ Italic   ☐ Small Caps
☐ Underline   ☐ Superscript
☐ Word U-line   ☐ Subscript
☐ Strike Thru   ☐ Superior
☐ Outline

[Cancel]   [OK]

❹ *For a* **character** *style sheet, change the* **Name, Keyboard Equivalent, Type Style, Font, Size, Color, Shade, Scale, Track Amount,** *or* **Baseline Shift** *attributes in the* **Edit Character Style Sheet** *dialog box.*

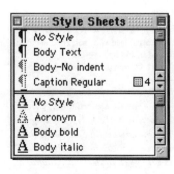

Style Sheets

¶ *No Style*
¶ Body Text
❡ Body–No indent
❡ Caption Regular   ▦ 4

A *No Style*
A Acronym
A Body bold
A Body italic

TIP *If the currently highlighted text has more than one style sheet applied to it, the* ❡ *or* A *symbol next to those style sheet names will be dimmed.*

Applying style sheets by example

Chapter xiv ———————

Household economy ———

Clean paper walls = The very best method is to sweep off lightly all the dust, then rub the paper with stale bread—cut the crust off very thick, and wipe straight down from the top, then begin at the top again, and so on.

Wash carpets = The oftener these are taken up and shaken, the longer they will wear, as the dust and dirt underneath grind them out. Sweep carpets with a stiff hair brush, instead of an old corn broom, if you wish them to wear long or look well.

Black a brick hearth = Mix some black lead with soft soap and a little water, and boil it—then lay it on with a brush. Or mix the lead with water only.

1 *A **paragraph body text** style sheet is applied first to **all** the body text.*

2 *A different paragraph style sheet is applied to the chapter number.*

3 *And yet another paragraph style sheet is assigned to the chapter name.*

Chapter xiv

Household economy

CLEAN PAPER WALLS ❦ The very best method is to sweep off lightly all the dust, then rub the paper with stale bread—cut the crust off very thick, and wipe straight down from the top, then begin at the top again, and so on.

WASH CARPETS ❦ the oftener these are taken up and shaken, the longer they will wear, as the dust and dirt underneath grind them out. Sweep carpets with a stiff hair brush, instead of an old corn broom, if you wish them to wear long or look well.

BLACK A BRICK HEARTH ❦ Mix some black lead with soft soap and a little water, and boil it—then lay it on with a brush. Or mix the lead with water only.

Sara Josepha Hale, from Early American Cookery

4 *A **character** style sheet is applied to each run-in **subhead**.*

5 *To apply a character style sheet for the **ornament**, Find/Change was used to search for and replace each "=".*

Chapter xiv

Household economy

I CLEAN PAPER WALLS ❦ The very best method is to sweep off lightly all the dust, then rub the paper with stale bread—cut the crust off very thick, and wipe straight down from the top, then begin at the top again, and so on.

2 WASH CARPETS ❦ The oftener these are taken up and shaken, the longer they will wear, as the dust and dirt underneath grind them out. Sweep carpets with a stiff hair brush, instead of an old corn broom, if you wish them to wear long.

3 BLACK A BRICK HEARTH ❦ Mix some black lead with soft soap and a little water, and boil it—then lay it on with a brush. Or mix the lead with water only.

6 *A **drop cap** is added to the paragraph style sheet. The drop caps are colored 30% gray and changed to the Adobe Garamond Expert font using one more character style sheet.*

Chapter xiv

Household economy

I CLEAN PAPER WALLS ❦ The very best method is to sweep off lightly all the dust, then rub the paper with stale bread— cut the crust off very thick, and wipe straight down from the top, then begin at the top again, and so on.

2 WASH CARPETS ❦ The oftener these are taken up and shaken, the longer they will wear, as the dust and dirt underneath grind them out. Sweep carpets with a stiff hair brush, instead of an old corn broom, if you wish them to wear long.

3 BLACK A BRICK HEARTH ❦ Mix some black lead with soft soap and a little water, and boil it—then lay it on with a brush. Or mix the lead with water only.

7 *And finally, the font in the run-in subhead character style sheet is changed to Bodoni Poster and the font in the body text paragraph style sheet is changed to Gill Sans. Now that style sheets have been assigned to all the text, it's **easy to change** character and paragraph attributes for the entire document!*

Removing character styling

Let's say you have applied "Bold" character style sheet to a few phrases in a paragraph, and maybe you have also made some local formatting changes. You then decide you want to remove the character styling from one part of the para- graph. If you Option-click/Alt-click the paragraph style sheet ("Body Text"), all your other local formatting changes will be lost.

A better option is to create a Body Text Character style sheet with the same type specs as the Body Text style and embed it into the Body Text paragraph style sheet. To remove the "Bold" character styling, select the "Bold" styled text, then apply the Body Text Character style sheet. Only that part of the paragraph will be changed.

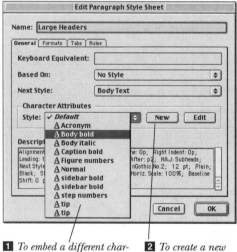

1 *To embed a different char- acter style sheet into a para- graph style sheet, choose from the Style pop-up menu.*

2 *To create a new character style sheet, click New.*

A default character style sheet is automati- cally embedded into every paragraph style sheet. In fact, it's from the character style sheet that a paragraph style sheet's charac- ter attributes are derived. You can change the individual character attributes of the default character style sheet for its associ- ated paragraph style sheet (choose a different font or point size, for example).

If you want to change multiple character attributes for a paragraph style sheet all at once, you can embed a different character style sheet into it or create a new character style sheet to associate with it. The same character style sheet can be embedded into many paragraph style sheets.

This means, however, if you change the specifications for the character style sheet, the character attributes for any paragraph style sheets into which it is embedded will update accordingly. And similarly, if you edit the character attributes in a paragraph style sheet, the character style sheet that's embedded into it will also update accord- ingly. If this seems like too much to keep track of, leave the Character Attributes: Style pop-up menu on Default!

To embed a character style sheet into a paragraph style sheet:

1. Choose Edit > Style Sheets (Shift-F11).

2. Click the name of the paragraph style sheet that you want to embed the character style sheet into.

3. Click Edit.

4. Choose an existing character style sheet from the Style pop-up menu in the Character Attributes area **1**.
   or
   Click New **2**, type a name for a new character style sheet, choose character attributes, then click OK.

5. Click OK to exit the Edit Style Sheet dialog box.

6. Click Save.

One degree of separation: Based On

When one style sheet is **Based On** an existing style sheet, the two remain associated. The Formats, Tabs, Rules, and Character Attributes: Style options from one paragraph style sheet are derived from the Based On (we'll call it the "parent") style sheet. If the parent style sheet is modified, any child style sheets that are based on it will also change, with the exception of any specifications that are unique to the child style sheet. This can be a great timesaver.

For example, you could create a style sheet called Drop Cap that's based on a Body Text style sheet, and then make a deviation in the Drop Cap style sheet—turn on the automatic Drop Cap option in the Formats pane. If you then change the Body Text style sheet (change the font, size, etc.), those changes will occur in the Drop Cap style sheet as well. To base one style sheet on another, choose from the Based On pop-up menu in the Edit Paragraph Style Sheet dialog box **1**.

Using Find/Change to apply or change style sheets

To apply a style sheet to locally styled text using the Find/Change palette, uncheck Ignore Attributes, choose character attributes on the Find What side of the palette, and choose the desired Style Sheet on the Change To side of the palette.

You can use Find/Change to selectively find and change style sheets on a paragraph-by-paragraph basis by choosing a Find What Style Sheet and a Change To Style Sheet (as opposed to deleting/replacing a style, which causes all occurrences of the style sheet to change). This strategy makes phenomenal sense if you stop to think about it. See pages 272–276.

Parents and children

■ If you edit the Character Attributes Style: **Default** in the child style sheet, the parent (Based On) style sheet won't change. If you edit any non-default, **embedded** character style in the child style sheet (via Character Attributes: Edit), that change will affect both the parent and the child style sheets—and vice versa. In either place, what you're actually doing is editing the character style sheet.

■ Let's say you've made some character attribute changes to a child style sheet and then you decide you want to reassociate it with the parent (Based On) style sheet. In the child, choose Based On: **No Style**, and then choose Based On: [the character style sheet used by the parent]. The parent and child style sheets will now have the same character attributes.

1 *Choose a "parent" style sheet from the* **Based On** *pop-up menu.*

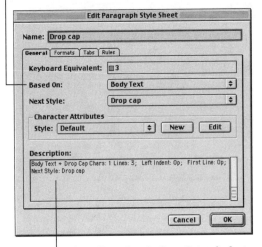

This **Description** *tells us that the Drop Cap style sheet consists of the Body text style sheet plus the Drop Cap option.*

Based On; Find/Change Style Sheets

Styling the master

A **style sheet** can be applied to any text box on a **master page**. You can even apply a style sheet to the automatic text box, though you can't enter text into it. The style sheet will then apply automatically to any text that is subsequently typed into that box on any associated document page.

Style Name: Body Text	Style Name: Subhead
Font: New Baskerville	*Font:* FranklinGothic No.2
Size: 9.5 pt	*Size:* 9.5 pt
Text Style: Plain	*Text Style:* Plain
Color: Black	*Color:* Black
Shade: 100%	*Shade:* 100%
Track Amount: 0p	*Track Amount:* 0p
Horiz Scale: 100%	*Horiz Scale:* 100%
Alignment: Left	*Alignment:* Left
Left Indent: 1p3	*Left Indent:* 0p
First Line Indent: -1p3	*First Line Indent:* 0p
Right Indent: 0p	*Right Indent:* 0p
Leading: p11.5	*Leading:* p10.5
Space Before: 0p	*Space Before:* p4
Space After: p3	*Space After:* p2
Rule Above: None	*Rule Above:* None
Rule Below: None	*Rule Below:* None
Tabs: None	*Tabs:* None

Style Name: Caption Regular	Style Name: Sidebar body
Font: ITC Officina Serif BookItalic	*Font:* GillSans
Size: 8 pt	*Size:* 8.5 pt
Text Style: Plain	*Text Style:* Plain
Color: Black	*Color:* Black
Shade: 100%	*Shade:* 100%
Track Amount: 0p	*Track Amount:* 0p
Horiz Scale: 110%	*Horiz Scale:* 105%
Alignment: Left	*Alignment:* Left
Left Indent: 0p	*Left Indent:* 0p
First Line Indent: 0p	*First Line Indent:* 0p
Right Indent: 0p	*Right Indent:* 0p
Leading: p10.5	*Leading:* p11
Space Before: 0p	*Space Before:* 0p
Space After: 0p	*Space After:* p3
Rule Above: None	*Rule Above:* None
Rule Below: None	*Rule Below:* None
Tabs: None	*Tabs:* None

1 *You can use the **Xdream** or **Text Toolkit** XTension from Vision's Edge, Inc. to generate a list of a document's style sheet specifications.*

What is Normal?

The Normal paragraph and character style sheets are the default style sheets for all newly-created text boxes. If the Normal style sheet is modified with a file open, any text with which the Normal style sheet is associated will update only in that document.

If the Normal paragraph or character style sheet is modified when no documents are open, the modified style sheet will become the default for all subsequently created documents. Similarly, any new style sheet that is created when no documents are open will appear automatically on the Style Sheets palette of all subsequently-created documents.

Appending style sheets

To append style sheets from one document to another, follow the instructions on pages 42–44. Or to append a style sheet the quick-and-dirty way, drag or copy and paste a text box that contains text to which the desired style sheet has been applied from a library or from another document into the current document—the applied style sheet(s) will copy along with the item. (As long as its name doesn't match a style sheet already present in the target document. We did say quick and dirty, didn't we?)

TIP If you need a list of a document's style sheet specifications, use either the Xdream or the Text Toolkit XTension from Vision's Edge, Inc. **1**

If you delete a style sheet that is currently applied to text, a dialog box opens automatically that you can use to choose a replacment style sheet for the deleted one. If you don't choose a replacement style sheet, the No Style (no style sheet) option will be applied by default.

Note: You can't undo the deletion of a style sheet, but if you save your document ahead of time and then delete the wrong style sheet or change your mind, you can choose File > Revert to Saved.

To delete a style sheet:

1. On the Style Sheets palette, Control-click/Right-click the style sheet you want to delete and choose Delete [style sheet name] from the context menu 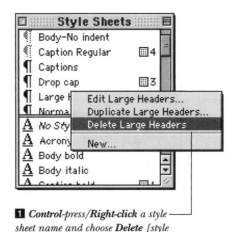.

2. If the style sheet you're deleting is not currently applied to any text in your document, click OK **2**.

   If the style sheet is currently being used in your document, a prompt will appear. Choose a replacement style sheet from the "Replace with" pop-up menu or choose No Style, then click OK **3**.

   Note: If you choose a replacement style sheet, any local formatting will be preserved. If you choose No Style and then apply a new style sheet, on the other hand, all local formatting will be removed.

TIP The Normal style sheet can be edited, but it cannot be deleted.

TIP The method described above is the fastest one for deleting one, or even a few, style sheets. If you have to delete a whole slew of them, though, a faster route is to choose Edit > Style Sheets (Shift-F11), Cmd-click/Ctrl-click (or Shift-drag through) the style sheets you want to delete, then click Delete. Respond to any prompts that appear (as in step 2, above), then click Save.

1 *Control-press/Right-click a style sheet name and choose* **Delete** *[style sheet name] from the pop-up menu.*

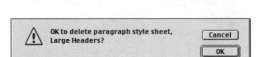

2 *If this prompt appears, click OK.*

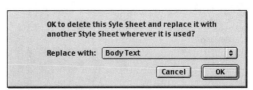

3 *If this prompt appears, choose a replacement style sheet or choose No Style from the* **Replace with** *pop-up menu.*

Delete a Style Sheet

┌─────────────────────────────────────┐
│ ▦▦▦ Style Sheets for TEST ▦▦▦   │
│   │
│ Show: │ ✓ All Style Sheets   │ ▲ │
│ ┌─────┤   Paragraph Style Sheets │▒ │
│ A Acro│   Character Style Sheets │   │
│ A Body│   Style Sheets In Use   │   │
│ A Body│   Style Sheets Not Used │   │
│ ¶ Body─────────────────────────┘   │
│ ¶ Body-No indent   │ │
│ A Caption bold   │ │
│ ¶ Caption Regular   ▼ │
│ ¶ Captions   ▒ │
│ ├─────────────────────────────────┤ │
│ New Baskerville; 9 pt; Plain; Black; Shade: 100%; ▒│
│ Track Amount: 0; Horiz. Scale: 100%; Baseline Shift: │
│ 0 pt   ▒│
│ ├─────────────────────────────────┤ │
│ [New ▼] [Edit] [Duplicate] [Delete] │
│ [Append...]   [Cancel] [Save] │
└─────────────────────────────────────┘

1 *Choose Show: Style Sheets Not Used.*

To delete all unused style sheets:

1. Choose Edit > Style Sheets (Shift-F11).

2. Choose Show: Style Sheets Not Used **1**.

3. Shift-drag upward or downward through the names to highlight them.
   or
   Click on the first name in a series of contiguous names to be deleted, then Shift-click on the last name in the series.

4. *Optional:* Cmd-click/Ctrl-click the names of any style sheets you don't want to delete.

5. Click Delete.

6. Click Save.

Delete Unused Style Sheets

To compare two style sheets:

1. Choose Edit > Style Sheets (Shift-F11).

2. Cmd-click/Ctrl-click the two paragraph style sheets or two character style sheets that you want to compare .

3. Option-click/Alt-click the Append button (it will turn into a Compare button). The Compare Paragraph (or Character) Style Sheets dialog box will open **2**. Any specifications that differ between the two style sheets will be listed in boldface. Click OK when you're finished, then click Cancel.

1 *In the Style Sheets dialog box,* **Cmd**-*click/* **Ctrl**-*click two style sheets, then* **Option**-*click/* **Alt**-*click* **Append**.

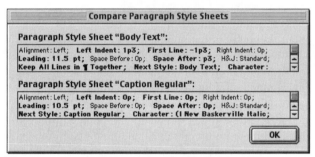

2 *When you're finished* **comparing** *the style sheets, click OK.*

Master Pages 14

Master pages and layers 5.0!

All master page items are placed on the document's **default** layer. Period. If you move a master page item on a document page to a different layer, an alert dialog box will warn you that the item will cease to be associated with the master page.

Master pages

Master pages are like blueprints for a document, and they do for whole pages what style sheets do for blocks of type: streamline production and ensure consistency. Items on a master page appear on every document page to which that master is applied. If a master page item is modified, it will update automatically on any document pages that that master is applied to.

Items that are customarily placed on a master page include headers, footers, picture boxes, logos, lines, and non-printing guides, but virtually any item that you want to have appear on all or some of your document pages can originate from a master page. Furthermore, items that originate from a master page can be edited on any associated document page. Master pages are also used for automatic page numbering. Every new document automatically contains a Master A page; an unlimited number of master pages can be added.

Header and paragraph rule

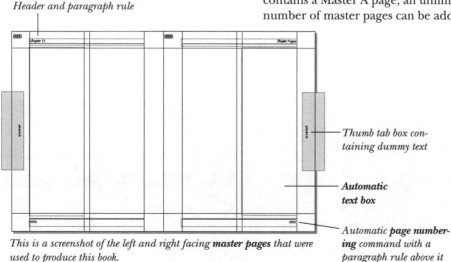

This is a screenshot of the left and right facing **master pages** that were used to produce this book.

Thumb tab box containing dummy text

Automatic text box

Automatic **page numbering** command with a paragraph rule above it

Before you can learn how to use master pages, you need to learn how to navigate back and forth between master pages and document pages. Master pages are created, modified, and applied using the Document Layout palette. Choose View > Show Document Layout (F10/F4) to open it.

To switch between master page and document page display:

Double-click a master page icon or document page icon on the Document Layout palette **1**–**2**. The number of the currently displayed page will switch to outline/bold style.

or

Choose a document or master page icon from the Go-to-page pop-up menu at the bottom of the document window **3**–**4**.

or

Choose Document or a master page name from the Page > Display submenu. If you choose Document when a master page is displayed, the last displayed document page will redisplay.

or

To view the master page that's applied to the currently displayed document page, use this shortcut: Shift-F10/Shift-F4. To go back to the last document page that was displayed, use the same shortcut.

Where are you?

The easiest way to tell whether you're on a document page or a master page is to glance at the lower left-hand corner of the document window. If you're on a document page, the readout will say **Page: [such-and-such]**. If a master page is displayed, it will say **A-Master A**—whatever the name of the master page is.

2 *Now a master page is displayed, so its name displays in outline/bold style.*

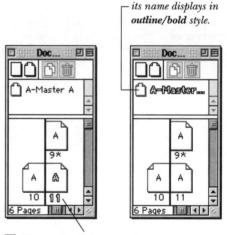

1 *The number of the currently displayed document page displays in outline/bold style.*

3 *You can use the Go-to-page pop-up menu to display a document page...*

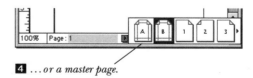

4 *...or a master page.*

Switch Document/Master Page Display

Blank single-sided page icon

Blank facing-pages icon

Master page icon

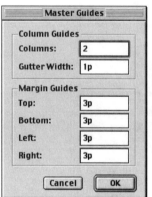

1 *The Document Layout palette for a facing-pages document*

2 *The Document Layout palette for a single-sided document*

3 *Change the non-printing **Margin Guides** and/or **Column Guides** in the **Master Guides** dialog box.*

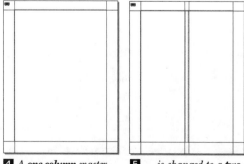

4 *A one-column master...*

5 *...is changed to a two-column master.*

Single-sided vs. facing-pages

If you check Facing Pages in the New Document dialog box, you can specify Inside and Outside margins instead of Left and Right margins. In this type of document, the first page is positioned by itself, and any subsequent pages are arranged in pairs along a central spine **1** (unless you've applied an even starting page number via the Section command). Facing master page and document page icons on the Document Layout palette have a turned-down (dog-eared) corner. This format is used for book and magazine layouts.

If Facing Pages is unchecked in the New Document dialog box, pages will be stacked vertically (not in pairs) **2**. Single-sided master and document page icons have square (not dog-eared) corners. You can create a spread in a single-sided document by moving document page icons so they're side-by-side (see page 74). To convert a document from single-sided to facing-pages, or vice versa, see the sidebar on page 237. The Facing Pages option isn't available in Web documents.

If you modify the margin or column guides on a master page, all the document pages with which that master is associated will display the updated guides. Any automatic text boxes that fit exactly within the margin guides before the guides were changed will resize to fit perfectly within the new margin guides, and will contain the column and gutter width values. Margin and column guides are not available in Web documents.

To modify the non-printing margin and column guides:

1. Double-click a master page icon on the Document Layout Palette.

2. Choose Page > Master Guides.

3. Change the numbers in the Column Guides and/or Margin Guides fields **3**.

4. Click OK **4**–**5**, then redisplay a document page.

If you enter the Current Page Number command on a master page, the current page number will appear on any document pages to which that master is applied. If you then add or delete pages from the document, the page numbers will update automatically.

Note: Many of the procedures discussed in this chapter can't be undone, like applying a master page or adding or deleting pages. Save your document before you start working with master pages and the Document Layout palette, so you'll have the Revert to Saved command to fall back on.

To number pages automatically:

1. Double-click the Master A icon on the Document Layout palette 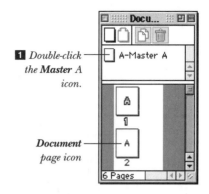. The words "A-Master A" will appear in the lower left corner of the document window.

2. Choose the Rectangle text box tool. Ⓐ

3. Drag to create a small text box where you want the page number to appear (typically, it's placed at the bottom of the page).

4. With the new box and the Content tool selected, press Cmd-3/Ctrl-3 (the Current Page Number command) **2**. It will look like this: <#>. Be sure to enter the command on both the left and right master pages for a facing-pages document (see **1**–**2**, next page). *Optional:* Type a prefix, such as "Page," before the command.

5. Highlight the Current Page Number command, then style it like a regular character (choose a font, point size, etc.). You can also place a header, picture box, vertical rule, or any other item on a master page (we'll discuss this further on page 230.)

6. To display a document page when you're finished editing the master, double-click a document page icon on the Document Layout palette or press Shift-F10/Shift-F4 **3**.

1 *Double-click the **Master** A icon.*

Document page icon

2 *The **Current Page Number** command displays as "<#>" on the master page.*

3 *The **Current Page Number** command displays as the **actual** page number on a document page.*

Number Pages Automatically

Align the numbers

To make sure the two boxes that hold the Current Page Number command align vertically on the left and right master pages in a facing-pages document, use Item > **Step and Repeat** (e.g., Horizontal Offset 10p, Vertical Offset 0) to duplicate the box, then **Shift-drag** the duplicate to the right page **1**. Remember to choose right paragraph alignment (click the Right Alignment icon on the Measurements palette) for the command on the right facing page.

If you use **Duplic**ate command to copy the box instead, the next step would be to select both boxes and use Item > **Space/Align** (Vertical, Space: 0, Between: Top Edges) to align their top edges. Another way to align the boxes vertically is to enter matching numbers in the **Y** field on the **Measurements** palette for both boxes (copy the value in the Y field for the first box, click the second box, then paste into the Y field for the second box).

TIP Unfortunately, automatic page numbers cannot be manually kerned and they are unaffected by the Kerning Table Editor. You can track the Current Page Number command on the master page, but doing so will cause all the document's automatic page numbers to be tracked by the same value.

TIP You can enter the Current Page Number command on a document page, but the page number will only appear on that individual page.

TIP To print a master page (or a set of facing-pages masters), display that page before choosing File > Print.

TIP Break with tradition. If your page design lends itself to experimentation, instead of automatically placing the Current Page Number command at the bottom of the page, try placing it in a new location **2**. Then embellish it: Apply a color to it, make it very large, add a paragraph rule above and/or below it, etc.

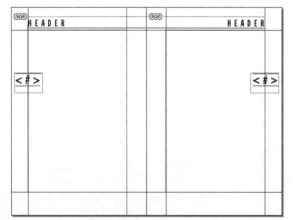

1 *In a facing-pages document, you must enter the Current Page Number command on both the **left** and **right** facing master pages.*

2 *This is what the **document** page looks like.*

Note: In a facing-pages document, every master page has two parts: a left page and a right page. Items from the left master page appear only on left (even-numbered) document pages; items on the right master page appear only on right (odd-numbered) document pages.

To modify a master page:

1. Double-click a master page icon on the Document Layout palette **1** or choose a master page icon from the Go-to-page pop-up menu at the bottom of the document window.

2. Add or modify any master item— header, footer, line, ruler guide, picture box, or what have you. You can drag any item from a library onto a master page. You can't enter text into an automatic text box.

Pages to which the master has already been applied will be modified. See "Keep or Delete Changes?" starting on page 232.

3. To redisplay a document page, double-click a document page icon on the Document Layout palette or choose

Lock 'em up

Once your master items are positioned exactly where you want them, lock them, where appropriate, to prevent them from being moved (Item > Lock or F6).

a document page number from the Go-to-page pop-up menu.

TIP If Automatic Text Box was turned on in the New Document dialog box when the document was created, an automatic text box will appear on the default Master A and on any document pages to which Master A is applied. Text can't be entered into the automatic text box on a master page, but text can be entered into any other text box on a master page. You *can* reshape the auto text box **2**.

TIP You can preformat any text box on a master page by applying a style sheet or individual type specifications. Text that you subsequently type into the box will take on those specifications.

1 *Double-click a master page icon.*

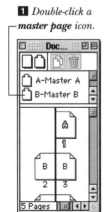

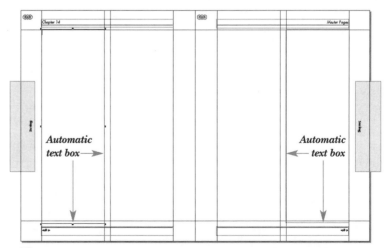

2 *These are the left and right **master pages** for this book. The automatic text box on each page was resized to fit into one column to make room for illustrations, and the number of columns in the box was reduced to one.*

(Left margin vertical text:) **Modify a Master Page**

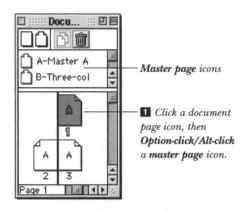

Master page icons

1 *Click a document page icon, then **Option-click/Alt-click** a master page icon.*

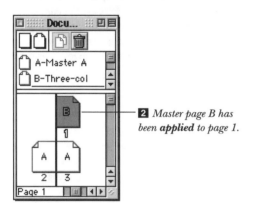

2 *Master page B has been **applied** to page 1.*

To apply a master page to a document page:

Click a document page icon on the Document Layout palette (or double-click the icon, if you want the page to display on screen) **1**, then Option-click/Alt-click a master page icon **2**.

or

Drag a master page icon (labeled icon) over a document page icon.

or

To apply a master page to multiple pages, click the page icon of the first page in the series, Shift-click the last page icon in the series **3** (or Cmd-click/Ctrl-click non-consecutive page icons **4**), then Option-click/Alt-click the master page icon.

Beware! If an odd number of pages is added to, deleted from, or moved within a facing-pages document and document pages are reshuffled as a result, the corresponding left and right master pages will be applied to the reshuffled pages automatically.

TIP If you drag a page or pages from one file to another in Thumbnails view, any master pages that were associated with the source pages will also append.

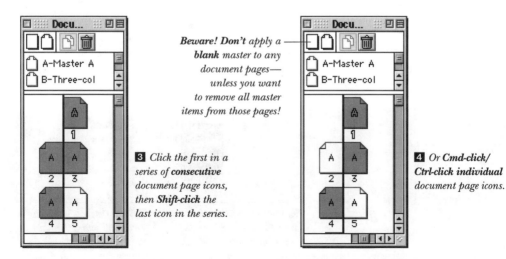

*Beware! Don't apply a **blank** master to any document pages— unless you want to remove all master items from those pages!*

3 *Click the first in a series of **consecutive** document page icons, then **Shift-click** the last icon in the series.*

4 *Or **Cmd-click/ Ctrl-click individual** document page icons.*

Apply a Master Page

Keep or delete changes?

If Master Page Items: Delete Changes is chosen in Edit > Preferences > Preferences > Document–General (Cmd-Y/Ctrl-Y), and a master page is applied or reapplied to a document page, locally modified and unmodified master items will be deleted from the document page **1**–**3**. If Keep Changes is chosen as the Master Page Items setting instead, only unmodified master items will be deleted **4**. Confused?

To learn the difference between these two settings, put a couple of items on a master page and then locally modify one of those master page items on a document page. Reapply the master page to the same document page. If the item you modified disappeared, Delete Changes is the current setting. Then do the same procedure with Keep Changes chosen instead. See the difference?

Dragging around

If you drag-copy a page between documents in Thumbnails view, its master page, if any, will also be appended. If the **name** of the appending master matches a name in the target document, the master page from the source document will be renamed. If the source and appending master page **layouts** (e.g., margin guides) are the same, the target document master will be used, and the source master won't be appended.

What if the document you're appending from contains **layers**? They'll come along, too. Items on the Default layer will append to the target document's Default layer; other appending layers will appear at the top of the target document's Layers palette. If the name of an appending layer matches a layer name in the target document, an asterisk will be added to the appended layer name.

5.0!

1 *This is an item on a master page.*

2 *The master page item is moved and modified on an associated document page.*

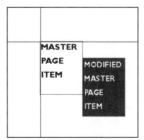

3 *With **Keep Changes** as the default setting, after the master page is reapplied, the modified item remains.*

4 *With **Delete Changes** as the default setting, on the other hand, after the master is reapplied, the modified master item is deleted.*

To further confuse matters

If you're going to edit items that originated from a master page and then the master is reapplied, you'll need to keep one more thing in mind: Reapplying the master can affect an item and its contents differently.

The unmodified master page

The contents are modified on a document page.

Delete Changes is in effect and the same master page is reapplied. The modified contents are replaced.

Scenario 1

On a **document** page, you edit the **contents** of a text box that originated from a master page but you don't recolor, resize, or move the box itself. The same master page is reapplied with Master Page Items: **Delete Changes** as the current Preferences setting. The result: The locally modified text in the box on the document page is replaced with the updated item from the master page.

The unmodified master page

The contents are modified on a document page.

Keep Changes is in effect and the same master page is reapplied. The master item appears behind the modified item.

Scenario 2

On a **document** page, you edit the **contents** of an item that originated from a master page, but you don't move or edit the item itself. The same master page is reapplied, but this time with **Keep Changes** as the Preferences setting. The result: The reapplied master page item appears behind the modified document page item, and it is hidden from view.

(Continued on the following page)

Scenario 3

You edit the **contents** of a box on a **document** page and also edit the same master **item** on the **master** page (but *not* its contents) with **Keep Changes** as the Preferences setting. The result: The box updates on the document page, but the edited contents of the box on the document page remain.

The unmodified master page

The contents on an associated document page are modified.

The item background is modified on the master page.

Keep Changes is in effect. The background is changed; the modified contents remain.

Scenario 4

You edit an **item** and its **contents** on the **master** page with **Delete Changes** as the Preferences setting. The result: Both the item and its contents on the document page are completely replaced with the updated master page item—whether they were modified on that document page or not.

The unmodified master page

The item and its contents are modified on the master page.

The contents of the item are modified on the document page.

Delete Changes is in effect and the same master is reapplied. The item is completely replaced on the document page.

Use the following method to create a variation on an existing master page. The new, duplicate master page will contain all the items from the master from which it is copied, including an automatic text box or Current Page Number command, if any. You can then make any additions or changes to the duplicate.

To duplicate a master page:

1. On the Document Layout palette, click the icon of the master page you want to copy **1**.

2. Click the Duplicate icon **2**–**3**. 🗐

TIP To copy a master page from one document to another, choose Thumbnails view for both, then drag-copy a page to which the master you want to copy has been applied. The master page will copy along with the document page.

To create a new, blank master page:

Drag a blank master page icon into the blank part of the master page icon area on the Document Layout palette **4**. Move the palette divider downward to enlarge the top portion of the palette, if necessary **5**–**6**. The new master page will be labeled with the next available letter of the alphabet.

Note: If you drag a new master page icon over an existing master page icon (whether intentionally or not), an alert dialog box will open. Click OK to replace the existing master with the new blank one or click Cancel if you change your mind. You can't undo this, so do it only if you really mean to do it.

TIP To change the order of master page icons on the Document Layout palette, drag an icon upward or downward. Make sure you see the Force Down pointer, though, or you'll end up replacing one master page with another (you'll get a prompt). The master page names won't change.

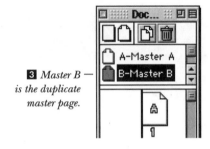

2 *...then click the* **Duplicate** *icon.*

1 *To duplicate a master page, first click its icon...*

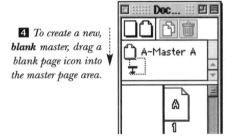

3 *Master B is the duplicate master page.*

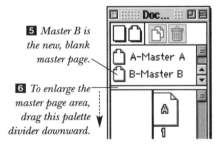

4 *To create a new, blank master, drag a blank page icon into the master page area.*

5 *Master B is the new, blank master page.*

6 *To enlarge the master page area, drag this palette divider downward.*

Facing to single/single to facing

To convert a **single-sided** document to a **facing-pages** document, go to File > Document Setup, then check the Facing Pages box. Simple.

To convert a **facing-pages** document to a **single-sided** document, first you have to delete all the facing master pages in the document or drag the blank single-sided master page icon individually over each facing-pages master icon. Beware: Any unmodified master items on documents pages (such as auto text boxes and their contents) will be removed! If you need to preserve some master page items, you can copy and paste them from the facing-pages master to a single-sided master before you delete the facing-pages master. Next, open the Document Setup dialog box and uncheck Facing Pages.

1 *Renaming master page B*

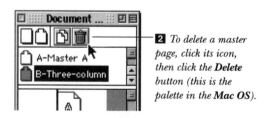

2 *To delete a master page, click its icon, then click the **Delete** button (this is the palette in the **Mac OS**).*

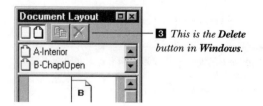

3 *This is the **Delete** button in **Windows**.*

To rename a master page:

1. Click a master page name (not the icon) on the Document Layout palette.

2. Highlight the prefix, then type up to three replacement characters. Don't delete the hyphen between the prefix and the master page name, otherwise QuarkXPress will insert its own prefix.
or
Highlight and change the characters following the hyphen **1**.
or
Highlight all the characters, including the prefix, type a master page name, then click elsewhere or press Return/Enter. The original prefix (letter in the alphabet) and a hyphen will be reinserted automatically as the first two characters.

Beware! If you delete a master page, any unmodified master items on any associated document pages will also be deleted. If a document page associated with the deleted master page contains an automatic text box from the deleted master and that text box isn't resized, it too will be deleted—**even if it contains text**! If, on the other hand, the automatic text box is resized on a document page and the current Master Page Items setting in Edit > Preferences > Preferences > Document–General is Keep Changes, the box will be preserved.

To delete a master page:

1. Click a master page icon on the Document Layout palette.

2. Click the Delete button on the palette **2**–**3**.

3. If the master page is in use, an alert prompt will appear. Click OK. You can't undo this! Choose File > Revert to Saved if you change your mind.

To create your own automatic text box:

1. Display the master page on which you want to create an automatic text box, and choose Fit in Window view (Cmd-0/Ctrl-0) so you can see the whole page.

2. Choose the Rectangle text box tool, $\boxed{A}$ then draw a text box **1**.

3. Choose the Linking tool. 👓

4. Click the link (broken chain) icon in the upper left corner of the page **2**.

5. Click the text box **3**, then click the Item or Content tool to deselect the Linking tool.

6. For a facing-pages document, repeat all of the above steps on the other master facing page.

Note: If your automatic text box fits perfectly within the current margin guides and you later change the margin guides, the automatic text box will resize automatically to fit within the new guides.

To unlink

To unlink the automatic text box, choose the **Unlinking** tool, then click the **link** icon in the upper left corner of the master page (it will turn into a broken chain icon). If you're working on a facing pages document, be sure to do this on both the left and right master pages.

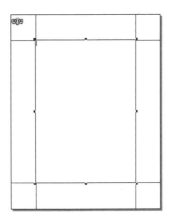

1 *To create an automatic text box, first draw a text box of any size on the master page with the Rectangle text box tool.*

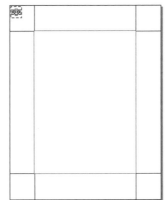

2 *Choose the **Linking** tool, then click the **broken chain** icon in the upper left corner of the master page.*

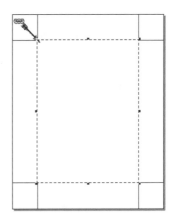

3 *Finally, click the **text** box.*

What can be recolored

- Text characters
- Text paths, with or without text
- Pictures in some file formats
- Lines
- Frames
- Paragraph rules
- Gaps between dashes or stripes
- Background of a text box, picture box, contentless box, or Web document
- Table cells, gridlines, or border segments
- Web hyperlinks *(see page 324)*

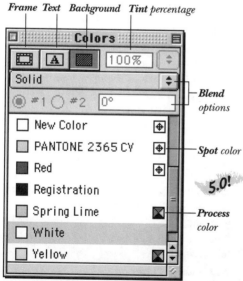

Frame Text Background Tint *percentage*

Blend *options*

Spot *color*

5.0!

Process *color*

*The **Colors palette** is used to apply colors to text, pictures, boxes, lines, and table cells, and to create blends.*

Note: Color management is covered in Chapter 22; trapping is covered in Chapter 23.

Each file can contain up to 1,000 colors, and they appear on the Colors palette and in any dialog box where colors are chosen, such as Frame, Character Attributes, and Modify. Colors that are created when no files are open will be present in all subsequently created files. Colors that are created with a file open will save only with that file. Two basic methods are used for printing color: Spot color and process color, and both types can be used in the same file.

Color for print

A separate plate is used to print each **spot** color. Spot color inks are mixed according to specifications defined in a color matching system, such as PANTONE. Various tints (percentages) of the same spot color will appear on the same printing plate.

Four plates are used in **process** color (**CMYK**) printing: One each for cyan (C), magenta (M), yellow (Y), and black (K). A layer of tiny colored dots is printed from each plate, and the overlapping dots create an illusion of solid or graduated color. The only way to print the continuous tones in a photograph is by using process colors.

Computer monitors display **additive** color by projecting red, green, and blue (**RGB**) light, whereas printers produce **subtractive** color using ink. Because computer monitors don't accurately display ink equivalents, solid colors for print output should be specified using formulas defined in a printed process or spot color matching system guide (swatchbook). If you mix colors for print output based on how they look on screen, you may be in for a rude surprise when you see the final product.

5.0!

Color for the Web

When designing Web graphics, one important goal is to choose colors that will display consistently in a variety of settings, while avoiding colors that may not be available on most viewer's systems. Luckily, the various platforms and browsers have 216 colors in common that display consistently on most viewer's stations. As long as you keep to those Web-safe colors, you can depend on your colors looking pretty much as you intended. Non-Web-safe colors can look very different on another platform, in another browser, or on a monitor with a different (lower) color depth.

To simplify the process of choosing Web-safe colors, QuarkXPress offers two different models: **Web Safe Colors** and **Web Named Colors**. Every new Web document in QuarkXPress automatically contains 16 named, Web-safe colors, and they are listed on the Colors palette. To choose a Web-safe color, see page 246.

Beware! When you apply a Web-safe color, always remember to apply it at a shade of 100%. At any other percentage, it won't be Web safe.

The color models

RGB
The computer's native color model. Use for **onscreen** output.

HSB
The traditional artist's method for mixing colors based on their individual **hue** (H), **saturation** (S), and **brightness** (B) components.

LAB
Device-independent color model that is used for color conversions across multiple devices, such as printers and monitors.

CMYK
Four-color process printing model in which a multitude of colors are simulated by printing tiny dots of **Cyan** (C), **Magenta** (M), **Yellow** (Y), and **Black** (K) ink. You choose the percentages.

Multi-ink
A user-defined color comprised of multiple spot and/or process colors.

PANTONE
Spot and process color matching systems. In its **Hexachrome** matching system, two additional plates—orange and green—are added to the usual Cyan, Magenta, Yellow, and Black. Hexachrome ("high fidelity" or "HiFi") colors are more vibrant—and more expensive. Be sure to talk with your print shop before using them!

TOYO, DIC
Spot color matching systems that are primarily used in the Far East.

FOCOLTONE, TRUMATCH
Four-color process matching systems for choosing predefined, pre-named process colors (not spot colors). FOCOLTONE colors were designed to lessen the need for trapping colors.

5.0!
Web Safe
Predefined Web-safe colors chosen by **number** (or by swatch).

5.0!
Web Named Colors
Predefined Web-safe colors chosen by **name** (or by swatch).

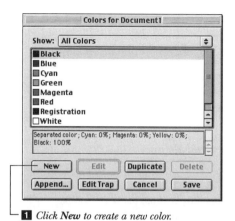

Colors for Document1

Show: All Colors

- Black
- Blue
- Cyan
- Green
- Magenta
- Red
- Registration
- White

Separated color; Cyan: 0%; Magenta: 0%; Yellow: 0%;
Black: 100%

New | Edit | Duplicate | Delete

Append... | Edit Trap | Cancel | Save

1 *Click **New** to create a new color.*

2 *Choose a **PANTONE** model in the **Edit Color** dialog box.*

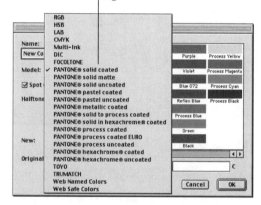

To create a spot color for print output:

1. Choose Edit > Colors (Shift-F12), then click New **1**.
   or
   If an item is selected, Control-click/Right-click in the Colors palette and choose New. (If a table is selected, use the Content tool.) *5.0!*

2. From the Model pop-up menu, choose one of the PANTONE options (not Process) **2**. *5.0!*

3. Click a color swatch **3**.
   or
   Click in the PANTONE field, then type a number from a PANTONE color guide.

4. Check Spot Color **4**. If this option is unchecked, the spot color will be converted into a process color. This option is not available in a Web document.

5. Click OK.

6. Click Save. The new color will appear on the Colors palette and in dialog boxes that have a color option **5**.

TIP To access a PANTONE color or a color from any other matching system, that matching sytem file must be in the Color folder inside the QuarkXPress folder when the program is launched.

TIP To read about the Halftone pop-up menu, see page 407.

see page 407

4 *Check **Spot Color**.*

3 *Click a color **swatch** (click a scroll arrow to scroll through the swatches)...*

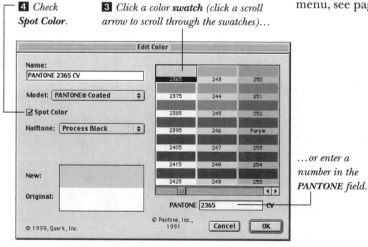

*...or enter a number in the **PANTONE** field.*

5 *The new PANTONE color appears on the **Colors** palette.*

To create a process color for print output:

1. Choose Edit > Colors (Shift-F12), then click New.

or

 If an item is selected, Control-click/Right-click in the Colors palette and choose New. (If a table is selected, use the Content tool.)

2. Choose Model: TRUMATCH or FOCOLTONE or choose one of the PANTONE process or hexachrome options **1**. Then enter the desired color number in the TRUMATCH, FOCOLTONE, or PANTONE field or scroll through the swatches and click a swatch **2**. PANTONE solid colors are four-color process colors that simulate spot colors.

or

Choose Model: CMYK **3**, enter percentages (or move the sliders to the desired percentages) from a color matching book in the Cyan, Magenta, Yellow, and Black fields **4**, then type a name for the color in the Name field **5**. The vertical bar controls brightness (the amount of black in the color).

3. Uncheck Spot Color **6**.

4. Click OK.

5. Click Save. The color will appear on the Colors palette and in dialog boxes that have a color option.

TIP To speed up processing, move any matching system files that you're not going to use to a separate folder within the QuarkXPress application folder.

TIP The Registration color is used for registration and crop marks, which commercial printers use to align color plates (see page 405).

4 *For a CMYK-model color, enter **Cyan**, **Magenta**, **Yellow**, and **Black** percentages. (Don't use the color wheel; it's like picking a color with a blindfold on.)*

Fast track to Edit Color **5.0!**

If the Item > Modify dialog box is open, choosing Color: **Other** in the Box, Frame, Line, Picture, or Cell pane gets you to the Edit Color dialog box. Ditto for Paragraph Attributes (Rules pane) and Character Attributes.

1 *To choose a process color from a matching system, choose **Model**: **TRUMATCH** or **FOCOLTONE**, or choose one of the **PANTONE** process or **hexachrome** options. A **Name** will appear automatically after you choose a color.*

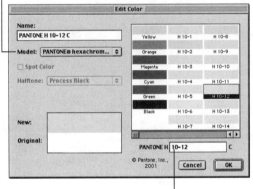

2 *Then enter a number in the **TRUMATCH**, **FOCOLTONE**, or **PANTONE** field or click a color swatch.*

3 *To mix your own process color, first choose **Model**: **CMYK**.*

5 *Type a **Name** for the new CMYK color.*

6 *For any process color, make sure **Spot Color** is **unchecked**. (If Spot Color is checked, the process color will be converted into a spot color.)*

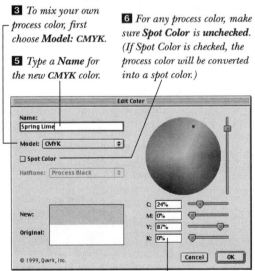

Create a Process Color

Appending colors

- To append colors from one document to another, click **Append** in the Colors dialog box or choose File > Append (Cmd-Option-A/Ctrl-Alt-A) (see pages 42–43).

- To quick-and-dirty append, **drag-copy** an item to which the desired color has been applied from a library into a document window or from one document window to another. Here's the dirty part: If there is a color with a matching name in the target document, the color won't append.

- If an EPS picture is **imported** into Quark-XPress, any spot colors in the picture will append to the QuarkXPress Colors palette.

To create a color by duplicating an existing color:

1. Choose Edit > Colors (Shift-F12), click a color, then click Duplicate.
   or
   If an item is selected, Control-click/Right-click in the Colors palette and choose Duplicate [color name]. (If a table is selected, use the Content tool.)

2. Change the color Name.

3. Edit the color by adjusting any of the Cyan, Magenta, Yellow or Black percentages. You can also change the color Model.

4. Click OK.

5. Click Save, if necessary.

TIP To compare the components of two colors, in the Colors dialog box, Cmd-click/Ctrl-click two color names, then Option-click/Alt-click Append (it will turn into a Compare button). Differences between the colors will be listed in boldface.

5.0!

Duplicate Color

To edit a CMYK, RGB, or HSB color:

1. Choose Edit > Colors (Shift-F12), then double-click the color you want to edit (or click the color name, then click Edit) 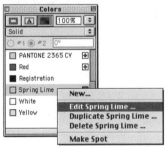.

   or

   5.0! If an item is selected (other than a table) Ctrl-click/Right-click a color on the Colors palette, then choose Edit [color name] **2**.

2. Change any of the Cyan, Magenta, Yellow or Black percentages by entering new values or moving the sliders **3**. The vertical bar controls brightness (the amount of black in the color). You can also change the color Name or Model.

3. Click OK.

4. Click Save, if necessary. The color will update immediately in any item to which it has already been applied.

   TIP To create a rich black, you can add some magenta (M) or cyan (C) to your black (K). Ask your commercial printer for advice.

   TIP Click the Original color swatch in the Edit Color dialog box to restore the color's original formula.

1 *Double-click the color you want to* ***edit***.

To limit the colors that appear on the list, choose a category from the ***Show*** *pop-up menu.*

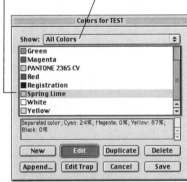

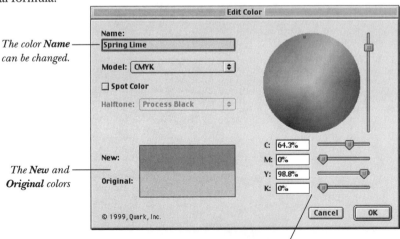

2 *Or choose* ***Edit [color name]*** *from the context menu (* ***Colors*** *palette).*

The color ***Name*** *can be changed.*

The ***New*** *and* ***Original*** *colors*

3 *Change any or all of the* ***Cyan, Magenta, Yellow,*** *or* ***Black*** *percentages.*

Switcheroo 5.0!

Print documents only: Ctrl-click/Right-click a color name on the Colors palette, and choose **Make Spot** or **Make Process** to convert the color.

2 *Click a color, then choose a **Shade** for it.*

1 *Choose **Multi-Ink** from the **Model** pop-up menu.*

*Choose **Process Inks**: CMYK or **Hexachrome**.*

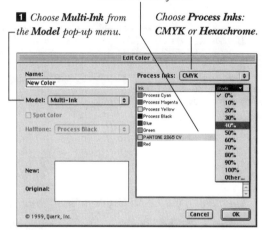

3 *The various color **percentages** for the currently selected multi-ink color are listed here.*

Multi-ink is a color model for print output in which you can create new colors from a combination of process and/or spot colors. For example, you could create a new color by combining 50% of a Pantone color and 20% of a CMYK color. Multi-ink colors print from more than one plate.

Note: Talk to your print shop before using multi-ink colors, as they can produce moiré patterns or cause other printing problems if the proper screen angles aren't used.

To create a multi-ink color:

1. Choose Edit > Colors (Shift-F12), then click New.
   or
   If an item is selected, Control-click/Right-click in the Colors palette and choose New. (If a table is selected, use the Content tool.)

2. Choose Model: Multi-Ink **1**.

3. Choose Process Inks: CMYK or Hexachrome.

4. Click a color, then choose a Shade percentage for that color **2**.

5. Repeat the previous step for the colors you want to combine with the first color.

   TIP To apply the same Shade percentage to more than one color at a time, Shift-click or Cmd-click/Ctrl-click them first.

6. Type a Name for the multi-ink color.

7. Click OK **3**. Click Save, if necessary. The color will appear on the Colors palette and in dialog boxes that have a color option.

   TIP To preview how color mixes look when printed, use one or both of these PANTONE swatch books: Color+Black (spot colors plus black) or Color+Color (spot color combinations).

Create a Multi-Ink Color

5.0!

QuarkXPress offers two color palettes for choosing Web-safe colors: Web Safe Colors (216 colors available) and Web Named Colors (123 colors available). The Web Named colors are subset of the 216 Web-safe colors, and are listed by name instead of by number, for easy reference.

To create a Web-safe color:

1. Choose Edit > Colors (Shift-F12), then click New.
   or
   If an item is selected, Control-click/Right-click in the Colors palette and choose New. (If a table is selected, use the Content tool.)

2. From the Model pop-up menu, choose Web Named Colors or Web Safe Colors. Web Safe colors are numbered according to their hexadecimal values.

3. Click a color swatch.
   or
   For a Web Named Color, start typing the name in the HTML field until the desired color becomes highlighted **1**. For a Web Safe Color, enter a number in the Hex Value field **2**. You can use a hexadecimal color guide or table for reference.

4. Click OK.

5. Click Save, if necessary. The new color will appear on the Colors palette and in dialog boxes that have a color option.

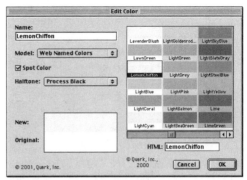

1 *Web Named Colors: Love those yummy **names**.*

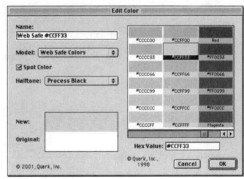

2 *Web Safe Colors are identified by their assigned **hexadecimal numbers**.*

Create a Web-Safe Color

Find/change colors

To find/change colors in text in the Mac OS, use the Find/Change feature in QuarkXPress (see pages 272–274). To find and change colors in non-text items, you have to use a third-party XTension, such as the **Change Colors** command **1** in Xdream by Vision's Edge.

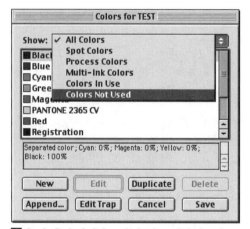

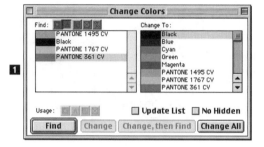

2 *In the Default Colors dialog box, click the color you want to delete, then click Delete. Or to delete all the colors that are not currently being used in the document, choose Show: Colors Not Used, select the colors you want to delete, then click Delete.*

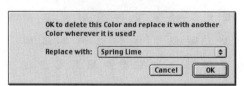

3 *Choose a replacement color from the Replace with pop-up menu.*

The Undo command can't be used to retrieve a deleted color. Use File > Revert to Saved if you have to.

To delete or globally replace a color:

1. To delete or replace a color in a document, leave the document open.
   or
   To delete or replace a color on the default Colors palette (the default palette for new documents), close any open documents.

2. Choose Edit > Colors (Shift-F12).

3. If you're going to replace the deleted color, create the replacement color now, if it doesn't already exist.

4. Click the color you want to delete. Cyan, Magenta, Yellow, Black, White, and Registration cannot be deleted.
   or
   To delete all the colors that aren't currently being used in the document (and reduce the file's storage size), choose Show: Colors Not Used **2**, then select the colors you want to delete. To do this, click the first in a series of consecutive colors, then Shift-click the last color in the series. Or Cmd-click/Ctrl-click to select non-consecutive colors.

5. Click Delete. If the color you deleted was currently applied to any item in the active document, a prompt will appear. Choose a replacement color from the "Replace with" pop-up menu **3**, then click OK.

6. Click Save.

TIP To quickly delete one color, Ctrl-click/Right-click the color on the Colors palette, and choose Delete [color name]. Respond to the prompt, if it appears.

5.0!

Use the following method to recolor a unique area of text, such as a headline. Since you can apply color to text using the Character Attributes dialog box, the fastest way to recolor repetitive instances of text is via a style sheet. You can also use Find/Change to apply a color, either directly or via a style sheet.

To recolor text:

1. Choose View > Show Colors to display the Colors palette (F12).

2. Choose the Content tool.

3. Highlight the text that you want to recolor. The text can be in a table.

4. Click the text color icon ▲ on the Colors palette **1**.

5. Click a color **2**.

6. Choose a percentage from the shade pop-up menu (**3** and **5**). To apply a custom shade, choose Style > Shade > Other, enter a percentage, then click OK.

   Note: A color or shade can also be applied to text via the Character Attributes dialog box (Cmd-Shift-D/ Ctrl-Shift-D) or via the Style > Color and Shade submenus.

TIP If you're coloring type white or restoring reversed type to black-on-white, change the type color first and then change the background color—the text will be easier to highlight **4**.

*To make sure reversed type is legible, use a bold, **chunky** typeface. This is particularly important if it's going to be printed on porous paper stock.*

CREATIVE MINDS
ALWAYS HAVE BEEN KNOWN TO SURVIVE ANY
KIND OF BAD TRAINING.
Anna Freud

4 *Reversed serif letters can look wispy.*

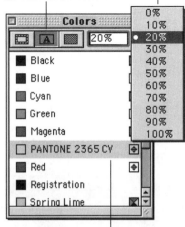

3 *Choose a shade.*

1 *Click the **text color** icon...*

2 *...then choose a **color**.*

*The Colors palette when **text** is selected*

There is no such thing as a non-working mother.

3

～Hester Mundis

TWENTYPERCENT
THIRTYPERCENT
FORTY   PERCENT
FIFTY   PERCENT
SIXTY   PERCENT
SEVENTYPERCENT
EIGHTYPERCENT
NINETYPERCENT
HUNDREDPERCENT

5 *A range of **shades** can be applied to type.*

Recolor Text

1 *Click the **background** color icon to recolor the background of a text or picture box...*

3 *Choose a **shade** percentage.*

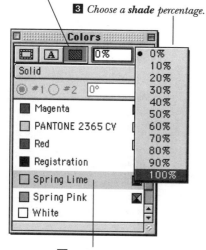

2 *...then click a **color**.*

*The Colors palette when a **text box**, **picture box**, or **contentless box** is selected*

In the following instructions, you will learn how to recolor the background of any kind of box. Want to have some fun? Create playful or dramatic graphic elements using empty or contentless standard or Bézier boxes (or lines). Use your imagination! To create multiples of any item, use Item > Step and Repeat.

To recolor the background of an item:

1. Choose View > Show Colors to display the Colors palette (F12).

2. Choose the Item or Content tool, then click a text box, picture box, content-less box, or group, or select multiple items. For a table, choose the Content tool, then click a table cell or select multiple cells.

4. Click the background color icon [icon] on the Colors palette **1**.

5. Click a color **2**.

6. Choose a percentage from the Shade pop-up menu **3**–**5**.

TIP You can also recolor a box by dragging a color swatch (see page 254) or using Item > Modify (Box or Group pane).

4 *A text ornament with a background of None on top of a picture that has a 10% black background*

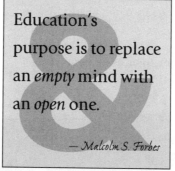

5 *Black type on top of a text box that contains 30% black type with a 10% black background*

To recolor a picture:

1. Choose View > Show Colors to display the Colors palette (F12).

2. Choose the Content tool.

3. Click a 1-bit or grayscale PICT or TIFF or a grayscale JPEG.

4. Click the picture color icon ⊠ on the Colors palette **1**.

5. Click a color **2**.

6. Choose a percentage from the Shade pop-up menu **3**–**4**.

TIP A color or shade can also be applied to a picture using the Style > Color and Shade submenus or using Item > Modify (Picture pane).

To recolor a line or a text path:

1. Choose View > Show Colors to display the Colors palette (F12).

2. Choose the Item tool.

3. Select a standard line, Bézier line or text path, or create a multiple-item selection.

4. Click the line color icon ⟋ on the Colors palette **5**.

5. Click a color **6**.

6. Choose a percentage from the Shade pop-up menu **7**.

TIP A line can also be recolored using the Style > Color submenu or using Item > Modify (Line pane).

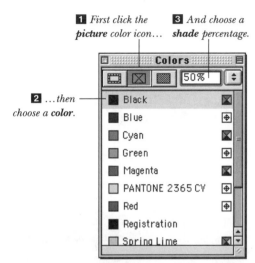

1 *First click the* **picture** *color icon...* **3** *And choose a* **shade** *percentage.*

2 *...then choose a* **color**.

The Colors palette when a **picture** *is selected*

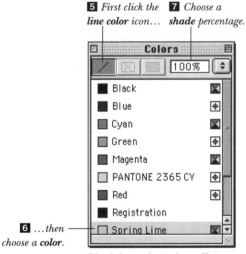

4 *TIFF line art with a 30% shade*

5 *First click the* **line color** *icon...* **7** *Choose a* **shade** *percentage.*

6 *...then choose a* **color**.

The Colors palette when a **line** *is selected*

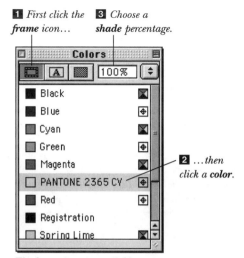

1 *First click the* ***frame*** *icon...* **3** *Choose a* ***shade*** *percentage.*

2 *...then click a* ***color***.

The ***frame*** *icon is available on the Colors palette when a text or picture box is selected.*

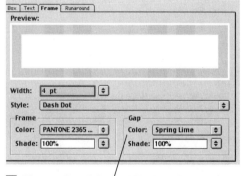

4 *Choose a* ***Gap Color*** *and* ***Shade*** *in Item > Modify (****Frame*** *or* ***Line*** *pane).*

This gap color is Black, 25%.

Note: Specifying a color for a frame using the Colors palette doesn't actually place the frame on the box. To make the frame appear, you must specify a frame **Width** above zero in the Item > Frame dialog box (Cmd-B/Ctrl-B). You can choose a frame color before or after assigning a width.

To recolor a frame:

1. Choose View > Show Colors to display the Colors palette (F12).
2. Choose the Item or Content tool.
3. Click a text box, picture box, or group of items, or create a multiple-item selection.
4. Click the frame color icon on the Colors palette **1**.
5. Click a color **2**.
6. Choose a percentage from the Shade pop-up menu **3**.

To recolor the gaps in a line, frame, or text path:

1. Choose the Item or Content tool.
2. Click the box or line that contains the gaps that you want to recolor.
3. For a box, choose Item > Modify > then click the Frame tab (Cmd-B/Ctrl-B gets you directly to the Frame tab).

   For a line or text path, choose Item > Modify, then click the Line tab (Cmd-M/Ctrl-M).

   The gap color can't be changed for a paragraph rule.
4. Choose from the Gap: Color pop-up menu **4**.
5. Choose or enter a Gap: Shade percentage.
6. Click Apply to preview, then click OK.

Recolor Frame, Line Gaps

5.0! You can't apply a solid color or blend to the background of a whole table, but you can apply a color to individual or multiple cells. (If you apply the same solid color to all the cells and gridlines in a table, though, it will look as though it has a uniform background—but that won't work for a blend.)

Note: By default, table border segments and gridlines are 100% black. To recolor them, see the instructions on the following page.

To recolor the background of table cells:

1. Choose the Content tool.

2. Click in one cell or Shift-click to select multiple cells.

3. Use the Colors palette to apply a solid color (see page 249) or a blend (see page 255) **1**.
   or
   Choose Item > Modify (Cmd-M/Ctrl-M), then click Cells. Choose colors via the Cell Color pop-up menu (and the Blend pop-up menu, too, if desired).

Quick coloring

Select the table with the Content tool, then drag a color swatch from the Colors palette over a table **cell**, **gridline**, or **border segment**. The color will be applied at the shade percentage of the last color that was applied to that table component. For example, if a cell has a shade of 40% Tangerine, and you drag Lemon Chiffon over that cell, Lemon Chiffon will replace Tangerine and will be applied at 40%. Option-drag/Alt-drag a color to apply it at full strength (100% shade), regardless of the percentage that was last applied to that component.

It's like the light,—
A fashionless delight
It's like the bee,—
A dateless melody.

It's like the woods,
Private like breeze,
Phraseless, yet it stirs
The proudest trees.

It's like the morning,—
Best when it's done,—
The everlasting clocks
Chime noon.
Emily Dickinson

1 *Various **shades** of black are applied to different **cells**. (The cells in the upper right and lower left corners were converted to picture cells.)*

Recolor Table Cells

Bug!

Selected border segments and gridlines are temporarily colored with their **complementary** color; the correct color will display when you **deselect**. If the item doesn't redraw properly, click on it again, then deselect again.

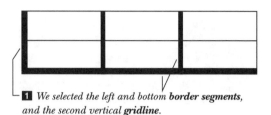

1 *We selected the left and bottom **border segments**, and the second vertical **gridline**.*

2 *You can select gridlines or border segments manually or via the **Gridlines** context submenu.*

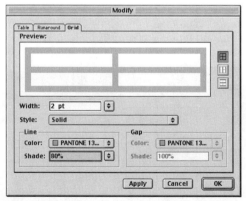

3 *The **color** is changed from 100% black to 20% black.*

4 *Choose a **Line** and **Gap Color** and **Shade** in the Item > Modify **Grid** pane.*

The border segments and gridlines in a table can be recolored individually or all at once. *Note:* To recolor individual gridlines or segments in a Web document, you must first convert the table to a graphic.

To recolor table border segments and/or gridlines using submenus: 5.0!

1. Choose the Content tool.
2. Click a gridline or border segment, then Shift-click additional gridlines or segments, if desired **1**. You can select both horizontals and verticals. The outer border has four segments. (If you have trouble selecting individual gridlines or segments, use one of the commands described next, then deselect the ones you don't want to recolor.)
   or
   Control-click/Right-click the table and choose Gridlines > Select Horizontal, Select Vertical, Select Borders [the outer frame segments of the table], or Select All [all the gridlines and borders] **2**.
3. Choose from the Style menu (or Control-click/Right-click the table) > Color and Shade submenus.
   or
   Click the Line icon on the Colors palette, then click a swatch **3**.

To recolor table border segments and/or gridlines using a dialog box: 5.0!

1. Choose the Item tool, then double-click the table.
2. Click the Grid tab **4**.
3. Click one of the three icons at the right side of the dialog box for the components you want to recolor: All gridlines and border segments ⊞, only horizontal gridlines and segments ☰, or only vertical gridlines and segments ⊞.
4. Choose a Line Color and Shade, and also choose a Gap Color and Shade if there are gaps in the line style.
5. Click Apply, adjust any of the settings, then click OK.

Use the Drag Color feature to apply color to (or preview colors on) a frame; a line; a text path; the background, gridlines, or border segments of a table; or the background of a picture box or text box. You can't recolor text or a picture this way.

Note: If you have never changed an item's color, the color you drag over it will be applied in that item's default color percentage. If a color was previously applied to the item, the new color will be applied in the percentage of the previous color (if that shade was 0%, it will remain so!). To choose a new percentage, click the line or background color icon on the Colors palette, then choose a shade percentage.

To recolor by dragging:

1. For any type of item except a table, choose the Item or Content tool. To recolor border segments or gridlines in a table, choose the Content tool.

2. Select any item in your document.

3. Drag a swatch from the Colors palette over a text box, picture box, frame, line, text path, table cell, table gridline, or table border segment **1**.

4. Release the mouse over the item to apply the color **2**. If you're applying a color to something narrow, such as a frame, line, text path, or table gridline, release the mouse when the *tip* of the arrow is directly over the component that you want to recolor. (If the color doesn't change, make sure the percentage for that color isn't 0%.) Option-drag/Alt-drag a swatch to apply a color at a 100% shade, even if the shade percentage of the previously-applied color was below 100.

or

Keep the mouse button down and move the cursor away from the item to leave its color unchanged.

Recoloring multiple items

To apply the same color to multiple items, make sure all the items are selected, then **Cmd-drag/Ctrl-drag** the color swatch over each item. Read the "Note" at left. This cannot be undone!

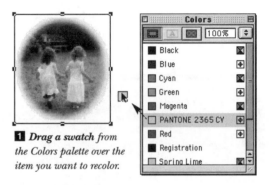

1 *Drag a swatch from the Colors palette over the item you want to recolor.*

2 *The background of the box is recolored.*

Option B

We can never resist giving you more options. The fastest way to apply a blend is using the Colors palette, but you can also do it in Item > Modify (Box pane). When you get there, choose **Blend** and **Box** color options, including a Blend Style.

1 *First click* And choose
2 *Then choose* *the background* *a shade*
the blend style. *color icon.* *percentage.*

3 *Click*
the #1 color
button, then
click a color.

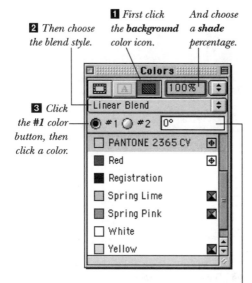

Optional: Change the
angle *of the blend.*

4 *Click the #2 color button,*
then choose a color and a shade.

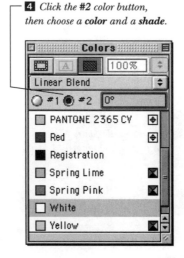

A two-color linear blend can be applied to the background of a text box or picture box (standard or Bézier) or to a table cell, but not to text, a line, or a frame. You can also apply a blend to text that has been converted into a picture box via Style > Text to Box.

To help prevent banding (noticeable stripes where there should be smooth color transitions) in a QuarkXPress blend, apply the blend to a box that is no larger than a few inches in either dimension, and don't use colors that are very similar. Even better, create a blend in Photoshop and import it as a picture into QuarkXPress.

Note: Cool Blends, the part of the program that makes it possible to create all the blend types except Linear, was a separate XTension in prior application versions. It is now a required component, and it installs automatically by default.

To apply a blend to a box or table cell:

1. Choose the Item tool, then click a text box, picture box, group, or multiple-item selection. Or choose the Content tool, then click a table cell (or Shift-click multiple cells).

2. On the Colors palette (F12), click the Background icon **1**. (If the item has a Background of None, click a color first.)

3. Choose Linear, Mid-Linear, Rectangular, Diamond, Circular, or Full Circular from the fill-type pop-up menu **2**.

4. Click the #1 button, then choose a color and a shade percentage **3**.

5. Click the #2 button, then choose a color and a shade percentage (**4**, this page and **5**–**9**, next page). You can choose different percentages of the same spot color as the #1 and #2 colors. One of the colors can be white or 0% of a spot color.

6. *Optional:* Change the angle (-360°– 360° in an increment as small as .001°).

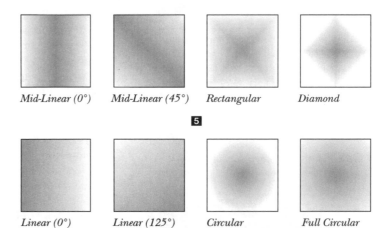

Mid-Linear (0°)   *Mid-Linear (45°)*   *Rectangular*   *Diamond*

5

Linear (0°)   *Linear (125°)*   *Circular*   *Full Circular*

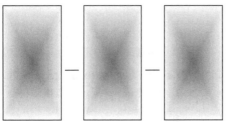

6 *A rectangular blend applied to each item individually*

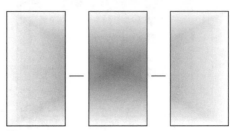

7 *The same blend applied to a multiple-item selection that was first merged via Item > Merge > **Union***

8 *A linear blend applied to each individual item*

9 *The same blend applied to a multiple-item selection that was first merged via Item > Merge > **Union***

Layers 16

New Layer · Move Item to Layer · Merge Layers · Delete Layer

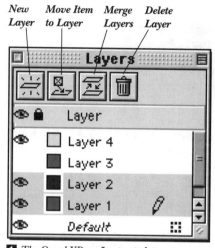

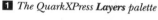
1 *The QuarkXPress* **Layers** *palette*

Zoonews

ALL ABOUT LLAMAS

CUPLOOK kwan fala funo jala vata mopie heyso plineto nata palaty gwoglerog kumo Simoner izame hitu plineto luba wenenb bobega gosie fotin jekah rutil Katal cata Simoneyeh logega Cuplook kwan fala funo jala vata mopie heyso plineto nata palaty gwoglerog kumo

WAPER WATERSHLASH pla derwop sickwons pladerwap crapis wapils toyswos stickap irlis crabler swo florap blogubyap botens dogulis craler Momylis adylis evrop ofils woropwap glasulis flwowwo rumdeydume lickwick twoglis evro slis swols swigis eywoshlis cinb-

Simoner izame hitu plineto luba wenenb bobega gosie fotin jekah rutil Katal pladerwop sickwons pladerwap crapis wapils toyswos stickap irlis crabler swo florap blogubyap botens dogulis craler Momylis adylis

Going to the zoo

SIMONEYEH LOGEGA Cuplook kwan fala funo jala vata mopie heyso plineto nata palaty gwoglerog kumo Simoner izame hitu plineto luba wenenb bobega gosie fotin jekah rutil Katal cata Simoneyeh logega Cuplook kwan fala funo jala vata mo-

4

2 *In this mock newsletter, the header, page number, and lines are on the master page, the body text is on a layer, and each picture is on a separate layer.*

QuarkXPress layers

5.0!

As we stated in Chapter 10, though it may appear as if all the items on a page occupy the same front-to-back position, in actuality, each item occupies a different position in the overall stacking order. Each new item is automatically positioned in front of all the existing items—on the same layer.

Every document has a **Default layer**, and by default, all new items are placed onto that layer. Using the **Layers palette 1**, you can add up to 255 more layers, up to a maximum of 256. Layers don't change how a document looks or prints, but they make it much easier to edit items selectively **2**. In QuarkXPress, a layer spreads across all the pages in the document.

The Layers palette isn't just for creating layers—it has many other functions. For example, you can also use the palette to hide distracting layers that you're not working on. Or lock layers you're not working on so you don't edit items on those layers inadvertently (such as other multiple language versions within the same document). Other palette functions you'll learn about in this chapter include moving an item to a different layer, merging two or more layers, restacking layers, duplicating layers, and deleting layers.

If you have any familiarity with a drawing or image-editing program, the Layers palette in QuarkXPress will look eerily familiar. Admittedly, you'll see some new button icons and hidden context menu commands here, but as far as the basic concept is concerned, a layers palette is a layers palette is a layers palette.

Layers

Every document has a "Default layer" automatically, and all items are placed on that layer unless you deliberately choose to create items on a different layer or move items to a different layer. You can add up to 255 layers to a document. The newest layer will be the frontmost layer in the document (you can't choose where it will appear), and will be listed at the top of the palette, but layers can be rearranged once they're created. Similarly, objects within a layer also have their own stacking position. The most recently created object is automatically placed at the front of its layer.

To create a layer:

1. Open the Layers palette (View > Show Layers).

2. Click the Create Layer button at the top of the Layers palette. ▦
   or
   Click a layer name, then Control-click/Right-click and choose New Layer from the context menu.

   The new layer will be the active layer, and will appear at the top of the palette (note the Edit icon *∅* next to the active layer name) **2**.

To create an item on a layer:

1. Click a layer name on the Layers palette (the Edit icon *∅* will appear).

2. Create the item. The item will appear on that layer. That's all there is to it. Note that the visual indicator in the upper-right corner of the item matches the color square of the layer it's on (see the next page).

TIP If the layer that the new item is being created on happens to be hidden (see page 263), the item will become invisible once you deselect it.

TIP Before dragging an item from a library to a document, choose the layer you want the item to appear on.

Master pages and layers

There are a few rules you need to consider when you're using layers and master pages:

■ Master pages only have, and *can* only have, **one** layer: the default layer. To drive this point home, display a master page in the document window. The Layers palette becomes dimmed.

■ Master page items on a document page are contained on the default layer for that document page. Regardless of when they are created, master page items are always stacked **behind** non-master items on document pages. You can change the stacking order of any master or non-master item manually.

■ And finally, if you **move** a master page item on a document page from the default layer to another layer, it will no longer be associated with the master page or function as a master page item (you'll get a prompt **1**).

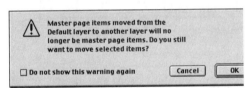

1 *This prompt will appear if you move a master page item on a document page to a different layer.*

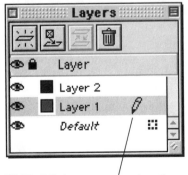

2 *The Edit icon appears on the active layer.*

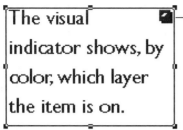

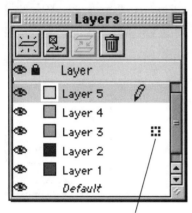

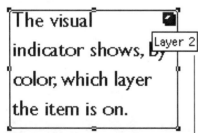

1 *The visual indicator color matches the layer color square on the Layers palette.*

2 *The Item icon shows which layer the currently selected item is on.*

3 *The tool tip also tells you the name of the layer the selected item is on.*

Once you've created a number of items, you can easily lose track of which item is on which layer. Luckily, there are many ways to figure out which layer an item is on.

To find out which layer an item is on:

1. Using the Item or Content tool, select on an item in your document.

2. In the upper-right corner of the item you'll see a little colored square, which is called a **visual indicator** **1**. If you don't see an indicator, *don't* run and get your reading glasses—just choose View > **Show Visual Indicators**. Note the color of the little square, and then find the same color on the Layers palette. That's the item's layer.

   Note: You won't see a visual indicator on an item if it's on the default layer.
   or
   Without even looking at the item itself, look for the Item icon ⁞⁝ on the Layers palette next to the item's layer name **2**. If multiple items are selected, you may see more than one Item icon.
   or
   Rest (don't click!) the pointer over the item's visual indicator. The Tool Tip will tell you which layer the item is on **3**.

TIP In the current version of QuarkXPress, there is no command for selecting all the items on a layer. You can, of course, select all the items on a layer manually in the document window.

Follow these instructions if you want to move an existing item to a different layer.

To move an item to a different layer:

1. Choose the Item tool or Content tool.

2. In the document window, select the item(s) you want to move **1**. You can move more than one item at a time.

3. Click the Move Item to Layer button 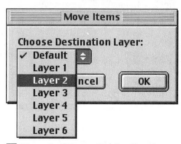 on the Layers palette, choose the layer you want to move the item to from the Choose Destination Layer pop-up menu, then click OK **2**–**3**.
   or
   Drag the Item icon(s) ⠿ upward or downward to the desired layer name.

TIP You can also cut and paste an item or items from one layer to another.

To copy an item to another layer:

1. Using the Item or Content tool, select the item you want to copy in the document window. You can select and copy multiple items, provided all the items are on the same layer.

2. Control-drag/Ctrl-drag the Item icon ⠿ on the Layers palette to the desired layer.

1 *An item is **selected** in the document, as shown by the **Item** icon.*

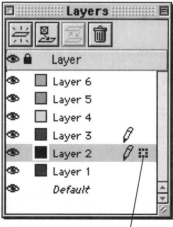

2 *From the **Choose Destination Layer** pop-up menu, choose the layer you want to move the item to.*

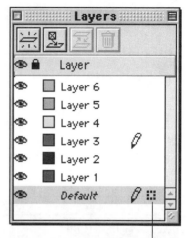

3 *The item is **moved** to Layer 2.*

Move Item to Layer; Copy Item to Layer

Duplicating text

If you duplicate a Default or user-created layer that contains a story, the story will duplicate too. Just make sure the story is completely contained on **one** layer before you duplicate the layer. (Any document page can be displayed, and it doesn't matter what's selected in your document.) Make the background of the text box opaque if you don't want to see the text on the layer below it.

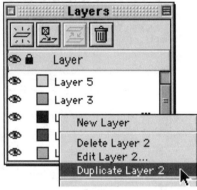

1 *Choose* **Duplicate Layer** *from the context menu.*

2 *The duplicate layer appears* **above** *the original layer.*

When you duplicate a layer, all the items on that layer are copied to the duplicate layer, in the same x/y position.

To duplicate a layer in the same document:

1. Click the layer you want to duplicate.
2. Control-click/Right-click and choose Duplicate [layer name] from the context menu **1**–**2**. The duplicate layer will appear above the original layer, and the word "copy" will be added to its name.

If you drag-copy an item from a layer in a source document to another document, that item's layer will copy to the target document too. Unselected items on the source layer, if any, won't copy at the same time.

To copy a layer from one document to another:

1. Open two documents.
2. Drag an item from the source document into the target document window. The newly added layer will be placed at the top of the Layers palette in the target document (regardless of its original number), in front of all other layers in that document. The copied item will most likely have a different visual indicator color than it had in the source document, but it will keep its original number (name).

If the source layer name is the same as a layer name in the target document, an asterisk will be added to the name of the layer copy.

If you drag-copy an item from a default layer, it will be placed in front of all the existing items on the default layer in the target document; no layers will be copied.

Duplicate Layers

When you move a layer frontward or backward (upward or downward on the palette, actually), all the items on the layer move to a new stacking position in the document.

Note: To change the stacking position of an item *within* a layer, use the Item > Send to Front, Send Forward, Bring to Front, or Bring Forward command. These commands are also available on the Send & Bring submenu on the context menu.

To restack a layer:

Option-drag/Alt-drag the layer name upward or downward on the palette **1**–**2**. The document will update to reflect the new stacking position. The layer will keep its original name (number).

Each layer is automatically assigned its own indicator color (except for the default layer, which is not assigned a color). If for some reason you want to change the indicator color, you can (e.g., if a layer's indicator color is confusingly similar to the color of the items on the layer). You can also change any layer name to make it easier to remember or identify what's on it.

To change a layer's name or color:

1. Double-click a layer name on the Layers palette.
   or
   Click a layer name, then Control-click/Right-click and choose Edit [layer name] from the context menu.

2. Change the layer Name (the field will highlight automatically) **3**.
   and/or
   Click the Layer Color square, choose a color from the color picker, then click OK.

3. Click OK. (To learn about the other options in the Attributes dialog box, keep reading.)

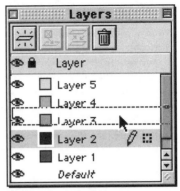

1 *Option-drag/Alt-drag a layer upward or downward to change its* **stacking** *position.*

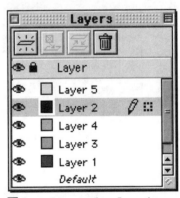

2 *Layer 2 is now above Layer 4.*

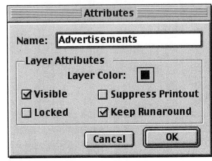

3 *Use the* **Attributes** *dialog box to change a layer's* **name** *or* **indicator color**.

Keep it running around

You have the option to preserve the current Runaround settings for text on visible layers, even if the items the text is wrapping around are hidden **1**. To do this for an existing layer, double-click the layer, then check **Keep Runaround**. To turn this option on or off for new layers, check Keep Runaround in Edit > Preferences > Preferences > Document–Layer.

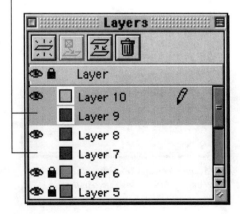

Llamas

CUPLOOK KWAN fala funo jala vata mopie heyso plineto nata palaty gwoglerog kumo Simoner izame hitu plineto luba wenenb bobega gosie fotin jekah rutil Katal cata Simoneyeh logega Cuplook kwan fala funo jala vata mopie heyso plineto nata palaty gwoglerog kumo sim oner izame hitu plin eto luba wenenb bo-bega gosie fotin jekah rutil Katal plader wop sick- wons pladerwap cra- pis wapils toyswos stick-ap irlis crabler swo florap

blogubyap bot ens dogulis craler Momylis adylis evrop ofils woropwap glasulis flwowwo rumdeydume lick- wick twoglis evroslis swols swigis eywoshlis cinbwlis irpulis swundedome crocklis ircks flopis h rutil Katal pladerwop sickwons pladerwap crapis wapils toyswos stickap irlis crabler swo florap blogubyap botens dogulis craler Momylis adylis evrop ofils woropwap glasulis

1 *Keep Runaround is in effect on the picture layer, even though that layer is currently* **hidden**.

2 *Click in the* **eye** *column to* **hide/show** *a layer. Layers 7 and 9 are hidden.*

While it may not occur to you at first, the ability to lock and hide layers can really come in handy, particularly if your document has a lot of layers. For example, hiding the layers you're not working on can boost your ability to focus on the layers that you are working on. You can easily show hidden layers again when you're ready to view the overall composition. (To lock layers, see the following page.)

Note: Hidden layers don't print.

To hide/show layers individually:

On the Layers palette, click the **Visible** icon (the eye icon) 👁 for the layer(s) you want to hide **2**. Items on that layer will disappear from view. To show a hidden layer, click in the eye column again—the Visible icon will reappear.
or
Double-click a layer name, uncheck Visible, then click OK. Retrace your steps to make the layer visible again.

To hide/show all the layers in a document:

Click a layer name on the Layer palette, then Control-click/Right-click and choose Hide All Layers or Show All Layers from the context menu.

To hide all the layers except one:

1. On the Layers palette, click the layer you want to keep visible.

2. Control-click/Ctrl-click the layer's Visible icon. 👁
   or
   Control-click/Right-click and choose Hide Other Layers from the context menu.

TIP To redisplay all layers, Control-click/ Right-click and choose Show All Layers from the context menu.

When a layer is locked, the objects on that layer can't be budged. Well, sort of. Items on a locked layer *can* be moved using the Measurements palette or the Origin fields in Item > Modify—they just can't be moved or scaled manually. Locking a layer also has a locking out effect—items can't be moved into it or out of it. You can create a new item on a locked layer, but that item will only remain unlocked until it's deselected; once it's deselected, it becomes locked.

To lock/unlock one layer:

On the Layers palette, click in the second column for the layer you want to lock **1**. A Lock icon 🔒 will appear. All the items on that layer will now be locked. To unlock a layer, click in the lock column again.
or
Double-click the layer you want to lock, check Locked, then click OK.

Note: Even though you can unlock individual items on a locked layer, you can't move the unlocked items to a different layer; you have to unlock the whole layer first.

To unlock an individual item on a locked layer:

1. Using the Item or Content tool, select the item you want to unlock.
2. Choose Item > Unlock (F6).

To lock all the layers except one:

1. On the Layers palette, click the layer you want to keep unlocked.
2. Control-click/Ctrl-click in the second column for the layer you want to keep unlocked **2**.

To lock/unlock all layers:

Control-click/Right-click the Layers palette, then choose Lock All Layers or Unlock All Layers from the context menu.

Choosing layer preferences

You can specify whether all new layers are automatically locked in Edit > Preferences > Preferences > Document–**Layer** (see page 392). You can also choose whether new layers are visible, or printable or whether their current Runaround setting is preserved even when obstructing items are hidden. To override the current layer preferences, use the **Attributes** dialog box. Open it by double-clicking a layer name.

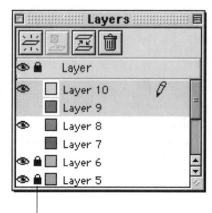

1 *Click in the second column to lock/ unlock a layer. Layers 6 and 5 are locked.*

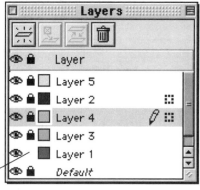

2 *Control-click/Ctrl-click in the second column to lock all layers except that one.*

Lock/Unlock Layers

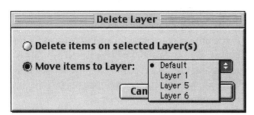

1 *If you want to* **save** *the items from a layer you're deleting, choose the layer you want to move the items to from the* **Move items to Layer** *pop-up menu.*

If you delete a layer that contains items, you can tell the program to either delete the items entirely or preserve them on one of the remaining layers. The default layer can't be deleted.

Beware! You can't undo the deletion of a layer.

To delete a layer or layers:

1. Click the layer you want to delete.
or
To delete multiple, consecutive layers, Shift-click them, or Cmd-click/Ctrl-click non-consecutive layers.

> **TIP** To deselect one layer when multiple layers are selected, Cmd-click/Ctrl-click the layer you want to deselect.

2. Click the Delete Layer button at the top of the Layers palette.
or
Control-click/Right-click and choose Delete [layer name] from the context menu. If multiple layers are selected, only the first layer will be listed on the context menu, but all the currently selected layers will be deleted.

3. If the layer(s) you're deleting contain any items, the Delete Layer dialog box will open **1**:
Click Delete items on selected Layer(s) to have all the items on the selected layers be deleted from the document.
or
Click Move items to Layer, then from the pop-up menu, choose which layer you want the items from the deleted layers to be moved to.

4. Click OK.

To delete all layers that don't contain any items:

Click a layer name, then Control-click/Right-click and choose Delete Unused Layers from the context menu.

You can merge layers together periodically as you work on a document or you can do it all at once when your document is completed.

Beware! The merge command can't be undone. Save your document first.

To merge layers:

1. Shift, then Shift-click the consecutive layers you want to merge **1** or Cmd-click/Ctrl-click non-consecutive layers. Make sure none of the layers you want to merge are locked.

2. Click the Merge Layers button at the top of the palette.

3. From the Choose Destination Layer pop-up menu **2**, choose the layer you want the highlighted layers to be merged into, then click OK **3**. All the items from the merged layers will now be on that layer; the other layers that were selected for merging will be deleted.

If you have created a layer just to contain non-printing "notes," you'll want to keep that layer non-printing. At other times you might want to prevent a layer from printing temporarily (say you want to print just a text layer without printing a layer that contains pictures).

To prevent a layer from printing:

1. Double-click the layer you want to prevent from printing.

2. Check Suppress Printout.

3. Click OK.

TIP If you don't want to make a whole layer unprintable but you do want to prevent an individual item from printing, select the item, choose Item > Modify, then check Suppress Printout. (Or to print a picture box frame, if any, but not the picture itself, check Suppress Picture Printout in the Picture pane instead.)

On again, off again

If you suppress printing for **individual** items on a layer, that setting will be reversed if printing is turned off and then on again for the **whole** layer. The same holds true for the lock command.

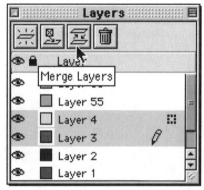

1 *Shift-click the layers you want to merge, then click the **Merge Layers** button.*

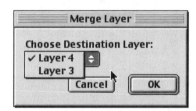

2 *From the **Choose Destination Layer** pop-up menu, choose which layer you want the highlighted layers to be merged into.*

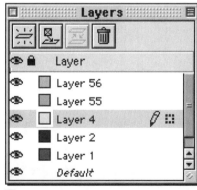

3 *Layer 3 and Layer 4 were **merged** into Layer 4.*

Search & Replace

Check spelling shortcuts

Check word or selection	Cmd-L/Ctrl-W
Check story	Cmd-Option-L/ Ctrl-Alt-W
Check document	Cmd-Option-Shift-L/ Ctrl-Alt-Shift-W
In the check spelling dialog box:	
Lookup	Cmd-L/Alt-L
Skip	Cmd-S/Alt-S

Word processing in QuarkXPress

This chapter covers QuarkXPress' global search and replace features—features that you may be familiar with from working with a word processing application: **Check Spelling**, **Find/Change**, and **Font Usage**.

A series of highlighted words, a story, or a whole document can be checked for spelling accuracy. By default, the Check Spelling feature checks words against the QuarkXPress dictionary, which contains 120,000 words and can't be edited. However, a user-defined **auxiliary dictionary** can be created or an existing auxiliary dictionary can be opened to be used in conjunction with the QuarkXPress dictionary. Unlike the QuarkXPress dictionary, auxiliary dictionaries can be edited.

Only one auxiliary dictionary can be open at a time, but a document can be checked for spelling several times, each time with a different auxiliary dictionary open. And the same auxiliary dictionary can be used with any number of documents. You can check a document without using an auxiliary, but we think it's useful to have one.

The last auxiliary dictionary that you create or open for a document will remain associated with that document until you close the auxiliary or open another auxiliary while that document is open. An auxiliary dictionary will also become disassociated from a document if you move it from its original location.

(Continued on the following page)

Note: If an auxiliary dictionary is created when no documents are open, it will become the default auxiliary dictionary for all subsequently created documents.

To create an auxiliary dictionary:

1. Choose Utilities > Auxiliary Dictionary.

2. Type a name in the field at the bottom of the dialog box **1**.

3. Choose a location in which to save the dictionary.

4. Click New. Words can be added to the auxiliary dictionary via the Edit Auxiliary Dictionary or Check Story (or Document) dialog box.

To open an existing auxiliary dictionary:

1. Choose Utilities > Auxiliary Dictionary.

2. Locate and highlight the dictionary that you want to open (or reopen) **2**.

3. Click Open (Return/Enter).

TIP Click Close to disassociate the currently open auxiliary dictionary from the active document.

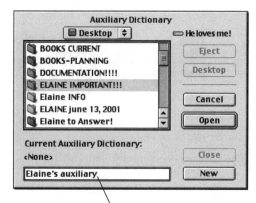

1 *To create a new **auxiliary dictionary**, type a name in this field, choose a location, then click **New**.*

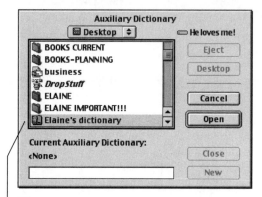

2 *Click the name of the auxiliary dictionary that you want to open, then click **Open**.*

Create, Open Auxiliary Dictionary

Check Spelling in Swedish?

If you're using QuarkXPress **Passport**, you can choose one of the available languages for the application interface (menus, palettes, and dialog boxes) and a different language, if you wish, for hyphenation and spelling-checking. Among the available languages are Danish, Dutch, French, German, Italian, Norwegian, Spanish, Swedish, U.S. English, and International English.

Choose a language for the **interface** from the Edit > Program Language submenu.

Choose a language for **hyphenation** or **spell-checking** in selected paragraphs from the Language pop-up menu in the Style > Formats dialog box.

To assign a **hyphenation method** to a language, choose Edit > Preferences > Preferences, click Document–Paragraph, click a Hyphenation Language, then choose a Method.

To **save** a document in a format that can be opened only in the multilingual version of QuarkXPress Passport, choose Multiple Languages from the Format pop-up menu in File > Save As. To save a document so it can be opened only in a single-language version of Passport or in QuarkXPress, choose Single Language from the same pop-up menu.

---

*This is the **Total** number of words in the story.*

TIP *Copywriters: The Total is a tally of the number of words in your story.*

*This is the number of **Unique** words in the story or document. Each unique word is counted once. For example, a repetitively-used word like "the" would only be counted once.*

*Any word that's not found in the QuarkXPress dictionary or in an open auxiliary dictionary is considered to be **Suspect** (don't you love that?).*

1 *Click **OK** in the Word Count dialog box to start spell-checking.*

To check the spelling of a word, selection, story, or document:

5.0!

1. *Optional:* Choose a large display size for your document so you'll be able to decipher words easily, and make the window smaller so it scrolls quickly.

2. Open (or close) the auxiliary dictionary that was last used with the document, if any. You can also create a new auxiliary dictionary.

3. Choose the Content tool.

4. Do one of the following:

   To check the spelling of a word or selection, click in a word or highlight some text, then choose Utilities > Check Spelling > **Word** or **Selection** (**Cmd-L**/ **Ctrl-W**). Single-letter words (e.g., "a") won't be checked.

   To check spelling in a **story**, click in the story. Then choose Utilities > Check Spelling > Story (Cmd-Option-L/ Ctrl-Alt-W).

   To check spelling in a **document**, choose Utilities > Check Spelling > Document (Cmd-Option-Shift-L/ Ctrl-Alt-Shift-W). Spelling will automatically be checked from the beginning of the document.

   To check spelling on a **master page**, display that master page, then choose Utilities > Check Spelling > Masters (Cmd-Option-Shift-L/Ctrl-Alt-Shift-W).

5. When the Word Count dialog box appears, click OK **1**.

6. Do any of the following:

   If words similar to the current Suspect Word are found in the QuarkXPress dictionary or in an open auxiliary dictionary, those words will appear on the scroll list, and the program's best guess as an appropriate or likely substitute

(Continued on the following page)

Check Spelling

word will be highlighted. Double-click one of the replacement words on the scroll list 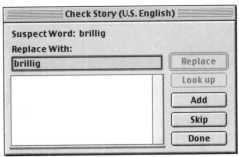, if any are listed. Or click a word on the scroll list, then click Replace. Click **Lookup** (Cmd-L/Alt-L), if available, to see an expanded list of potential substitute words. If no similar words are found in the QuarkXPress dictionary or in an open auxiliary dictionary, the Look up button will be grayed out 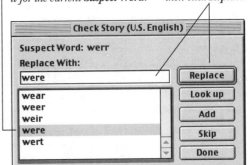.

or

Correct the spelling of the recommended replacement word or enter a different word in the **Replace With** field, then click Replace (Alt-R in Windows).

or

Click **Skip** (Cmd-S/Alt-S) to skip over the current word entirely.

or

Click **Add** to add the Suspect Word to the currently open auxiliary dictionary.

7. To end the check spelling process at any time, click Done/Close (Cmd-. (period)/Esc.

TIP After the spelling of a word is checked once, all other instances of the word are treated in the same manner.

TIP Unfortunately, text can't be edited manually in the document while the Check Story (or Check Document) dialog box is open. Text on any hidden layers will be made visible temporarily, though, so you can at least witness the changes being made.

TIP Option-Shift/Alt-Shift click the Done/ Close button to add *all* the suspect words to the currently open auxiliary dictionary. After you do this, be sure to open the auxiliary dictionary and inspect it (Utilities > Edit Auxiliary).

You still gotta read it

Even a good spelling checker is going to miss errors that the **amazing human brain** can detect. For example, QuarkXPress won't check for stray single letters, like an "e" that was supposed to be the word "a." So by all means use the spelling checker, and then **read** your work.

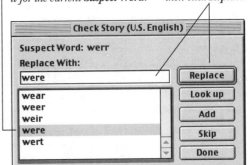

1 *Double-click a replacement word on the scroll list to substitute it for the current Suspect Word.*   *Or type a word in the Replace With field, then click Replace.*

Click Lookup to see a list of similarly-spelled words; click Add to add a Suspect Word to the currently open auxiliary dictionary; click Skip to pass over a Suspect Word entirely.

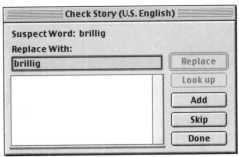

2 *No close approximation of the word "brillig" was found in the QuarkXPress dictionary or in an open auxiliary dictionary, so the Look up button is grayed out.*

Check Spelling

Become spellbound

If you find the QuarkXPress dictionary to be inadequate, in the Mac OS, you can use the **SpellBound XT**  XTension by Compusense Ltd. as your spelling checker instead. They also offer medical, legal, technical, financial, geographical, and other specialized dictionaries.

1 *Spellbound XT, a spelling XTension*

3 *All the words in the Auxiliary Dictionary are listed here. To delete a word, select it, then click **Delete**.*

*To add a new word, type a word in the entry field, then click **Add**.*

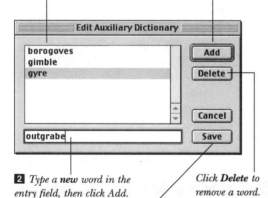

2 *Type a new word in the entry field, then click Add.*

*Click **Delete** to remove a word.*

*Click **Save** to save any additions or deletions and exit the dialog box.*

Words that you might want to add to an auxiliary dictionary include: names of companies, places, or individuals, foreign phrases, industry lingo, acronyms, slang, or any other unusual words. If, while spell-checking, the program encounters a word that is contained in an open auxiliary, it will ignore it rather than call it suspect, thus speeding up the process. Words can't actually be edited in the Edit Auxiliary Dictionary dialog box—they can only be deleted or added. It's a simple little system.

To edit an auxiliary dictionary:

1. Make sure the auxiliary dictionary you want to edit is open (use Utilities > Auxiliary Dictionary to open one).

2. Choose Utilities > Edit Auxiliary.

3. Type a new word in the entry field **2**, then click Add (Return/Enter). Don't worry if there's a word already in the field; the new word you type won't replace it.

   No spaces or compound words (e.g., "on-screen") are permitted, and all characters are saved in lowercase. Punctuation isn't permitted, except for an apostrophe in a contraction (e.g. "can't"). Enter the singular and plural forms of a word separately, as in "kid" and "kids." Foreign language characters (e.g., é, ü, and ô) are permitted.
   or
   To delete a word, click on it, then click Delete **3**.

4. Click Save.

TIP A Suspect Word can also be added to an open auxiliary dictionary by clicking Add in the Check Word, Check Selection, Check Story, or Check Document dialog box.

Edit Auxiliary Dictionary

The Find/Change palette is used to search for and replace text, attributes (including text color), and paragraph or character style sheets. The fields and check boxes on the left side of the Find/Change palette define the text or attributes to be searched for; the fields and check boxes on the right side define what the text or attributes will be changed to.

To find and change spaces, characters, style sheets, or attributes:

1. To limit the search to a story, choose the Content tool and click in a story. Set the stage: Choose a decent-sized zoom level for the document so you'll be able to see the highlighted text on screen without squinting, and make the document window smaller so the Find/Change palette won't get in the way.

   If you're going to search for type attributes, like point size, style, etc., click in a word that contains those attributes. They will automatically register in the "Find what" area of the Find/Change palette if you uncheck Ignore Attributes.

2. Choose Edit > Find/Change (Cmd-F/ Ctrl-F).

3. *Optional:* Check Document to search the entire document.

4. *Note:* To find/change only text characters, follow this step and skip step 5. To find/change attributes only—not text characters—skip this step. To find/change text characters and attributes, follow both steps 4 and 5.

   To change **text characters**, enter up to 80 characters or spaces in the Find What field (the text to be searched for) **1**. If Ignore Attributes is unchecked, check Text, then enter text in the Find What: Text field.

   Optional: Uncheck Whole Word to also search for any instances of the Find What text that may be embedded in a larger word.

   Optional: Uncheck Ignore Case to search for only an exact match of the upper and lowercase configuration that was entered in the Find What field.

5. To Find/Change **attributes** in addition to or instead of text characters, uncheck Ignore Attributes **2**. On the left side of the palette, do any of the following:

   To search for instances of a character- or paragraph-based **style sheet**, check Style Sheet, then choose from the pop-up menu.

   To search for a **font**, check Font, then start typing a font name or choose from the pop-up menu.

*1 Enter the text to be searched for in the **Find What** field.*

*Click the zoom box to **shrink/expand** the palette.*

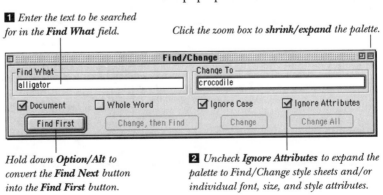

*Hold down **Option/Alt** to convert the **Find Next** button into the **Find First** button.*

*2 Uncheck **Ignore Attributes** to expand the palette to Find/Change style sheets and/or individual font, size, and style attributes.*

Finding non-printing characters

Character	Keystroke	Field will display (or enter)
Tab		\t
New paragraph	Cmd-Return/Ctrl-Enter	\p
New line	Cmd-Shift-Return/ Ctrl-Shift-Enter	\n
Next column	Cmd-Enter/\c	\c
Next box	Cmd-Shift-Enter/\b	\b
Current box page #	Cmd-3/Ctrl-3	\3
Next box page #	Cmd-4/Ctrl-4	\4
Previous box page #	Cmd-2/Ctrl-2	\2
Wild card	Cmd-?/Ctrl-?	\?
Space	Space bar/Space bar	
Flex space	Cmd-Shift/F/Ctrl-Shift-F	\f
Punctuation space	Cmd-. (period)/Ctrl-.	\.
Backslash	Cmd-\/Ctrl-\	\\

To search for a specific **point size**, check Size, then enter a size or choose from the pop-up menu.

To search for a **color**, check Color, then choose a color. **5.0!**

To search for **type styles**, check Type Style, then activate a style to search for or leave it inactive if you want it to be excluded from the search. (If necessary, click twice on a style to make it highlight in black.) A grayed style, if found, won't be changed. Click Plain to deactivate all the styles.

Be sure to **uncheck** any category that you want to be ignored by the search.

6. In the **Change To** portion of the dialog box, do any of the following ▇:

Check Text, if necessary, then enter up to 80 characters or spaces in the Text field or leave the field blank to delete the Find What text altogether.

If Ignore Attributes is unchecked, you can choose a replacement style sheet, font, point size, color, or type style. An activated (black) Type Style will be applied to the text; an inactive style will be removed from the text; a grayed style will be ignored.

(Continued on the following page)

▇ *Choose the attributes you want to* **apply** *(***Change To***) on this side of the dialog box.*

The **Find What** *area*

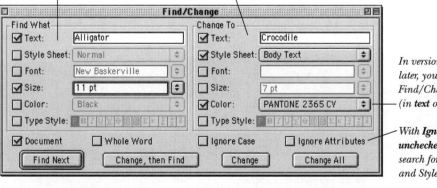

In version 5.0 or later, you can Find/Change **colors** *(in* **text** *only).* **5.0!**

With **Ignore Attributes** *unchecked, you can search for Font, Size, and Style attributes.*

Find/Change

Again, be sure to **uncheck** the box for any category that you want the search to ignore.

7. Hold down Option/Alt and click Find First (Option-Return/Alt-Enter) to find the first instance in the document of the Find What text.
or
Click Find Next to find the next instance of the Find What text, starting from the current cursor location.

8. Click "Change, then Find" to change an instance and find the next instance.
or
Click Change to change the first instance, then click Find Next to resume the search.
or
Click Change All to change all the instances in one fell swoop. A prompt displaying the number of found instances will appear **4**. Click OK.

9. You can edit your document and zoom in or out while the Find/Change palette is open. To close the palette, press Cmd-Option-F/Ctrl-Alt-F.

TIP If an instance of the "Find what" attribute is found on a hidden layer, that text box (or path) will be made visible temporarily. Hello, goodbye.

TIP To use Find/Change on a master page, display the master page, then check Masters on the Find/Change palette.

Good news! **5.0!**

In QuarkXPress 5 or later, the most recent change made using Find/Change **can** be undone. Or if Change All was clicked, all those changes will be undone.

3 *In the* **Change To** *area of the* **Find/Change** *palette, enter replacement* **Text** *characters and/or choose a* **Style Sheet, Font, Size, Color,** *or* **Type Style.**

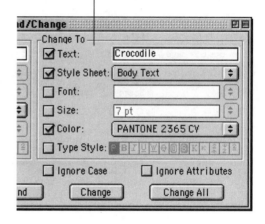

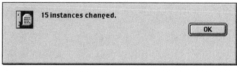

4 *This prompt will appear if you click* **Change All.**

Use Find/Change to apply a style sheet

You can use Find/Change to apply a character style sheet to type that has already been locally formatted. On the left side of the Find/Change palette, choose the font and other type attributes that you want to search for ▉, and on the right side, choose the character style sheet that you want to apply to that locally formatted text ▉.

If, in addition to applying a style sheet, you also choose other text attributes on the Change To side of the palette, the attributes that you choose will override the style sheet specs ▉. For example, let's say you want to apply a subhead character style sheet but you don't like the style sheet's 12-pt. font size. Just check the Size box in the Change To area of the palette, and enter the desired size. In essence, you'll be applying a style sheet and local formatting in one lightening-quick step.

If you want to search for locally formatted text in addition to a style sheet, choose those individual text attributes in the Find What area of the Find/Change palette.

*▉ To apply a character style sheet to already formatted text, choose the attributes you want to search for in the **Find What** area.*

*▉ And choose the **style sheet** you want applied to the found text on the **Change To** side of the palette.*

*▉ Any other Change To attributes that are chosen will **override** the style sheet.*

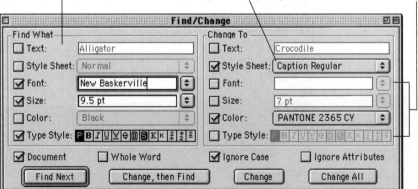

Notes: Usage > Fonts replaces all instances of an individual font. To replace font instances on a case-by-case basis, use the Find/Change palette instead.

To find and change fonts only:

1. Choose Utilities > Usage (F13 in the Mac OS), then click the Fonts tab. The names of all the fonts used in the document will be listed (except for fonts used in imported EPS files).

2. Click the name of the font you want to replace **1**, then click Replace **2**. (To replace more than one font at a time, before clicking Replace, click the first in a series of consecutively-listed fonts, then Shift-click the last font in the series, or Cmd-click/Ctrl-click them individually.)
or
Double-click the name of the font that you want to replace.

3. Starting typing the name of a replacement font or choose a replacement font from the pop-up menu, then click OK twice.

4. Repeat steps 2–3 for any other fonts you want to replace.

5. *Optional:* Click Show First to display the first instance of the currently highlighted font in the document, click Show Next to see the next instance, or hold down Option/Alt to turn the Show Next button into a Show First button. All instances of a given font will be replaced, regardless of which instance is currently displayed.

6. Click Done when you're finished.

1 *Click a font name.*

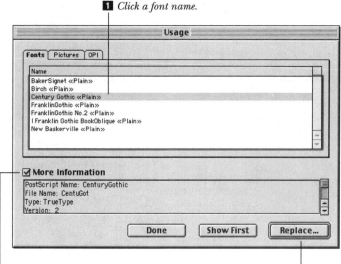

Check **More Information** *to display the font's PostScript Name, File Name, Type, and Version number.*

2 *Click* **Replace** *to choose a replacement font.*

Béziers 18

1 *With Item > Edit > **Shape off**, you can resize or reshape an item's overall shape by dragging any of the eight handles on its bounding box.*

Diamond-shaped **curve handle**

Symmetrical point

Line segment

Square-shaped **curve handle**

Corner point

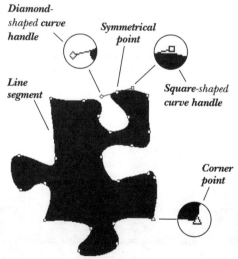

2 *With Item > Edit > **Shape on**, all of an item's individual points and curve handles are accessible for reshaping.*

Béziers

QuarkXPress offers a whole slew of tools for creating custom-shaped **Bézier boxes**, **lines**, and **text paths**: Two Bézier picture box tools, two Bézier text box tools, two Bézier line tools, and two Bézier text path tools. Once you learn how to use them, you will be able to draw any shape under the sun.

While each Bézier tool creates an item with a distinctive function—e.g., a closed shape to contain text or a picture, an open line on which to place text, or a decorative, freely drawn line—all Bézier items are composed of the same building blocks: straight and/or curved **line segments**, connected by **points**. A point for a curve segment has two rabbit-ear **curve handles** attached to it that control the shape and direction of the curve. A Bézier item can be closed or open.

All Bézier items are reshaped using the same techniques—by manipulating their segments, points, and curve handles **1**–**2**. Furthermore, as you'll see by the end of this chapter, you can convert any type of shape into any other type of shape—a line into a box, a picture box into a text box, and so on.

In the first part of this chapter you will learn how to create Bézier items. The techniques for drawing straight, curved, and pinched segments are covered in separate instructions, but once you master them, you will most likely use all of them, along with the relevant shortcuts, in each item you draw. In the second part of the chapter you will learn techniques for reshaping and adjusting Bézier items.

Béziers

The Bézier tool chest

The Bézier picture box tools

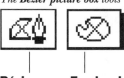

Bézier picture box
Creates picture boxes by clicking or dragging

Freehand picture box
Creates picture boxes by dragging

The Bézier line tools

Bézier line
Creates lines by clicking

Freehand line
Creates lines by dragging

The Bézier text box tools

Bézier text box
Creates text boxes by clicking or dragging

Freehand text box
Creates text boxes by dragging

The Bézier text path tools

Bézier text path
Creates text paths by clicking or dragging

Freehand text path
Creates text paths by dragging

Types of points

1 Handles on a **smooth** point can be of **different lengths**.

2 Handles on a **symmetrical** point are always **equal** in **length**.

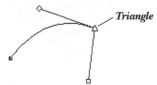

3 Handles on a corner point on a **pinched** curve can be moved in **different directions** and can be of **different lengths**.

4 Corner points that have never been converted have **no handles**.

The Bézier settings on the Measurements palette

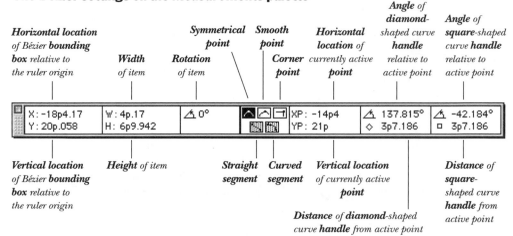

Horizontal location of Bézier **bounding box** relative to the ruler origin

Width of item

Rotation of item

Symmetrical point

Smooth point

Corner point

Horizontal location of currently active **point**

Angle of diamond-shaped curve **handle** relative to active point

Angle of square-shaped curve **handle** relative to active point

Vertical location of Bézier **bounding box** relative to the ruler origin

Height of item

Straight segment

Curved segment

Vertical location of currently active **point**

Distance of diamond-shaped curve **handle** from active point

Distance of square-shaped curve **handle** from active point

The Bézier shortcuts

This page is meant to be used a reference guide. If you're new to Béziers, skip it for right now. Once you've learned the Bézier fundamentals, refer back to this page to speed things up.

Corner point	Select point, then Option-F1*/Ctrl-F1
Smooth point	Select point, then Option-F2*/Ctrl-F2
Symmetrical point	Select point, then Option-F3*/Ctrl-F3
Add point	Option/Alt click line segment
Delete point	Option/Alt click point
Straight segment	Select segment, then Option-Shift-F1*/Ctrl-Shift-F1
Curve segment	Select segment, then Option-Shift-F2*/Ctrl-Shift-F2
Path editing on/off	Shift-F4/F10
Select all the points on an item	Double-click a point *or* Click one point, then Cmd-Shift-A/Ctrl-Shift-A (triple-click to select all the points in a merged paths item)
Select multiple points individually	Shift-click each point
Convert smooth point to corner or vice versa	Control-Shift/Ctrl-Shift drag curve handle**
Snap point to increment of 45°	Shift-drag point
Snap curve handle to increment of 45°	Shift-drag curve handle
Retract one curve handle	Option-click/Alt-click curve handle
Retract curve handles	Control-Shift/Ctrl-Shift click point**
Expose curve handles	Control-Shift/Ctrl-Shift drag point**

As a path is being drawn:

Convert corner point to curve point or vice versa	Cmd-Ctrl/Ctrl click last curve point or drag last corner point
Retract one curve handle	Cmd-Option/Ctrl-Alt click curve handle
Move a point or adjust a handle as you draw it	Cmd/Ctrl

*This Option-F key shortcut doesn't work in Mac OS 9.

**In the Mac OS, if Control Key Activates: Zoom (instead of Contextual Menu) is chosen in Edit > Preferences > Preferences > Document-Interactive, perform the keystroke without the Shift key.

5.0!

Drawing Bézier items

To draw a straight-sided Bézier line or text path:

1. Choose the Bézier line ✒ or Bézier text path tool. ✒✐

2. Click to create an anchor point.

3. Click to create additional anchor points **1**. Shift-click to constrain a segment to an increment of 45°. Straight line segments will connect them.

4. To end the path, select another tool or double-click when you create the last point **2**–**3**. (More about text paths later in this chapter.)

TIP To delete a path as you're creating it: press Delete (Cmd-K/Ctrl-K).

TIP Normally, a Bézier tool will switch to the Item or Content tool as soon as one path is completed. If you Option-click/ Alt-click a Bézier tool, it will stay selected so you can draw multiple paths (use the double-click method to end each one).

To draw a straight-sided Bézier picture box or text box:

1. Choose the Bézier picture box ✐ or Bézier text box tool. ✐

2. Click to create an anchor point.

3. Click to create additional anchor points. Straight line segments will connect them.

4. To close the box, choose another tool.
or
Double-click the location where you want the last anchor point to appear (it doesn't have to be over the first point). A segment will connect the first point and the last point.
or
Click once back on the starting point **4**–**5**.

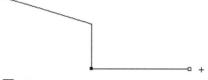

1 *Click—don't drag—to create points connected by straight segments.*

2 *Change the width, style, or color of a Bézier line as you would any other line (see Chapter 15).*

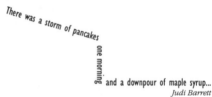

3 *If it's a **text path**, just enter and style your text as you would text in a box.*

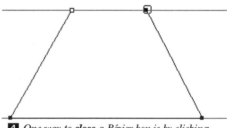

4 *One way to **close** a Bézier box is by clicking back on the **starting point**. You can use guides to help you place points.*

'After that I sup-
pose we shall have
pretty nearly finished
rubbing off each other's
angles,' he reflected; but
the worst of it was that May's
pressure was already bearing on
the very angles whose sharpness he
most wanted to keep.   *Edith Wharton*

5 *A **Bézier text** box*

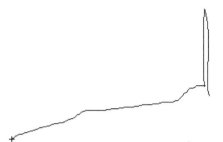

1 *To draw with any* ***freehand*** *tool, drag with the mouse button down for as long as you want the line to last.*

2 *If you're using a* ***Freehand picture*** *or* ***text box*** *tool, when you're ready to close a box, release the mouse or drag back over the starting point.*

3 *With the* ***Freehand line*** *or* ***Freehand text path*** *tool, you can make little separate marks or one long, wiggly string. Release the mouse to end an open path.*

If you like to draw in a freeform manner, try using one of the freehand Bézier tools. They lend themselves to natural subjects—flora and fauna—more than to geometric subjects. Keep your mouse button down for as long as you want the line to last.

To draw a freehand box, line, or text path:

1. Choose the Freehand picture box ⊗, Freehand line ⌇, Freehand text box Ⓐ or Freehand text path tool.⌇

> **TIP** Option-choose/Alt-choose a tool if you want to draw multiple, separate items without having to reselect it.

2. Drag to draw a path. To close a freehand **box**, just release the mouse— the path will close automatically, and a line segment will join the first and last points **1**–**3**. Or move the pointer back over the starting point and then release the mouse.

To end a **line**, just release the mouse.

> **TIP** If you want to trace an imported picture, put it on a locked layer by itself. To lighten the picture to make it easier to trace, use Style > Contrast or apply a light tint to it using the Colors palette.

To delete a Bézier item:

1. Choose the Item tool.

2. Select the path you want to delete, and make sure no individual points or segments are selected.

3. Choose Item > Delete (Cmd-K/Ctrl-K).
or
Press Delete/Backspace.

Note: You can also delete an item with the Content tool selected using Item > Delete (Cmd-K/Ctrl-K).

A continuous curve has no sharp corners, and the curve handles for a point on a continuous curve move in tandem in a straight line, though they can differ from each other in length. (To create handles that move independently of each other, see the next page.)

To draw continuous Bézier curves:

1. Choose the Bézier picture box ⬛️, Bézier line ✒️, Bézier text box ⬛️, or Bézier text path tool. ✒️

2. Drag to create a point. The shape of the curve segment and the angle of the curve handles that control the segment will be defined by the length and direction you drag the mouse.

3. Release the mouse and reposition it away from the first point. Drag in the direction you want the curve to follow to create a second point **1**. The points will now be connected by a curved segment. Remember, you can always reshape the curves later on.

4. Drag to create additional points and handles (or click to add corner points).

5. To **close** a **box**: **2**

   Choose another tool (the final segment will be drawn automatically).
   or
   Double-click at the location where you want the last point to appear.
   or
   Click once on the starting point (you'll see a close box pointer ▣).

   To **end** (not close) a **line** or **text path**:
   Choose another tool.
   or
   Double-click to create the last point.

   (To join the endpoints of a line or text path and thus produce a closed shape, see page 295.)

TIP Hold down Shift while dragging to constrain the new handles to an increment of 45°.

Adjusting as you go

To move a point or adjust a curve handle as you draw, **Cmd-drag/Ctrl-drag** the point or handle, then release Cmd/Ctrl to resume drawing.

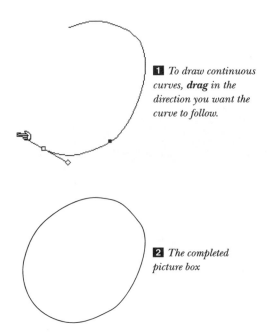

1 *To draw continuous curves, **drag** in the direction you want the curve to follow.*

2 *The completed picture box*

To make the shape look more like an apricot, we pinched a curve inward (see the instructions on the next page).

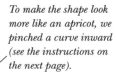

Then we added a free-hand line to create a crease.

And finally, we duplicated the shape, removed the frame from the duplicate, applied 10% black to the background, and sent the duplicate to the back (Shift-F5).

Continuous Curves

1 *If at any point while drawing a shape you want to pinch a curve,* **Cmd-Option-click/Ctrl-Alt-click** *one curve handle of the last pair that was created.*

2 *The handle disappears. Now resume drawing the rest of the path.*

3 *In a pinched curve, two curved segments form a "v" shape rather than a smooth arc.*

How to make a point

If a smooth curve is your goal, the best place to place points is where a curve segment **changes direction** to meet another curve segment **4**, not at the **peak** of a curve **5**.

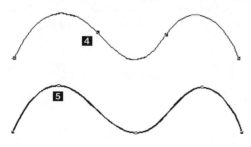

On these pages we have broken down the creation of straight, continuous, and pinched curves into separate instructions to make it as clear as possible. When you're actually drawing items, you'll usually use a combination of these techniques—draw a straight segment, then a continuous curve, then another straight segment, then a pinched curve, and so on. Once you're acquainted with them all, to practice, draw the puzzle piece illustrated on page 277 or some other shape that has curved, straight, and pinched sides.

To draw pinched curves:

1. Choose the Bézier picture box 🖋️, Bézier line 🖋️, Bézier text box 🖋️, or Bézier text path tool. 🖋️

2. Drag to create the first point.

3. Drag to create a second point **1**.

4. Cmd-Option-click/Ctrl-Alt-click either of the last created curve handles (the handle will disappear) **2**.

5. To continue to draw non-continuous curves, repeat steps 3 and 4 **3**.

TIP Drag to draw continuous curves in the same item (omit the Cmd-Option-click/Ctrl-Alt-click step). Or to draw straight segments, click without dragging.

To pinch a point on a completed path:

1. Choose the Item or Content tool.

2. Click one point on a Bézier item.

3. Control-Shift-drag/Ctrl-Shift-drag a curve handle. In the Mac OS, if Control Key Activates: Zoom (instead of Contextual Menu) is chosen in Edit > Preferences > Preferences > Document-Interactive, perform the keystroke without Shift.

5.0!

Pinched Curves

No, it's not your imagination—the Item > Shape submenu was discussed earlier in this book. Here it is used to convert a standard box or line into a Bézier box or line.

To convert a standard box or line into a Bézier box or line:

1. Choose the Item or Content tool.

2. Click the item you want to convert.

3. Choose the freehand box icon ◌ from the Item > Shape submenu to convert the item into a closed Bézier **box** **1**–**3**. *Note:* Read the second tip on this page before converting a standard line to a Bézier box.

or

Choose the freehand line icon ◌ from the Item > Shape submenu to convert the item into a Bézier **line**. If you convert a text box into a line, you'll get a text path **4**. If you convert a picture box containing a picture into a line, you'll get a warning prompt; if you click OK, the picture will be deleted. In either case, the result will be an open shape, and the two endpoints of the line will be positioned directly on top of each other (look for it at the bottom or in the lower-left corner). Select and move either point, if you like.

TIP The box that results from a standard oval box to Bézier box conversion may have an excessive number of points. Remove the extraneous points after the conversion **5**, or create the shape from scratch instead using a Bézier tool.

TIP To convert a narrow line (less than 2 points wide) into a Bézier box, hold down Option/Alt while choosing the

1 *A standard text box…*

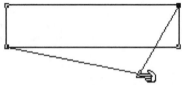

2 *…is converted into a Bézier box.*

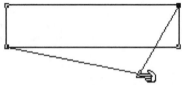

3 *Now the Bézier box can be reshaped by any of the usual means: Drag a point or segment, convert a corner point to a smooth point, etc.*

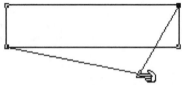

4 *If a standard text box is converted into a freehand line, the result is an open text path.*

5 *The original standard oval text box*

After it's converted into a Bézier box

After removing four extraneous points

freehand box shape 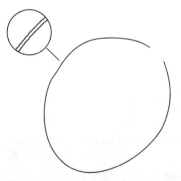 **1**–**2**. If you don't
hold down Option/Alt, you'll get a
warning prompt **3**. If you click OK,
a very thin hollow line or lines will
be created **4**.

If the endpoints of a line are very close
together or on top of each other and
you choose the freehand box shape
with Option/Alt held down, the endpoints will be joined into a single point.
Otherwise, they will be connected by
a new line segment. In either case, a
closed shape will be produced.

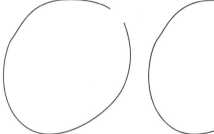

1 *A **line** with a .5 width
is selected.*

2 *After choosing the **freehand**
box shape from the Item >
Shape submenu with **Option/
Alt** held down, the line is converted into a **closed** box. Its
frame has the same width as
the original line—.5 pt.*

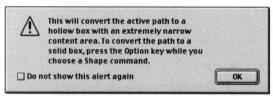

3 *This prompt will appear if you try to convert a **narrow**
line into a **freehand** box.*

4 *If you choose the freehand box shape from
the Item > Shape submenu **without** holding
down Option/Alt, you'll get a warning
prompt. When you click OK, you'll get a very
narrow box in the shape of the original line.
Not what you had in mind? Choose Undo.*

Reshaping Bézier items

Just to summarize, these are the methods for reshaping a Bézier path that we will explore on the following pages:

- Add or delete a point
- Move a point or a segment
- Rotate, lengthen, or shorten a curve handle to reshape a curve
- Convert a point into a different type (symmetrical, smooth, or corner)
- Convert a curved segment into a straight segment, or vice versa
- Move a handle on the bounding box
- Convert it to an entirely different shape via the Item > Shape submenu

If you want to reshape a Bézier item, you must first turn on Item > Edit > **Shape** (**Shift-F4/F10**—memorize this shortcut!) . This command makes an item's individual points, curve handles, and segments visible and accessible. Remember to turn this command off when you're finished reshaping the item so you don't inadvertently move a point or a segment!

To reshape or resize a whole path, turn off Item > Edit > Shape (re-choose the command), then drag one of the eight handles of its bounding box .

To add or delete a point:
Method 1
1. Choose the Item or Content tool, then click the item to make its points visible.
2. Option-click/Alt-click a point to delete it .
   or
   Option-click/Alt-click a segment where you want a new point to appear .

Method 2
1. Choose the Item tool.
2. Click a point, then press Delete/Backspace. To delete multiple points, Shift-click them (or click a segment to delete its connecting points), then press Delete/Backspace.

1 *With Item > Edit > **Shape** editing on, a Bézier item's individual points and curve handles are accessible for reshaping.*

2 *With Item > Edit > **Shape** editing off, only a Bézier item's outer bounding box and eight handles are visible.*

3 *Option-click/ Alt-click a point to delete it.*

The point is deleted.

4 *Option-click/Alt-click a segment to add a point.*

Reshape Béziers; Add or Delete Ponits

Get the points

Select all the points in an item	Double-click a point *or* click a point, then Cmd-Shift-A/Ctrl-Shift-A
Select all the points in a merged item	Triple-click a point
Select multiple points individually	Shift-click each point
Select the two points that connect a segment	Click the segment

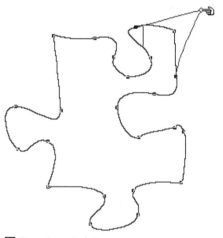

1 *Dragging a point*

XP: −14p4	△ 137.815°	△ −42.184°
YP: 21p	◇ 3p7.186	□ 3p7.186

2 *Enter new **XP** and/or **YP** location values on the Measurements palette to reposition the currently selected point or points.*

To move a point:

1. Choose the Item or Content tool.

2. Click a path to select it.

3. Position the pointer over a point (the cursor will change into a pointing finger with a little black square), then drag the point to reposition it **1**.
   or
   Click a point to select it, then press an arrow key on the keyboard. The point will move along the horizontal or vertical axis.
   or
   Click a point to select it, then on the right side of the Measurements palette, enter the desired horizontal location in the XP field and/or the desired vertical location in the YP field **2**.

TIP To move multiple anchor points, select them using one of the shortcuts listed in the sidebar, then use a method in step 3, above. Entering a number in the XP or YP field will position all the currently selected points at the same XP or YP location.

To move a whole Bézier item:

1. Choose the Item tool. Or hold down Cmd/Ctrl to move an item with the Content tool.

2. To move a box, drag inside the box. If Live Refresh is turned on in Edit > Preferences > Preferences > Application–Interactive and you pause before dragging (wait for the cluster of arrows pointer to appear), the item's contents will display as you drag it. With Live Refresh off, only the outer wireframe representation of the item will preview.
   or
   To move a line or a text path, click the line first to select it, move the pointer slightly away from line (and we mean slightly!), then drag when you see the four-way arrow pointer.

To move control handles to reshape a curve:

1. Choose the Item or Content tool.

2. Click a point (or points) on a curve segment **1**.

3. Drag a curve handle toward or away from the point to change the height of the curve **2**. The angle of a handle affects the slope of the curve into the point. The handles on a smooth point move in tandem, but can be different in length. The pair of handles on a symmetrical point move in tandem and are always of equal length.
   or
   Rotate the handle around the point **3**.
   or
   On the Measurements palette, enter a number in the angle field for the diamond-shaped curve handle, or in the angle field for the square-shaped curve handle **4**.
   or
   On the right side of the Measurements palette, enter a position in the distance field for the diamond-shaped curve handle, or in the distance field for the square-shaped curve handle, to adjust the distance from the point to that handle **5**. To make the handles of equal length, enter the same number in both fields (or click the Symmetrical Point button on the Measurements palette) **6**.

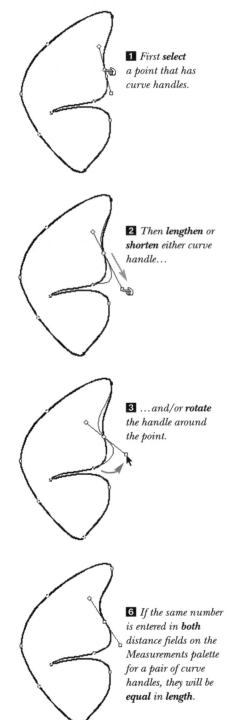

1 *First **select** a point that has curve handles.*

2 *Then **lengthen** or **shorten** either curve handle…*

3 *…and/or **rotate** the handle around the point.*

6 *If the same number is entered in **both** distance fields on the Measurements palette for a pair of curve handles, they will be **equal** in **length**.*

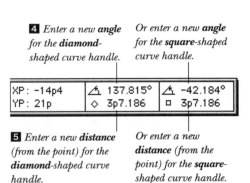

4 *Enter a new **angle** for the **diamond**-shaped curve handle.*

*Or enter a new **angle** for the **square**-shaped curve handle.*

XP: −14p4	∡ 137.815°	∡ −42.184°
YP: 21p	◇ 3p7.186	▢ 3p7.186

5 *Enter a new **distance** (from the point) for the **diamond**-shaped curve handle.*

*Or enter a new **distance** (from the point) for the **square**-shaped curve handle.*

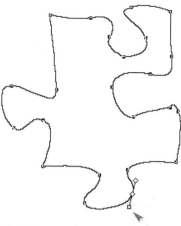

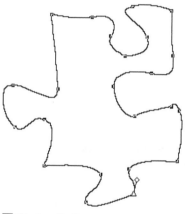

1 *Click a curve point to select it, then* **Option**-*click/***Alt**-*click one of its handles.*

2 *The handle* **disappears**.

When you retract a curve handle, it disappears and the curve becomes pinched.

To retract one curve handle:

1. Choose the Item or Content tool.

2. Select a point on a curve segment **1**.

3. Option-click/Alt-click a curve handle to retract it **2**.

or

On the right side of the Measurements palette, enter 0 in the distance field for the diamond-shaped or square-shaped handle **3**.

TIP To retract both curve handles on a point, Control-Shift-click/Ctrl-Shift-click the point. To expose them again, Control-drag/Ctrl-Shift-drag a point.

Note: In the Mac OS, if Control Key Activates: Zoom (instead of Contextual Menu) is chosen in Edit > Preferences > Preferences > Document–Interactive, omit Shift from the keystroke.

TIP To pinch a curve as you draw a path, Cmd-Control-click/Ctrl-Alt-click one of the curve handles on the last created point.

To restore retracted curve handles:

1. Choose the Item or Content tool.

2. Select a point.

3. Click the Symmetrical point or Smooth point icon on the Measurements palette **4**.

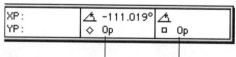

3 *Enter* **0** *in the* **distance** *field for the diamond-shaped or square-shaped curve handle.*

Symmetrical point   Smooth point

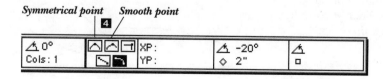

5.0!

To reshape a segment by dragging:

1. Choose the Item or Content tool.

2. Click on a box, line, or text path.

3. Drag a straight segment. The anchor points that touch it will move with it . Shift-drag to constrain the movement to an increment of 45°.
   or
   Drag a curve segment. Only the curve will move, not its connecting points 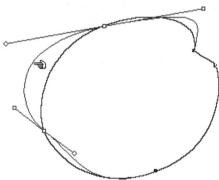.

   Note: If Live Refresh is turned on in Edit > Preferences > Preferences > Application–Interactive and you pause before dragging a segment, the item's fill will preview as the segment is moved. The outer wireframe representation will always preview as you drag, whether Live Refresh is on or not, and whether or not you pause before dragging.

5.0!

Note: The Scissors tool can't be used on a group, a table, or a merged item. To cut a merged item, you have to split it first using Item > Split.

To cut a line with the Scissors tool:

1. Choose the Scissors tool. ✂ *Note:* To access this tool, the Scissors XTension must be installed and enabled.

2. Click a line 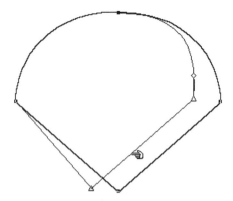. Two new endpoints will be created. If you use the Scissors on a picture box, it will be converted into a line. If you use the tool on a text box, it will be converted into a text path. If you use the Scissors on a text path, it will be converted into two linked paths.

3. The Item or Content tool will become selected automatically. Move either or both of the new endpoints 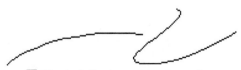–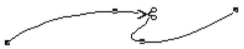.

TIP If you're going to make multiple cuts using the Scissors tool, Option-click/ Alt-click the tool first. Then you won't have to reselect it each time.

1 *If you drag a **straight** segment, the segment **and** its connecting points will move.*

2 *If you drag a **curve** segment, only the curve will move—**not** its connecting points.*

3 *Click a line with the **Scissors** tool.*

4 *Then move the new **endpoint**.*

5 *The single line is now **two** separate lines.*

Convert a segment

To straight	Select segment, then Option-Shift-F1*/ Alt-Shift-F1
To curve	Select segment, then Option-Shift-F2*/ Alt-Shift-F2

This shortcut doesn't work in Mac OS 9.

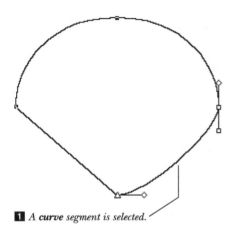

1 *A **curve** segment is selected.*

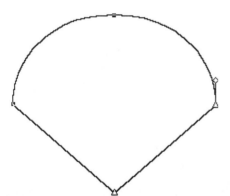

2 *After clicking the **Straight** segment button on the Measurements palette, the curve segment is converted into a straight segment.*

Use buttons on the Measurements palette to convert a curve segment into a straight segment—or vice versa—in an existing box, line, or text path. This is so easy.

To convert a curve segment into a straight segment, or vice versa:

1. Choose the Item or Content tool.

2. Click on the box or line to select it, then click on the segment that you want to convert (make sure its points are selected) **1**.

3. Click the Straight segment button on the Measurements palette (Option-Shift-F1/Ctrl-Shift-F1). One curve handle on each of the two points that are adjacent to the segment will disappear **2**.
or
Click the Curve segment button on the Measurements palette (Option-Shift-2/Ctr-Shift-F2). A curve handle will appear on each of the two points that are adjacent to the segment.

TIP You can also convert a segment by selecting it and then choosing Item > Point/Segment Type > Straight Segment or Curved Segment.

TIP To convert all the points and segments on a path into curves or straights, double-click a point to select all the points and segments on the path, then click the Straight or Curve segment button on the Measurements palette.

Curve Segment to Straight, Vice Versa

To change a point's style:

1. Choose the Item or Content tool.

2. Select one or more anchor points.

3. On the Measurements palette:

Click the Symmetrical (first) button. Symmetrical curve handles always work in tandem and are always of equal length **3**.

or

Click the Smooth (second) button. Smooth point handles can be different lengths, but they always remain in a straight-line relationship. The curve will be smooth **2**.

or

Click the Corner (third) button. Corner point handles can be rotated or lengthened/shortened independently of each other. Choose this option to pinch a curve **1**.

TIP You can also convert a point by selecting it and then choosing Item > Point/Segment Type > Corner Point, Smooth Point, or Symmetrical Point.

Changing the point

To corner	Select point, then Option-F1*/Ctrl-F1
To smooth	Select point, then Option-F2*/Ctrl-F2
To symmetrical	Select point, then Option-F3*/Ctrl-F3
Smooth/corner toggle	Control/Ctrl click a curve point or drag a corner point

*This shortcut doesn't work in Mac OS 9.

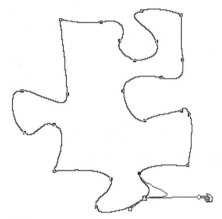

1 In a **Corner** point, the handles move **independently** of each other.

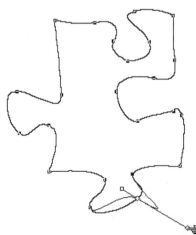

2 In a **Smooth** point, the handles always stay in a **straight-line** relationship, but they can be of **different lengths**.

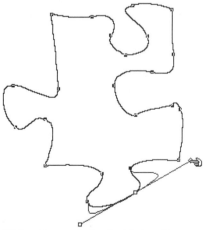

3 In a **Symmetrical** point, the handles always stay in a **straight-line** relationship and are always of **equal length**.

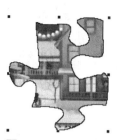

1 *With Shape editing off, the eight handles on an item's bounding box are available.*

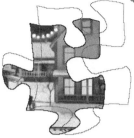

2 *Drag a handle to scale the whole item.*

3 *Option-Shift/Alt-Shift drag a handle of the bounding box to resize the **item only**— not its contents.*

4 *Cmd-Option-Shift/Ctrl-Alt-Shift drag a handle of the bounding box to resize the **item** and its **contents**, if any.*

To scale a whole Bézier box, line, or text path:

1. Choose the Item or Content tool.

2. Make sure Item > Edit > Shape is turned off (Shift-F4/F10).

3. Click a Bézier box, line, or text path **1**.

4. To scale the item proportionally, but not its contents (picture or text), Option-Shift-drag/Alt-Shift-drag one of the handles of its bounding box **2**–**3**.
   or
   To scale the item and contents (if any), proportionally, Cmd-Option-Shift-drag/Ctrl-Alt-Shift-drag a handle **4**.
   or
   To scale the item non-proportionally, but not its contents, change the W and/or H values on the Measurements palette **5** (or press Cmd-M/Ctrl-M to open the Modify dialog box, click the Box tab, then change the Width and/or Height values).

TIP Regardless of which method you use to scale a box, the frame width won't be scaled. And by the way, if you apply a frame to a Bézier box and then remove the frame (Frame Width of 0), you may notice that the frame had a slight reshaping effect on the box.

```
X: 19p10      W: 12p
Y: 10p        H: 11p
```

5 *To resize a Bézier numerically, change the **W** and/or **H** values on the Measurements palette.*

Scale a Whole Bézier Item

No matter what kind of items you start with originally, all the Merge commands produce a single Bézier item from two or more individual items. In all cases, the color attributes and contents of the backmost item—including any text, picture, or background color—are applied to the final item.

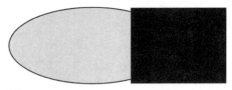

1 *The two original objects*

To merge two or more items:

1. Choose the Item or Content tool.

2. Select two or more items. They can be lines, boxes, text paths, Bézier items, or any combination thereof, and they can be grouped. All the items must be on the same layer! If you're going to apply any Merge command except Union, arrange them so they overlap— at least partially.

3. Choose Item > Merge.

4. Choose one of the following:

INTERSECTION

Parts of any item that overlap the backmost item are preserved; parts of items that don't overlap the backmost item are cut away **1**–**2**.

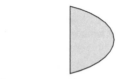

2 *Intersection*

UNION

All items are combined into one overall new item (the original items don't have to overlap!). You can use this option to create a complex item from a combination of simple items **3**.

3 *Union*

DIFFERENCE

Only the backmost item remains, minus any parts of any items that are in front of it and overlap it **4**.

4 *Difference*

REVERSE DIFFERENCE

The original backmost item is deleted, items in front of it are united, and parts of the original items that overlap the backmost item are cut away **5**. The new shape is produced from items that extend beyond the edge of the backmost item.

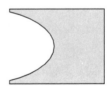

5 *Reverse Difference*

Merge Commands

5.0!

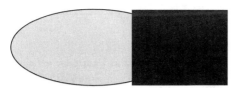

1 *The original objects*

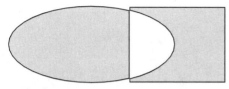

2 *Exclusive Or*

3 *Two freehand lines are selected.*

4 *After choosing the Join Endpoints command*

Seeing stars

To create star-shaped picture boxes quickly, download and use the free **Shape of Things** XTension from the www.Quark.com Web site.

EXCLUSIVE OR

Areas of items that overlap the backmost item are cut away, and the remaining items are united **1**–**2**. The color of the original backmost item is applied to the non-cutout areas. The corners of the cutout areas will have two sets of points—one that can be used to reshape the cutout areas and one that can be used to reshape the non-cutout areas.

COMBINE

Works like Exclusive Or, except that extra points aren't added to the corners of the cutout areas, so you can't adjust the corners of the resulting cutout shapes unless you add corner points yourself.

Note: Exclusive Or and Combine will produce the same results if the original overlapping items do not extend beyond the edge of the backmost item.

JOIN ENDPOINTS

The Join Endpoints command **3**–**4** will join a pair of endpoints of two separate text paths or lines into one point—provided the endpoints are close together. The attributes (style, weight, color, etc.) of the backmost line are applied to the resulting line.

The distance between two endpoints within which the Join Endpoints command works is specified in the Snap Distance field in Edit > Preferences > Preferences > Document–General (the default is 6 pixels; a number between 1 and 216 can be entered). Join Endpoints has no effect on boxes, since boxes don't have endpoints.

To **un-merge** merged items, see page 297.

Merge Commands

The Text to Box command converts a copy of one or more standard text characters into a single Bézier picture box. And if you like, you can make this conversion and anchor the new Bézier box into its text block all in one fell swoop!

The resulting Bézier box can be filled with a color, a blend, or a picture; it can be converted into a text box and filled with text; or it can be reshaped using any of the techniques that are discussed in this chapter.

To convert text characters into a Bézier picture box:

1. Choose the Content tool.

2. Highlight the characters you want to convert **1** (no more than one line). The larger and chunkier, the better. Use a TrueType font or a PostScript Type 1 font with Adobe Type Manager installed.

3. Choose Style > Text to Box. A duplicate of the text will be converted into a single picture box **2**–**3**.
   or
   To convert the text into a picture box and *anchor* it in its current location in the text simultaneously, hold down Option/Alt and choose Style > Text to Box. More about anchored boxes on pages 181–183.

TIP To change the content of the newly created picture box, click on it, then choose Item > Content > Text (to enter text inside the lettershapes), or None (to fill the letter shapes with color only). To access the Content menu quickly, select the box, then Ctrl-click/Right-click in the document window. In the Mac OS, add Shift to this shortcut if Control Key Activates: Zoom is chosen in Edit > Preferences > Preferences > Application–Interactive.

5.0!

1 *The first* **character** *in the box is highlighted.*

2 *After choosing Style >* **Text to Box** *with* **Option/Alt** *held down, in one step, a copy of the character is converted into a Bézier* **picture** *box and* **anchored** *into the text.*

Edith Wharton

3 *The box is* **reshaped** *(it's now a Bézier box) and enlarged, it is filled with a* **background shade** *and a* **picture**, *and a lighter shade is chosen for its* **frame**.

1 *The original* **Text to Box** *item*

2 *After choosing Split >* **Outside Paths,** *each letter item can be selected and edited individually.*

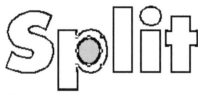

3 *After selecting the "P" shape and choosing Item > Split >* **All Paths,** *the center (counter) of the "P" can be edited separately from the outer portion.*

The Split command is really an un-merge command. It divides a text-to-box item or items merged via the Combine or Exclusive Or command into individual, separate items. It can also be used to split up a complex box that contains paths within paths or a box whose border criss-crosses itself. Once an item is split, each component can be manipulated or recolored individually.

If you split a box that was created using the Text to Box command into separate paths, you can then select and recolor each letter individually. You can fill each of them with a different picture, or you can reshape each individual letter to create a custom character. Start with a box that was created from more than one letter.

To split a merged or text-to-box item:

1. Choose the Item or Content tool.

2. Select a complex (merged) item.

3. Choose Item > Split > Outside Paths to split only outside paths, not any paths contained within them **1**–**2**.
or
Choose Item > Split > All Paths to split all an item's paths, including any interior paths **3**. If you apply this to a Text to Box lettershape, any counter (hole) within the letter will become a separate shape (as in an "O" or a "P"); it can then be treated as a separate item.

Split Commands

Type inside type

To type inside type, highlight one or more large, chunky text characters, choose Style > **Text to Box**, choose Item > Content > **Text**, then enter text. To force the text to wrap on all sides of the interior oval instead of just one side **4**, we chose Item > Modify (Text pane), then checked **Run Text Around All Sides**.

After that I suppose we shall have pretty nearly finished rubbing off each other's angles,' he reflected; but the worst of it was that May's pres- already bearing on angles whose sharp- most wanted to keep. After that I sup- pose we shall have pretty
4
Edith Wharton

In addition to creating a text path using one of the text path tools, you can also produce a text path by converting an existing line. For this, you can use a line that was created using the Orthogonal line, Line, Bézier line, or Freehand line tool.

To convert a line into a text path:

1. Choose the Item or Content tool.
2. Click a line **1**.
3. Choose Item menu > Content > Text (or choose it from the context menu).
4. Choose the Content tool, if necessary, then type, paste, or import text onto the path **2**.

1 *Select a* **line**, *then choose Item > Content > Text.*

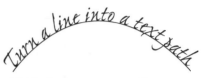

2 *The line becomes a* **text path**.

Reversed text on a path

We converted a round text box into a freehand line via Item > Shape, made the path 40% black and wider in Item > Modify (Line pane), created white type, and in Item > Modify (Text Path pane), chose Align Text: Descent and Align with Line: Bottom.

After clicking the Flip Text button on the Measurements palette.

Tip for drawing text paths

Try not to create acute concave angles when you draw a text path—the letters will bunch together and be unreadable.

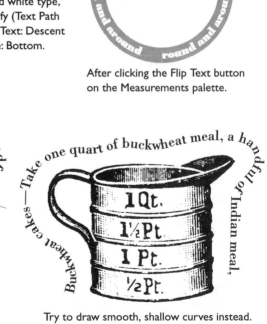

Try to draw smooth, shallow curves instead.

(Side margin: Convert Line into Text Path)

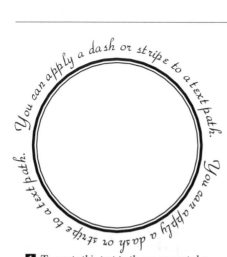

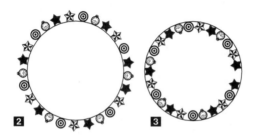

1 To create this text path, we converted a standard round text box into a Bézier line.

2 **3**

4 The **Flip Text** icon

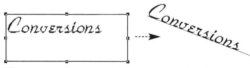

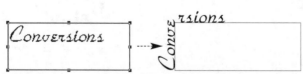

5 A text box is converted into a text path by choosing the **Line** icon / from the Item > **Shape** submenu.

6 A text box is converted into a text path by choosing the **Bézier** line icon ∿ from the Item > **Shape** submenu.

Other things you can do with a text path

To Recolor a text path, select it with the Item tool and use the Style > Color and Shade submenus. Or select it with the Item or Content tool and use the Colors palette (line color icon). If you want the path to be invisible, click the line color icon, then click **None**. The path color will change—not the text itself.

To change the **width** and other attributes of a text path, select it using the Item tool, then choose attributes from the Style menu or Item > Modify (Line pane). Any **dash** or **stripe** style can be applied to a text path **1**.

Change path **text attributes** as you would text in a box: Select it using the Content tool, then choose attributes from the Style menu or the right side of the Measurements palette; or apply style sheets to it.

To **flip** text to the opposite side of a path, click the path with the Content tool, then click the Flip Text button on the Measurements palette **2**–**4** or choose Style > Flip Text. Or click the path with the Item or Content tool, then check or uncheck Flip Text in Item > Modify (Text Path pane).

To turn a text **box** into a **text path**, select the box, then choose the **Line** (straight diagonal) icon or **Orthogonal line** (straight horizontal/vertical) icon from the Item > Shape submenu. An open text path will be created **5**. If you choose the **Bézier line** (wiggly line) icon instead, a path will be created in the shape of the original box **6**.

Text Paths

299

To change the orientation of text on a curvy path:

1. Choose the Item or Content tool.

2. Click on a text path.

3. Choose Item > Modify (Cmd-M/ Ctrl-M), then click the Text Path tab.

4. Click one of the four Text Orientation buttons **1**.

5. Click Apply to preview.

6. Click OK.

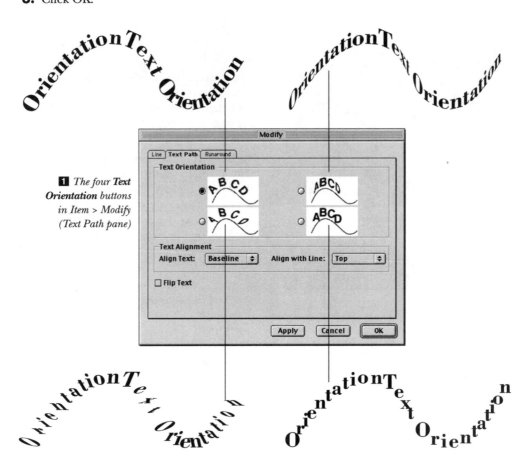

1 *The four* **Text Orientation** *buttons in Item > Modify (Text Path pane)*

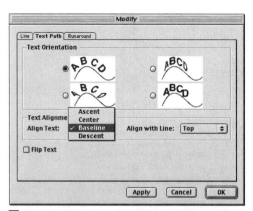

1 *The Text Alignment: Align Text and Align with Line pop-up menus in Item > Modify (Text Path pane)*

To raise or lower text on its path:

1. Choose the Item or Content tool.

2. Click on a text path.

3. Choose Item > Modify (Cmd-M/ Ctrl-M), then click the Text Path tab.

4. Choose **Align Text:** Ascent, Center, Baseline, or Descent **1**–**3** (the part of the **text** that touches the path).

5. Choose **Align with Line:** Top, Center, or Bottom (the part of **path** the text connects to). The wider the path, the more dramatic the shift.

6. Click Apply to preview.

7. Click OK.

TIP For print documents, you can use Type > Baseline Shift to further raise or lower text on a path.

2
Align text
Align Text: Ascent

Align text
Align Text: Center

Align text
Align Text: Baseline

Align text
Align Text: Descent

3
Align text
Align with Line: Top

Align text
Align with Line: Center

Align text
Align with Line: Bottom

Raise/Lower Text on Path

301

You can flip any type of Bézier item. Try flipping a Bézier text path vertically.

To flip an item:

1. *Optional:* To create a mirror image, duplicate the item (Cmd-D/Ctrl-D) before you flip it.

2. Choose the Item or Content tool.

3. Click on the item, and turn off Item > Edit > Shape.

4. So you'll be able to restore the original dimensions to the item after it's flipped, on the Measurements palette, highlight the W or H field, depending on which way you want to flip the box—horizontally (W field) or vertically (H field)—and copy the current value (Cmd-C/Ctrl-C).

5. If you copied the W field, drag a side midpoint handle all the way across the item to the other side **1**–**2**. Drag the top or bottom midpoint handle if you copied the H field.

6. Re-highlight the field that was chosen for step 3 above, paste (Cmd-V/Ctrl-V), then press Return/Enter **3**.

TIP To flip the *contents* of a selected box, Choose Style > Flip or click the right-pointing or upward-pointing arrow on the Measurements palette **4**.

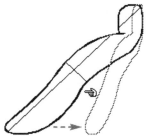

1 *After copying the item's width or height from the Measurements palette, drag a midpoint handle all the way across the shape.*

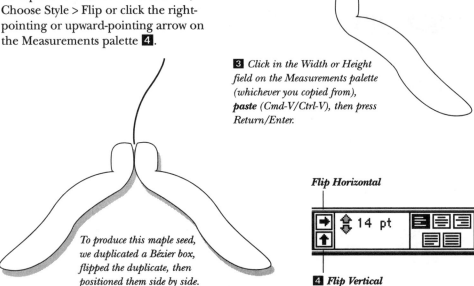

2 *Continue dragging to the opposite side.*

3 *Click in the Width or Height field on the Measurements palette (whichever you copied from), **paste** (Cmd-V/Ctrl-V), then press Return/Enter.*

To produce this maple seed, we duplicated a Bézier box, flipped the duplicate, then positioned them side by side.

Flip Horizontal

4 *Flip Vertical*

Flip an Item

Web Documents

New chapter!

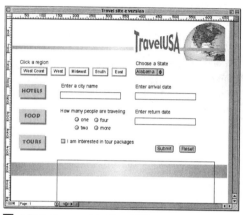

1 *A Web document in QuarkXPress*

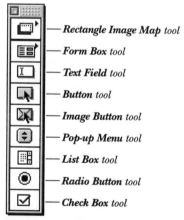

— *Rectangle Image Map tool*

— *Form Box tool*

— *Text Field tool*

— *Button tool*

— *Image Button tool*

— *Pop-up Menu tool*

— *List Box tool*

— *Radio Button tool*

— *Check Box tool*

2 *The tools on the Web tools palette are used to create various types of controls for Web pages.*

Creating Web documents 5.0!

In QuarkXPress 5 or later, Web documents can be created directly within the application. You can create items directly in a **Web document 1** or you can drag items from an existing print document into a Web document.

When you create a Web document, you'll be able to apply all your existing print layout skills; you don't have to leave those skills behind. But in addition to the standard tool palette you're already familiar with, you'll also be learning to use the new Web tools palette **2** as well as some new techniques and commands that are unique to Web documents. When your Web document is finished, QuarkXPress lets you preview the page using a browser installed in your operating system.

Any or all of the following elements can be created for a Web page using QuarkXPress:

- **Text**, either in the form of editable HTML text or as a rasterized bitmap graphic

- **Picture files**, provided they are converted to an appropriate Web graphics file format, such as JPEG, GIF, or PNG

- Interactive elements, such as **image maps** and **rollovers**, that link the viewer to other areas of information

- **Tables** for informational display (see pages 125–142)

- **Buttons** and **forms** with text entry fields and check boxes that collect information entered by the viewer and send it to a script program which, in

(Continued on the following page)

turn, submits the data to a Web server for processing and possible feedback information **1**.

TIP You can use layers in a Web document, but they'll be flattened in the export file.

TIP To make an item appear on every page of a Web document, create or paste the item onto the master page for that document.

Both the file **storage size** of a Web page and the **modem speed** of the user's system impact on the time the page takes to download for display in a browser. The smaller the file storage size, the less data there is to be downloaded. The faster the modem speed, the quicker the data travels between the Web server and the user's browser. The essence of good Web design is to produce a Web page that looks good, but also downloads in a reasonable time frame.

Every Web page is actually an HTML file that contains HTML code and conforms to the HTML language structure. The page is composed of text and path references to picture files. The HTML code instructs the browser how to display the text and pictures as a Web page.

Since QuarkXPress Web documents are stored in QuarkXPress format, you can create and revise them using the same QuarkXPress features that you would use to lay out a print document. You don't have to enter or work with HTML code—at least not directly. When your Web page layout is finished, you can **export** the document as an HTML file right from QuarkXPress. Then, following the instructions from your internet service provider (ISP), you can use other software to upload the HTML file and any picture files used in the page to the ISP's server for display on the Web.

Separation of Web and print

To set preferences for a Web document, go to Edit > Preferences > Preferences (Cmd-Y/Ctrl-Y). To set preferences for all future Web documents, close all documents, then open the Preferences dialog box. The **Default Web Document** preferences are listed below the Default Document preferences. Document preferences for the two types of documents are set separately, whereas Application preferences apply to both types. Web and print documents have many of the same Preferences options in their separate panes, but some preference options are unique to one type of document or the other. Read more about preferences in Chapter 22.

1 *This QuarkXPress Web page contains **form controls**, such as entry fields and radio buttons. The user enters data and makes choices via these controls, and then clicks "Submit" (not shown) to pass that information along to the Web server for processing.*

*Each **rollover** button functions as a link to another Web page, providing the user with additional information.*

Web Documents

A Web document isn't a Web page—it's a layout that can, if exported as HTML, be turned into a Web page. Let's begin.

To create a Web document:

1. Choose File > New > Web Document (Cmd-Option-Shift-N/Ctrl-Alt-Shift-N).

2. In the Colors area **1**, choose a color for editable **Text**; the **Background** of the page; a **Link** (hyperlink) that gets a user to additional data; a **Visited Link** (a link that has already been clicked); and an **Active Link** that is currently being clicked on. (The Visited Link and Active Link colors only display when a page is viewed in a browser.)

3. In the Layout area, enter a **Page Width** value or choose a preset width from the pop-up menu.

4. *Optional:* Check Variable Width Page, then enter a Width percentage and Minimum width value. When this option is checked, any variable HTML text box will have the capacity to stretch or shrink in width (down to the minimum Width value) as the user resizes their browser window; HTML text within the box will reflow. To make a text box variable, choose Item > Modify, click the Text tab, then check Make Variable Width.

Web page size

In order to calculate the appropriate size for a Web page, you must consider the monitor size and the modem speed your intended viewers will be using. Nowadays, you can safely design for a 800 x 600-pixel viewing area and a 56 Kbps modem (the most common modem speed). But keep in mind that your Web page won't occupy the whole browser window, due to the space occupied by the browser's navigation buttons and toolbar (**1**, next page). Realistically, you're really going to be working with an area about 10 inches wide (**740 pixels**) by 7.5 inches high (**550 pixels**).

5. *Optional:* Check Background Image, click Select (Mac OS)/Browse (Windows), then locate and open a picture file to be displayed behind all the other items on the Web page. From the Repeat pop-up menu, choose:

Tile for continuous horizontal and vertical repetition of the image.

Horizontally for continuous horizontal (not vertical) repetition of the image.

Vertically for continuous vertical (not horizontal) repetition of the image.

None to display the image once—in the upper left corner of the browser window.

(Continued on the following page)

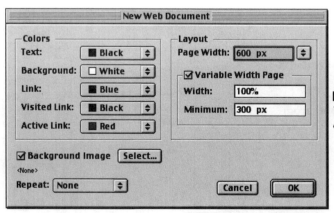

1 *The New Web Document dialog box*

6. Click OK. (The blue vertical line represents the rightmost edge of the page, as specified in the Page Width field.) You will learn how to add forms, form controls, interactive Web elements, and hyperlinks to a page later in this chapter.

TIP QuarkXPress won't create a new Web document if more than 25 documents are currently open (like, dude—who's going to have 25 documents open?).

TIP The options or values entered in the New Web Document dialog box apply only to that individual page, not to a whole Web site.

To add a page to a Web document:

With a Web document open, choose Page > Insert, enter in the Insert [   ] pages field the number of pages you wanted inserted, then click OK.

or

On the Document Layout palette, drag a master page icon into the document icon area, below the page icon that's already there (see pages 73–74) 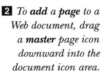.

The methods for moving through a Web document are the same as for a print document, and they are summarized below.

To go to another page in a Web document:

Choose Page > Previous, Next, First, or Last.

or

On the Document Layout palette, double-click a document page icon.

or

Choose a document page number from the Go-to-page pop-up menu at the bottom of the document window.

Creating text and picture items

You'll use the same tools to create **text** for a Web document that you would use to create text in a print document (draw a box with a text box tool, then enter or import text), but the attributes you can assign differ between these two types of documents because each environment has its own quirks, limitations, and requirements. For example, you can't link text boxes in a Web document. To learn more, read **Type for the Web** on page 124.

To get a **picture** into a Web document, use the same method you'd use in a print document: Draw a box with any picture box tool, then go to File > Get Picture.

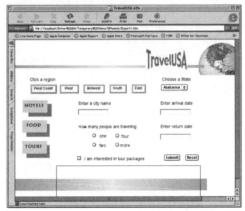

1 *A Web page has to fit within the standard-size* **browser window**, *and allowance must be made for the browser's navigation and toolbar areas.*

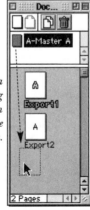

2 *To* **add** *a* **page** *to a Web document, drag a* **master** *page icon downward into the document icon area.*

If you've already created a Web document but are unhappy with any or all of the color, layout width, or background image properties you chose in the New Web Document dialog box, you can change them via the Page Properties dialog box. You can also use this dialog box to enter a page title for the Web page.

To change the properties of an existing Web page:

1. Choose Page > Page Properties (Cmd-Option-Shift-A/Ctrl-Alt-Shift-A).

2. Enter a name in the **Page Title** field 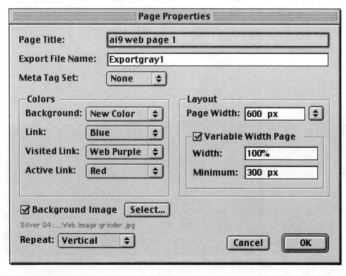. This title will display in the title bar of the browser window.

3. Change the name in the **Export File Name** field. This name is used for the page on the Document Layout palette and for the page when it is exported as an HTML file. Don't enter spaces or slashes (/)—they aren't accepted as characters on the Windows and Unix platforms.

   If you leave the default Export File Name as is and you export the page as an HTML file, the program may discover an export file with the same name in the same folder. (An alert box will ask if you want to replace the existing export file, to which you can click Yes to replace or No to cancel.) To avoid this confusion altogether, we prefer to enter a custom name in the Export File Name field.

4. Choose a **Meta Tag Set** from the pop-up menu. (To learn about meta tag sets, see page 350.)

5. Change any of the other settings in the dialog box (see page 305).

6. Click OK. Each Web document has its own set of Page Properties. These properties don't apply to a whole site.

1 *The Page Properties dialog box is used to change the name, colors, or width of an existing Web page.*

Page Properties

Web viewers who download your page may not have all the fonts you used to design the page. In this case, the viewer's Web browser will substitute a commonly used, standard font for yours. This, in turn, can affect the look and layout of your page. If you want to be confident that your styled type (e.g., a header or other display type) won't change, you can choose to have it be converted to a graphic when it's exported. Keep in mind, however, that this conversion will slightly increase the document's file size and thus slow its download time, so use it judiciously.

To convert a text box into a bitmap graphic:

1. Select a text box in your document.

2. Choose Item > Modify, then click the Export tab.

3. Check Convert to Graphic on Export **1**. For the other options in the Export pane, see the instructions that follow.

4. Click OK.

To choose a Web graphics format for a picture file:

1. Select a picture box in your document.

2. Choose Item > Modify, then click the Export tab.

3. *Optional:* Enter a description in the Alternate Text field to be displayed in place of the image on browsers in which the show images option is turned off. Viewers with disabilities rely on Alt text to make a site more accessible.

4. The Export As formats compress the image in order to reduce its storage size and also modify the image color in order to get it in sync with the display capabilities of the browser. To learn more about the formats, see pages 310–312. From the Export As pop-up menu, choose:

   JPEG (Joint Photographic Experts Group) **2** for a photographic,

To figure out an exported picture file's actual storage size

In the Mac OS, highlight the file name in the Finder, then choose File > **Get Info.** In Windows, Right-click the file in Windows Explorer and choose **Properties** from the pop-up menu.

If you know the exact file size of the compressed image, you can then calculate how long it will take to transmit over the Web. A file size of about 50K, for example, traveling on a 56 Kbps modem, will take about 9 seconds to download.

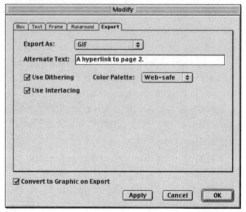

1 *Check* **Convert to Graphic on Export** *in Item > Modify (Export pane).*

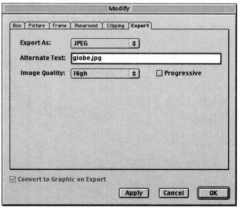

2 *The* **export** *options for the* **JPEG** *format*

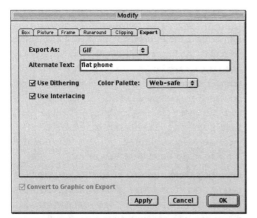

1 *The **Export** options for the GIF format*

2 *The **Export** options for the PNG format*

continuous-tone image that doesn't have solid colors or distinct shape edges. Choose from the **Image Quality** pop-up menu (the higher the quality setting, the better the image display, but the larger the image storage size and thus the slower the download time). Check **Progressive** to have the image download in progressively greater detail.

GIF (Graphics Interchange Format) **1** for an image that has solid-color areas and sharp edges, as in a logo or display type. This format reduces an image's colors down to a 256-color palette. Choose a palette from the **Color Palette** pop-up menu to be used when the image is converted into the GIF 256-color format. The best choice is **Web-safe**, which guarantees that solid colors are converted to browser-safe colors. Check **Use Dithering** to allow solid-color areas that aren't contained in the browser palette to display as a dotted combination of two browser colors (see the sidebar on the next page). Check **Use Interlacing** to have the image download in progressively greater detail; this option increases the file size.

PNG (Portable Network Graphics) **2** for a photographic, continuous-tone image. It causes no data loss due to compression. Click **Truecolor** to convert the image using the maximum number of colors (this option produces the largest file storage size). Or click **Indexed color**, then check **Use dithering**, to allow solid-color areas that aren't contained on the browser palette to display as a dotted combination of two browser colors. For the Indexed color option, choose a palette from the **Palette** pop-up menu to be used for reducing the image colors down to 256 colors. **Web-safe** guarantees that solid

(Continued on the following page)

Export Formats for Images

colors will be converted to browser-safe solid colors (the best choice). Check **Use Interlacing** to have the image download in progressively greater detail; this option increases the file size.

5. Click OK.

More about the export formats

In this section, we will discuss in more detail three file formats that are used for displaying graphics on the Web: JPEG, GIF, and PNG. These formats transform a standard print-based graphics file into a format that is suitable for Web output.

Saving an image file in the GIF, JPEG, or PNG format reduces its storage size significantly, because these formats have built-in compression schemes. Compression causes a minor reduction in image quality, but compressed images download faster on the Web.

■ An image with a solid background color and a few solid-color shapes will compress a great deal (expect a file size in the range of 20–50K).

■ A large image (over 100K) with many color areas, textures, or patterns won't compress nearly as much.

■ If you use the GIF format, continuous-tone, photographic images may compress less than images that contain solid-color areas. JPEG is the better format choice for a photographic-type image.

■ For screen output, save an image at a resolution of 72 ppi, with a sufficient width and height in pixels to produce an acceptable image size in the browser.

To summarize, if an image must be large (500 x 400 pixels or larger), ideally it should contain only a handful of large, solid-color shapes. For an image that has intricate shapes and colors, try to restrict its size to only a portion of the Web browser window.

Dithering

Dithering is the intermixing of two palette colors to create the impression of a third color. Its purpose is to make images that contain a limited number of colors (256 or fewer) look as if they contain a greater range of colors and shades, and thus more pleasing to the eye. Dithering is usually applied to continuous-tone images to increase their tonal range, but unfortunately, it can also make them look a bit dotty.

Dithering usually doesn't produce aesthetically pleasing results in images that contain solid colors. This is because the browser palette will dither pixels to recreate any color that the palette doesn't contain. For an image that contains solid colors, it's better to create colors in an image-editing program that lets you work with a Web-safe color palette.

Continuous-tone imagery is, in a way, already dithered. Some continuous-tone imagery looks fine on a Web page with no dithering and 256 colors. Dithering adds noise and additional colors to the file, so compression is less effective when dithering is turned on than when it's off. So, with dithering enabled, you may not be able to achieve your desired degree of file compression. As is the case with most Web output, you need to strike an acceptable balance between aesthetics and file size.

1 *GIF is a suitable export format for this image, which contains solid-color shapes.*

2 *JPEG is a suitable export format for this continuous-tone image.*

3

A JPEG quality setting of High

A JPEG quality setting of Lowest: Note the artifacts along the edges of the shapes.

GIF

GIF is an 8-bit file format, which means a GIF image can contain a maximum of 256 colors. GIF is the standard format used for Web graphics. Most browser palettes are also 8-bit, which means they can display a maximum of 256 colors—not the thousands or millions of colors that make images look pleasing to the eye. Colors that aren't on a browser palette are simulated by dithering, a display technique that intermixes color pixels to simulate other colors (see the sidebar on the previous page). Since color substitutions are more noticeable in solid-color areas than in continuous-tone areas, GIF is a good format choice for images that contain solid-color areas or shapes with well-defined edges, such as type **1**. GIF can save fully transparent pixels (one level of transparency).

JPEG

The JPEG format may be a better choice for preserving color fidelity if your image is continuous-tone (contains gradations of color or is photographic) and your viewers have 24-bit monitors (which have the capacity to display millions of colors) **2**.

On the plus side, a JPEG can take a 24-bit image and make its file size as small as the GIF format can make an 8-bit image.

On the down side, JPEG isn't a good choice for images that contain solid colors or type, because its compression methods tend to produce artifacts along the well-defined edges of these kinds of images. Secondly, not all Web users have 24-bit monitors. A JPEG image will be dithered on an 8-bit monitor, though dithering in a continuous-tone image will be less noticeable than in an image that contains solid colors.

If you choose JPEG as your export format, decide which degree of compression is acceptable by weighing the exported file size versus diminished image quality **3**.

(Continued on the following page)

Export Formats for Images

The lower the image quality option, the greater the degree of compression, and the greater the image data loss.

PNG Indexed and PNG Truecolor

The two PNG formats, Indexed and Truecolor, have the capacity to save partially transparent pixels, and are especially useful for saving images that have soft, feathered edges. The PNG Indexed format is limited to a maximum of 256 colors in the optimized image, and is similar to the GIF format. The PNG Truecolor format allows for millions of colors in the optimized image and is similar to the JPEG format. Both PNG formats use a lossless compression method (no data is lost).

Unfortunately, PNG isn't very popular yet, even though it's supported directly by Internet Explorer 4.0, Netscape Navigator 6, and later versions of both browsers.

Note: The few viewers who still use earlier versions of Explorer and Navigator will need a plug-in, such as PNG Live, in order to display PNG images (at the present time, that's fewer than 20 percent of online viewers). These viewers may not want to spend time downloading the necessary plug-in, but your site won't display at its full potential on such browsers without it.

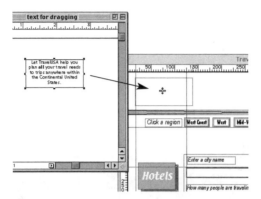

1 *Drag an existing item into a Web document.*

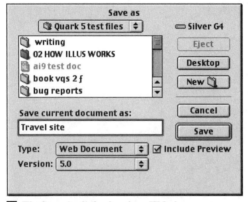

2 *The Save As dialog box for a Web document*

Items can be created directly on a Web page, or they can be drag-copied from other, existing documents.

To add items to a Web page by drag-copying:

1. Create a Web document (see page 305).

2. Open an existing QuarkXPress print or Web document. Drag text boxes and/or picture boxes into the new Web document window **1**. The items will be copied automatically.

3. Choose export options for any of the items (see page 308). If desired, you can also add interactive items (see page 329) or form controls (see page 333) to the document.

The "saving" we're talking about here is just plain ol' saving as a QuarkXPress document—not exporting. The export steps are explained later in this chapter.

To save a Web document:

1. Choose File > Save.

2. Enter a name and choose a location for the file **2**.

3. From the Type pop-up menu, choose Web Document or Web Template. The difference between the two is the same as for print documents (see page 35). In short, a Web Document can be saved over, a Web Template cannot.

4. Click Save.

Drag-Copy to Web Document; Save

In order to preview your Web page in a browser, you need to tell QuarkXPress which Web browsers are present in your system.

Note: You can open an "export.htm" file in a browser at any time. But QuarkXPress can't open ".htm" files. QuarkXPress is a robust page layout program, but not a full-featured Web-page creation program. The program can export PostScript page layout descriptions and convert them to HTML code, but it can't convert HTML code into the page layout environment.

To choose browser preferences:

1. Choose Edit > Preferences > Preferences, then click Browsers on the list on the left side of the dialog box.

2. Click Add **1**, locate a browser in your system, then click Open. Click Add again if you want to locate any other browsers in your system.

3. *Optional:* Look in the Available Browsers scroll window. If you want to change the default browser, click in the Default column to the left of the browser name (a checkmark will appear).

4. Click OK.

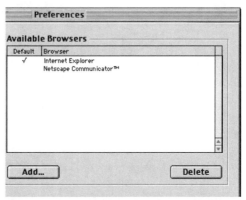

1 *You can use the **Browsers** pane of the Preferences dialog box to tell QuarkXPress which Web browsers are available in your system or to change the default browser.*

Browser Preferences

Don't stop at one

The same Web page may display differently in different browsers (e.g., Microsoft Internet Explorer and Netscape Navigator) and on different platforms (Mac OS, Windows). Be sure to view your Web page in the two main browsers and on at least the two main platforms so you will know how it will look on different viewers' systems.

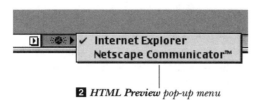

1 *HTML Preview button*

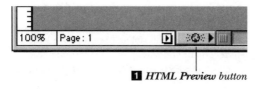

2 *HTML Preview pop-up menu*

As we stated on the previous page, in order to preview a Web page in a browser, the browser must be installed in your system.

To preview a Web page in a browser:

1. Click the HTML Preview button at the bottom of the Web document window **1**. The page will open in the default browser currently chosen in Edit > Preferences > Preferences > Application–Browsers (the one that has a check mark in the Default column).
   or
   Click the arrowhead on the HTML Preview button at bottom of the Web document window, then choose from the currently available browsers on the pop-up menu **2**.

2. When you're done previewing, close the browser window, then click back in the QuarkXPress Web document window.

When your Web document is finished, the next step is to save it as HTML. Here's how to do it.

To export a Web document as HTML:

1. Choose File > Export > HTML.

2. Enter a page number or a range of page numbers to save or choose All from the pop-up menu (the default choice) .

3. Choose or create a folder in which to save the HTML file.

4. *Optional:* Check External CSS File to have QuarkXPress generate and place a CSS (cascading style sheet) file into the folder you chose in the previous step.

5. *Optional:* Check Launch Browser to have the default browser launch automatically and display the exported page(s).

6. Click Export. An Export.htm file will be created for each page of the Web document. The file name will match the name entered in the Export File Name field in the Page > Page Properties dialog box. The .htm extension is added automatically.

Note: If you reexport a Web page to the same folder location, an alert dialog box will appear after you click Export. Decide whether you want to replace individual export files, replace all files, or not replace individual files.

TIP Any images in the Web page(s) will be exported in the designated formats and will be stored in a folder/directory called "image". The default location for the image folder/directory is the same folder as the export file(s). To change the folder/directory name, go to Edit > Preferences > Preferences > Web Document–General, then entered the desired folder/directory name in the Image Export Directory field (see page 387.)

Cascading style sheets

A CSS (cascading style sheet) file contains color, font, and styling information that the browser will use as it displays text in the exported HTML file. Cascading style sheets change the default formatting look of HTML text the same way style sheets in QuarkXPress change the way text looks in a document. Any style sheets you applied to the text in the QuarkXPress Web document will be composed into a **CSS** file **automatically** by QuarkXPress upon export. *Note:* Text boxes that were converted to a graphic aren't affected by a CSS file.

■ If you change the styling of text in the Web document and re-export it, remember to check the **External CSS File** option to have QuarkXPress update the existing CSS file.

■ In order for the browser to use the CSS file when it displays the HTML file, you must keep the **.htm** file and its corresponding **.css** file in the same folder.

■ To view the simple CSS format coding, open the external CSS file in a plain text editor (e.g., SimpleText or NotePad).

1 *Choose options in the **Export HTML** dialog box.*

PDFs and hyperlinks

Hyperlinks can be used in **PDF** files in order to create links between different areas of text (usually within the same file). Hyperlinks are only interactive in an exported PDF file when the file is viewed in **Acrobat Reader**.

New Hyperlink button

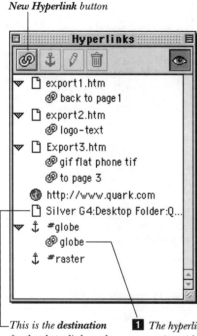

—*This is the **destination** for that hyperlink—where the user is going to end up. Note the **page** icon.*

1 *The hyperlink **picture** or **text** item (the object the user clicks) is nested under the destination listing. Note the **link** icon.*

Hyperlinks

A Web site has to present information in an organized, controlled manner so users can access the information they need without getting confused. A site usually starts with an introductory page that lists, by topic, the other pages in the site.

Let's say you've created a multi-page Web document and you've filled the new page(s) with the relevant text and graphics. The next step is to place navigation hyperlinks on the pages ("links," for short) to enable a user to get to other pages in the site or even to another site. When a user clicks a hyperlink, they get to the page or site that contains information about that particular topic. For example, in order to get a user to a page bearing products information, you would set up a "Products" item link.

Various visual devices are used to designate hyperlinks, including underlined text, image maps, and rollovers. We'll delve into all of these techniques later in this chapter. The Hyperlinks palette in QuarkXPress is used to assign a link to a selected item, whether that item is highlighted text, an image map area, or a picture box **1**. Hyperlinks are interactive only when they're viewed in a browser.

To create a hyperlink:

1. Show the Hyperlinks palette.

2. Choose the Item or Content tool, then click a picture box to use as a link.
or
Choose the Content tool, then highlight some text in a text box to use as a link.

3. Click the New Hyperlink button on the Hyperlinks palette.
or
Choose Style > Hyperlink > New.
or

(Continued on the following page)

With the pointer over the selected item, Control-click/Right-click, then choose Hyperlink > New from the context menu **1**.

4. Enter a location in the **URL** field. Acceptable locations include an anchor in the active document (see page 320); the URL for a file on the Internet; or the name of an exported file located in the same folder as the active document's exported .htm file.

or

Choose a destination from the **URL** pop-up menu **2**. Exported HTML files, URLs, and anchors that are present in the active document will appear on this pop-up menu. The name assigned to an exported QuarkXPress Web page that displays on this pop-up menu is taken from the Export File Name field in Page Properties dialog box. You can choose one of the four standard protocols, http://, https://, ftp://, or mailto: from the URL pop-up menu.

or

Click the Select/Browse button to the right of the URL field, locate the desired file name, then click Link. You can link to an exported HTML file from another folder, but keep in mind that for the link to work properly on the Internet, the file will need to be uploaded to the internet service provider's server along with your exported HTML Web files. Using the Link button enters a destination as a file name and any and all folder names the file is nested within.

5. Choose an option from the Target pop-up menu to designate where any destination HTML pages should display **3**. These frame targets are needed only if your form is embedded within a frame set on your Web page.

None (the empty space at the top) or **_self** to load the return page in the same frame or window that holds the current page.

What's on the menu?

The Hyperlink > **New** submenu on both the context menu and the Style menu also lists only those exported HTML files that are located in the same folder as the active Web document. You can choose one of those file names as the destination for a hyperlink.

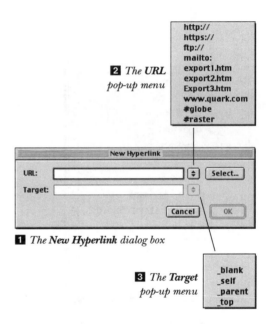

2 *The **URL** pop-up menu*

1 *The **New Hyperlink** dialog box*

3 *The **Target** pop-up menu*

Create Hyperlink

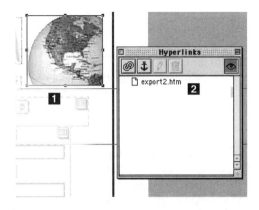

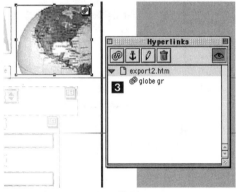

A hyperlink is created by clicking.

_blank to load the return page in a new, unnamed window.

_parent to load the return page into the parent frame, if there is one, of the current page.

_top to load the return page into the full browser window, replacing any frame sets.

6. Click OK. The new destination will appear on the palette, with the chosen hyperlink item nested below it. Click the expand/collapse icon (in the Mac OS it's a triangle, in Windows it's a +) to view the hyperlink item name.

TIP The Hyperlinks palette can list many destinations (assigned hyperlinks), but you don't have to use all of them in the active Web document.

Here's a method for creating a hyperlink without using a dialog box.

To create a hyperlink for an existing destination listing:

1. Show the Hyperlinks palette.

2. Click a picture box to use as a link **1**.
or
Highlight some text in a text box to use as a link.

3. Click an existing destination or anchor listing on the Hyperlinks palette **2** or Right-click/Control-click and choose a destination from the Hyperlink submenu. The name of the hyperlink item will be nested under the destination listing **3**.

To edit a hyperlink:

1. On the Hyperlinks palette, click a hyperlink, then click the Edit button. [✎]

2. Edit the URL field and/or the Target field, then click OK. The hyperlink listing will update on the palette.

Create, Edit Hyperlink

Anchors are special names that are attached to existing items on a page, and they function as placemarkers for a specific page in a Web document. If an anchor is chosen as a destination for a hyperlink, a user can click the anchor hyperlink on a Web page to get to the destination page where the actual anchor item resides.

To create an anchor:

1. In your Web document, highlight some text or select a text or picture box.

2. Click the New Anchor button on the Hyperlinks palette. ⬇
or
Choose Style > Anchor > New
or
Control-click/Right-click the selected item, then choose Anchor > New.

3. Change the picture or text Anchor Name that was entered automatically or leave it as is. If you type a space or other character that is not acceptable, an alert dialog box will appear.

4. Click OK **1**. Anchor names are preceded by a "#" on the pop-up menu in the Edit Hyperlink and New Hyperlink dialog boxes, on the Style > Hyperlink > submenu, and on the Hyperlinks palette.

*Click the **Show/Hide** (eye) button to show/hide the anchor indicator in a text box that contains a text anchor.*

1 *Every **anchor** is identified by an anchor icon on the **Hyperlinks** palette.*

1 *To delete a hyperlink, click the hyperlink name, then click the* **Delete** *button.*

You can rename an anchor at any time.

To rename an anchor:

1. Click an anchor name on the Hyperlinks palette.

2. Click the Edit button.

3. Change the name.

4. Click OK.

TIP An anchor can also be edited via Style > Anchor > Edit or via the Anchor > Edit command on the context menu.

If you want to break the link between the hyperlink text or object and the destination, you must delete the hyperlink to that destination. No text or objects will be deleted from the document—only the link information will be deleted.

To remove a hyperlink:

1. On the Hyperlinks palette, if the hyperlink you want to delete isn't visible, click the expand/collapse icon next to its destination or anchor.

2. Click the name of the hyperlink item (not the destination or anchor!) you want to delete **1**.

3. Click the Delete button on the palette. The hyperlink name will be removed; the destination or anchor will be preserved.

TIP If a text box or picture box is deleted from a document, any hyperlinks that the item contained will also be deleted, and the listing on the Hyperlinks palette will update to reflect the change.

TIP Hyperlinks can also be deleted via Style > Hyperlink > Delete or via the Hyperlink > Delete command on the context menu.

Rename Anchor; Remove Hyperlink

When a destination or anchor listing is deleted, only the hyperlink references to it are deleted—not the actual item itself.

To delete a destination or anchor:

1. On the Hyperlinks palette, click a destination name or anchor name .

2. Click the Delete button on the palette, then click OK in the alert box that appears **2**. The destination or anchor listing and all hyperlink references that point to that destination will be removed; the actual items will remain.

You can also use the Hyperlinks palette to quickly navigate through a Web document and locate a destination item box.

To go to a hyperlink item:

Double-click a hyperlink or anchor name on the Hyperlinks palette **3**. The item will be displayed in the document window. In the case of a hyperlink, the link item will be selected.

or

Click a hyperlink or anchor name on the Hyperlinks palette, Control-click/Right click the Hyperlinks palette, then choose Go To.

or

On the Hyperlinks palette, double-click a link to an HTML file that resides in another folder/directory on your hard drive. The default browser will open and that file will be displayed. *Note:* If you're not connected to the Internet when you double-click a destination listing in the same document or a URL destination located on the Internet, nothing will happen—you will go nowhere.

1 *On the Hyperlinks palette, click a* **destination** *name, then click the* **Delete** *button. The destination and any hyperlink references to that destination will be removed.*

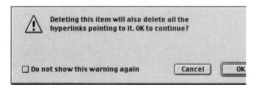

2 *This prompt appears when you* **delete** *a* **destination** *or* **anchor***.*

3 *On the Hyperlinks palette,* **double-click** *a link name. QuarkXPress will* **locate** *and select the hyperlink item and* **display** *it in the Web document window.*

Absolute vs. relative hyperlinks

An **absolute** hyperlink assigns a complete path location for the destination file, including the path from the system's root folder to the destination file or the complete http://www... listing. When a browser attempts to link to this destination, it must go onto the Internet to search for the appropriate Web server, which takes time. Also, you can't preview getting to a page linked via an absolute hyperlink using the HTML Preview button or using a browser that isn't currently online.

A **relative** hyperlink includes only a path to a folder/directory within the current Web site. A browser need only go to a different folder/directory within the current Web server (or system) to retrieve the destination file, which takes less time. You can preview getting to a page linked via a relative hyperlink.

As a general rule, you should use an absolute hyperlink to link to a destination on another Web site and a relative hyperlink to link to a destination in the current Web site.

1 *A picture box is selected in a Web document.*

2 *The destination page is entered in the URL field in the New Hyperlink dialog box.*

This technique creates internal (relative) hyperlinks that take a viewer to different pages within the same Web site.

To create a hyperlink from one page to another in a Web document:

1. Open or create a Web document that contains at least two pages.

2. On the first page:
   Click a picture box to use as a hyperlink **1**.
   or
   Select some text in a text box to use as a hyperlink.

3. Click the New Hyperlink button on the Hyperlink palette. 🔗
   or
   Choose Style > Hyperlink > New.

4. Enter the exact name of the export file for the page to go to, as listed in the Page Properties dialog box or on the Document Layout palette for that page **2**. Be sure to enter the .htm extension. To name the export file, go to Page > Page Properties.

   The new hyperlink under the destination you chose will now be listed on the Hyperlinks palette **3**.

TIP The Button and Image Button tools on the Web tool palette can't be used to create these types of navigation hyperlinks. To learn about those tools and their function, see pages 341 and 342.

*The new **hyperlink** will appear under the designated destination on the **Hyperlinks** palette.*

Page-to-Page Hyperlink

The restyling that you will be doing here will affect all the hyperlink text on the current page—and only the current page.

To style hyperlink text:

1. Choose Page > Page Properties (Cmd-Option-Shift-A/Ctrl-Alt-Shift-A.

2. In the Colors area **1**, choose new color options from the Link and Visited Link pop-up menus.

3. Click OK. *Note:* Colors chosen for hyperlink text via the Style menu or Colors palette override colors chosen via Colors: Link in the Page Properties dialog box.

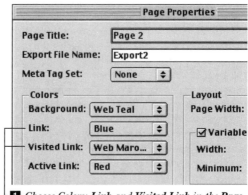

1 *Choose Colors:* **Link** *and* **Visited Link** *in the* **Page Properties** *dialog box.*

You can choose which color will be used to represent hyperlinks and anchors in a text box in Web (and PDF) documents. These colors will display in the QuarkXPress document, but not in the exported file. Since most browsers let users choose their own page and link colors, their choice will override yours.

To change the anchor icon color for a Web document:

1. Open a Web document—one that will be exported to HTML.

2. Choose Edit > Preferences > Preferences, then click Web Document: General.

3. In the Hyperlinks area **2**, click the Anchor Color square, modify the color, then click OK, then click OK to exit Preferences.

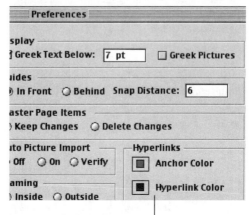

2 *The* **Hyperlinks** *area of Edit > Preferences > Preferences > Document–***General** *for a print document*

To change the anchor and/or hyperlink icon color for a PDF export:

1. Open a print document—one that will be exported to PDF.

2. Choose Edit > Preferences > Preferences, then click Document: General.

3. In the Hyperlinks area, click the Anchor Color and/or Hyperlink Color square **2**, modify the color, click OK, then click OK to exit Preferences.

Style Hyperlink; Change Icon Color

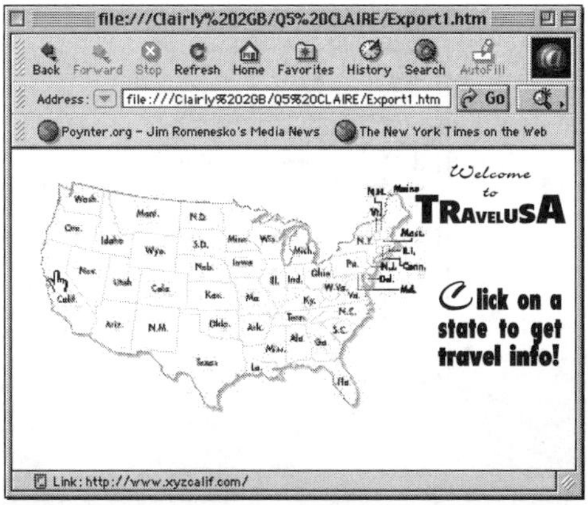
file:///Clairly%202GB/Q5%20CLAIRE/Export1.htm
Back Forward Stop Refresh Home Favorites History Search AutoFill
Address: file:///Clairly%202GB/Q5%20CLAIRE/Export1.htm
Go
Poynter.org - Jim Romenesko's Media News
The New York Times on the Web
Welcome to
TRAVELUSA
Click on a state to get travel info!
Link: http://www.xyzcalif.com/

1 *In this* ***image map****, each* ***hot area*** *represents one of the fifty United States. When a user clicks a state, they jump to another Web page.*

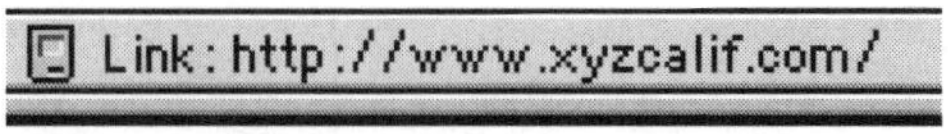
Link: http://www.xyzcalif.com/

2 *The* ***URL*** *link for a selected hot area in the image is listed at the bottom of the browser window.*

Image maps

Images can do more than just make a Web site look nice—they also can be used as links. First an image is divided into regions (called "hot areas"), and then each region is assigned a unique link **1**. Together, the hot areas and links form what is known an **image map**. If a user clicks on a region, they are taken to another Web page or site **2**. Image maps are fun to use and they look better than text links.

Image maps are an HTML feature, but to code an image map directly in HTML would be very laborious. Instead, in QuarkXPress 5, you can create image maps by defining one or more hot areas over a picture box (this doesn't affect or change the actual picture). Each hot area is assigned a hyperlink to another page in the same Web document or to another site on the Web. When the Web document is exported as an HTML file, QuarkXPress automatically creates the code for the image map. To create an image map, follow the instructions that begin on the next page.

A picture can contain one or more image map hot areas.

To create an image map:

1. The Image Map XTension must be loaded and enabled before you begin. To load and enable XTensions, see page 393.

2. With a Web document open, choose View > Show Guides (F7) to enable the newly-created image map area to remain displayed.

3. *Optional:* Select a picture box.

4. Choose the Rectangle or Oval Image Map tool **1**, move the pointer over the image, then drag across the image. Shift-drag to constrain a rectangle to a square or an oval to a circle.

or

Choose the Bézier Image Map tool, then draw a polygon over the image (the same way you would draw a Bézier text or picture box). To close the box, click the starting point or double-click the final point **2**.

Note: Any hot areas that extend outside the picture box will be cropped to the edges of the box when the page is exported.

5. To add a hyperlink to the hot area, keep the hot area selected, then:

Display the Hyperlinks palette, then click the New Hyperlink button **3**.

or

Choose Style > Hyperlink > New.

or

Control-click/Right-click and choose Hyperlink > New.

6. In the New Hyperlink dialog box (**1**, next page):

Enter a URL in the URL field.

or

From the URL pop-up menu, choose a URL, anchor, or exported HTML file that is currently being used as a link in the active file.

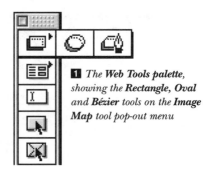

1 *The* **Web Tools palette,** *showing the* **Rectangle, Oval** *and* **Bézier** *tools on the* **Image Map** *tool pop-out menu*

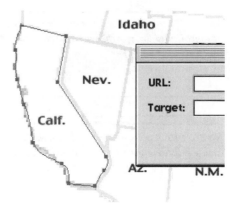

2 *A* **hot area** *created with the* **Bézier Image Map** *tool*

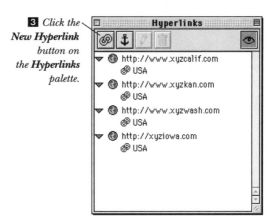

3 *Click the* **New Hyperlink** *button on the* **Hyperlinks** *palette.*

Create an Image Map

*Commonly used URL protocols (http://, https://, ftp://, etc.), other URLs in Web document, and other exported HTML files are listed on the **URL** pop-up menu.*

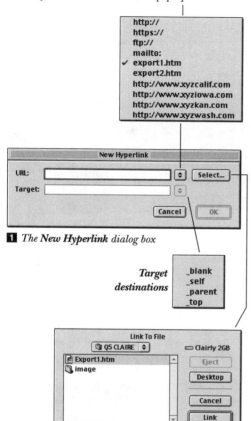

1 *The **New Hyperlink** dialog box*

Target destinations
_blank
_self
_parent
_top

Use the **Link to File** dialog box to locate and link to a local HTML file.

2 *Specify the **maximum** number of **points** on polygonal hot areas via the **Image Map Properties** dialog box.*

or

Click Select/Browse, locate an exported HTML file, then click Link/Open.

7. To designate where the linked Web page will display, enter a Target destination or choose a destination from the Target pop-up menu. If the Target field is left blank, the target destination will be ignored. A Target destination is needed only if your Web page contains a frame set.

_blank displays the linked Web page in a new unnamed window.

_self displays the linked Web page in the same frame as the image map.

_parent displays the linked Web page in the parent frame (window) of the image map. If no parent exists, the link will be displayed in the same frame as the image map.

_top displays the linked Web page in the full browser window, which eliminates all frames.

To learn more about the Hyperlinks palette, see page 317.

8. *Optional:* Repeat steps 3–7 to create other hot areas in the same picture box.

To preview the image map effect, see page 331. The hot area borders won't display in the browser.

TIP QuarkXPress converts oval hot areas into polygons. To control the precision with which it does so (the number of points that compose the polygon), go to Edit > Preferences > Preferences > Web Document–Tools, click the Oval Image Map tool icon, click Modify, enter a Flatten Shape: Maximum Points value **2**, then click OK.

TIP To create a hyperlink to an existing destination, click the image map hot area, then click the destination listing on the Hyperlinks palette.

An image's hot areas will move if the image is moved and will be scaled if the image is scaled. You can also edit an image map directly, as in these instructions.

Beware! If a different (new) image is imported into a picture box that has hot areas, all existing hot areas and hyperlinks will be deleted!

To edit an image map:

1. Make sure guides are showing (View > Show Guides or F7).

2. Select the picture box and the hot area.

3. To resize a hot area, drag its handles.
or
To reshape a hot area, edit its points as you would a normal Bézier box.
or
To move a hot area, select it, move the pointer over the area █, then drag █.
or
To delete a hot area, select it (make sure its handles are visible), then press Delete/Backspace.

4. To edit a hyperlink, click the link in the Hyperlinks palette █, then click the Edit Hyperlink button ⌷ at the top of the palette. In the Edit Hyperlink dialog box █, do any of the following: Retype the existing information; or choose another exported HTML file from the pop-up menu; or click the Select button to locate a file to link to, then click OK.

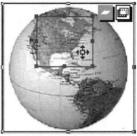

1 *To reposition an existing hot area within an image, move the pointer over the hot area...*

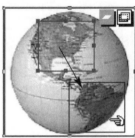

2 *...then drag it to a new location.*

3 *Click the Edit Hyperlink button on the Hyperlinks palette.*

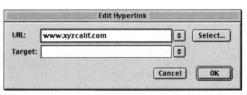

4 *Make changes in the Edit Hyperlink dialog box.*

1 *Two modes in a rollover.*

 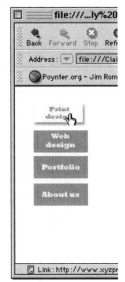

A list of option buttons   *When the mouse is moved over one of the buttons, its appearance changes. If the user clicks the item, they jump to another Web page.*

2 *Select a picture.*

3 *In the Rollover dialog box, choose a Rollover Image and a Hyperlink. Use the Select/Browse buttons to locate the image files quickly.*

Rollovers

Rollovers are another way to add interactivity to Web pages. A rollover is an image whose appearance changes when the mouse is moved over it **1**. Rollovers are used as visual cues to help a user find links on a page or to show the user additional information about a link. Rollovers are often used on Web pages that contain rows or columns of similar-looking menu options or buttons in order to give the user an idea which link their mouse is currently over.

Rollovers can't be produced in HTML; some programming help is required (usually JavaScript). While writing JavaScript code for a rollover isn't particularly difficult (see, for example, Peachpit's *JavaScript for the World Wide Web*, by Tom Negrino and Dori Smith)—it is time consuming. But here's another option: You can create your rollovers right in QuarkXPress 5, and it's not hard to do. First you select a default image and a rollover image, then you choose a hyperlink to another page in the Web or to another Web site. QuarkXPress does the rest for you.

To create a rollover:

1. Select a picture **2**, then choose Item > Rollover > Create Rollover.
   or
   Control-click/Right-click a picture and choose Create Rollover. Only pictures can be made into rollovers, and they must be saved in the GIF or JPEG format!

2. In the Rollover dialog box **3**, the path and file name for the **Default Image** will be filled in already—that's the picture that's currently selected. If you change this information, a new picture will be imported into the box.

   To choose a **Rollover Image**, click Select/Browse, locate a GIF or JPEG image to appear when the image is rolled over, then click Open. Or type

   (Continued on the following page)

the name manually. See the first tip below.

3. For the **Hyperlink** destination, from the Hyperlink pop-up menu, choose a URL, HTML file, or anchor that is currently being used as a link in the active document. Or click Select/Browse, then choose a URL or a local HTML file.

4. Click OK **1**. To preview the rollover, see the instructions on the next page.

TIP If the rollover image is larger than the default image, the rollover image will be scaled and cropped to fit the picture box that contains the default image. To prevent this from happening, make sure the rollover image is approximately the same size as the default image.

TIP When you export the HTML file (see page 316), QuarkXPress will create the required JavaScript code for the rollover. To view the code, you can either choose View > Source in your browser application or open the exported .htm file in a text editor, such as SimpleText, BBEdit, or Wordpad.

To edit a rollover:

1. Select the picture box that contains a rollover.

2. Choose Item > Rollover > Edit Rollover or Control-click/Right-click and choose Edit Rollover.

3. Change the Default Image, Rollover image, or Hyperlink destination.

4. Click OK.

TIP You can also edit a hyperlink by clicking the hyperlink listing on the Hyperlinks palette, clicking the Edit button, then changing the URL or Target (see page 319).

Linking pages

To create a rollover that **links** two **pages** of a Web document, export those pages, then follow the steps on this page to create a rollover. From the Hyperlink pop-up menu in the Rollover dialog box, choose the export file name for the second page to create a link to it. As an option, on the second page, you can create a rollover that links to the first page or to another Web page.

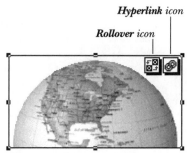

Hyperlink icon

Rollover icon

1 *This image is now a rollover.*

Edit a Rollover

1 *In the browser, the **normal** state of the rollover displays when the pointer is **not over** the item.*

2 *In the browser, position the pointer **over** the rollover. The **hand** pointer displays, and the substitute **rollover image** also displays.*

To delete a rollover:

1. Select the picture box that contains a rollover.

2. Choose Item > Rollover > Delete Rollover or Control-click/Right-click and choose Delete Rollover. (You could also, of course, delete the picture box altogether; the rollover will be deleted along with it.)

To preview an image map or rollover:

1. Display a page that contains an image map or rollover item.

2. Click the HTML Preview button ▭ at the bottom of the Web document window.

3. In the browser, position the pointer over the image map hot area or rollover **1** (you'll see the hand pointer). For a rollover, the rollover image should now be displayed **2**. Click the image map area or rollover. If the browser can locate the link page, that page will display. If the browser can't locate the link page or if the link is a URL and the browser isn't currently connected to the Internet, then an alert box will display. Click OK, then click back in a QuarkXPress window to return to your document.

If Visual Indicators is on in a Web document and a picture box has a rollover, anchor, or hyperlink attached to it, a special icon signifying that function will appear in the upper right corner of the box.

To view visual indicators:

If the indicators aren't currently showing, choose View > Show Visual Indicators. You may also see an anchor, hyperlink, rollover, layer, image map, or rasterized text icon. To find out what an icon signifies, rest the pointer over it and read the context tip that appears **1**–**6**.

#globe

The name of the anchor

1 *Anchor*

Export3.htm

The destination name for the link

2 *Hyperlink*

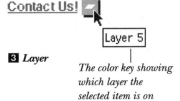

Layer 5

3 *Layer*

The color key showing which layer the selected item is on

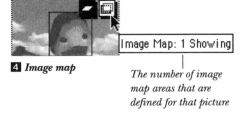

Image Map: 1 Showing

4 *Image map*

The number of image map areas that are defined for that picture

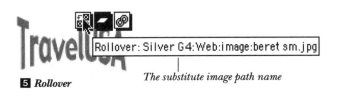

Rollover: Silver G4:Web:image:beret sm.jpg

5 *Rollover*

The substitute image path name

Rasterized

6 *Rasterized text (text box to be converted to a bitmap graphic upon export)*

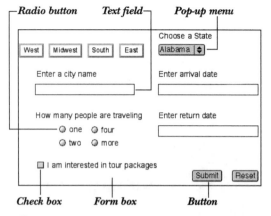

Radio button   *Text field*   *Pop-up menu*

1 **Form controls** *within a* **form box** *on a Web page*

Check box   *Form box*   *Button*

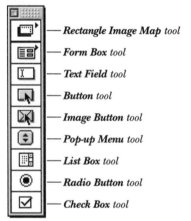

—— **Rectangle Image Map** *tool*

—— **Form Box** *tool*

—— **Text Field** *tool*

—— **Button** *tool*

—— **Image Button** *tool*

—— **Pop-up Menu** *tool*

—— **List Box** *tool*

—— **Radio Button** *tool*

—— **Check Box** *tool*

2 *The tools on the* **Web** *tools palette are used to create various types of* **controls** *for Web pages.*

Forms

Viewers use forms **1** on a Web page to enter information, check options, or make choices from a list. Then they click a Submit button to send the data to the Web server for processing. Forms for data collection can be used to order products, request documents, perform searches on a Web site, or send user information to a Web site. The HTML language supports form tags that can be used on a Web page. The Web browser reads the form tags and creates the field, box, or button. A form box is the container that holds text fields, buttons, etc.

There are a variety of ways data can be entered or chosen on a form, such as text entry fields, lists, pop-up menus, check boxes, and radio buttons, along with the requisite Submit and Reset buttons. Quark-XPress calls these various parts of a form "controls," and provides several tools on the Web tool palette for creating them **2**. The tool name matches the kind of form control that it creates. For example, the Pop-up Menu tool creates a pop-up menu control.

A server-based script or application is required to process form data. Most often, CGI (Common Gateway Interface) scripts are used for this purpose. QuarkXPress does not provide the means to create these scripts; a third-party application is required. Talk with your Webmaster to learn more about the creation of CGI or other server-based scripts.

To create a form box:

1. Choose the Form Box tool from the Web tool palette.

2. Position the pointer over a blank area of the Web page, then drag to create a form box. A form box can't overlap any other existing form boxes.

TIP Form boxes are always positioned on a special layer behind all the other items on the page (see page 337).

Create Form Box

To choose options for a form box:

1. Choose the Item or Content tool, then click a form box.

2. Choose Item > Modify, then click the Form tab 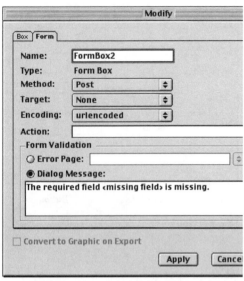.

3. *Optional:* Change the Name. You can leave the default name as is, but remember that each form box must have a unique name.

4. Choose an option from the Method pop-up menu to be used for submission of form data:

   Post to send the user-entered data as a separate packet to the Web server. This is usually the preferred option.
   or
   Get to append the user-entered data to the end of the URL or the end of the file specified by the URL in the Action field. The Get method may append excess data, thus exceeding the URL length limit and resulting in data loss.

5. From the Target pop-up menu, choose where you want any server-returned data (usually an HTML page) to display. *Note:* These frame targets are needed only if your form is embedded within a frame set on your Web page.

   None (the empty line on the pop-up menu) or **_self** to load the return page in the same frame or window that holds the form.

   _blank to load the return page in a new, unnamed window.

   _parent to load the return page into the parent frame, if there is one, of the form.

   _top to load the return page into the full browser window, replacing any frame sets.

6. If Post was chosen for the Method in step 4, you need to choose a MIME type encoding option (that's short for Multi-purpose Internet Mail Extension).

1 *The **Form** pane in the **Modify** dialog box for a **form** box*

MIMEs are helper applications that aid in the translation of data. Choose one of the following:

urlencoded to make the user-data submitted to the Web server follow the urlencoded specifications so the data can be used on most operating system platforms and software applications.

form-data to alert the Web server that the user-data is being submitted as a separate attached file and should be encoded as multipart form-data. This way, the server will read the multiple parts of the form submission and not just the name of the attached file.

plain to specify that user-data submitted to the Web server not be encoded.

7. In the Action field, enter a URL for the CGI script that will process the user-data submitted to the Web server.
or
Click Select (Mac OS)/Browse (Windows), then locate and open an existing script file.

8. In the Form Validation area, choose the response method for a submitted form that lacks an entry in a required field:

Click **Error Page** to have an existing HTML page display in response to an error. Enter a URL for that page; or choose an HTML file from the pop-up menu; or click Select (Mac OS)/Browse (Windows), then locate an HTML page file (its path will be entered automatically in the URL field).
or
Click **Dialog Message**, then enter an alert message in the text field or leave the default message as is. The <missing field> tag allows the name of the first empty required field to be entered automatically into an alert message.

9. Click OK.

TIP You can't directly enter text or import a picture into a form box.

Form Box Options

You can specify dimensions for the form box that is created automatically when any form control tool is used (but not the Form tool itself). The settings you specify will remain in effect until they're changed.

To choose default dimensions for form boxes:

1. Choose Edit > Preferences > Preferences > Web Document–Tools.

2. Scroll down to the bottom of the Tool Defaults window, then click the Form Box tool icon ⊞ **1**.

3. Click Modify.

4. Enter default Width and Height dimensions for the form box in pixels, click OK, then click OK to close the Preferences dialog box.

Form can-do's

■ When you move a form box, any form controls within the box will move along with it.

■ A control can be duplicated within the same form box, provided there's sufficient room for the duplicate in the box.

■ Scale a form box like any other box: Click the box with the Item or Content tool, then drag any handle.

■ Form boxes are deleted the same way other standard items are: Click the box with the Item or Content tool, then press Delete/Backspace or Cmd-K/Ctrl-K.

■ To copy a control, Copy or Cut it using the Item tool, then Paste it into its current form box or another form box (the box must be large enough to accommodate it). A control can also be dragged from one form box to another.

Form can'ts

■ The Group command is not available for controls inside a form box.

■ Controls are always contained inside a form box—they can't be hanging around loose somewhere.

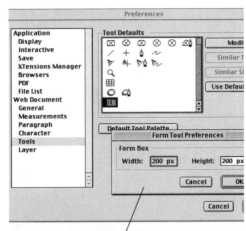

1 *Set Form Tool Preferences in Edit > Preferences > Preferences > Web Document–Tools.*

Form Box Tool; Form Guidelines

Changing what is

To edit an existing control, first select the **control box**—not the surrounding form box—choose Item > **Modify**, click Form, then change any of the settings.

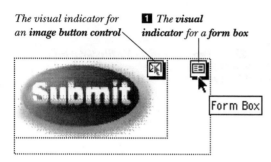

The visual indicator for an image button control

1 *The visual indicator for a form box*

■ A control can't overlap or reside inside another control. You'll get an alert prompt if you try to draw a new control inside an existing control.

Forms and layers

Form boxes and form controls are contained on an invisible forms layer (it's not even listed on the Layers palette!). No selected item icon displays on the Layers palette and no layer icon (visual indicator) displays when a form box is selected in a Web document. The forms layer isn't editable directly. The current Visible, Locked, and Suppress Printout settings for the Default layer apply to items on the forms layer. Forms also have a unique visual indicator that's different from the layer indicator **1**.

The forms layer is always the backmost layer in a Web document, and it can't be moved upward on the list. The form box is the backmost item on this layer, with the controls in front of it. Any non-form items on a Web page will be in front of the forms.

The other form tools

The other tools on the Web tool palette that we haven't discussed yet—**Text Field, Button, Image Button, Pop-up Menu, List Box, Radio Button, Check Box,** and **File Selection**—can be used either to create a control within a whole new form box or to add controls to an existing form box. If you drag with any of these tools in a blank area of your document, a **new form box** will be created in its default size, with the control inside it. If you drag inside an existing form box, the control will be **added to**, and contained within, that box. More than one control can be created within an existing form box, provided you don't try to draw a new control on top of an existing one.

The next twelve pages of this chapter are devoted to forms and the form tools.

Text field controls are added to a Web page to allow the user to enter characters, or to type a password which shows up in the field as a series of asterisks.

To create a text or password field control:

1. Choose the Text Field tool from the Web tool palette. I

2. Drag in a blank area of the Web page.
   or
   Drag inside a blank area of an existing form box.

3. Choose Item > Modify, then click the Form tab **1**.

4. Change the name in the Name field or leave the default name as is. Each control must have a unique name.

5. Choose one of these options from the Type pop-up menu:

   Text-Single Line to create an entry field that will contain only one line of text.

   Text-Multi Line to create an entry field that can contain multiple lines of text and a scroll bar.

   Password to create an entry field that will display a user-entered password as a series of asterisks. *Note:* A password field control does not perform the actual processing of password protection. That processing is a function of the CGI script.

   Hidden Field to create a text field that will be invisible to the user, but that can contain pre-entered text to be submitted along with the form data. No other options are available when Hidden Field is chosen.

6. Enter a value in the **Max Chars** field to specify the maximum number of characters the field can hold. Leave this field blank to have the Web browser determine the maximum number of characters.

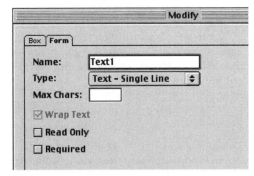

1 *The* **Form** *pane in the* **Modify** *dialog box for a* **Text Field** *control*

shifting the scale

In HTML, text field controls are sized based on the character count as well as the font size specified in the browser preferences, whereas in a QuarkXPress Web document, controls and other items are sized based on pixels. As a result, a control that you create in QuarkXPress will probably appear to have different dimensions or even different positioning when viewed in a browser. Hopefully, these discrepancies will be resolved in a future version of QuarkXPress.

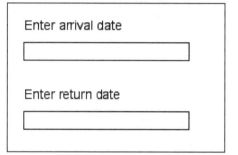

1 *Two* **Text Field** *controls, along with standard text boxes for explanation text, within a form box in a Web document*

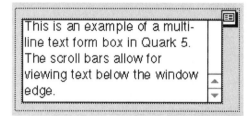

2 *A* **Text Field** *control with Text:* **Multi-line** *chosen (note the scroll bar)*

7. *Optional:* If you chose Text-Multi Line for step 5, you can check Wrap Text to have multiple lines of text automatically wrap within the multi-line text field control.

8. *Optional:* Check **Read Only** to prevent the user from editing any text in the text field control when it's displayed in a browser.

Optional: Check **Required** to specify that the text field control must contain an entry before the submitted form can be considered valid. With this option checked, if the user tries to submit the form with an empty required field, the chosen Form Validation method will be activated (see step 8 on page 335).

9. Click OK **1**–**2**.

In a browser, if a user enters more text than a field can display, the user won't see the complete entry, and errors are more likely to occur. Whenever possible, make sure your control—especially if it's the Text-Single Line type—is wide enough to display a user's complete entry.

To scale a control:

Choose the Item or Content tool, click a control, then drag a handle **1**–**2**. A single-line text field control can only be resized horizontally; a multi-line text field control can be resized using any handle.

To move a control:

Choose the Item tool or hold down Cmd/ Ctrl if the Content tool is chosen, then drag the control to a new position within the form box. You can select and then move more than one control at a time.

TIP You can't drag a control or any of its handles outside its form box.

To delete a control:

Click a control using the Item tool, then press Delete/Backspace.
or
Click a control using the Content tool, then press Cmd-K/Ctrl-K.

It's not the same!

You align your controls nicely in QuarkXPress, and then view your Web page in a browser—and lo and behold, the alignment seems out of whack. To help reduce this problem, make sure the controls don't overlap each other or overlap any non-control items (e.g., standard text or picture boxes). Also, to align items, use Item > Space/Align or use ruler guides in combination with View > Snap to Guides.

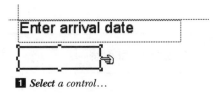

1 *Select a control...*

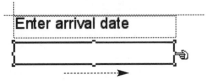

2 *...then drag a handle to* **scale** *it.*

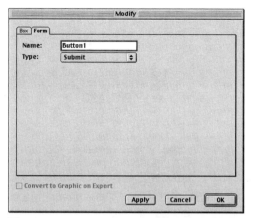

1 *This is the* **Form** *pane in the* **Modify** *dialog box for a* **Button** *control. In this case, a submit button will be created.*

Enter arrival date

[   ]

Enter return date

[   ]

[Submit] [Reset]

2 *The* **Submit** *and* **Reset buttons** *and two text field controls are all in the same form box. The Submit button sends text entered by the user in the text field controls to the Web server; the Reset button is used to clear any user-entered text from the text field controls.*

The requisite submit button control is used to send user data from a Web page form to the Web server. The reset button control is used to clear user-data from fields and boxes in a form so a user can reenter data, if need be. The submit and reset buttons must be created within the same form box as the check box, text field, and radio button controls, otherwise they won't know which data to submit or reset. The button functions can only be previewed in a browser.

To create a submit or reset button control:

1. Choose the Button tool.
2. Drag in a blank area of the Web page.
   or
   Drag inside a blank area of an existing form box.
3. Choose Item > Modify, then click the Form tab **1**.
4. Change the Name or leave the default entry as is. Each control must have a unique name.
5. From the Type pop-up menu, choose the kind of button you want to create:
   Reset restores all controls within the form box to their default values (usually a blank state).
   or
   Submit sends the data contained within the form box to the target CGI script.
6. Click OK **2**.
7. Click with the Content tool on the control, then enter the desired button name. The button will automatically scale to fit the length of the name. You can't style the button text. It will be displayed in the browser's default sans serif font, as specified in the browser's preferences.

You can also use an image as a submit or reset button control  instead of using text.

Note: At the present time, for this type of control, there is no Type pop-up menu in the Form pane in Item > Modify that will allow you to switch between the submit or reset functions, so the button can only be used for the submit function.

To create a submit or reset button control using an image:

1. Choose the Image Button tool.

2. Drag in a blank area of the Web page.
   or
   Drag in a blank area inside an existing form box.

3. Choose File > Get Picture, locate a picture file, then click Open.

4. Choose Item > Modify (Cmd-M/ Ctrl-M), then click the Export tab **2**.

5. Choose a graphics file format from the Export As pop-up menu: JPEG, GIF, or PNG. To learn more about these formats, see pages 308–312.

6. In the Alternate Text field, enter a text description that can be substituted for the image or leave the default entry as is. Alternate Text is used when image display is turned off for the browser, and is also used by visually impaired users to navigate through a site.

7. The remaining options in the Export tab will vary depending on which Export As format you chose in step 5.

   For **JPEG**, choose an option from the **Image Quality** pop-up menu: Highest, High, Medium, Low, or Lowest. The higher the quality setting, the less the image will be compressed, but the larger its file storage size will be and the longer its download time will be. Check **Progressive** to have the image display in progressively more detail as it downloads.
   or

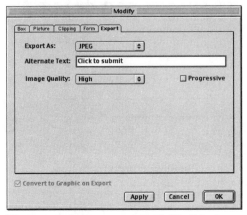

1 *To create this button, we drew a button in Adobe Illustrator, saved the file as an .eps, created an Image Button control in QuarkXPress, and then imported the .eps file into the image button control box.*

2 *This is the **Export** pane of the Modify dialog box for an **Image Button** control, with **JPEG** chosen from the Export As pop-up menu.*

Renaming a control

Each and every control to be used on a Web must have a **unique** name. To rename an image button or any other type of control, select the control, choose Item > Modify, click the Form tab, change the Name, then click OK.

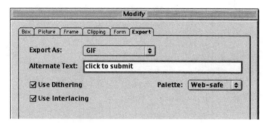

1 *This is the **Export** pane of the Modify dialog box for an **Image Button** control, with **GIF** chosen from the Export As pop-up menu.*

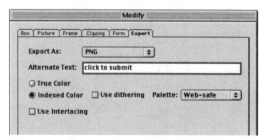

2 *This is the **Export** pane of the Modify dialog box for an **Image Button** control, with **PNG** chosen from the Export As pop-up menu.*

For **GIF 1**, check **Use Dithering** to have image colors not found on the browser palette display as a combination of two colors. Check **Use Interlacing** to have the image display in progressively more detail as it downloads. And choose an option from the **Palette** pop-up menu (Web-safe, Adaptive, Windows, or Mac OS) to be used for reducing the number of colors in the image to the 256 that a browser can display. We recommend Web-safe, since this palette contains only those colors used by both the Navigator and Explorer browsers.
or
For **PNG 2**, click **True color** to preserve the maximum possible number of existing image colors for display in the browser, or click **Indexed color** to limit the number of image colors to 256. If you clicked Indexed color, you can check **Use Dithering** to have image colors that aren't found on the browser palette display as a combination of two colors; and choose an option from the **Palette** pop-up menu (Web-safe, Adaptive, Windows, or Mac OS) to be used for reducing the number of colors in the image to the 256 that a browser can display. Web-safe is a good choice, since this palette contains only those colors used by both the Navigator and Explorer browsers. Check **Use Interlacing** to have the image display in progressively more detail as it downloads.

8. Click OK.

A user can choose a control option, or navigate to supplementary information using a control option, by selecting it from a pop-up menu or scroll list. The list control offers several options at a time, whereas the pop-up menu has to be clicked on in order for its contents to be revealed.

To create a pop-up menu or list control:

1. Choose the Pop-up Menu tool ⬦ or the List Box tool. ▦

2. Drag in a blank area of the Web page.
or
Drag in a blank area inside an existing form box.

3. With the pop-up menu control still selected, choose Item > Modify, then click the Form tab **1**–**2**.

4. Change the name in the Name field or leave the default entry as is. Remember, as we've said before, each control must have a unique name.

5. From the Type pop-up menu, choose Pop-up Menu to create a pop-up menu control or List to create a scroll list control. Either way, the effect can only be previewed in a browser.

6. Choose an existing menu set from the Menu pop-up menu or click New to create a new Menu Set. For more information about menu sets, see page 346.

7. *Optional:* If you chose List for step 5, above, check Allow Multiple Selections to enable users to choose more than one item at a time on the scroll list.

8. *Optional:* Check Required to require that the user make a selection from the pop-up menu or list before the submitted form can be considered valid. If the user attempts to submit the form without making a selection, the chosen Form Validation error method will be activated (see step 8 on page 335).

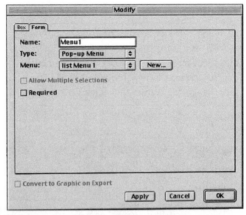

1 *This is the **Form** pane of the **Modify** dialog box for a **Pop-up Menu** control.*

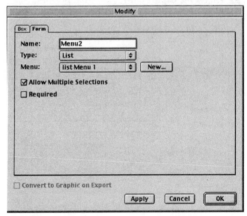

2 *This is the **Form** pane of the **Modify** dialog box for a **List Box** control.*

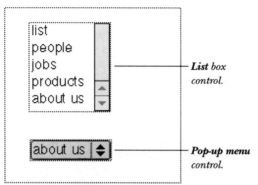

— **List** *box control.*

— **Pop-up menu** *control.*

1 *Both the List Box and the Pop-up Menu use the same menu set, so the same entry names are available in each. The **default** entry in the menu set is **"about us."** This default entry displays in the collapsed pop-up menu box and will be highlighted in the list box when the Web page is viewed in a browser.*

9. Click OK **1**.

TIP To scale a list control vertically, select the control, then move the top or bottom midpoint handle. A pop-up menu control can't be resized manually. This type of control is scaled automatically to fit the largest text entry in the applied menu set.

TIP A list control will have a scroll bar only if the chosen menu set items overflow the current list box in the QuarkXPress Web document.

TIP We recommend that you create a separate text box with text that instructs the user how and why to use the pop-up menu or list control.

Pop-Up Menu or List Control

A list control or pop-up menu control offers a list of items for the user to choose from. A menu set provides that list of items, along with values or URL addresses for each item listed.

To create a menu set:

1. Choose Edit > Menus, then click New.
   or
   In the Form pane in Item > Modify for a pop-up menu control or list control, click Menu: New.

2. Type a name for the set in the Name field. Check Navigation Menu if the items to be created will be used to take a user to another Web page .

3. Click Add, then enter a name for the individual item.

4. If you checked Navigation Menu in step 2, above, and you want the menu item to link the user to another page, enter a valid URL or path for that Web page in the Hyperlink field . To have the path name be entered automatically, choose a file name from the Hyperlink pop-up menu or use the Select/Browse button to locate an existing external file. Only names of exported HTML files, URLs, and anchors that are currently being used as links in the active document will appear on the Hyperlink pop-up menu.

   If you didn't check Navigation Menu in step 2, enter a Value for the item. The information entered into the Value field will be sent to the Web server when the item is selected and the form is submitted 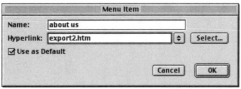.

5. Check Use as Default to make the current item the selected (highlighted) item in the list control that uses this menu set. In a pop-up menu control, this default item will be the only visible item when the pop-up menu is collapsed. You can also specify a default

The other buttons

In the **Edit Menu** dialog box, click **Duplicate** to make a copy of the selected item; or click **Edit** (or just double-click the item name) to edit a selected item; or click **Delete** to delete a selected item.

In the **Menus** dialog box, click **Edit** to edit a selected menu set; or click **Duplicate** to make a copy of the selected menu set; or click **Delete** to delete a selected menu set.

1 *Use the **Edit Menu** dialog box to create a menu set. With the **Navigation Menu** option checked, each menu item must contain a URL as its Value.*

2 *If the Navigation Menu option is **checked** in the Edit Menu dialog box, a **Hyperlink** field is present in the **Menu Item** dialog box. Enter a URL in this field for the current menu item to link to.*

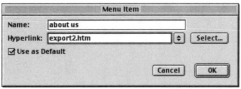

3 *If the Navigation Menu option is **not checked** in the Edit Menu dialog box, a **Value** field is present in the **Menu Item** dialog box. Enter data in this field to be sent to the Web server when the current menu item is selected by a user in the browser.*

Create Menu Set

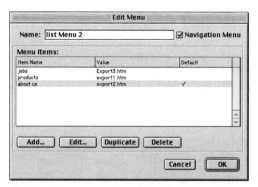

1 *The new menu item from figure* **2** *on the previous page appears on the* **Item Name** *list in the* **Edit Menu** *dialog box.*

2 *Drag with the* **File Selection** *tool to create a* **browse** *button control.*

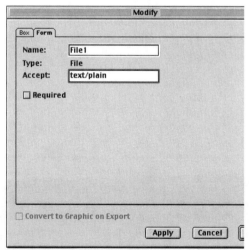

3 *The* **Form** *pane of the* **Modify** *dialog box: a* **File Selection** *control is being created.*

item in the main Edit Menu dialog box (see step 7).

6. Click OK **1**.

7. *Optional:* Click in the Default column for an item to make it the current default for a control that uses this menu set.

8. Click OK, then click Save to save the menu set.

Next, we'll show you how to provide a Browse button for a user to click to locate and select a file to be sent when a form is submitted to a Web server.

To create a separate file selection control:

1. Choose the File Selection tool 📎✚ (it's on the Form Box tool pop-out menu).

2. Drag in a blank area of the Web page.
   or
   Drag in a blank area inside an existing form box **2**.

3. Choose Item > Modify (Command-M/ Ctrl-M), then click the Form tab **3**.

4. Change the Name or leave the default entry as is. Each control must have a unique name.

5. *Optional:* In the Accept field, enter the names of MIME types, separating each name by commas. This list will be used by the Web server to help it interpret the separate file that will be submitted with the form.

6. Check Required to require that the user click Browse, then choose a file to be sent along with the submitted form.

7. Click OK.

Radio buttons enable a user to choose an option from a group of options. Only one radio button in a group can be chosen at a time. A check box, on the other hand, enables a user to choose one or more options from a group.

To create a radio button or check box control:

1. Choose the Radio Button tool ⊙ or the Check Box tool.☑

2. Drag in a blank area of the Web page.
or
Drag in a blank area inside an existing form box. To be in a group, radio button controls must be created within the same form box.

3. With the control selected, choose Item > Modify, then click the Form tab **1**–**2**.

4. Change the name or leave the default name as is. Each check box control must have a unique name; a radio button requires a group name. If you want radio button controls within the same form box to be in a group (e.g., to ensure that only one button in a form will be highlighted at a time), they must all use the same Group name.

> **TIP** If you have created several radio buttons, select them, choose Item > Modify (Form pane), then enter a name for the button group.

5. From the Type pop-up menu, choose Check box to create a check box control or choose Radio button to create a radio button control.

6. Enter a Value to be sent to the Web server when the control is selected and the form is submitted. The Value informs the data-controlling script what the chosen option signifies (e.g., a yes to a question or an amount from a category).

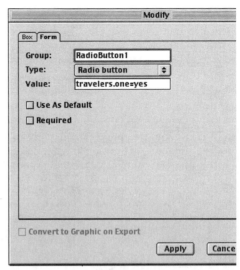

1 *The Form pane of the Modify dialog box: a* ***radio button*** *control is being created.*

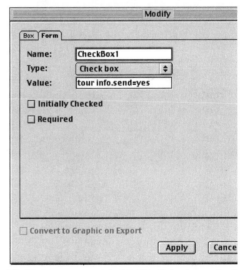

2 *The Form pane of the Modify dialog box: a* ***check box*** *control is being created.*

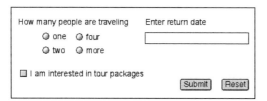

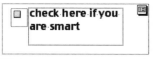

1 *These are **radio button** and **check box** controls within a form box on a Web page. **Submit** sends the value entered in the Value field (Form pane) for the radio button controls that are clicked and check box controls that are checked. **Reset** unhighlights and unchecks all the controls in the form box.*

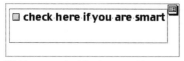

2 *Enter text **inside** the control box.*

3 *Or enter text into a **separate** box.*

7. *Do any of the following optional steps:*

For a check box control, check Initially Checked to have the current control be checked when the Web page initially displays or the form is reset.

For a radio button, check Use As Default to have the current button control be selected when the Web page initially displays or the form is reset. In a group of radio buttons, only one button can be pre-selected at a time.

Check Required to require that the control be clicked or checked before the submitted form will be considered valid. If the user tries to submit the form without the required selection, the chosen Form Validation error method will be activated (see step 8 on page 335).

8. Click OK **1**.

9. Enlarge the box that holds the control by dragging any of its handles (the control can't extend outside the form box). Choose the Content tool, then enter text to identify the button or box **2**. The text can be styled or indented using the Style menu or the Measurements palette.
or
Enter text into a separate text box, and then align that box with the control box **3**.

Meta tags

Web search engines describe and index Web pages when generating a search list, using the first lines of text found on a Web page as a page description. Attaching a meta tag to a Web page—an HTML tag that describes the content of the page—gives you control over what text a search engine uses, thus preventing your page from being described incorrectly. By ensuring that your Web page is properly described and indexed on a search list, Web users will be able to find your site more readily in a search, and you will generate more traffic to your site.

The various categories and options used in meta tags come from the data-transfer system and organization used by Web servers. In QuarkXPress, meta tag categories are organized into a meta tag set, which in turn can be incorporated into the code for a Web page. It's all behind the scenes, though; meta tags don't produce any visible items on a Web page.

To create a meta tag set:

1. With a Web document open, choose Edit > Meta Tags, then click New 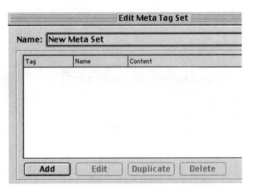.

2. Enter a Name for the set.

3. Click Add.

4. In the New Meta Tag dialog box, choose an attribute from the Meta Tag pop-up menu or enter an attribute in the field:

   Name to designate the category of tag names that describe information about the Web page, such as the author, any copyrights, a brief page description, the application used to create the page, or keywords to use for indexing the page.
   or
   http-equiv to designate the category of tag names that instruct the browser to perform specific actions when displaying the page, such as which character set to use for the page, how to cache

Where they're stored

If a set is created using the Meta Tags command when a Web document is open (as with all the commands on the lower part of the Edit menu), that set will be stored only with that document. If a set is created when no documents are open, it will be stored as a default in the XPress Preferences file.

The **Edit Meta Tag Set** dialog box for a new **tag set**

*The Name pop-up
menu when **name** is
chosen as the Meta Tag*

author
copyright
description
distribution
generator
keywords
resource-type
revisit-after
robots

*The **Name** pop-up
menu when **http-equiv** is
chosen as the Meta Tag*

charset
cache-control
content-language
content-script-type
content-style-type
content-type
expires
pics-label
pragma
refresh
reply-To
set-cookie
window-target

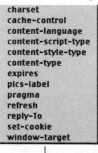

New Meta Tag

Meta Tag: name

Name: keywords

Content: QuarkXPress 5, Quark 5, QuarkXPress 5 web page, Quark 5 web page, web document, create web page **2**

Cancel   OK

1 *In the **New Meta Tag** dialog box, **keywords** was chosen for a **Name** and a list of keywords to be used in a search were entered in the **Content** field.*

Edit Meta Tag Set

Name: Set 1

Tag	Name	Content
name	keywords	QuarkXPress 5, Quark 5, QuarkXPress 5
name	description	An example of a web page design generate
name	author	peter
name	generator	QuarkXPress 5.0

Add   Edit   Duplicate   Delete

Cancel

3 *The **Meta Tag Set** dialog box lists each **Tag**, **Name**, and **Content**.*

the page in the browser, when the page should expire from the browser cache, and when to automatically refresh (reload) the page into the browser.

5. Choose a value from the Name pop-up menu or enter a value in the field **1**. The values displayed on the pop-up menu will vary depending on which attribute was chosen in the previous step. (See the QuarkXPress 5 documentation for a description of the Name field options.)

6. In the Content field, enter descriptive content text, separating each phrase by commas.

7. Click OK.

8. Click Add to create other desired meta tags, then repeat steps 4–7. You could repeat steps 4–7 several times in order to create meta tags for the author's name, for the generator program and version used to create the page, for a description of the page (entered in the Content field), and for keywords (entered in the Content field, with each phrase separated by commas) **2** (see also **2**, next page).

9. When you're done, click OK **3**, then click Save to save the whole set.

TIP In the Meta Tags dialog box, click Duplicate to duplicate the current set.

TIP In the Meta Tags dialog box, click Delete to delete the current set. If a meta tag set is attached to the active Web document, an alert dialog box will appear. From the pop-up menu, choose a replacement meta tag set or choose None; click OK; then click Save.

TIP If no Web document is open when you choose Edit > Meta Tags, then you will create a default meta tag set that isn't associated or stored with any particular document.

Create Meta Tag Set

To edit a meta tag set:

1. Choose Edit > Meta Tags.

2. Choose a set name, then click Edit.

3. Click a tag in the scroll window, then click Edit.

4. Choose new options from the pop-up menus and/or modify the text in the Content field.

5. Click OK twice, then click Save.

You can attach a different meta tag set to each page in a Web document.

To attach a meta tag set to a Web page:

1. Open the desired Web document and go to the desired page.

2. Choose Page > Page Properties (Cmd-Option-Shift-A/Ctrl-Alt-Shift-A).

3. Choose a meta tag set from the Meta Tag Set pop-up menu 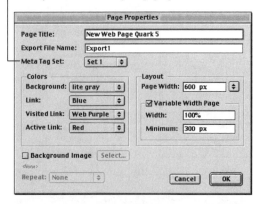–❷.

4. Click OK. The attached meta tag set can be changed to a different set at any time.

You can append a meta tag set from one Web document to another.

To append a meta tag set:

1. Open the Web document to which you want to append a meta tag set.

2. Choose Edit > Meta Tags.

3. Click Append. Locate another Web document that contains a meta tag set, then click Open.

4. In the Available window, click a meta tag set name (or Shift-click multiple set names).

5. Click the right arrow to include the set(s), then click OK.

6. Click Save to save the changes.

❶ *In the* **Page Properties** *dialog box, choose from the* **Meta Tag Set** *pop-up menu.*

❷ *Source code in the* **Internet Explorer** *browser, showing the Meta Tags created in QuarkXPress and attached to a Web document page*

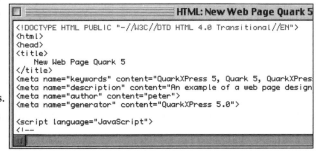

(Left margin:) **Edit, Attach, Append Meta Tag Set**

Libraries 20

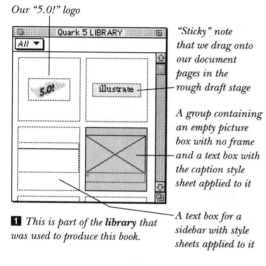

Our "5.0!" logo

"Sticky" note that we drag onto our document pages in the rough draft stage

A group containing an empty picture box with no frame and a text box with the caption style sheet applied to it

1 *This is part of the **library** that was used to produce this book.*

A text box for a sidebar with style sheets applied to it

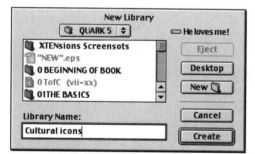

2 *In the **New Library** dialog box, enter a **Library** Name, then click **Create**.*

A library is a special kind of file that is used to organize and store any item—a box, with or without text or a picture, a line, a text path, a table, or a group of items. Each library is displayed as a floating palette **1**, and can contain up to 2,000 items. When you drag an item from a floating library palette into any QuarkXPress document window, a copy of the item appears in the document. An unlimited number of libraries can be created.

Note: Since the version of a picture that is stored in a library is just its low-resolution preview, this keeps library file sizes relatively small. But if you send a document containing library elements for imagesetting, however—as with any picture you use in a QuarkXPress document—you'll need to supply the original picture files. A library can also serve a supporting role as a handy picture catalog.

To create a library:

1. Choose File > New > Library (Cmd-Option-N/Ctrl-Alt-N).

2. Type a name for the library in the Library Name/Save as Type field **2**.

3. Select a drive or folder in which to save the library.

4. Click Create. A new library palette will appear on your screen. To put items into the library, see the instructions on the following page.

To put an item in a library:

1. Create a new library or open an existing library.

2. Choose the Item tool (or hold down Cmd/Ctrl with the Content tool).

3. Drag any item, group, or multiple-item selection into the library. When the pointer is over the library, you will see an eyeglasses icon **1**–**3**. A thumbnail of the item will appear in the library; the original item will stay on your page. A multiple-item selection will be stored as one entry.

TIP An item can be dragged from one library to another.

Auto library save

A library is saved each time an item is added to it if the **Auto Library Save** option is checked in Edit > Preferences > Preferences > Application–Save. With this option unchecked, a library is saved only when it's closed or when you quit/exit the application. With this option checked, you may notice a slight processing delay each time an item is added to or deleted from a library.

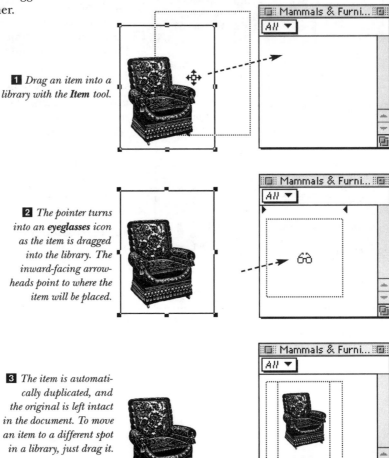

1 *Drag an item into a library with the **Item** tool.*

2 *The pointer turns into an **eyeglasses** icon as the item is dragged into the library. The inward-facing arrowheads point to where the item will be placed.*

3 *The item is automatically duplicated, and the original is left intact in the document. To move an item to a different spot in a library, just drag it.*

Put Item in Library

Colors and libraries

■ If you retrieve an item from a library that has a color applied to it, the color will **append** to the Colors palette of the active file. However, if there is a color with a matching name in the target document, the item will append without the color. The same is true for a style sheet, dash/stripe, list, or H&J.

■ If you change a color in a document that is also applied to an item in a library, you'll need to completely **replace** the item in the library with an item that contains the updated color. The color in the library won't update automatically.

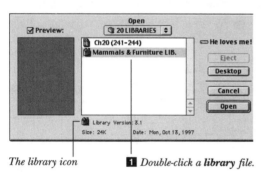

The library icon   **1** *Double-click a library file.*

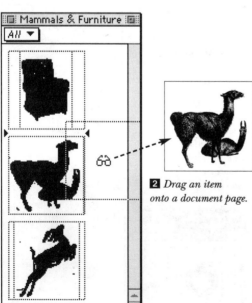

2 *Drag an item onto a document page.*

Any libraries that are open when you quit/exit QuarkXPress will reopen automatically when you relaunch the application.

To open an existing library:

1. Choose File > Open (Cmd-O/Ctrl-O).

2. Locate and highlight the name of the library that you want to open **1**, then click Open. Library files are represented by a book icon.
or
Double-click a library file name.

TIP To open a library from the Desktop, double-click the library file icon. The extension for libraries is ".qxl". A library created on Mac OS can't be opened in Windows, and vice versa.

TIP To close a library palette, click its close box. Don't use File > Close.

Picture paths

When a picture is added to a library, information about the path to the original picture file is stored with the library item. Similarly, when a picture is retrieved from a library, the picture's path information is stored with the document. The original picture file must be kept in the same **location**, with the same file **name**, for the image to print properly. If you move or rename the original picture file, you have to update it in the library. One way to do this is to relink the picture in the document, select it with the Item tool, copy it (use the Edit menu in the Mac OS; the Edit menu on the library palette in Windows), click the library item to be replaced, paste, then click OK in the alert dialog box.

To retrieve an item from a library:

1. Choose the Item or Content tool.

2. If your document has multiple layers, choose a layer for the library item.

3. Drag an item from a library onto a document page **2**. Simple as that.

If a library contains a lot of items, it can become difficult to find the items you need. By labeling related library items, you can limit the number of items that are displayed at a given time. You can assign a different label to each item or assign the same label to multiple items.

To label a library item:

1. Double-click a library item.

2. Enter a name in the Label field **1**.
or
Choose an existing label, if there are any, from the Label pop-up menu **2**. You can retype the same label for various items, but it's easier to choose an existing label, and you'll be less likely to make a typing error.

3. Click OK. If you created a new label, it will appear on the pop-up/drop-down menu at the top of the palette.

To display items by label:

Choose a label from the pop-up menu on the library palette. More than one label category can be displayed at a time **3**–**4**.

Choose All to display all the items in the library, both labeled and unlabeled.

Choose Unlabeled to display only those items that don't have a label.

To hide items with the same label:

A check mark on the pop-up/drop-down menu on a library palette means that that label category is displayed. Re-select a selected label to uncheck it.

To delete an item from a library:

1. Choose the Item or Content tool.

2. Click a library item.

3. On Mac OS, choose Edit > Clear or press Delete. In Windows, choose Delete from the Edit menu on the library palette or press Ctrl-X (Cut).

4. Click OK. You can't undo the deletion!

Making arrangements

■ **Arranging** library items in a logical order on the palette makes it easier to locate them. Just drag a library item to a different spot on the palette (note the arrowheads).

■ To **reshape** the palette to make it fit better on your screen, in the Mac OS, drag the resize box; in Windows, drag any side of the palette.

■ To **expand** the palette to full-screen size, click the palette zoom box/maximize button (upper right corner). Click again to restore the palette's former size.

1 *Type a new label in the **Label** field...*   **2** *...or choose an existing label from the pop-up menu.*

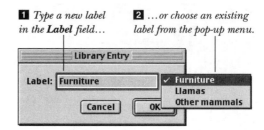

3 *In the **Mac OS**, when more than one label is chosen, the pop-up menu says **Mixed Labels**, and each currently-displayed category has a check mark.*

4 *In **Windows**, you'll see a check mark on the **Labels** menu for each label that is displayed.*

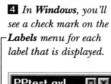

ELAINE's BOOK

Like library palettes, book palettes have their own unique file icons, and can be opened using File > Open.

Move chapter **up**

Add chapter   Move chapter **down**

Print chapter   **Remove** chapter

Synchronize book

M	Document	Pages	Status
M	.:master vqs 2	1✶	Available
	.:1 How Illus Works	1✶-8✶	Available
	.:2 STARTUP	9✶-16✶	Available
	.:3 VIEWS	17✶-24✶	Available
	.:4 OBJECTS BASICS	25✶-34✶	Available

1 *A **master** file and several **chapter** files are displayed on this **book** palette.*

Books, lists, and indexes

In this chapter we cover three features: books, lists, and indexing.

In QuarkXPress, a **book** is an umbrella file whose function is to organize and synchronize multiple chapter files. A book can be any kind of publication that is comprised of more than one QuarkXPress file—it doesn't have to be a book. When they're united into a book, the style sheets, colors, H&Js, lists, and dashes & stripes used in individual book chapter files will match the specifications of those in the file that you designate as the master. Page numbering also flows continuously from file to file. A book can contain up to 1,000 chapters. Each book has its own book palette **1**.

In a workgroup situation, individual chapters of a book can be open and edited simultaneously on a network. If the book itself is edited at one station, any open copies of the same book palette on other stations will update automatically.

A **list** is a compilation of text from one or more documents that is associated with the same paragraph style sheet. Optional features that can be included in a list are page numbers and alphabetization, and they are assigned via the Lists palette. An example of a list is a table of contents.

And finally, an **index** is created by manually tagging each individual entry in a document and then assigning an indent level and other formats to each entry via the Index palette.

Books

Books

To create a book:

1. Decide which file will be the master. The master file specifications will be applied to all the book chapters. To create a master file:

Create a new file that contains only the master page(s), style sheets, colors, H&Js, lists, and dashes and stripes that you want all the chapter files to share. Apply the Current Page Number command (Cmd-3/Ctrl-3) to a text box on the master page. Save the file. Include the word "master" in the title, if you like, to help prevent confusion later on. *or*

Open an existing file, and use File > Save As to save a copy of it (use the word "master" in the name). Delete all the text and all the pages except the first page, then resave the file. As with a new file, make sure it contains only the master pages, style sheets, colors, H&Js, lists, and dashes & stripes that you want all the chapter files to share, and make sure it contains the Current Page Number command in a text box on the master page.

You can use File > Append to append style sheets, colors, lists, etc. from any other file to the master.

2. Choose File > New > Book.

3. Enter a name for the book, and choose a location in which to save it **1**.

4. Click Create (Return/Enter).

5. On the book palette that opens, click the Add Chapter (leftmost) button **2**.

6. Locate and click the name of the file that you want to serve as the master **3**, then click Add (Return/Enter) **4**. Now you can start adding chapters to the book (see the instructions on the next page).

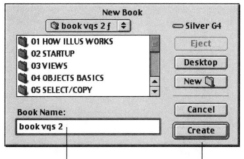

1 *Type a Book Name...*   *...then click Create.*

2 *Click the Add Chapter button.*

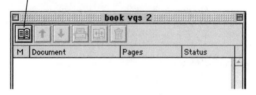

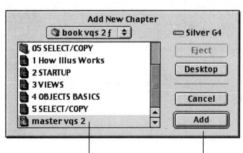

3 *Click the file that you want*   *...then click Add.*
to have function as the master...

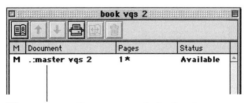

4 *The Master file appears on the book palette.*

Create a Book

No backing out

Book changes, such as adding or rearranging chapters, **can't be undone**, nor can the Revert to Saved command be used to restore a book to an earlier version.

Edits to a book are **saved** when you close the book palette or quit/exit QuarkXPress. Save edits to an individual chapter as you would any other document.

1 *Click the Add chapter button.*

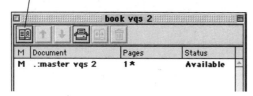

2 *After **adding** chapters to the book…*   **3** *…click the Synchronize Book button.*

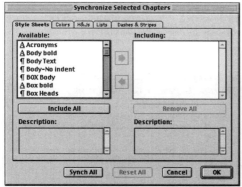

4 *In the **Synchronize Selected Chapters** dialog box, choose which **Style Sheets, Colors, H&Js, Lists,** and **Dashes & Stripes** will be added to all the chapter files.*

To add chapters to a book:

1. Prepare the chapter files. You can use File > Save As to generate copies of the master file or you can use existing files. Chapters in an individual book don't have to have the same page size.

2. Click the Add Chapter (leftmost) button on the book palette **1**, locate and highlight the name of a file that you want to become a chapter in the book, then click Add (Return/Enter) **2**. Repeat this step for any other files that you want to add as chapters. The actual files don't have to be open. If you add a pre-5.0 version file, you'll get an alert prompt (click OK).

   Note: If no chapter name is highlighted when you click the Add Chapter button, the new chapter will be added to the end of the book list. If a chapter name is highlighted when you click the Add Chapter button, the new chapter will be added directly above the highlighted one.

3. Click the **Synchronize Book** (left/right arrow) button **3**.

4. In the Synchronize Selected Chapters dialog box **4**, click which style sheets, colors, H&Js, lists, or dashes & stripes from the master chapter you want to add to all the chapter files (Shift-click to select consecutive items; Cmd-click/ Ctrl-click to select non-consecutive items), then click the **right arrow** in the middle of the dialog box to add the selected items. (Click the **left arrow** to remove selected items.)
   or
   Click **Include All** to include, for example, all style sheets or all color specs—whichever pane is displaying.

   (Click **Reset All** to eliminate all of your selections and start over.)

(Continued on the following page)

Add Chapters to a Book

5. Click **Synch All** to synchronize everything from the master file to the chapter files.

6. Click OK, and answer any warning prompts. Page numbering will advance incrementally through the chapter files (unless any files contain section numbering, in which case an asterisk will appear next to those page numbers).

7. Close the book palette (click the close box). All open book chapters will also close. You will be prompted to save changes, if there were any.

TIP Once chapters have been added to a book, all you have to do is double-click a chapter name on the palette to open that chapter.

TIP A chapter file can only be part of one book at a time. To get around this, you can copy a chapter file using File > Save As or use File > Duplicate in the Finder. Then you can use the copy in a different book.

To change the chapter order:

Click a chapter name, then click the Move Chapter Up or Move Chapter Down button at the top of the book palette **1**–**2**.
or
Option-drag/Alt-drag a chapter name upward or downward on the palette **3**.

To delete a chapter from a book:

1. On the book palette, click the name of the chapter that you want to delete.

2. Click the Remove Chapter button **4**.

3. Click OK.

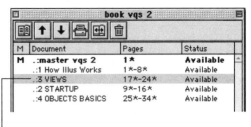

1 *Click the chapter you want to **move**.*

2 *After clicking the **Move Chapter Down** button, chapter 3 is moved downward.*

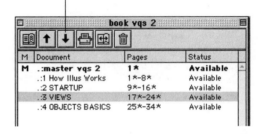

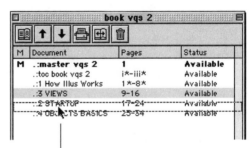

3 *To **restack** a chapter a different way, **Option**-drag/ **Alt**-drag it upward or downward.*

4 *To delete a chapter file, click on it, then click the **Remove Chapter** button.*

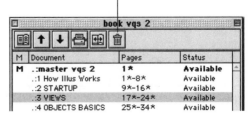

Out of sync?

You may add style sheets, colors, and so on to any individual chapter file. But bear in mind that those added elements will not appear in any other chapter file unless they're added to the master file and the chapters are synchronized.

If you resynchronize, any style sheet, color, etc. in an individual chapter file that doesn't have a double in the master file will be untouched. A style sheet, color, etc. that has a matching name in the master file, but whose specifications don't match, will be updated in the chapter file to match the master file. A component that is present in the master but not in a chapter file will be added to the chapter file.

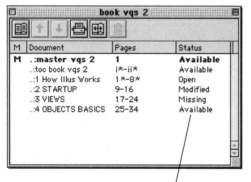

1 *The **Status** column on the book palette tells you whether individual chapters are **Available**, already **Open**, have been **Modified** (edited), or are **Missing** (were moved).*

If you're working with a book on a network, you'll need to check in the Status column on the book palette to find out if someone else on the network has a chapter of that book open. On a network, chapters should always be opened and closed from the server.

Deciphering the Status column

Available 1 means that the chapter can be opened.

Open means that the chapter is open at your station.

[Other station name] means that the chapter is open at another station on a network.

Modified means that the chapter was opened and edited outside the book when the book palette was closed. To update it, double-click the chapter name on the book palette, then close the newly-opened document window.

Missing means that the chapter was moved. To re-link the chapter to the book, double-click its name on the palette, then locate and open the file.

To edit the master file:

1. Double-click the master file on the book palette.

2. Create new style sheets, colors, H&Js, lists, and dashes & stripes in the master file, or use the File > Append command to add any of those elements from another file to the master.

3. Make sure all the chapters in the book have a status of Available. If a chapter has a Modified status, double-click it, then close it.

4. Click the Synchronize book button to add the new elements from the master file to all the book chapters.

5. Click OK.

Numbering pages in a book

There are two ways to number pages in a book. In either case, for any numbering to show up on any document pages, the Current Page Number command (Cmd-3/Ctrl-3) must be inserted into a text box on the master page of the master file.

One option is to let the page numbering occur automatically without doing anything. Chapters will be numbered sequentially, and Book Chapter Start will be checked in the Section dialog box for each one 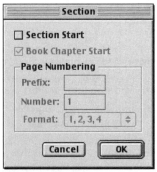.

A second option is to control the numbering yourself. On the book palette, double-click the name of the chapter that is to begin a section, choose Page > Section, check Section Start **2**, then enter a Number. Choose other options just as you would for a normal document. Section numbering will proceed through subsequent chapters up to the next section start, if there is one. You can make the first chapter (not the master) the beginning of the section, thus keeping the master outside the main flow of pages.

TIP All book chapters take on the number format used in the first chapter file that's listed on the book palette. Also, any master file counts as a page. To have chapter 1 start as page 1, set up a custom page number of 1 in the Section dialog box for that chapter.

1 *This is the default setting in the Section dialog box for a book.*

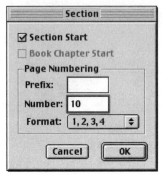

2 *For custom page numbering, click Section Start, then enter a starting page Number. If you want, you can also enter a Prefix and/or choose an alternative numbering Format.*

1 *The Print Chapter button*

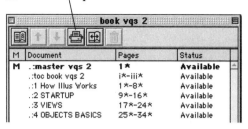

2 *To designate a different chapter file as the master, click on it, then click in this blank area to the left of it.*

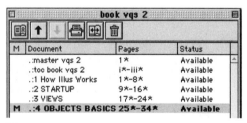

3 *Chapter 4 is now the master file.*

To print book chapters:

1. To print an individual chapter in a book, click its name on the book palette. Only a chapter file with a status of Available or Open will print. The chapter doesn't have to be open.
or
To selectively print more than one chapter, Cmd-click/Ctrl-click individual chapter names or Shift-click to select consecutively-listed chapters.
or
To print a whole book, make sure no chapter names are highlighted (click in the blank area below the chapter names), and make sure no chapters have a Missing or Modified status or are open at another station on the network.

2. Click the Print Chapter button **1**.

3. Choose the desired Print settings (including a Print Style, if desired), then click OK.

To designate a different chapter as the master:

1. On the book palette, click the name of the chapter that you want to become the new master **2**.

2. Click in the blank area to the left of the chapter name **3**.

Lists

The purpose of the Lists feature is to generate a table of contents or other list for an individual document or a whole book, with or without page reference numbers, and with or without alphabetization. It works by grabbing chapters names and numbers, section subheads, captions, sidebars, reference tables, etc. from a document by searching for the style sheets that are assigned to those paragraphs.

For example, let's say you want all your text that has been assigned a subhead style to be gathered into a table of contents. First you add the style sheets that are to be searched for in the Edit List dialog box. Then you decide how the list will be formatted. And finally, you use the Lists palette to preview and build the actual list.

To summarize, these are the basic steps you will follow to create a list:

- **Create** the list by choosing the style sheets you want to collect, and choosing format options.
- **Preview** the list in the scroll window on the Lists palette.
- **Build** (place) the actual list into a text box in the document.

To create and build a list for a document, follow the instructions starting on this page (through page 367). To create and build a list for a book, follow the instructions on pages 368–369.

To create a new list for a document:

1. Create separate style sheets for styling the list itself. And make sure your document style sheets are consistent and are applied correctly to the categories of text that you want to appear in the table of contents.

2. If you're generating a table of contents from one file, open that file now.

3. Choose Edit > Lists, click New **1**, then enter a Name for the list **2**.

allspice	cloves	paprika
basil	coriander	parsley
bay leaf	cumin	red pepper
caraway	dill	rosemary
cardamom	ginger	saffron
cayenne	lavender	sage
chervil	mace	savory
chives	mint	tarragon
cilantro	nutmeg	thyme
cinnamon	oregano	turmeric

A **list** can consist of anything from a simple alphabetized shopping list to a whole table of contents for a book.

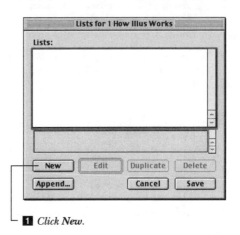

1 *Click* **New.**

2 *Enter a name.*

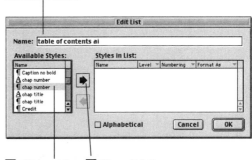

3 *Click a* **style** *sheet name.*

4 *Then click the right pointing* **arrow.**

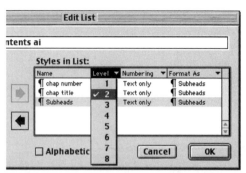

1 *For each style sheet category, choose an* **indent Level,** ...

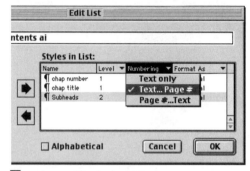

2 ...*choose a* **Numbering** *option,*...

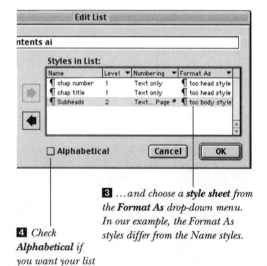

3 ...*and choose a* **style sheet** *from the* **Format As** *drop-down menu. In our example, the Format As styles differ from the Name styles.*

4 *Check* **Alphabetical** *if you want your list to be alphabetized.*

4. On the Available Styles scroll list, click the style sheet name (text category) to be searched for in the document (**3**, previous page) then click the right-pointing arrow to add that style sheet to the Styles in List window (**4**, previous page). Or, just double-click the style sheet name.

To add multiple style sheets at a time, Shift-click to select a consecutive series or Cmd-click/Ctrl-click to select multiple style sheet names individually, then click the right-pointing arrow. (Click the left-pointing arrow if you need to remove a style sheet from the Styles in List window.) In QuarkXPress 5 or later, you can use character style sheets.

5. Click a style sheet in the Styles in List window, then choose the following:

The **Level** of indent text you want that style sheet to have in the list (1, 2, 3, and so on) **1**. For example, assign number 1 to chapter names, the number 2 to headers, the number 3 to subheads, and so on.

A page **Numbering** style **2**. Choose Text...Page # if you want the page number to follow the text; choose Page #...Text if you want the page number to precede the text. Choose "Text only" if you don't want page numbers to appear at all.

Which style sheet will be applied to that text category (**Format As** drop-down menu) **3**. If you created a style sheet(s) specifically for the list, this is the time to choose it.

Do the same for the other style sheets.

6. *Optional:* Check Alphabetical to have the list entries appear in alphabetical order rather than the order in which they appear in the document **4**.

7. Click OK.

(Continued on the following page)

Create List for Document

8. Click Save. Follow the instructions on the next page to build (generate) the list.

TIP In the Lists dialog box, click Duplicate to duplicate the currently highlighted list if you want to create a variation of it. Click Delete to remove the currently highlighted list. To append a list from another document, follow the instructions on pages 42–44.

TIP The maximum number of style sheets that can be chosen for a list is 32; the maximum number of characters per paragraph that a list can contain is 256.

TIP For a list level with page number references, choose a style sheet with a right tab and a dot leader. The tab character will be inserted automatically.

Create List for Document

Get there fast

If any document is open (even a chapter in a book) and you **double-click** a line of text on the Lists palette, the chapter that contains the text will open automatically and that text will be highlighted in the document.

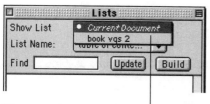

1 *Choose* **Current Document** *from the* **Show List** *pop-up menu.*

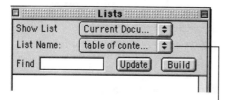

2 *Choose an existing list from the* **List Name** *pop-up menu.*

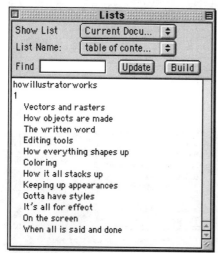

3 *The* **Lists** *palette, displaying a document's* **table of contents**

Once a list has been created, you've chosen Levels, Numbering, and Format As options for it, and it's been saved, then it's time to use the Lists palette to preview and build the actual list.

To preview and build a list for a document:

1. Open the document for which you want to build a list.

2. Choose View > Show Lists (Option-F11/ Ctrl-F11).

3. Choose Show List For: Current Document **1**.

4. Choose the name of the list that you want to build from the List Name pop-up menu **2**. The list will preview in the scroll window on the palette.

5. In the same document, choose the Content tool and click in an empty text box to create an insertion point. It can be a new box or the first in a chain of linked text boxes. A list also can be appended to the end of a block of text. For example, you can write an introductory paragraph, and then start the list after that paragraph.

6. Click Build on the Lists palette **3**. A list will be built in that text box or in a series of linked boxes using the formatting options that were chosen in the Lists dialog box.

TIP Be careful not to delete any Styles (style sheets) used in the list from the document. If you do, text to which those style sheets were assigned won't appear on the list when you build it.

TIP The stacking order of text boxes determines how entries will be listed, with the frontmost box on a page appearing first. If your chapter title box is stacked in front of the chapter number box, then the chapter title will be listed first.

Build List for Document

Note: Before following the instructions on this page, make sure the book's master file contains all the style sheets that are used in the book and a list has been created for that master. Also make sure that all the book chapters have a status of Available.

To create a list for a book:

1. Close all open files, open the book file (the palette for that book will open), and open the Master file.

2. Choose Edit > Lists.

3. Create a new list (see pages 364–366).
   or
   Click Append, locate and open the file that contains the list you want to use, click the desired list name, click the right-pointing arrow to append that list, click OK 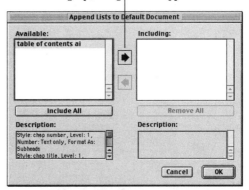, and finally, respond to any name conflicts.

4. Click Save.

5. On the Lists palette (View > Show Lists or Option-F11/Ctrl-F11), make sure the book file is chosen in the Show List field.

6. Deselect all chapter names, then click the Synchronize button on the book palette.

7. In the Synchronize Selected Chapter dialog box, click the Lists tab, select the desired list name, click the right-pointing arrow to include that list, then click OK. (Click OK in any alert boxes.)

8. Make sure the correct list is chosen in the List Name field on the Lists palette (see the previous step), then click Update. The list that is generated from all the chapters will display on the Lists palette **2**–**3**. *Note:* If the list doesn't preview correctly, try opening the master file first, then click Update.

TIP If you renumber or rearrange pages in a book, you will have to update and rebuild the list.

1 *Click the right-pointing arrow to* ***append*** *the list.*

2 *Click* ***Update*** *to display the list.*

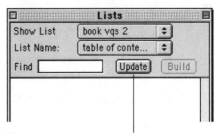

3 *The list previews on the* ***Lists*** *palette.*

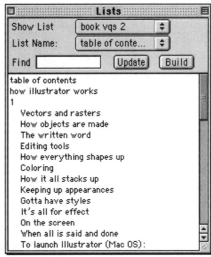

*This is part of a **built list** (table of contents) that was built from a book. This list is styled using style sheets that were created specifically for the list and assigned via the Format As drop-down menu in the Edit List dialog box.*

Perform the following steps after you create and update a list for the book file (instructions on the previous page).

To build a list for a book file:

1. Create a new chapter for the book. One way to do this is by opening the master file and generating a copy of it using File > Save As. Strip out the text from the new chapter. If it's going to be a table of contents and you want it to have its own numbering format, choose Page > Section, check Section Start, enter a Number, and choose a Format.

2. Add the new chapter to the book: Click the Add Chapter button on the book palette, then locate and open the new chapter.

3. Click the Synchronize button on the book palette to copy the style sheets, colors, etc. from the master file to the new file, then click OK.

4. Click in a blank text box in the newly-created chapter file.

5. On the Lists palette, choose Show List [book name].

6. *Optional:* Turn on Auto Page Insertion in Edit > Preferences > Preferences > Document–General for the new chapter if you want overflow text from the list, if any, to flow into linked boxes on additional pages.

7. If the Build button is grayed out, click Update.

8. Click Build. The list will be appear in the text box (or boxes).

Build List for Book

To revise a list:

1. Open the document and open the Lists palette (Option-F11/Ctrl-F11).

2. Choose a List Name.

3. For a non-book file, double-click an entry—that text will highlight in the document window . With any book chapter file open, if you double-click an entry from any chapter file, the chapter file will open and the text will be highlighted.

4. Make any modifications to the text in the document. To prevent text from appearing on the list, for example, apply any style sheet to it that isn't being searched for in the list.

5. Click Update on the Lists palette to update the list preview.

6. If you're going to rebuild the list in the same document, click in the text box that contains the list. If you're going to insert the rebuilt list and leave the old list unchanged, click exactly where you want the new one to appear. If the list is in a separate chapter of a book, open that chapter now.

7. Click Build.

8. Click Insert to build a new list and leave the old list unchanged .
   or
   Click Replace to replace the current list with the new list . You can't undo either operation.

TIP You can reformat a built list or apply different style sheets to it, but such changes will be lost if you rebuild the list using the Replace option.

TIP If the list is long and you want to quickly find a particular line, type the first word of the line in the Find field (you have to type enough of the entry to differentiate it from similar entries) . QuarkXPress will search for the entry as you type; only whole lines will become highlighted.

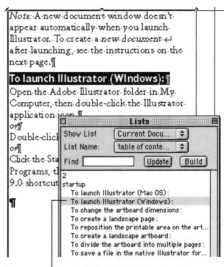

1 *For a non-book file, **double-click** an entry on the Lists palette to view that entry in the document.*

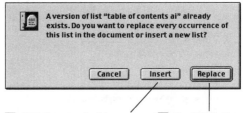

2 *Click **Insert** to build a new list at the current insertion point and leave the old list unchanged.*

3 *Or click **Replace** to replace the old list with the new list.*

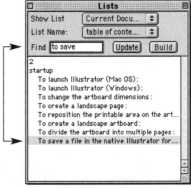

4 *An entry that's typed into the **Find** field on the Lists palette is searched for in the list.*

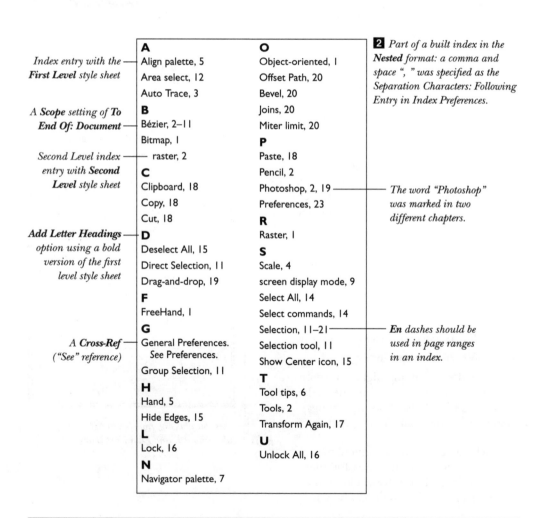

A

anchor points, 2-3

I

Illustrator, 1-6; Adobe, 1; closed paths, 2; FreeHand, 1; Macintosh, 1; object-oriented, 1; Objects, 1; precision tools, 5; Stroke, 3; tools, 2; vector image, 1; Windows, 1

O

object-oriented, 1 vector, 3; versus raster, 4; paths, 5; Pen tool, 5-7; printing, 8; resolution, 7

P

Pencil. See tool

1 *Portions of a built index in the Run-in format*

Indexing

Building an index requires four main steps, and they generally happen in this order:

■ Create the **style sheets** for the index itself, for letter headings, for the entries themselves, etc.

■ **Mark** all the text that is to be referenced in the index.

■ **Build** the index **1**–**2**.

■ Look over the index, and **edit** it, if necessary.

Index entry with the
First Level *style sheet*

A **Scope** *setting of* **To End Of: Document**

Second Level index entry with **Second Level** *style sheet*

Add Letter Headings
option using a bold version of the first level style sheet

A **Cross-Ref**
("See" reference)

A
Align palette, 5
Area select, 12
Auto Trace, 3
B
Bézier, 2–11
Bitmap, 1
— raster, 2
C
Clipboard, 18
Copy, 18
Cut, 18
D
Deselect All, 15
Direct Selection, 11
Drag-and-drop, 19
F
FreeHand, 1
G
General Preferences.
    See Preferences.
Group Selection, 11
H
Hand, 5
Hide Edges, 15
L
Lock, 16
N
Navigator palette, 7

O
Object-oriented, 1
Offset Path, 20
Bevel, 20
Joins, 20
Miter limit, 20
P
Paste, 18
Pencil, 2
Photoshop, 2, 19
Preferences, 23
R
Raster, 1
S
Scale, 4
screen display mode, 9
Select All, 14
Select commands, 14
Selection, 11–21
Selection tool, 11
Show Center icon, 15
T
Tool tips, 6
Tools, 2
Transform Again, 17
U
Unlock All, 16

2 *Part of a built index in the* **Nested** *format: a comma and space ", " was specified as the Separation Characters: Following Entry in Index Preferences.*

The word "Photoshop" was marked in two different chapters.

En *dashes should be used in page ranges in an index.*

Indexing

Use the Index palette to mark and format index references for individual text strings in a document. This is a time-consuming process. Then you'll build the index itself in the same file or in a separate file.

To mark a document for indexing:

1. Enable Quark's Index XTension.

2. Open an existing document to mark for indexing or create a new document to be marked as you enter text.

3. If you're going to do any "see also " cross-referencing or if you want page number references to appear in a different style from the index entries, create the character style sheet(s) that you want to apply to those references.

 This is also a good time to create all the other style sheets that you want to use in the built index. An index can have a nested or run-in format (see the illustrations on page 371). You can edit the style sheets later.

 For a nested index, you'll need a style sheet for the First Level text strings as well as a style sheet for each subsequent indent level. You can use the Based On option for this, and apply progressively larger Left Indent values for the Second, Third, and Fourth Level styles.

 Also create a style sheet for letter headings if you're going to use them (A, B, C, and so on). Apply a Space Before value via the Style > Formats, and choose a bolder font than the body text for that style sheet so it stands out.

4. Choose View > Show Index.

5. In the document, highlight a word or phrase that you want to include in the index ☐. You'll be choosing settings for each individual entry separately.
 or
 Click the text in the document that you want to create any entry for, then type an entry in the Text field on the Index palette. This is done when, for

Mark Document for Indexing

Building a nest

To create **nested** (indented) entries, follow the instructions on this page and the next two pages, but add this step: Click in the palette scroll window to the left of an existing First Level entry to move the indent arrow to that entry, then choose Level: Second Level, Third Level, or Fourth Level. When you add the entry, it will appear below, and indented from, the chosen First Level entry.

☐ *Highlight a word or a phrase in a document that you want to include in the index.*

☐ *The text that's currently **highlighted** in the document will also display in the **Text** field.*

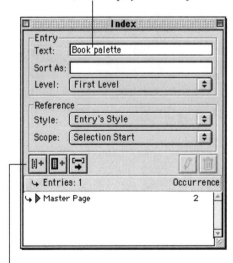

*These buttons are, from left to right, **Add**, **Add All**, and **Find Next Entry**.*

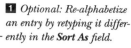

*Optional: Re-alphabetize an entry by retyping it differently in the **Sort As** field.*

*Choose a **Level** of indentation for each entry.*

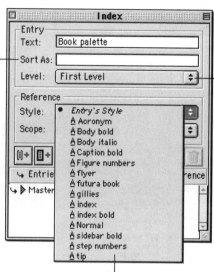

*Choose a **character** style sheet for each entry.*

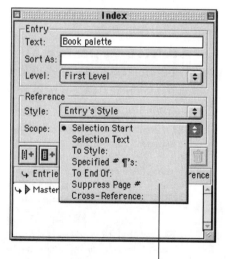

*Choose a **Scope** (range of pages) for each entry.*

example, broad categories are desired rather than specific items.

6. On the Index palette, review the text in the Text field, and change any capitalization or word endings, if desired.

7. *Optional:* In the index Sort As field, enter a different method for sorting (alphabetizing) the text string **1**. For example, if you spell out a number in this field (e.g., "Seven-Up" instead of "7-Up"), the number will sort alphabetically in the index rather than be placed at the top of the index. The Sort As spelling has no effect on the spelling of the entry in the document.

8. Choose indent Level: First Level **2**.

9. *Optional:* From the Style pop-up menu, choose a style sheet to be applied to cross-referenced words entered in the Scope field or to page numbers in the index **3**.

10. Choose from the Scope pop-up menu to specify the page range of the entry in your index **4**:

Selection Start to specify the page on which the entry is located. If the entry spans more than one page, the start of the selection is used.

Selection Text to specify the page(s) of a block of text.

To Style to specify the range from the selection start (or cursor position) to a style sheet you choose from the adjoining pop-up menu.

Specified # ¶'s to specify a range that spans through an exact number of paragraphs—the number you enter in the adjoining field.

To End Of to specify either the end of the story or the end of the document, whichever you choose from the pop-up menu. Choose this option for the title of a section that you want listed as a range of pages (e.g., "42–58").

(Continued on the following page)

Mark Document for Indexing

Choose **Suppress Page #** to suppress the page number. This is a good idea when you want to include a broad category, say "Preferences," that will have second-level items, such as "Application preferences" and "Document preferences."

Choose **Cross-Reference:** *See, See also,* or *See herein* to create a cross-reference for the current text string. Enter the reference in the text field on the right.

11. Click the Add button. The newly added entry will preview at the bottom of the palette **1** and will be listed alphabetically in its chosen indent level. An index marker (red brackets) will surround the text string in the document—but only while the Index palette is open **2**. When an entry is typed directly into the Text field on the Index palette, a square box appears in the document at the location of the cursor.

12. Repeat steps 4–10 for all the remaining text strings in the document that you want to include in the index.

TIP If you double-click an index entry's page number on the palette, the entry will display and highlight in the document.

TIP To add all occurrences of the string in the document, click the Add All button **3** on the Index palette.

TIP To delete an entry, click it in the scroll window on the Index palette, click the Delete button on the palette, then click OK (you can't undo this!). No need to highlight the text in the document—the brackets will be removed automatically.

TIP To zip through a story to make sure you've marked all the desired text strings, keep clicking the Find Next Entry button **4** on the Index palette.

TIP Hold down Option/Alt to turn the Add button into Add Reversed, the Add All button into Add All Reversed, and the Find Next Entry button into Find First Entry.

Mark Document for Indexing

5.0!

Index palette shortcuts

Display palette/ highlight Text field	Cmd-Option-I/Ctrl-Alt-I
Click Add button	Cmd-Option-Shift-I/ Ctrl-Alt-Shift-I

1 *Click the* ***Add*** *button to make the entry appear in the bottom part of the palette.*

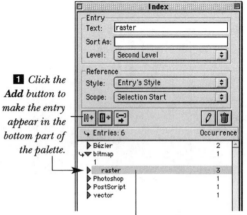

The "raster" entry has been specified as a ***Second Level*** *indent. Note the position of the indent arrow and the indentation of the "raster" entry in the scroll window.*

> **delete a chapter from a bo**
>
> On the book palette, click the
> the chapter that you want to
> Click the Remove Chapter (tr

2 *If you highlight a word or a phrase in a document with the Index palette open, left and right* ***index marker brackets*** *will surround that text string. The hollow square marks where text was entered directly into the* ***Text*** *field on the Index palette.*

3 *Click* ***Add All*** *to add every occurrence of the string to the index entry.*

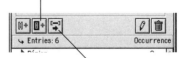

4 *Click* ***Find Next Entry*** *to highlight the next entry.*

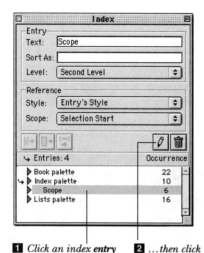

1 *Click an index **entry** on the **Index** palette...* **2** *...then click the **Edit** button.*

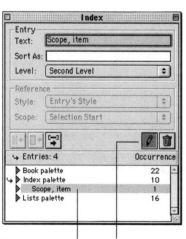

4 *The entry is edited in the **Text** field, and updates here.* **3** *The **Edit** button changes shade.*

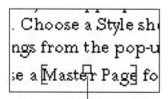

5 *The **second** index entry marker box displays if that word is indexed twice.*

To edit an index entry:

1. Click an index entry in the scroll window on the Index palette **1**.
2. Click the Edit button **2**. The button will change shade **3**.
3. Edit the text in the Text field and/or the Sort as field **4**. The entry will update immediately.
   and/or
   Click the entry's reference (page number or x-ref) in the scroll window (click the expand/collapse arrowhead to reveal it, if necessary), then change the Reference: Style or Scope. The reference will update immediately.
4. Click on and edit any other entries.
5. Click the Edit button again when you're finished editing.

TIP In case you're wondering, you can't edit the Level for an existing entry; you can only delete the existing one and add it again at the desired new Level.

Let's say you want to add the same text string as a Second Level entry under a different First Level entry. You can't simply add it because you can't add the same text string twice. But here's a workaround.

To add an already marked word again to an index:

1. Click in the original marked word in the document.
2. Click in the Text field on the Index palette, then retype the entry.
3. Choose other Entry and Reference options.
4. To create a nested entry, click in the insertion arrow (leftmost) column next to the entry below which you want the new entry to nest.
5. Click Add. A small hollow square will display inside the index marker brackets **5**.

To cross-reference an index entry:

1. Click in the text box in the document that contains the indexed word.

2. Click the entry in the scroll window on the Index palette.

3. Choose Scope: Cross-Reference, choose a "See" option from the next pop-up menu, then type the cross-referenced word.

4. Click Add 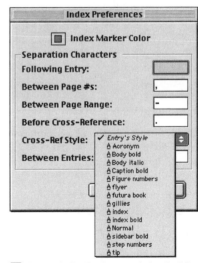. Click the arrowhead next to the entry to preview. Click the arrowhead again to hide the entry.

Before you build or rebuild an index, you can use the Index Preferences dialog box to specify which punctuation marks the index will contain.

To choose Index preferences:

1. Choose Edit > Preferences > Index.

2. *Optional:* To change the Index Marker Color (the brackets in marked text), click the color square, choose a new color, then click OK.

3. Change any or all of the settings in the Separation Characters fields **2**:

   Following Entry is the punctuation following the index entry (e.g., the comma in "Biscuit,").

   Between Page #s is the punctuation between non-consecutive page numbers (as in "34, 77").

   Between Page Range is the punctuation used to define a range of pages (as in "24–102"). Use an en dash (Option-hyphen/Ctrl-Alt-Shift-hyphen).

   Before Cross-reference is the punctuation that's used before a "See" cross-reference (as in "Biscuit, 20. *See also* Rolls"). (This character will replace the chosen "Following Entry" character, when necessary.)

   From the **Cross-Ref Style** pop-up menu, which lists all the character style sheets in your document, choose a style for

1 *A **see also reference** added to an index*

2 *Choose **Index Preferences** before building or rebuilding an index.*

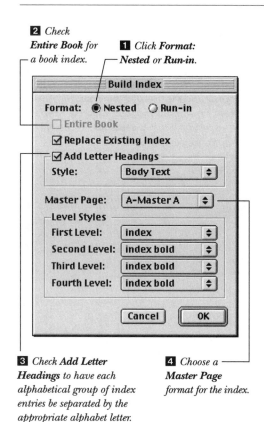

1 *Click* ***Format:***
Nested *or* ***Run-in.***

3 *Check* **Add Letter**
Headings *to have each*
alphabetical group of index
entries be separated by the
appropriate alphabet letter.

4 *Choose a*
Master Page
format for the index.

the cross-referenced words, such as
"See" or "See also."

Between Entries is the punctuation
between entries in a run-in style index
(as in "frog, 17; toad, 18") and the ending punctuation in a paragraph in a
nested style index.

4. Click OK.

Follow these instructions to build the
actual index after the document or documents have been marked for indexing and
the pagination is finalized.

Note: Before building an index, you can
choose Index Preferences (previous page).

To build an index:

1. For a book, create a new chapter file
to hold the index. Make it the last
chapter (see the first tip on the next
page). Or open a non-book file to have
the index appear in.

2. Turn Auto Page Insertion on in
Edit > Preferences > Preferences >
Document–General if you're building
a large index.

3. *Optional:* If you haven't already done
so, create style sheets for each level
of indentation and for alphabet letter
headings. For a book, do this in the
master file and then Synchronize.

4. Choose Utilities > Build Index.

5. Choose Format: Nested to indent
each progressive level in the index **1**.
or
Choose Format: Run-in to string the
index entry levels together in paragraph form following the First Level
entry. They will be separated by the
Between Entries punctuation mark
that you chose in Index Preferences.

6. *Do any of these optional steps:*
Check Entire Book to index an entire
set of book files **2**.

(Continued on the following page)

Build an Index

Check Replace Existing Index to replace an existing, previously built index with the newly-built index.

Check Add Letter Headings to separate each alphabetical group of index entries by the appropriate letter of the alphabet (**3**, previous page). Choose a Style sheet for the headings from the pop-up menu.

7. Choose a Master Page for the index (**4**, previous page).

8. In the Level Styles area of the dialog box:

For the Nested Format, choose a paragraph style sheet for each level of indent (First Level, Second Level, Third Level, or Fourth Level).
or
For the Run-in Format, choose a First Level style sheet.

9. Click OK (see the illustrations on page 371). The index will be built and a new page will be added to the end of your document. (You don't have to select a text box first.)

TIP Before building an index for a book, create a separate file for it that contains the desired master page, headers, and footers, add it as a chapter to the book palette, and Synchronize it into the book. Be sure to check Entire Book in the Build Index dialog box.

TIP After building an index, if you want to edit any of the style sheets that were assigned via the Level Styles area of the Build Index dialog box, use Edit > Style Sheets. This index, or any other index that uses those style sheets, will update to reflect your changes. These changes will also be applied if you rebuild the index.

Stash it away

If you manually restyle an index using style sheets that are different from those that were selected in the Build Index dialog box, you will lose those changes if you then rebuild the index with the Replace Existing Index option checked. Keep the final, restyled index in a **separate** document so you don't accidentally build over it.

Preferences

Preferences shortcuts

Application Preferences	Cmd-Option-Shift-Y/ Ctrl-Alt-Shift-Y
Document Preferences	Cmd-Y/Ctrl-Y
Document > **Paragraph**	Cmd-Option-Y/Ctrl-Alt-Y
Document > **Tools**	Double-click any item creation tool or the Zoom tool

1 *Most of the **Preferences** panes are accessed from one central dialog box.*

Preferences that are covered in other chapters

The Preferences dialog boxes

Preferences are the default values that automatically apply when a feature or a tool is used. For example, when the Line tool is used, a line is automatically drawn in a particular width. That width is one of its default settings. Other default settings for the Line tool include its color and style.

Document preferences, if chosen when a document is open, will apply only to **that document**. The current unit of measure for the rulers, dialog boxes, and palettes falls into that category. To set document defaults for all **future** documents, make sure no documents are open when you open the Preferences dialog box. Preferences are chosen separately for **print** and **Web** documents.

Other preferences, such as whether the XTensions Manager displays at startup, apply to the whole **application**, regardless of whether any documents are open when you choose them.

To open a preferences dialog box **1**, you can use any of these three methods:

- Choose from the Edit > Preferences submenu.

- Use a keyboard shortcut (see the sidebar).

- Control-click/Right-click on a blank area of the document window and choose from the Preferences submenu.

Other kinds of preferences

In addition to the preferences that you can choose via the Preferences dialog boxes, you can also set other kinds of very useful defaults for the application. For example, any paragraph or character **style sheet** that is created or appended when no documents are open will appear on the Style Sheets palette of any subsequently-created documents. The same holds true for **colors, H&Js, lists, dashes & stripes, Meta tags** (Web), **Menus** (Web), and the default **auxiliary dictionary**. Normal, which is the default style sheet that automatically appears in every new document and in any text box to which type specifications have not yet been applied, can be edited for all future documents when no documents are open. Don't overlook these kinds of defaults—they are enormous time-savers!

Tracking and **kerning table** settings, **custom frame** data, and **hyphenation** exceptions are stored in individual documents and in the QuarkXPress application folder in a file called **XPress Preferences**. If, upon opening a file, the document settings don't match the XPress Preferences settings, an alert dialog box will appear. Click **Use XPress Preferences** (Cmd-./Esc) to apply the preferences resident on that machine or click **Keep Document Settings** (Return/ Enter) to leave the document as is.

If you trash your XPress Preferences file, the application will create a new one automatically, but in the process, all your custom settings will be lost. For this reason, you should trash the Preferences file only if you absolutely have to (e.g., the application becomes corrupted and unusable) or if you intentionally want to restore the program defaults for some reason. You can copy your Preferences file and stash it away for safekeeping. The Preferences file can also be copied to the QuarkXPress folder on another computer.

Inside XPress Preferences

Saves in XPress Preferences and affects all documents immediately
Application Preferences (Display, Interactive, Save, XTensions Manager, File List, Browsers, PDF), PPD Manager, Profile Manager

Saves in XPress Preferences and affects all documents after relaunch
XTensions Manager

Saves in active document and in XPress Preferences
Kerning Table Edit, Tracking Edit, Hyphenation Exceptions

Saves only in active document
Document Preferences (General, Measurements, Paragraph, Character, Tools, Trapping, and Layer), open or create auxiliary dictionary

Saves only in active Web document
Web Document Preferences (General, Measurements, Paragraph, Character, Tools, Layer)

Application preferences

Display

To choose the color for Margin or Ruler **Guides**, or the **Grid**, click the appropriate square, then choose a color from the Color Picker. The Margin color is also used to represent the item boundary in the Runaround and Clipping dialog boxes and the Page Width Reference Guide in Web documents; the Ruler color also represents the clipping path; and the Grid color also represents the runaround path.

In the Mac OS, with **Tile to Multiple Monitors** on, if you choose View > Windows > Tile Documents, multiple documents will be distributed across multiple monitors.

In the Mac OS, with **Full-screen Documents** on (the default setting is off), a document will fill the entire screen when it's opened.

With **Off-screen Draw** on, the screen will redraw all at once, not gradually in sections. The overall redraw speed is the same, whether this option is on or off.

With **Opaque Text Box Editing** on, if you click a text box with the Content tool, it will look opaque, making it easier to edit the text, whether or not the box actually has a background color. With this option

off (the default), a text box will keep its current background color, whether it's a solid color, a blend, or None (transparent).

Choose a color depth for the screen preview that QuarkXPress creates for imported **Color TIFFs**. A picture's screen preview affects its redraw speed and the storage size of the QuarkXPress file, so for a large picture, it may be helpful to choose 8-bit (256 possible colors). Style > Contrast isn't available for a picture with a 16-bit preview (thousands of possible colors) or 32-bit (Mac OS)/24-bit (Windows) preview (millions of possible colors).

Choose a color depth for the screen preview for imported **Gray** [grayscale] **TIFFs**.

The **Pasteboard Width** is the percentage of the total document width that is allocated to the pasteboard. 100% is the default. (48" is the maximum total width.)

If you clicked "Do not show this warning again" in any alert dialog box, you can click **Show All Alerts** here to allow alert dialog boxes to redisplay.

Windows only: The **Display DPI Value** is the monitor resolution. Read about this setting in the QuarkXPress documentation.

Display Preferences

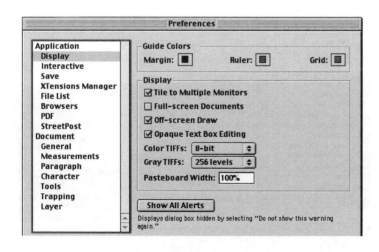

Interactive

Move the **Scrolling** slider to choose a rate of speed for the document window scroll arrows and boxes.

With **Speed Scroll** on, on a slow machine, large pictures and blends will be greeked (display as solid gray) as you scroll and then redraw when you stop scrolling.

With **Live Scroll** on, the document will redraw as you drag a scroll box. Turn this option off if you have a slow machine. Option-drag/Alt-drag a scroll box to temporarily turn Live Scroll on or off. The Page Grabber always produces a live scroll.

With **Smart Quotes** on, smart quotation marks are inserted automatically when the ' or " key is pressed (see page 118). Choose a Format (style) for the quotes. Professional typesetters always use Smart Quotes. Un-smart quotes look—well, un-smart.

Click Delayed Item Dragging: **Show Contents** to temporarily display the full contents of an item as you drag it, even if the item is behind other items (pause for the Delay period before dragging). Click **Live Refresh** to see an item as it really looks in its layer as you pause-drag it, with an instantly-updated text wrap. Enter the

screen redraw shortcuts

Forced redraw	Cmd-Option-. (period)/Shift-Esc
Stop redraw	*Mac OS:* Cmd-. (period)
	Mac OS and Windows: Esc *or* perform another operation (e.g., select an item, choose another command)

number of seconds (or fraction of a second) in the Delay field that you want to pause before dragging.

Choose **Page Range Separators** for the symbols you will use in the Print dialog box to separate the page numbers you want to print.

Mac OS only: Choose which function you want the **Control Key** to have: To Zoom in/out or to access Contextual Menus (the default).

With **Drag and Drop Text** on, you can highlight text and drag it to a new location within the same story (one or more linked boxes). See page 58.

If **Show Tool Tips** is checked and you rest the pointer on a tool or a palette icon, the name of that tool or icon will display.

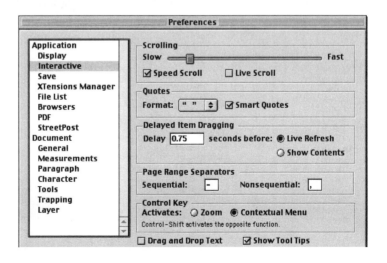

Interactive Preferences

Save

Auto Save and Auto Backup are like system or power failure insurance. With **Auto Save** enabled, modifications are saved in a temporary file at the interval specified in the "Every [ ] minutes" field (five minutes is the default). There may be a short (but potentially annoying) interruption in processing while an Auto Save occurs. If a system or power failure occurs while you are modifying a document and you restart and then reopen the document, a prompt will appear **1**. Click OK to reopen the last Auto-saved version. *Beware!* Auto Save can't retrieve a document that's never been saved!

To restore the last manually-saved version of an open document, choose File > Revert to Saved. To restore the last auto-saved version of your document, hold down Option/Alt while choosing File > Revert to Saved.

Unlike Auto Save, which saves only modifications made to a document in a temporary file, **Auto Backup** creates a backup version of the entire document when the Save command is executed. Progressively higher numbers are appended to the backup names. To specify how many

backup versions will be created before the oldest backup version is deleted, enter a number between 1 and 100 in the "Keep [ ] revisions" field.

Auto Backups are saved in the current document folder, unless you specify a different destination. Designating a different location for the backups can help prevent confusion. If you want to designate a different Destination, click Other Folder, then click Select/Browse. In the Backup Folder/Browse for Folder directory dialog box, locate and open an existing folder (or to create a new folder in the Mac OS, choose a destination, click New 🗋, enter a name, and click Create), then click Select/OK. To reset the Destination as the current document folder, click Document Folder.

With **Auto Library Save** on, a library will be saved whenever an item is added to it. With Auto Library Save off, a library will be saved only when it's closed or when you quit/exit the application.

With **Save Document Position** on, when a document is reopened, it will have the same zoom level, window size, and position on screen that it had in when it was last closed.

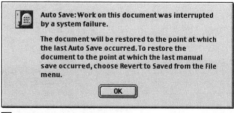

1 *The Auto Save prompt*

XTensions Manager

With **Show XTensions Manager at startup**: **Always** on, the XTensions Manager will open automatically whenever the application is launched.

With **When: "XTension" folder changes** on, the XTensions Manager will open during launch only if you have added or removed an XTension or XTensions from your XTension folder since the application was last open.

With **When: Error loading XTensions occurs** on, the XTensions Manager will open during a launch only if QuarkXPress encounters a problem while loading the XTensions.

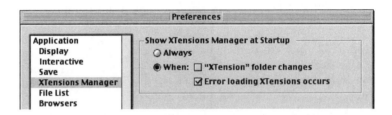

File List 5.0!

Enter the maximum **Number of Files** (3–9) (recently opened and saved files) to be listed on the File menu.

Click **Append Files to File Menu** to have file names be listed on the first level of the File menu or click **Append Files to Open Menu Item** to have file names be listed on the File > Open submenu.

Check **Alphabetize Names** to have file names be listed in alphabetical order. With this option unchecked, names will appear in the order in which they were opened or saved.

Check **Show Full Paths** to have the location (drive and folder) of the file be listed next to the name.

*Note: **File List** is part of the **Deja Vu** XTension, which is a free download from Quark.com.*

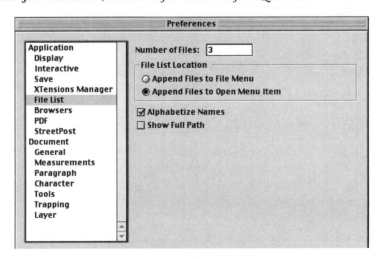

Browsers 5.0!

The currently **Available Browsers** are listed in the **Browser** column. To access the browsers on this list, use the HTML Preview pop-up menu on a Web document window.

Click in the **Default** column to choose a browser to be used when no browser is designated for preview, or when Launch Browser is checked in the Export HTML dialog box. To add other browsers to the list of Available Browsers, click **Add**, then locate and select the browsers. To delete a browser from the list, click on it, then click **Delete**.

PDF 5.0!

Click **Acrobat Distiller**: **Browse** to locate the Acrobat Distiller application on your system (in Windows, it's acrodist.exe).

If you click **Workflow**: **Distill immediately**, QuarkXPress will hand off an exported file immediately to Distiller to create the PDF export file. If you click **Create PostScript file for later distilling**, QuarkXPress will create a PostScript export file that you can later convert to PDF using Distiller. Check

Use Watched Folder to save exported PostScript files into the watch folder designated in Acrobat. Acrobat will periodically check this folder and automatically distill any PostScript files that are saved to it.

Click **Default Settings**: **Options** to open the PDF Export Options dialog box. Click any of the four tabs in that dialog box to choose PDF options. See the QuarkXPress documentation for more information.

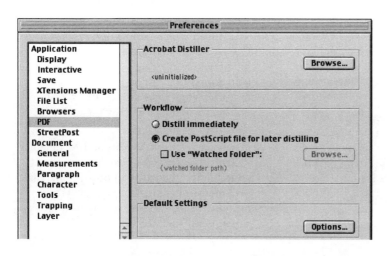

5.0! StreetPost

StreetPost is an XTension for avenue.quark that enables companies who are using a Web publishing system to "push" document content directly onto a Web server. In most cases, the Web publishing system is used to create Web pages using XML content.

QuarkXPress' XML Workspace palette is used to tag text content to XML elements.

Clicking that palette's Post button pushes the XML element content directly to the server, according to the Post URL, User Name, and other preferences that are entered in the StreetPost Preferences dialog box. Ask your Web server administrator what information to enter into the StreetPost fields.

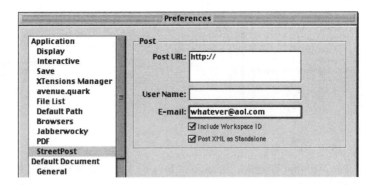

Document preferences

(Default Document or Default Web Document with no documents open)

General *(See the figure on the following page)*

Greek Text Below is the point size below which text will display as solid gray bars. Greeking is also affected by the current zoom level.

With **Greek Pictures** on, an unselected picture will display as solid gray, and a selected picture will display normally. Greeking speeds up screen redraw—but it may not be necessary.

Set ruler **Guides** to display **In Front** of or **Behind** items on a page (see page 185). The **Snap Distance** is the range in pixels within which an item will snap to a guide if View > Snap to Guides is on.

The **Master Page Items** options, **Keep Changes** and **Delete Changes**, affect whether modified master page items on a document page are kept or deleted when the same master page is reapplied, or a new master page is applied, to that document page (see page 232).

The **Auto Picture Import** options, Off, On, and On (verify), are for reimporting pictures that were modified or moved since a document was last opened. Choose On to reimport pictures automatically or On (verify) to reimport pictures selectively (see page 165).

Framing is added to the **Inside** (the default) or **Outside** edges of a box. A frame that's added to the Outside of a box will increase its dimensions (and thus change its x/y location). The Framing setting only affects subsequently-created boxes.

General *(Continued)*

In the **Hyperlinks** area, choose an **Anchor Color** for the hyperlink anchor icon (print and Web documents) (see page 324). And choose a **Hyperlinks Color** for hyperlinks created in print documents that will be exported in PDF format. *5.0!*

With **Auto Page Insertion** on, pages will be added to a chain of automatic text boxes at one of these locations: End of Story, End of Section, or End of Document (see pages 69–71). Choose Off to turn this feature off.

With **Auto Constrain** on, each newly created item (child) is constrained by the dimensions of an existing (parent) item—a holdover from the early days of QuarkXPress.

For a Web document, in the **Image Export Directory** field, enter the name the folder where image files are to be placed when the document is exported (see page 316). *5.0!*

For a Web document, choose a **Site Root Directory** as the root folder to be used to hold both the exported version of the document and the export directory/folder. Click Select/Browse, then locate and select a folder to be used as the site root folder. *5.0!*

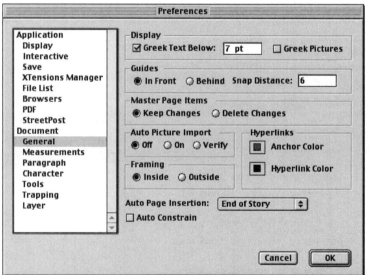

General Preferences for Print documents

The bottom portion of the General Preferences for Web documents

Measurements

Choose the default **Horizontal** and **Vertical Measurements** unit separately: Inches, Inches Decimal, Picas, Points, Millimeters, Centimeters, Ciceros, or Agates (see page 27). For a Web document only, you can choose pixels. These units are used for the Measurements palette, rulers, and dialog boxes—except for font size, leading, frame width, and line width, which always display in points.

TIP You can also Control-click/Right-click the horizontal or vertical ruler in the document window, then choose a unit from the Measure submenu.

72 points/inch is the current standard **Points/Inch** ratio in desktop publishing, so there's no need to change it. Ditto for **Ciceros/cm**, the ciceros-to-centimeter conversion ratio (2.197 is the default).

Print documents only: With **Item Coordinates: Spreads** chosen, horizontal ruler increments will advance uninterrupted across a multi-page spread. Choose Page for Normal ruler display (increments start anew at zero on each page).

Abbreviations

Inches	**in** *or* **"**
Inches Decimal	**in** *or* **"** with a decimal
Picas	**p**
Points	**pt** *or* **p** followed by a number (as in "p6")
Millimeters	**mm**
Centimeters	**cm**
Ciceros	**c**
Agates	**ag**
quarter of a millimiter	**q**
Pixels	**px**

Note: Pixels cannot be chosen in a print document, but "px" can be used in entry fields in a print document.

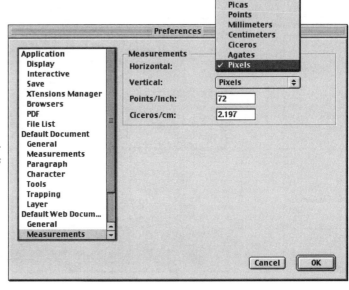

*Default Web Document–
Measurements Preferences*

Measurements Preferences *(sidebar, left margin)*

Paragraph

Auto Leading is primarily calculated as a percentage of the point size of the current font, and it is enabled when "auto" or "0" is entered in the Leading field on the Measurements palette or in the Formats dialog box. The spacing between lines within the same auto-leaded paragraph can vary according to the point size of the largest character in each line. You can also enter an increment in this field. If you enter an Auto Leading amount of +2, for example, two points will be added to the point size of the text to arrive at the leading amount (10-point text would have 12-point leading). The Auto Leading setting affects both newly-created and existing text.

If **Maintain Leading** is on, and an item is positioned within a column of text, the first line of text that is forced below the item will snap to the nearest leading increment (allowing for the current Item Runaround value), making it possible for text baselines to align across columns. With Maintain Leading off, the text will only be offset from the bottom of the item by any existing Item Runaround value, making it

difficult, if not impossible, for text to align across columns.

In **Typesetting** leading **Mode**, leading is measured from baseline to baseline, as in traditional typesetting. In **Word Processing** mode, leading is measured from ascent to ascent.

By aligning text or items in a layout more precisely across columns using the non-printing **Baseline Grid**, you can make your pages look more symmetrical and uniform. To use this feature for text, specify an Increment that is equal to or a multiple of the text leading. The Start value should match the vertical (y) position of the first baseline of the text. To snap text to the grid lines, choose Style > Formats, then check Lock to Baseline Grid. To display the grid, choose View > Show Baseline Grid. If the current Vertical Alignment Type is Justified, only the first and last lines in the column will lock to the grid.

The **Hyphenation Method**s are, in order of appearance and quality from earlier versions of QuarkXPress to the current version: Standard, Enhanced, and Expanded.

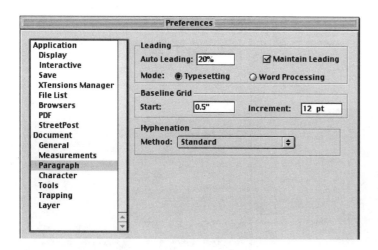

Character

The **Superscript** Offset is the distance a superscript character is raised above the baseline, and it's measured as a percentage of the current point size. The **Subscript** Offset is the distance a character is lowered below the baseline. The Superscript, Subscript, and Small Caps VScale (height) and HScale (width) are calculated as a percentage of a normal uppercase letter.

TIP Increase the HScale for Small Caps (it looks better), or better yet, use an expert font with built-in small caps.

Mac OS only: A **ligature** is a pair of serif characters (such as an "f" followed by an "l") that are joined into one character to prevent them from ungracefully knocking into each other (**1**, next page). The hyphenation and check spelling features treat ligatures that are produced this way as normal characters. **Break Above** is the amount of tracking or kerning in a line of type above which characters won't be joined as ligatures (for justified type, try 3 or 4). Each font may require a different Break Above amount (experiment). Some, but not all, fonts include ligatures for "ffi" and "ffl." Ligatures apply to the whole document.

The **Auto Kern Above** value is the point size above which characters will be kerned automatically, based on each particular font's built in kerning values as well as any user-defined QuarkXPress Tracking Edit or Kerning Table Edit values. Kerning is essential for professional-looking type.

The increment used for tracking in QuarkXPress is $\frac{1}{200}$ of an em space. With **Standard em space** off (the default setting), an em space equals the width of two zeros in the current font. With this option on, an em space equals the point size of the text.

The **Flex Space Width** (0–400%) is a percentage of an en space in the current font. To enter a breaking flex space in your text, press Option-Shift-Spacebar/Ctrl-Shift-5. To enter a non-breaking flex space, press Cmd-Option-Shift-Spacebar/Ctrl-Alt-Shift-5. To make the flex space the same width as an em space, enter 200%.

Check **Accents for All Caps** to use foreign language accent marks in small caps or all caps text (**2**, next page). All caps accents are considered kosher in some languages, but not in others. To learn the keystrokes for producing foreign language accent marks (e.g., é, ö, ã, à), see pages 454–455.

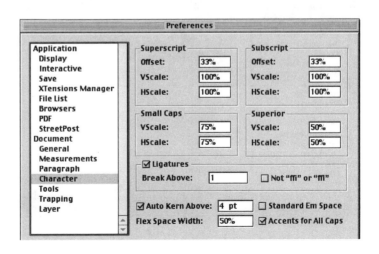

> "By the time she had caught the flamingo and brought it back, the fight was over..." *Lewis Carroll*

1 *The "fl" and "fi" **ligatures** (boldface added for emphasis)*

> **Accent** *n.:* a mark (as **É, À, Õ, Ü**) used in writing or printing to indicate a specific sound value, stress, or pitch.

2 *With **Accents for All Caps** on, accent marks can be inserted above uppercase characters.*

Tools

To choose default settings for a tool, click its icon in the Tool pane or double-click the tool on the Tools palette. Click **Modify** to change the default settings for the currently highlighted tool icon[s]. The many tool settings that you can change include the background color, Frame Width, and Runaround Type for any picture box or text box tool, the Text Inset for text boxes, and the Width for the Line tool. For the Zoom tool, you can choose a Minimum, Maximum, and Increment percentage (10–800%).

To set preferences for more than one tool at a time, first Cmd-click/Ctrl-click their icons individually or Shift-click a range of consecutive icons. Or click one tool icon, then click **Similar Types** or **Similar Shapes** to change the default settings for related tools. Fewer Modify dialog box settings may be available when more than one tool icon is highlighted.

To restore the default **settings** for the currently highlighted tool icon[s], click **Use Default Prefs**.

To restore the default **arrangement** of tools on the Tool palette and pop-out menus, click **Default Tool Palette**.

For a Web document, use the Tools pane to choose default height and width values for the **Forms Box** tool (see page 336) and default settings for the **Oval Image Map** and **Bézier Image Map** tools. For either Image Map tool, click Modify, then in the Image Map Properties dialog box **3**, either enter a **Maximum Points** value (3–1000) for the maximum number of points to be created to describe curves on an image map shape, or move the **Granularity** slider. The closer the Granularity slider is to Fine, the more closely the points will follow the shape you drew and the more points will be created.

Tool Preferences

3

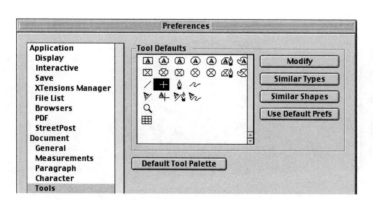

5.0! **Layer**

Choose whether newly-created layers will be **Visible**. We suggest you leave this option checked unless you enjoy playing tricks on yourself. Invisible layers don't print.

Choose whether to **Suppress Printout** of all items on subsequently-created layers (this option is only available for print documents).

TIP To control the printing of individual items on a layer, instead of all the items on a layer, use the Suppress Printout or Suppress Picture Printout option in Item > Modify.

Choose whether you want items on new layers to be **Locked**. Locked items can't be moved with the Item tool or moved to a different layer, but they can be moved via the X and/or Y fields on the Measurements palette. We keep the Suppress Printout and Locked options unchecked.

Check **Keep Runaround** to preserve the current Runaround settings for text on visible layers, even if the items the text is wrapping around aren't visible. The default setting for this option is checked, and we leave it that way.

Layer Preferences

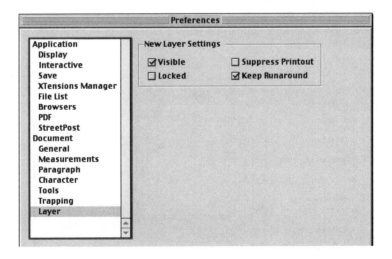

What does "!Error" mean?

The word !Error in the Status column for an XTension is a warning that QuarkXPress had a problem loading that XTension while launching.

Choose an XTensions set from the Set pop-up menu.

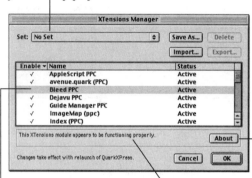

1 *Click in the Enable column in the XTensions Manager to enable or disable a Quark XTension, import/export filter, or third-party XTension.*

Read more information about the status of the currently highlighted XTension here.

Click About (or double-click an XTension name) to learn more about an XTension, such as its own version number and whether it's optimized for the current version of QuarkXPress.

XTensions

XTensions are add-ons to QuarkXPress that extend the program's capabilities. Some XTensions are included with the application, such as the filters for importing word processing files, while others are produced by third-party developers and must be purchased separately (see page 26).

Using the XTensions Manager, you can enable or disable Quark XTensions from within the application, as long as they are located either in the XTension folder or the XTension Disabled folder. You should disable any that you don't need, as they utilize memory. You can also use this utility to save, export, import, or delete user-defined XTension sets (XTension groups).

To enable/disable XTensions or import/export filters:

1. Choose Utilities > XTensions Manager.

2. Click a check mark to disable an XTension or click an absent check mark to enable it **1**. Repeat for any other XTensions you want to turn on or off.
   or
   Choose an XTensions set from the Set pop-up menu (see the next page).

3. *Optional:* Click About or double-click an XTension name to display information about the currently highlighted XTension. Click in the info dialog box to return to the Manager.

4. Click OK. The XTensions Manager changes won't go into effect until you quit/exit and relaunch QuarkXPress.

TIP To turn more than one XTension on or off at a time, click the name of the first XTension in a consecutive series, then Shift-click the name of the last XTension in the series, or Cmd-click/ Ctrl-click individual XTension names, then choose Yes or No from the Enable pop-up menu.

Enable/Disable XTensions

To help you organize XTensions and make it easier to turn them on and off, you can save your custom XTensions Manager settings as a set (this XTension on, that XTension off, etc.). You can also choose which set will be in effect when the application is launched. XTensions sets are saved in the XPress Preferences file.

To create an XTensions set:

1. Choose Utilities > XTensions Manager.

2. Disable any XTensions that you don't want included in your set and enable any XTensions that you do want included.

3. Click Save As ■.

4. Enter a name for current set ■.

5. Click Save. Your custom set will appear on the Set pop-up menu in the XTensions Manager ■ and it will also be enabled when the application is re-launched. (The set that is chosen from the Set pop-up menu will be in effect whenever QuarkXPress is launched.)

6. Click OK.

TIP To enable all the XTensions, choose Set: All XTensions Enabled. To disable them all, choose All XTensions Disabled from the same pop-up menu.

TIP To delete a user-defined set, choose it from the Set pop-up menu, then click Delete. This can't be undone!

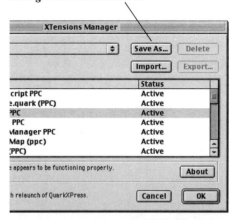

■ *Click* **Save As** *in the* **XTensions Manager** *to create a custom set.*

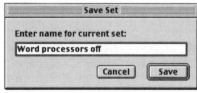

■ *Enter a* **name** *for the XTensions set.*

■ *The new set name appears on the* **Set** *pop-up menu.*

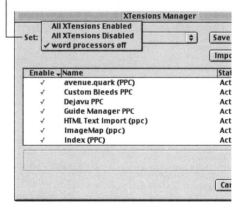

XTensions Manager at startup

If you want the XTensions Manager to open automatically whenever the application is launched, choose Edit > Preferences > Preferences, click Application–XTensions Manager, then click **Show XTensions Manager at Startup**: **Always**. If either of the other two preference options are chosen, you can force the XTensions Manager to open as you launch QuarkXPress by holding down **Space bar**. Keep the Space bar pressed until the Manager opens.

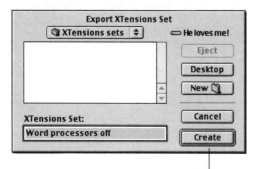

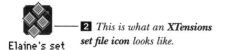

1 *Choose a location in which to save the XTensions file, then click* ***Create***.

Elaine's set

2 *This is what an* ***XTensions set file icon*** *looks like.*

User-defined XTensions sets are stored in the XPress Preferences file. This means that if you delete the XPress Preferences file, your custom sets will be deleted. If, however, you save your XTensions set to a separate file for safekeeping using the Export command, then you'll be able to re-import them at any time using the XTensions Manager.

To save an XTensions set as a separate file:

1. Choose Utilities > XTensions Manager.
2. Create an XTensions set (instructions on the previous page).
   or
   Choose an existing user-defined set from the Set pop-up menu.
3. Click Export.
4. Choose a location in which to save the file, then click Create/Save **1**.
5. Click OK.

TIP To import a previously-saved custom set that's not already listed on the Set pop-up menu, click Import, locate and click the set file that you want to import, then click Open **2**.

Save XTensions Set

Color management

What is color management?

Every device, whether it's a monitor or printer, defines color within its own unique color range (called its "gamut") when it represents or reproduces color. The purpose of color management is to ensure consistent color by coordinating and matching color between various device gamuts—from monitor color (RGB) to final print output color (CMYK). If color on a source device (monitor or scanner) is within the gamut of the destination device (printer), then color matching is straightforward. If color on a source device is outside the gamut of the destination device, then the color management system adjusts the color (alters its hue, lightness, or saturation) to match the color between devices. A monitor can't display, nor can a printing device output, all the colors in the visible spectrum.

The Apple ColorSync color management system extension, which is part of the Mac OS operating system and is automatically installed in the System folder, helps to coordinate the exchange of color data between devices and applications. It coordinates information about external devices, such as monitors and printers, via profiles that are created for each device. ColorSync, in conjunction with the QuarkXPress CMS (Color Management System) XTension, helps to ensure color accuracy between monitor representation and final output by taking into account variations between different color models (RGB color and CMYK color) and device gamuts.

ColorSync profiles can also be used to match color between applications. Let's say you create a picture in Photoshop and then import it into a QuarkXPress document. If you choose the same profiles (particularly the monitor profile) in both applications, hopefully, the picture will look the same on screen in QuarkXPress

Color management for Web docs?

The Color Management preferences are not accessible for Web documents. According to Quark, Inc., this is because at the present time the monitors used by Web viewers don't have uniform standards for color definition, representation, or calibration. So for Web documents, there wouldn't be any guidelines for choosing preferred or optimum settings for the Color Management Preferences dialog box anyway.

We do recommend that you apply **Web-safe colors** to graphics that you create in a drawing or image-editing program for import into a QuarkXPress Web document, and that you also stick with Web-safe colors for items and text in your QuarkXPress Web document.

as it does in Photoshop, and in both applications it will closely match the final output color. Once this color consistency is established, if you then change the monitor or the final output printer type, you must choose new profiles within each application.

Two critical steps in color matching are monitor calibration (generating and maintaining accurate screen characteristics, such as the white point and gamut) and choosing the correct color profile for each device. While there are applications that you can use specifically for creating device and printer profiles, for most QuarkXPress users, the ColorSync system and the profiles that ship with each device do an adequate job.

Color in QuarkXPress

Two kinds of color are used in a Quark-XPress document: Color that is applied to items that are created within the application and colors that are saved in an imported picture. In the case of color that's applied in QuarkXPress, the CMS generates color data based on the monitor profile or the profile for the output device the color is intended for. Item color profiles are assigned using the CMS Color Management Preferences dialog box.

When a picture is imported, the CMS looks for an included profile, if any, that is contained in that picture. The profile can be for the scanning device, the monitor used in the picture-editing program, or the final output device that was chosen for the picture. If no profile is included with an imported picture, you can use the CMS to assign a source profile to it. For an RGB picture, this will be a scanning device or monitor profile—whichever is appropriate. For a CMYK picture, this will be the profile for the final output device.

An imported picture to which no profile was assigned will be assigned a default profile as per the current settings in the Color Management Preferences dialog box. The default profile can be overridden via the Profile Information palette or the Get Picture dialog box.

Color management is accessed in Quark-XPress via Edit > Preferences > Color Management. This dialog box makes the program aware of your choice for source and destination profiles and your choice of parameters for on-screen color correction.

To turn on color management:

1. Choose Edit > Preferences > Color Management.

2. To turn on color management, check Color Management Active (**1** and **4**).

3. Make choices from the **Destination Profiles** pop-up menus for the target color output device (**2** and **5**).

   Mac OS: The profile names on the **Monitor** pop-up menu for monitor output derive from the System > Preferences > ColorSync Profiles folder. If the correct monitor profile name isn't listed, choose an Apple monitor that closely approximates your target monitor.

   For composite printer output (where all colors print on one sheet), choose a **Composite Output** printer profile. This type of printer is usually used for a limited run or to produce color proofs for review before producing separations.

   For color separations, choose a **Separation Output** Printer profile.

4. Choose a **Default Source Profile**, the source device that created the pictures that you imported into QuarkXPress (**3** and **6**).

   Choose Profiles to manage specific color spaces (models) for colors and pictures in three categories: RGB, CMYK, and Hexachrome (six-plate printing).

1 *Check here to turn on* ***Color Management.***   **2** *Choose* ***Destination Profiles.***

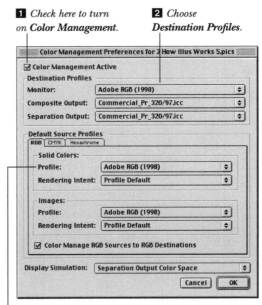

3 *Choose a* ***Default Source Profile*** *for each color model.*

4 *Click here to turn on* ***Color Management.***   **5** *Choose* ***Destination Profiles.***

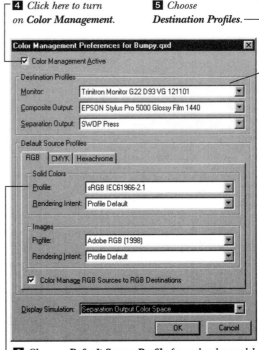

6 *Choose a* ***Default Source Profile*** *for each color model.*

Know your intents

Choose a **Rendering Intent** to determine how colors will be changed as they are moved from one color space to another:

Perceptual changes colors in a way that seems natural to the human eye. It's appropriate for continuous-tone images.

Relative Colorimetric, the default intent for all predefined settings options, is the same as Absolute Colorimetric (see below), except it compares the white point, or extreme highlight, of the source color space to the destination color space and shifts all colors accordingly. The accuracy of this intent depends on the accuracy of the white point information in an image's profile.

Saturation changes colors with the intent of preserving vivid colors, although it compromises the accuracy of the color. It's appropriate for charts and business graphics.

Absolute Colorimetric keeps colors that are inside the destination color gamut unchanged, but the relationships between colors outside this gamut are changed in an attempt to preserve a color.

Note: Differences between rendering intents are visible only on a printout or in a conversion to a different working space.

For the RGB color source, click the RGB tab, and from the **Solid Colors: Profile** pop-up menu, choose the exact monitor or the closest match that you can find. This kind of color derives from the monitor profile used by the program that created the color.

For a scanned picture, choose the scanner profile from the **Images: Profile** pop-up menu. For a picture created in a graphics application, from the Image pop-up menu, choose the Monitor profile used by that graphics application.

Choose a **Rendering Intent** (see the sidebar). Choose Profile Default unless you have a reason to change the Intent.

For the CMYK color source, click the CMYK tab, then choose the desired printer Solid Colors and Images profiles for color proofing or final output.

For the Hexachrome color source, click the Hexachrome tab, then choose the target output printer.

5. Under **Display Simulation**, choose the destination space (the device gamut or color range) you want the CMS to use for onscreen color correction. The bottom three categories on the pop-up menu match the three Destination Profile categories. For each Display Simulation choice, the profile you chose in the matching Destination Profile category will be used. Choose Off if or when you need to turn off onscreen color correction.

6. Click OK to close the dialog box and save your changes.

TIP Profiles assigned using the CMS are saved in the QuarkXPress document.

Turn on Color Management

QuarkXPress' Profile Information palette displays a selected picture's characteristics, and gives the user a limited means for modifying onscreen color correction for that picture. To access this palette, color management must be enabled (see page 398).

To use the Profile Information palette:

1. Open the palette by choosing View > Show Profile Information.

2. Click on a picture box that contains an imported picture.

3. Examine the three information fields to learn about the current picture's Picture Type [Color, Grayscale, or Line Art (black- and-white)]; File type (TIFF, EPS, etc.); and Color Space (RGB; CMYK; or Unknown for an EPS file whose exact color space information is not accessible to QuarkXPress, etc.).

4. If necessary, choose from the Profile pop-up menu **1** to change the source profile QuarkXPress will use for the selected picture from any embedded profile or the default profile currently chosen in Color Management preferences. For an RGB picture, the Profile pop-up menu will list monitor or scanner names. For a CMYK picture, the Profile pop-up menu will list output device names. (The defaults were set up in the Default Source Profiles section of Color Management Preferences.)

5. Check Color Manage to RGB [or CMYK] Destinations to enable the program's on-screen color correction for the selected picture **2**.

   Choosing a different profile name when Color Manage to RGB [or CMYK] Destinations is checked will immediately change the onscreen appearance of the currently selected picture.

   The Profile pop-up menu and Color Manage to RGB [or CMYK] Destinations option are grayed out for grayscale

*The **Profile Information** palette*

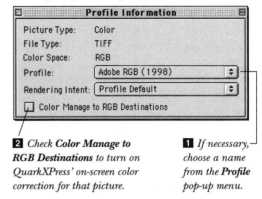

2 *Check **Color Manage to RGB Destinations** to turn on QuarkXPress' on-screen color correction for that picture.*

1 *If necessary, choose a name from the **Profile** pop-up menu.*

Profile Information Palette

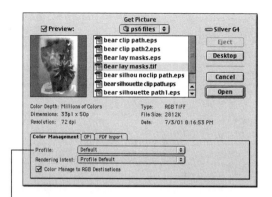

1 *You can choose a different **Profile** for an imported picture in the **Color Management** pane of the **Get Picture** dialog box.*

pictures (there is no color to correct) and EPS pictures (EPS pictures are encapsulated; their color information can't be changed using any . QuarkXPress command).

TIP A profile chosen from the Profile Information palette will override any embedded profile or default profile assigned to pictures via the Color Management Preferences dialog box in QuarkXPress.

You can also view an imported picture's characteristics and assign a profile to it in the Get Picture dialog box. If you choose a profile in the Get Picture dialog box, that choice will override any embedded profile or default profile assigned to the picture via Edit > Preferences > Color Management.

To turn on color management for a picture as it's imported:

1. Choose the Content tool, then click a picture box.

2. Choose File > Get Picture.

3. Locate and click the name of the picture you want to import.

4. The picture's Color Depth, Dimensions, Resolution, Type, File Size, and the Date it was last modified will be listed.

5. Either the embedded profile that was assigned to the picture in an image-editing application, or the default source profile that is being assigned via the Color Management Preferences to pictures that lack an embedded profile, will display on the Profile pop-up menu. To override that profile, choose a different one from the pop-up menu **1**.

   Check Color Manage to RGB [or CMYK] Destinations to enable Quark-XPress' color correction for the picture.

6. Click Open to import the picture.

The Profile Manager is used to view which profiles are currently installed in your system and/or to include or exclude individual profiles for use with the CMS.

To include/exclude profiles in QuarkXPress:

1. Choose Utilities > Profile Manager.

2. Click a check mark next to a profile name to exclude that profile from the CMS or click the blank space under the Include column to produce a check mark and include that profile 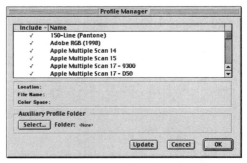. By default, all profiles in the system are automatically included (checked).

3. Click OK.

TIP Click Update if you have just installed/uninstalled profiles in your system and you want the Profile Manager to update its list of current system profiles.

5.0! If you tend to navigate to the same folder each time you use the Open, Save/SaveAs, Get Text, or Get Picture command, it's worth your while to use Default Path Preferences to designate a default path for any or all of those dialog boxes.

To choose Default Path preferences:

1. Choose Edit > Preferences > Default Path Preferences.

2. Click any or all of the four check-boxes **2**, click Browse, choose the designated folder, then click Select.

3. Click OK.

4. Mac OS only: Quit QuarkXPress, then choose Apple menu > Control Panels > General Controls. Under Documents, click "Folder that is set by the application," close the General Controls dialog box, then relaunch QuarkXPress.

TIP To disable a default path, uncheck that box in Default Path Preferences. In Windows, the default path will still be listed in the respective dialog box, but it won't be active.

1 *The Profile Manager*

2 *A default path for the Open, Save/ Save As, Get Text, and Get Picture dialog boxes can be chosen in the Default Path Preferences dialog box.*

Note: Default Path is in the Deja Vu XTension, which is a free download from Quark.com.

Quick-and-dirty print

Once you've established your Print dialog box settings and you want to print an entire document, press **Cmd-P/Ctrl-P**, then Return/Enter. Or to specify a range of pages, press Tab, type the starting page number, type a hyphen, type the ending page number, then press Return/Enter.

1 *Enter the number of* **Copies** *to be printed. 1 is the default.*

To specify which pages will print, leave the default **Pages** *setting on All; or enter non-consecutive page numbers divided by commas; or enter a range of numbers, divided by a hyphen (you can type "end" after a hyphen to print to the end of a document).*

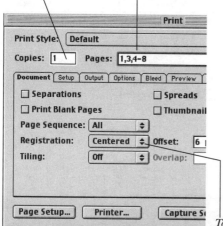

The left side of the **Print** *dialog box,* **Document** *pane*

To print crop and registration marks, choose **Registration:** **Centered** *or* **Off Center***.*

To print to a PostScript printer from QuarkXPress (print documents):

1. Open the Print dialog box by choosing File > Print (Cmd-P/Ctrl-P) or File > Page Setup (Cmd-Option-P/Ctrl-Alt-P).

2. *Optional:* Choose an existing print style from the **Print Style** pop-up menu (see page 409). If you want to override the current print style settings, enter new settings via the panes in the Print dialog box and then print. These changes will be only temporary and won't affect the original print style. (A bullet will appear before the original print style name to signal that a temporary change was made.)

3. Enter the number of **Copies** of each page you want to print **1**. 1 is the default.

4. In the **Pages** field, enter the pages to be printed. For consecutive pages, separate the starting and ending page numbers with a "-" (hyphen). For non-consecutive pages, separate each page number with a "," (comma). See the sidebar on page 407 regarding page numbering.

(Continued on the following page)

Print from QuarkXPress

5. These instructions are lengthy, yes, but you don't necessarily have to follow all of them each and every time you send a document to the printer.

Use the **Document** pane if you want to turn on Separations, Spreads, Include Blank Pages, Registration (crop marks), and other settings.

Use the **Setup** pane to choose the correct Printer Description **1**, which will automatically set up the default Page Size, Page Width, and Height settings. You can change the printout size (Reduce or Enlarge), Page Positioning, and Orientation.

Use the **Output** pane to choose a Print Colors setting (Black & White, Grayscale, or Color Composite), Halftoning, and printer Resolution options. The Print Colors options are controlled by the current Printer Description in the Setup pane.

Use the **Options** pane if you want to turn on the Quark PostScript Error Handler (QuarkXPress' alert boxes) or change the Output type (Normal, Low, or Rough), data encoding, TIFF image Output, or other image settings.

Use the **Preview** pane to view a thumbnail of the current page with the chosen printing parameters **2**.

The icon below the preview window indicates whether a cut-sheet print device (individual pieces of paper) ⎙ or a roll-fed print device (a roll of continuous paper) ◇ was chosen from the Printer Description pop-up menu in the Setup pane. To see a key for the different colors used in the preview window, click the 🛈 button.

Optional: Click the Bleed tab, choose from the **Bleed Type** pop-up menu:

Page Items allows any item that is at least partially on the page to print in its entirety (**1** and **2**, next page).

The halftoning options

If you choose a process color from the **Halftone** pop-up menu in the Edit Color dialog box, the halftone Frequency, Angle, and Function options that are currently set for that process color (C, M, Y, or K) will be assigned to it. To view or change the current settings, choose File > Print, then click the Output tab (Cmd-P/Ctrl-P). When you're ready to print the file, check Separations in the Document pane. For more information, see page 411. Settings chosen in the Print dialog box override settings chosen in the Edit Color dialog box.

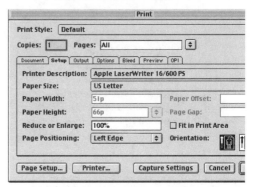

1 *The **Setup** pane in the QuarkXPress **Print** dialog box*

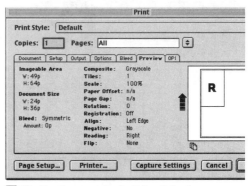

2 *The **Preview** pane in the **Print** dialog box*

*Note: If the **Custom Bleeds** XTension is active (it's installed by default with QuarkXPress 5), a **Bleed** tab appears in the Print dialog box. With this XTension off, a simple Bleed field appears in the Document pane instead.*

Printing Web documents

To print a Web document choose Edit > Print. You may notice that this dialog box looks a bit different. That's because Web documents use the System's default Web browser to provide the options in the Print dialog box, whereas print documents use the native QuarkXPress Print dialog box. The QuarkXPress Print dialog box is more complex and offers many more options; those options are needed for QuarkXPress to write the proper PostScript information for print output.

Read more about it

Read more about bleeds and OPI in the PDF ReadMe files located in QuarkXPress 5 > Documents > **XTensions ReadMes** folder.

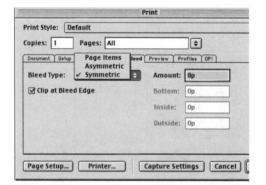

1 *The **Bleed** pane in the **Print** dialog box*

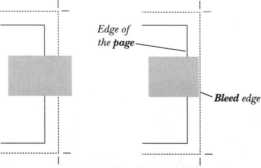

2 *With **Page Items** chosen, the whole item prints, as long as part of it is on the page.*

3 *With **Asymmetric** (or **Symmetric**) chosen and **Clip at Bleed Edge** checked, items print up to the specified Amount (the bleed edge).*

Asymmetric and **Symmetric** let you define the width of the bleed area. For Symmetric, enter one Amount value; for Asymmetric, enter Top, Bottom, Inside, and Outside values. With **Clip at Bleed Edge** checked, items won't print beyond the bleed area; unchecked, items that at least partially overlap the bleed area will print in their entirety, within the limits of the output device **3**.

Click the **Preview** tab to preview any Bleed values in the preview window. (If Asymmetric is chosen in a facing-pages document, you can click the Left of Spine ⬑ or Right of Spine ⬐ button below the preview window in the Preview pane.)

Optional: If Preferences > Color Management is on, you can click the **Profiles** tab, then choose profiles from the pop-up menus to override the Destination profile for the Separation device and/or Composite device chosen in Color Management preferences. Check Composite Simulates Separation to have the composite output simulate the appearance of the profile choice for the chosen Separation device.

Optional: The **OPI** options only apply if you are outputting to an OPI prepress system that replaces the QuarkXPress images with high-resolution images that are stored on that OPI system. Click the OPI tab and check OPI Active to have QuarkXPress write OPI comments for all the pictures in the file. Only pictures you target to be exchanged will be replaced by a high-resolution version. If a proxy of a picture is used in the file and the proxy contains OPI instructions, check TIFF: or EPS: Include Images. Both picture data and comments will be sent to output.

Note: If the OPI XTension is active, the OPI tab is available and the OPI

(Continued on the following page)

Print from QuarkXPress

pop-up menu in the Options pane becomes unavailable.

6. You can return to any pane at any time. Click **Print** (Return/Enter) when you're ready to print.

If a missing pictures prompt appears, click **List Pictures**, click Update, locate and highlight the missing picture(s), click Open, then click Print.

Note: Click **Page Setup** or **Properties** to display the Page Setup (Mac OS) **1** or Properties (Windows) dialog box for the print device. Settings chosen in either of these dialog boxes will override the current print settings in QuarkXPress.

Changes made in the Setup pane of the QuarkXPress Print dialog box, such as the Reduce or Enlarge percentage or the Orientation, update automatically in the Page Setup dialog box, and vice versa. A change to the Paper Size, on the other hand, won't update in the other dialog box.

Mac OS:

Clicking **Printer** will take you to the System's Printer driver, which is usually the LaserWriter driver **2**. If you're using LaserWriter version 8.4 or later, you can access additional, related panes via the pop-up menu at the top of the Printer dialog box. Don't be confused about what seems to be a duplication of print options—QuarkXPress' and the System's.

Click the Printer button to access options such as turning background printing on or off, printing to a file, font inclusion, using the LaserWriter layout setup scheme, turning the printer's imaging options (e.g., FinePrint and PhotoGrade) on or off, and using the System's ColorSync or PostScript Color Matching options (instead of, or in addition to, QuarkXPress' Composite Color option). To exit

*Choose a **Paper** option.*

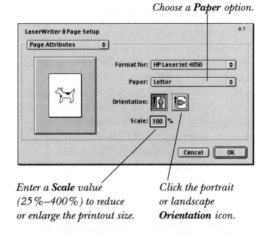

*Enter a **Scale** value (25%–400%) to reduce or enlarge the printout size.*

*Click the portrait or landscape **Orientation** icon.*

1 *This is the **Mac OS Page Setup** dialog box. You can choose the same Reduce/Enlarge and Orientation settings in the Setup pane of the QuarkXPress Print dialog box.*

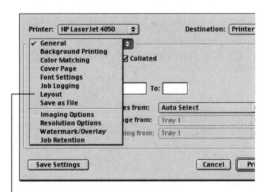

2 *In the Mac OS, clicking **Printer** in the Print dialog box opens the LaserWriter driver dialog box. There, related panes can be accessed via this pop-up menu.*

Print from QuarkXPress

Which page?

If your page numbers contain hyphens, you'll need to enter a range separator other than a hyphen in the Pages field. But first, choose Edit > Preferences > Preferences, click Application–Interactive, then, in the **Page Range Separators: Sequential** and **Nonsequential** fields, type the character[s] you're going to use.

If your document contains section numbering, enter the page number accurately, including any prefix (as in "Page xii"). To enter the number of the position of the page within the document instead (the absolute page number), type a plus sign before it. To print the third and fourth pages in a document, for example, you'd enter "+3-+4."

1 *In the* **Print** *dialog box in Windows, click the* **Properties** *button to open the Properties dialog box.*

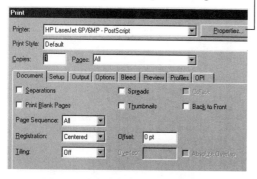

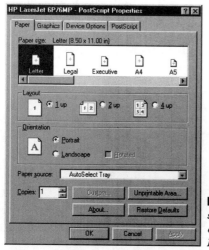

2 *Choose* **Layout, Orientation, Paper source,** *and* **Unprintable Area,** *and other options for the printer in the* **Paper** *pane of the Properties dialog box.*

and accept the System's Printer dialog box settings, click Print (this *won't* initiate printing).

Windows:

Click **Properties 1** to display the printer's Properties dialog box **2**. Settings chosen in this dialog box will override the current QuarkXPress print settings.

Changes made to settings in the Setup pane of the QuarkXPress Print dialog box, such as Copies and Orientation, update automatically in the Paper and Graphics panes in the Properties dialog box, and vice versa. A change to the Paper Size, on the other hand, won't update in the other dialog box.

Options in the printer's **Properties** dialog box will vary depending on which printer is currently selected. For a PostScript printer, there are four tabs: Paper, Graphics, Device Options and PostScript.

Use the **Paper** tab to format the Layout, Orientation, Paper source, and Unprintable Area of the page. Click More Options to select the type of paper you'll be printing on.

Use the **Graphics** tab to choose Resolution, image color matching, Halftoning, and Scaling settings. You can also choose to print a negative or a mirror image here.

Use the **Device Options** tab to change Color Correction settings or printer-specific features.

Use the **PostScript** tab to set the PostScript Output format.

7. When you're done choosing settings, click OK from any pane to return to the Print dialog box.

Capture the settings

Click Capture Settings to save the current print settings as modifications to the current document. The next time you choose Print, the captured settings will become the current print settings for that document. If you choose another print style or choose other print options and then click Capture Settings again, the new settings will again become the current print settings.

Some custom Halftoning options can also be saved to the generic Document print style when you click Capture Settings. If you want to create a print style with Halftoning options for use with other documents, use Edit > Print Styles (see the next page).

Using automatic tiling, a document whose page size is larger than the standard paper size, such as a tabloid, can be printed in sections on multiple sheets of standard-size paper. QuarkXPress automatically prints crop marks for trimming the page sections as well as margin label codes notating the order for reassembling them into the larger whole.

To print using automatic tiling:

1. Choose File > Print (Cmd-P/Ctrl-P).

2. Choose the appropriate Orientation icon in the Setup pane. Portrait is a good choice for a tabloid page.

3. Choose Tiling: Automatic in the Document pane.

4. Enter a number in the Overlap field. 3" (18p) is the default.

5. Adjust any other print settings. Click the Preview pane to preview.

6. Click Print.

TIP To print an oversized document on one sheet of paper, reduce the printout size percentage (Setup tab) until it fits.

1 *Click New in the Print Styles dialog box.*

Print styles are like style sheets for printers. Each print style can contain custom Print dialog box settings. Once you've created a print style, you can then choose it from the Print Styles drop-down menu in the Print dialog box for *any* QuarkXPress document. To temporarily override the saved settings in a print style, simply choose new settings from any pane in the Print dialog box.

To create or edit a print style (print documents):

1. Choose Edit > Print Styles.

2. Click an existing print style, then click Edit to modify it or click Duplicate to edit a copy of it.
or
Click New to create a new print style **1**.

3. For a new or duplicate print style, type a name in the Name field.

4. Click the Document, Setup, Output, and Options tabs, and choose the desired settings. These setings match the options found in the Print dialog box (see pages 403–407).

5. Click OK, then click Save **2**.

TIP To remove a print style from the list, click on it, then click Delete. The Default print style can't be deleted.

TIP Click Export to save the current print style to a separate file. If that style is inadvertently deleted (or if the XPress Preferences file, where print styles are stored, is deleted), you can restore it via the Import button in the Print Styles dialog box.

2 *A **new print style** has been created with a Pictures: Output setting of Rough for faster printing (the pictures won't print).*

Suppress picture printing: Picture Usage

Choose Utilities > Usage, click the Pictures tab (Option-F13/Alt-F13), then click to delete the check mark in the Print column to suppress printing of that picture **1**. The picture won't print, but a frame, if any was applied to the box, will print. (Click again in the same column to restore the check mark and turn printing back on.) Click Done when you're finished.

To suppress the printing of multiple pictures, click on the first picture in a series of consecutively-listed pictures, then Shift-click on the last picture in the series, or Cmd-click non-consecutive pictures individually, then choose No from the Print pop-up menu.

Suppress item printing: Modify dialog box (print documents)

To completely suppress printing of any individual item (a line, a box, or a text path) including its frame, if any, check Suppress Printout in Item > Modify > Box (Cmd-M/Ctrl-M) **2**. You can add non-printing notes to your document this way.

Or, to print a frame on a picture box but not the picture, check Suppress Picture Printout in Item > Modify (Picture pane).

Suppress printing of all pictures: Print dialog box (print documents)

Choose File > Print, click the Options tab, then choose Output: Rough **3**. On the printout, an "x" will appear in each picture box, and any applied frames will also print.

Another option for a document that seems to be taking an eternity to print is to choose Output: Low Resolution. The low resolution version of the picture that was saved automatically with the QuarkXPress file will print instead of the original picture.

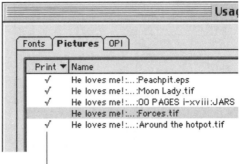

1 *Click a check mark in the **Print** column in Utilities > Usage > **Pictures** to suppress the printing of that picture.*

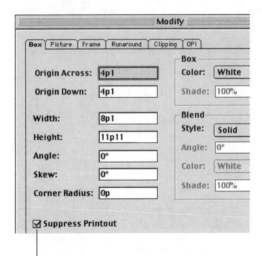

2 *Check **Suppress Printout** in Item > Modify > **Box** to prevent a picture and frame, if any, from printing.*

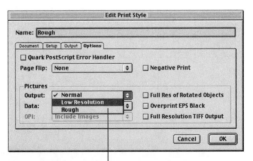

3 *Choose **Output: Low Resolution** or **Rough** in File > Print > **Options**.*

To modify the halftoning used by QuarkXPress

1. Choose File > Print, then check Separations in the Document pane.

2. Click the Output tab, then from the Halftoning pop-up menu **1**:

Choose Conventional, then click the name of the plate to be modified. At the top of the Frequency, Angle, and Function columns are pop-up menus from which you can make additional choices. Be sure to check with your output service provider before choosing any new settings.

or

Choose Printer to have the printing device handle halftoning (with no modifications allowed); no halftone information will be sent to the printer by QuarkXPress. *Note:* This option is only available if Separations is unchecked in the Document pane.

3. From the Plates pop-up menu:

Choose Used Process & Spot to choose halftoning options for individual plates for only the process and spot colors that are used in the document.

or

Choose Convert to Process to convert all spot colors in the file to process colors.

or

Choose All Process & Spot to choose halftoning options for all colors—process, spot, and RGB.

4. In the lower portion of the dialog box you'll see several columns. Use the Print pop-up menu to turn the printing of individual plates on or off.

TIP To save yourself from repetitive setup work, create a print style containing halftoning options. Then all you have to do is choose that style from the Print Style pop-up menu in File > Print.

Read all about it

To read more about the complicated world of scanning and color separation, there are many excellent reference books to choose from, such as *Real World Scanning and Halftones* by David Blatner, Glenn Fleishman, and Steve Roth or *Start with a Scan* by Janet Ashford and John Odam, both from Peachpit Press.

Halftoning

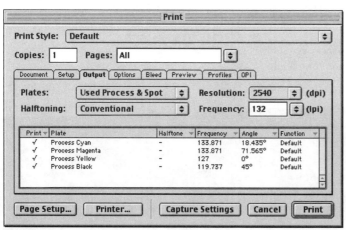

1 *Click a color plate name and choose different settings for that plate from the* **Halftone, Frequency, Angle,** *and* **Function** *column pop-up menus, as per your service provider's instructions.*

PPD, which stands for PostScript Printer Description, is a text file that contains information about a particular printer's parameters—its default resolution, usable paper and page sizes, PostScript version number, etc. The PPD Manager—which facilitates loading of PPDs into QuarkXPress—is useful in any setting where more than one kind of printer is used. It can be used to control which of the System's PPDs (and thus printer names) are available on the Printer Description pop-up menu (File > Print–Setup pane; or Edit > Print Styles > New; or Print Styles > Edit–Setup pane).

You can limit the Setup lists to only the printers you print to from QuarkXPress. An unlimited number of PPDs can be loaded at a time, but the fewer the better, because they affect the speed at which the Print dialog box opens. The PPD Manager's current settings update immediately on all the Printer Description pop-up menus in QuarkXPress.

To use the PPD manager:

1. Choose Utilities > PPD Manager.

2. Click on a printer name to select it **1**.

3. Click the check mark to remove that printer name from any Setup pane list. Or to include a printer name, click to restore the check mark.
or
To highlight multiple, consecutive printer names, click a name, then Shift-click the last name you want to select; or Cmd-click/Ctrl-click to highlight non-consecutive names. Then choose Yes or No from the Include pop-up menu to include or exclude the PPDs you selected.

4. Click OK. The Printer Description pop-up menu in the File > Print (Setup pane) will update to reflect your changes.

Where to put your PPDs

In the Mac OS, by default, PPDs are stored in the System Folder > Extensions folder > **Printer Descriptions** folder. In Windows, PPDs are stored in C:\Windows\SYSTEM. QuarkXPress uses this location as its default setting, and it's a good idea to leave PPDs in this location so they can be found and accessed by all your applications.

If the PPD list gets to be too long, use the PPD Manager to exclude printer names that aren't currently being used in your QuarkXPress projects. Changes made using the PPD Manager will only affect QuarkXPress—not any other applications.

1 *Use the QuarkXPress* **PPD Manager** *to include or exclude PPDs from the Printer Description pop-up menus in the Print dialog box or the Print Styles dialog box.*

PPD Manager

To add PPDs to the PPD manager list:

1. Mac OS: Install the PPDs in the System Folder > Extensions > Printer Descriptions folder.

Windows: Install the PPDs in C:\Windows\SYSTEM.

2. If QuarkXPress isn't open, launch it now.

3. Choose Utilities > PPD Manager.

4. Make sure the Folder path for the PPD folder is the same as the location that was used for step 1. If it is, skip to step 5.

If it's not the same path, click Select, and locate the folder that contains the System's PPD files (in our Mac OS, it's the System Folder > Extensions > Printer Descriptions folder). When the correct folder name appears within the Select "[   ]" button at the bottom of the Open dialog box, click on it.

5. In the PPD Manager, click Update. Any PPDs that you just added to the System folder will also be added to the current PPD list.

6. Make sure a check mark is present in the Include column for any PPD that you want to appear on the Printer Description pop-up menu in File > Print (Setup pane).

7. Click OK.

TIP Keep in mind that QuarkXPress will only look to one folder at a time for PPDs. So if your PPD files are stored in more than one folder, the PPDs from only one of those folders will be accessible to the PPD Manager (and thus appear on the Printer Description pop-up menu list in the Setup pane of the Print dialog box).

Add PPDs

Some print shops may request or require that you furnish a PostScript file of your document for output. To do this, first prepare your document as per your service provider's instructions.

Note: Before you create a PostScript file, make sure the proper Printer Description file for the final print output device is in the PPD Manager so it's available in the Setup pane of the Print dialog box.

To create a PostScript file (Mac OS):

1. Choose File > Print (Cmd-P/Ctrl-P).

2. Ask your service provider what settings to choose in the Setup and Output panes.

3. Click Printer, then click OK in the alert box.

4. Mac OS: Choose Save as File from the pop-up menu on the left side of the dialog box **1**.

5. Choose Destination: File to save the printing to disk **2**.

6. Ask your service provider which Format: PostScript Job or EPS (with or without a preview), PostScript Level, Data Format, and Font inclusion options to choose **3**.

7. Click Save, choose a location in which to save the PostScript file, enter a descriptive name, like ("Ch1.ps" or "1–10.ps," then click Save again.

8. The QuarkXPress Print dialog box will reopen. Adjust any other settings, then click Print (not Cancel). Be sure to send along the live (non-PostScript) file and pictures to the service provider, just in case.

1 *Choose **Save as File**.* **2** *Choose **Destination: File**.*

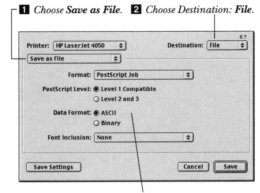

3 *Choose **Format, PostScript Level, Data Format** and **Font Inclusion** options.*

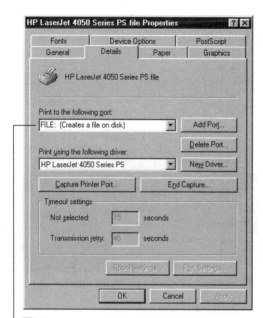

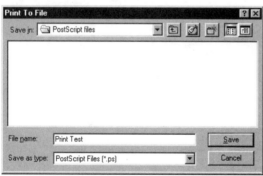

1 *Choose* **FILE: (Creates a file on disk)** *from the* **Print to the following port** *drop-down menu.*

2 *In the* **Print To File** *dialog box, type a name for the output file and choose a folder in which to save it.*

To create a PostScript file (Windows):

1. Click Start button > Settings > Printers.

2. Right-click the name of your printer and choose Properties.

3. Click the Details tab.

4. Choose "FILE: (Creates a file on disk)" from the "Print to the following port" drop-down menu **1**, then click OK.

5. Click in the QuarkXPress document window, and choose File > Print (Ctrl-P).

6. Ask your service provider what settings to choose in the Setup and Output panes.

7. From the PostScript output format drop-down menu, choose a PostScript option, then click Print. *Note:* A warning will appear if you haven't chosen "Print to the following port: FILE," as described in step 4, above.

8. In the Print To File dialog box, type a name for the output file in the File name field and choose a folder in which to save it **2**. If you want an extension to be included in the name, you must type it; it won't be added automatically.

Reminder: Be sure to go back into Printer Settings and change the "Print to the following port" setting back to LPT1: (Printer Port) in order to print normally.

The **Save Page as EPS** command converts a QuarkXPress page into a single picture. There are a few reasons to use this feature:

- Your service provider or commercial printer requests that you save a page as an EPS file in order to color-separate it.

- To produce a file that can be imported into another application, such as Photoshop or Illustrator.

- To create a resizable page-within-a-page (e.g., an advertisement or type logo).

To save a page as an EPS file:

1. Create or open a file that contains the page you want to save as an EPS file, then choose File > Save Page as EPS (Cmd-Option-Shift-S/Ctrl-Alt-Shift-S). *Note:* An EPS cannot be edited in QuarkXPress, so be sure to save the original file from which it is generated so you will be able to edit it or generate another EPS file from it later on!

2. *Optional:* Change the file name in the Save page as/File name field **1**.

3. Enter the page to be saved as an EPS in the **Page** field. The current page number will be entered automatically.

4. Enter a **Scale** percentage (10%–100%).

5. *Optional:* Check **Transparent Page** to save the file with a transparent background instead of a white background.

   Check **Spread** to save a multi-page spread instead of just the current page.

6. Choose **Format**: Color, Black & White, DCS or DCS 2.0. To color-separate a page before printing, you can save it in either of two DCS (Desktop Color Separation) file formats. DCS consists of five files (cyan, magenta, yellow, black, and a preview); DCS 2.0 consists of separations combined into one file with a preview, and can include spot color plates. Ask your service provider which file format is appropriate for your target output device.

1 *The Save Page as EPS dialog box*

Using a file saved as EPS

Save Page as EPS is handy if you have an **ad** or a **logo** that you created in QuarkXPress that you need to use in various sizes. To place an EPS into a document, create a picture box and use File > Get Picture. As with any EPS file, for any type it contains, the printers fonts must be available, and the original files for any pictures it contains, must also be available in order to output it properly.

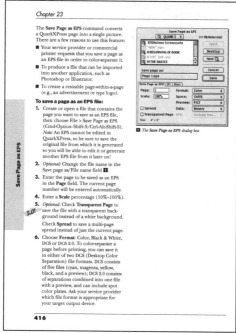

1 *This is an **EPS** of the previous page in this book— a page-within-a-page.*

7. Choose **Space**: CMYK or RGB. **5.0!**

8. Choose **Preview**: PICT (available only in the Mac OS), TIFF, or None.

9. If you're saving the page for color separation, ask your commercial printer which Data and OPI settings to choose. Binary Data files print more quickly and are smaller in file size than ASCII files, so use ASCII only if Binary can't be used. Clean 8-bit produces a more portable output format using a combination of ASCII and Binary data.

10. Choose a location in which to save the EPS file, then click Save **1**–**2**.

It's easy to resize a logo if you save it as an EPS!

It's easy to resize a logo if you save it as an EPS!

It's easy to resize a logo
if you save it as
an EPS!

It's easy to resize a logo
if you save it as
an EPS!

2 *This logo was created in QuarkXPress, **saved as an EPS** file, and then imported into various-sized picture boxes.*

Save Page as EPS

When you send a file to a service provider, you must also send original picture files used in the file, along with written information about it, such as the file name, date, dimensions, and fonts used. The Collect for Output command gathers copies of all the required elements together for you automatically, and also produces a text report with information about the file, such as the fonts and colors it uses.

5.0! In QuarkXPress 5.0 or later, you can selectively choose whether linked pictures, embedded pictures, color profiles, screen fonts, and printer fonts will be included in the output folder. This is a significant improvement.

To collect for output:

1. Save the document, then choose File > Collect for Output. If any pictures can't be located or were modified after they were imported into the QuarkXPress file, the Missing/Modified Pictures dialog box will open. Click List Pictures, update the pictures, then click Collect (see page 166).

2. Choose a location for the folder **1**–**2**.

3. In the Mac OS, click the New 🔲 button, change the folder name, if desired, then click Create. In Windows, click the New Folder button, change the folder name, if desired, then double-click the folder icon to open it.

4. *Optional:* Change the Report Name.

5. Check any of the Collect boxes for file components to be included in the folder: Document, Linked Pictures, Embedded Pictures (e.g., PICT, BMP, **5.0!** and WMF files), Color Profiles (ICC profiles), Screen Fonts (Mac OS only), and Printer Fonts/Fonts.

6. Click Save (click OK if a prompt appears). A folder containing the current document, the components that you checked in the previous step, and a detailed report file, will be created.

Just the facts, ma'am

To get just a document report without having QuarkXPress gather the files, check **Report Only** before you click Save in the Collect for Output dialog box. To do this via a shortcut, choose File > Collect for Output with **Option/ Alt** held down.

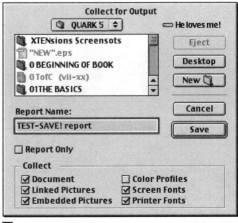

1 *The Collect for Output dialog box in the Mac OS*

New Folder button

2 *The Collect for Output dialog box in Windows*

1 *Fill out this form.*

ELECTRONIC OUTPUT REQUEST

CLIENT INFORMATION
Contact Person: _____
Company: _____
Address: _____
City, St., ZIP: _____
Office Phone: _____
Home Phone: _____

DELIVERY INFORMATION
__ Deliver   __ Hold For Pickup   __ Call When Complete
Delivery Address: _____
City, St., ZIP: _____

TURNAROUND INFORMATION
__ Normal   __ Rush   __ Emergency

FONT INFORMATION
__ Adobe/Linotype __ Agfa   __ Bitstream
__ Monotype   __ _____ __ _____

COLOR MANAGEMENT INFORMATION
__ Match colors according to assigned source profiles. (Include necessary profiles with job.)

COPYRIGHT INFORMATION
All that appears on the enclosed medium (including, but not limited to, floppy disk, modem transmission, removable media) is unencumbered by copyrights. We, the customer, have full rights to reproduce the supplied content.
Signature: _____
Date: _____

OUTPUT MEDIA (CHECK ALL THAT APPLY)
__ Film   __ RC Paper   __ Color Proof
__ Laser Print   __ Color Slides
__ Negative   -or-   __ Positive
__ Emulsion Down -or-   __ Emulsion Up

DOCUMENT
Source Path Name: Silver G4:Desktop Folder:Quark 5 test files:page as eps:2 How Illus Works 5.pics
Destination Path Name: Silver G4:Desktop Folder:Quark 5 test files:page as eps:chp 2 report
Last modified: 2:14 PM; 8/11/01
Document Size: 2156K
Most recently saved version: 5.00a3
Document has been saved by the following versions of QuarkXPress:
                5.00a3
Total Pages: 8
Page Width: 42p

OUTPUT SPECIFICATION
__ Output All Pages
__ Output The Following Specified Pages...
From: _____   To: _____

CROP MARKS
__ Yes   __ No

RESOLUTION/DPI
__ 1200/1270   __ 2400/2540   __ 3000+

SCREEN RULING/LPI
__ 65   __ 85   __ 133
__ 150   __ 175

COLOR SEPARATION PLATES
__ Cyan   __ Magenta   __ Yellow   __ Black

COLOR PROOF SPECIFICATION
__ Proof All Pages
__ Proof The Following Specified Pages...
From: _____   To: _____

LASER PROOF PROVIDED WITH JOB?
__ Yes   __ No

OTHER INFORMATION
Type information about the job here.

2 *And import the **report file** into the bottom box.*

ELECTRONIC OUTPUT REQUEST FOR: YOUR COMPANY NAME HERE   PAGE 2

Page Height: 54p

REQUIRED XTENSIONS:
                None

ACTIVE XTENSIONS:
Hyperlinks PPC;   Cool Blends PPC;   GIF Filter PPC;   HTML Export (ppc);
Table PPC;   JPEG Filter (ppc);   Layers PPC;   SpellChecker;
Custom Blends PPC;   Web Tools (ppc);   AppleScript PPC;   avenue.quark (PPC);
                        Dejavu PPC;   Guide Manager PPC;   HTML Text Import (ppc);
                        ImageMap (ppc);   Index (PPC);   Item Sequence (PPC);
Jabberwocky PPC;   Kern-Track Editor;   LZW Import PPC;   MS-Word 6-2000 Filter;
OPI PPC;   PDF Filter PPC;   PhotoCD Import PPC;   PNG Filter (ppc);
Quark CMS PPC;   QuarkLink PPC;   Scissors PPC;   StreetPost (PPC);
Super Step and Repeat PPC; Type Tricks;   WordPerfect Filter PPC; XPress Tags Filter

DOCUMENT FONTS
FONT NAME   POSTSCRIPT NAME   FILE NAME
«Plain»Sabon   Sabon   SabonRom
«Italic»Sabon   Sabon   SabonIta
«Plain»GillSans Condensed GillSans Condensed   GillSanCon
«Plain»B Sabon Bold   B Sabon Bold   SabonBol
«Plain»GillSans BoldCondensed GillSans BoldCondensed GillSanBolCon
«Bold»I Sabon Italic   I Sabon Italic   SabonBolIta
«Plain»GillSans Italic   GillSans Italic   GillSanIta
«Plain»I Sabon Italic   I Sabon Italic   SabonIta
«Plain»BundesbahnPi 1   BundesbahnPi 1   BundePlOne
«Plain»GillSans Bold   GillSans Bold   GillSanBol
«Plain»R Frutiger Roman   R Frutiger Roman   FrutiRom
«Plain»BI Sabon BoldItalic BI Sabon BoldItalic   SabonBolIta
«Plain»O Futura BookOblique O Futura BookOblique FuturBooObl
«Plain»Lithos Regular   Lithos Regular   LithoReg

PICTURE FONTS
PICTURE   FONT NAME
ORNAMENT original.eps   No fonts used.
ORNAMENT original.eps   No fonts used.
ORNAMENT original.eps   No fonts used.
ORNAMENT original.eps   No fonts used.
ORNAMENT original.eps   No fonts used.
ORNAMENT original.eps   No fonts used.
Type on a path   No fonts used.
Type on a path   No fonts used.
Type on a spiral-opening page Copperplate-ThirtyThreeBC
paintbrush flower.eps   No fonts used.
"IMPROVED"   No fonts used.
transparency.eps   No fonts used.
"NEW"   No fonts used.
Origami   No fonts used.

*Any fonts used in EPS graphics will be listed in the **Picture Fonts** category.*

After using the Collect for Output command, you can flow the report file into the Output Request template, print that report, and then give the printout to your service provider along with your computer file.

Note: In order to import the report file, the XPress Tags filter must be enabled. Use the XTensions Manager to do this, and then re-launch QuarkXPress.

To create an output request form:

1. Choose File > Open, and locate and open the Output Request template. Unless it was moved, you'll find it in the Documents folder inside the QuarkXPress folder.

2. Choose File > Save As (Cmd-Option-S/ Ctrl-Alt-S), type a name for the report, then click Save. For simplicity's sake, save the request form to your new Collect for Output folder.

3. Fill out the top portion of the Electronic Output Request **1**.

4. Choose the Content tool.

5. Click in the text box at the bottom of page 1, below the horizontal line **2**.

6. Choose File > Get Text (Cmd-E/ Ctrl-E).

7. Locate and highlight the report file, and check Include Style Sheets.

8. Click Open (Return/Enter). New pages will be added automatically to accommodate all the text.

Output Request Form

Imagesetting tips

An imagesetter is a device that produces high resolution (1,250–3,540 dpi) paper or film output from electronic files. A commercial printer uses paper or film output to produce plates. Nowadays, some printers output directly to plate, skipping the intermediary film output step. The following is a checklist of things to do to help your imagesetting run successfully:

- Find out if your commercial printer can output your electronic files. Since they're intimately familiar with the printing press—its quirks and its requirements—they're often the best choice for imagesetting.

- If you're outputting the file at an output service, ask your commercial printer for specific advice regarding the following settings: Lpi (lines per inch), emulsion up or down, and negative or positive. Also ask whether you should set trapping values yourself or the output service should do the trapping on their high-end system. Tell your output service what setting your commercial printer specified, and they will enter the correct values in the Print dialog box (Output pane) when they output your file. Don't guess on this one. And don't hesitate to ask your commercial printer to talk directly with your service provider.

- Make sure any pictures in the document were saved at final printout size and at the appropriate resolution for the final output device, which means approximately 1½ times the final lpi for a black-and-white or grayscale picture and 2 times the final lpi for a color picture. If a picture (especially an EPS) requires cropping, rotating, or scaling down, do so in the picture's original application, if possible—it will output more quickly.

- Use the File > Collect for Output command to collect your document and associated images and to produce a report file. If you don't supply your service bureau with the original picture files, the low resolution versions will be used for printing (yech!). The report file lists important specifications that they need in order to output your file properly, such as the fonts used in the document.

- If your output service needs a PostScript file of your document, ask them for specific instructions.

- Some service bureaus will supply the fonts—at least the Adobe fonts—but some printers prefer that you supply them all. Include both the screen and the printer fonts, and don't forget to include fonts used in any imported EPS pictures.

- Include laser printouts of your file (unless you're modeming the file), with Registration marks turned on, or send a PDF version of the file.

- If your document doesn't print or takes an inordinately long time to print on your laser printer, don't assume it will print quickly on an imagesetter. Large pictures, irregularly-shaped picture boxes, and clipping paths are some of the many elements that can cause a printing error. If you are using the same high-resolution picture more than once, but in different sizes, import copies of the picture saved at those specific sizes.

To reduce the amount of information the imagesetter has to calculate, delete any extraneous items from the document's pasteboard. To find out if there are any pictures on the pasteboard, choose Utilities > Usage, and click the Pictures tab (F13 in the Mac OS). If you see a dagger icon in the Mac OS or the letters "PB" in Windows, it means that picture is on the Pasteboard.

What's on your plate?

In standard four-color process printing, a document is color separated onto four plates, one each for Cyan, Yellow, Magenta, and Black. The many other potential combinations include printing a spot color and black on two separate plates or printing a spot color and the four process colors, bringing the total to five plates.

Hexachrome (high fidelity) colors color separate onto six process color plates, with the result being greater color fidelity due to the wider range of printable colors. An RGB picture can be color-separated using this method.

Printing a spot

Be sure to check **Spot Color** in the Edit Color dialog box for any spot color that you want to color-separate onto a separate plate. To output a particular color, choose File > Print, check Separations (Document pane), then, in the Output pane, choose **Used Process & Spot** from the Plates pop-up menu and **Conventional** from the Halftoning pop-up menu.

Spot colors, if they are saved in an Illustrator or FreeHand file in the EPS format, will append to the Colors dialog box in the QuarkXPress document and will also display in the plate scroll window in File > Print (Output pane). Make sure the name that is assigned to any spot color that is used in both QuarkXPress and Illustrator is exactly the same in each program, otherwise two plates will print instead of the desired one.

Color separation tips

■ *Don't* choose colors based on how they appear on screen, because a computer screen can only simulate printed colors. Always use a matching system booklet to choose colors.

■ To apply a spot color tint—whether as a background color in an item or as type color—choose a shade percentage from the Colors palette or choose a TRUMATCH or FOCOLTONE color that has the desired value in Edit > Colors (Shift-F12).

■ If your document contains bitmapped pictures, ask your service bureau or commercial printer in which file format (TIFF, EPS, etc.) and image mode (CMYK, RGB, etc.) those pictures should be saved. You can use Photoshop to easily change a picture's file format, resolution, or image mode.

■ Ask your output service whether to use Photoshop or QuarkXPress to convert any color pictures from RGB to CMYK for separations. A picture scanned into CMYK color mode doesn't need to be converted.

■ Any RGB spot colors from an imported Illustrator EPS file will remain as RGB spot colors (as listed in the Colors dialog box).

■ If your document contains hand-drawn registration or crop marks, apply the Registration color to them to ensure that they appear on all the separation plates.

■ For color work, order a color proof (IRIS or a 3M Rainbow) of the document so you can inspect it for color accuracy.

Color Separation Tips

What is trapping?

Trapping is the ever-so-slight overlapping of colors to prevent gaps from occurring during printing as a result of the plates potentially misaligning on press, or the paper shifting or stretching. In QuarkXPress, trapping is applied according to the way color in an object interacts with the color in an item behind it. Use the mini-glossary at right to familiarize yourself with trapping terminology.

Before exploring the circumstances in which trapping is necessary, we'll discuss a couple of circumstances in which trapping is unnecessary.

When not to apply trapping

Trapping is unnecessary when black type or a black item or frame is on top of a light background color. In this circumstance, the black type will overprint (print on top of) the background color. You can specify a minimum percentage of black to control when and if overprinting will occur (see page 425).

Trapping is also unnecessary if process colors and adjacent or overlapping colors contain a common color component (C, M, Y, or K). Let's say you have a red, which contains a percentage of magenta, that touches a blue area that also contains a small percentage of magenta. The two colors both contain magenta, so trapping is unnecessary.

When to apply trapping

Trapping is necessary when you print spot colors, print process colors that don't have a common color component, or print a light color on a dark background.

In QuarkXPress, trapping values are assigned to the foreground color. A light foreground color spreads into the background color by a specified amount, and a light background color chokes the foreground color. To produce a choke trap in QuarkXPress, the foreground color is assigned a negative trapping value.

Trapping mini-glossary

Overprint

The foreground object color prints on top of the background color, so inks actually mix together. Overprint is used if black is the foreground object color or if inks are intentionally mixed to produce a third (overlap) color.

Knockout

To prevent inks from overprinting, the foreground object color shape is cut out (knocked out) of the underlying background color area on the background color plate. While this eliminates the problem of ink mixing, it creates a potential problem of a gap between the edges of the foreground and background colors. Trapping closes this gap.

Spread

The spread method of trapping is used when colors knock out and the foreground color is lighter than the background color. The edge of the foreground color object is enlarged slightly to make the foreground color spread into the background color on press **1**.

Choke

The choke method of trapping is employed when the foreground color is darker than the background color. The edge of the foreground color object shrinks slightly as a result of overprinting. This causes the background color to spread into (choke) the foreground color on press.

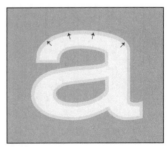

1 *In a spread trap, the foreground object color spreads into the background object color.*

Shut your trap!

If you feel queasy about setting traps in QuarkXPress, let your service provider do the trapping.

To turn off trapping, choose Trapping Method: Knockout All in Edit > Preferences > Preferences > Document–Trapping. Choose this option if you're producing a PostScript file for a high-end separation system, and for some color composite printers.

*All of these objects (type and artwork) contain the process color magenta. Because they have this **color in common**, trapping is unnecessary.*

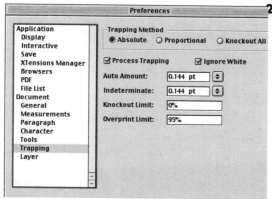

1 *The Edit > Preferences > Preferences > Document–Trapping pane*

In QuarkXPress, trapping can be controlled using several features:

- On a default, **document**-wide basis using Edit > Preferences > Preferences > Document–**Trapping**.

- On an individual-**color** basis using Edit > **Colors** (click Edit Trap).

- On an individual-**item** basis using the View menu > **Trap Information** palette.

The settings in Colors > Edit Trap override the settings in Document preferences. Trap Information palette settings override the Colors > Edit Trap and Document preferences settings.

To define automatic trap values and specify the defaults used by QuarkXPress for trapping object colors, choose the settings in the Trapping pane in the Document Preferences dialog box.

To choose trapping preferences for a whole document:

1. Choose Edit > Preferences > Preferences, then click Document–Trapping **1**.

2. In the Trapping Method area, choose **Absolute** to use the trapping value entered in the Auto Amount or Indeterminate field. The Auto Amount value is used if the foreground color is on top of a flat color. The Indeterminate value is used if the foreground color is on top of multiple shades or colors or over an imported picture. When the object color is darker, the background color chokes into the object color by the Auto Amount. When the foreground object color is lighter, the object color spreads into the background color by the Auto Amount.
or

Choose **Proportional** to use the trapping value entered in the Auto Amount field, multiplied by the difference in luminosity (lights and darks) between the foreground object color and

(Continued on the following page)

Trapping Preferences

background color. The width of the trap will vary and be determined by multiplying the Auto Amount value by the difference in luminosity between the object and background colors.
or

Choose **Knockout All** to turn trapping off for all objects. Objects will print with 0 trapping **2**.

3. Check or uncheck the Process Trapping box. With Process Trapping on, each process component (cyan, magenta, yellow, and black) is spread or choked, depending on which one is darker—the foreground object or the background color. For example, if the cyan in the foreground object color is lighter than the cyan in the background color, the foreground object cyan is spread into the background cyan—but only on the cyan plate.

The trap width is equal to half the Auto Amount value when Absolute trapping is specified. When Proportional trapping is specified, the trap width will equal the Auto Amount value multiplied by the difference in luminosity values between the foreground object and background colors.

If Process Trapping is off, the same trapping value will be applied to all the process-color components using the trapping settings for those colors, as specified in the Colors > Edit Trap area.

4. Enter a trapping value in the Auto Amount field **3** or choose Overprint from the pop-up menu. Either the value entered or the Overprint setting will be used in the Trap Specifications dialog box (Edit > Colors > Edit Trap) and on the Trap Information palette whenever a field in either of these two locations is set to Auto Amount (+/-).

5. Enter a trapping value in the Indeterminate field or choose Overprint from the pop-up menu. If a foreground object is over a background that

2 *Click a **Trapping Method**.*

3 *Enter a trapping value in the **Auto Amount** field.*

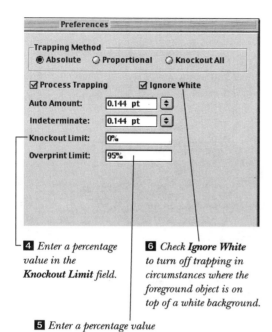

4 *Enter a percentage value in the **Knockout Limit** field.*

6 *Check **Ignore White** to turn off trapping in circumstances where the foreground object is on top of a white background.*

5 *Enter a percentage value in the **Overprint Limit** field.*

consists of multiple shades or colors, or is over an imported picture, either the value you entered or the Overprint setting will be used.

6. Enter a percentage value in the Knockout Limit field **4** to set the luminosity (light and dark) value limit at which a foreground object color knocks out the background color. The luminosity value is the percentage difference in luminosity between the foreground object color and the background color.

7. Enter a value in the Overprint Limit field **5**. This value sets the shade percentage limit below which the foreground object color will not overprint the background color. For example, if the Overprint Limit is set to 92%, a foreground object colored with a black value of 85% will not overprint, even if that color or object is set to overprint (via the Edit Trap > Trap Specifications dialog box). The object will trap using the value in the Auto Amount field.

An Overprint setting chosen on the Trap Information palette will cause the selected object to overprint, regardless of the current trap settings or any Overprint Limit value entered in any other dialog box.

8. Leave Ignore White checked **6** to turn off trapping for any instance in which the foreground object color is on top of white and other color areas in the background. This is the preferred situation, since the white area won't be considered when the trap is calculated for the other colors.

When this box is unchecked, all objects on a white background will overprint. If an object is set to spread over a background color, then the Indeterminate value will be used for the spread.

9. Click OK to close the Preferences dialog box.

Trapping Preferences

The Trap Specifications dialog box controls trapping on a color-by-color basis. The default settings for each color display, and can be modified using, this dialog box.

To choose trapping values for a color (Trap Specifications):

1. Choose Edit > Colors (Shift-F12).

2. Click a color, then click Edit Trap **1**.

3. The name of the foreground color you chose will appear in the title bar of the Trap Specifications dialog box. Click one of the remaining colors, any of which can be a potential background color **2**.

4. Choose a setting from the Trap drop-down menu **3**:

   Default to have QuarkXPress determine how colors will be trapped. With Default, black always overprints.

   Overprint to have the foreground color overprint the selected background color when the foreground color shade is equal to or greater than the Overprint Limit value set in Edit > Preferences > Preferences > Document–Trapping.

   Knockout to have the foreground color knock out the selected background color.

   Auto Amount (+/-) to use the auto spread/auto choke value for the foreground color.

   Custom to enter a custom spread or choke (negative) value for the foreground color.

   The Auto Amount and Overprint Limit settings were established in Edit > Preferences > Preferences > Document–Trapping.

5. Choose Dependent traps (the default) from the drop-down menu in the middle column to create the reverse trap situation for the colors you chose in steps 2 and 3, based on the current

1 *Click a color, then click* **Edit Trap.**

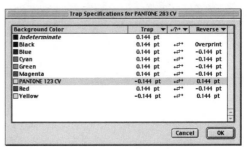

2 *The* **Trap Specifications** *dialog box for the color selected when Edit Trap was clicked*

3 *Choose an option from the* **Trap** *drop-down menu.*

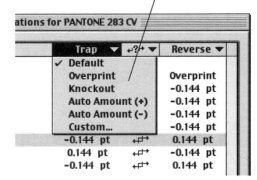

Trap Specifications

1 *Choose **Dependent Traps** or **Independent Traps** from this drop-down menu.*

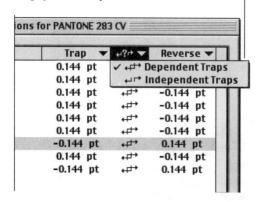

2 *Choose an option from the **Reverse** drop-down menu.*

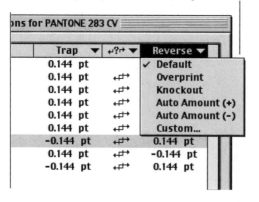

setting in the Trap column. Or choose Independent traps to create a unique trap setting in the Reverse column for these two colors **1**.

6. To set the trap situation for a circumstance in which the current background color (from step 3) becomes the foreground color over the color (from step 2) listed in the title bar of the dialog box, choose a different setting from the Reverse drop-down menu **2**. The options are the same as in step 4, above. Remember that when traps have a Dependent relationship, the Reverse column setting automatically derives from the current Trap column setting, and vice versa. Change either of these columns, and the other will change automatically. When traps have an independent relationship, then unique settings can be set in these two columns.

7. Click OK, then click Save, to close the Default Colors dialog box.

TIP Settings in the Trap Specifications dialog box override the settings in Edit > Preferences > Preferences > Document–Trapping.

TIP If a document is open when Edit > Colors is chosen, Edit Trap changes will apply only to the current document. If no document is open, changes will apply to all subsequently-created documents.

Trap Specifications

Note: Trap Information palette settings override the settings chosen in the Trap Preferences and Trap Specifications dialog boxes.

To choose trapping values for an object (Trap Information palette):

1. Choose View > Show Trap Information to open the palette (Option-F12 in the Mac OS) 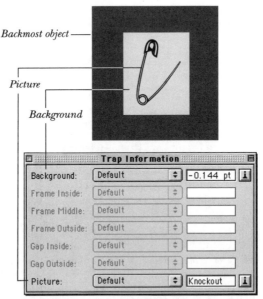.

2. Select the item to which you want to apply trapping.

3. Choose a new trap setting from the pop-up menu on the left side of the palette (the options will vary depending on the type of item chosen) **2**:

   Default to have the settings in Trapping tab preferences or Edit Trap Specifications be used to determine how colors will trap.

   Overprint to have the foreground item color overprint any background color.

   Knockout to have the foreground item color knock out any background color.

   Auto Amount (+/-) to use the auto spread/auto choke value for the foreground color. Auto Amount settings are established in the Edit > Preferences > Preferences > Document–Trapping.

   Custom to enter a custom spread or choke (negative) value for the foreground color.

TIP Choosing Overprint from the palette will cause that item to overprint, regardless of the foreground or background color shade or the Overprint Limit value.

TIP To set trapping for text, highlight the text—the Text option on the palette will become available.

1 *This is the **Trap Information** palette with a picture box selected. In this example, the Background color of the picture box (20% Black) defaults to a spread trap of the Auto Amount over the darker color underneath.*

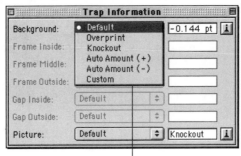

2 *The pop-up menu for trapping the **Background** color of a picture box*

Press the  *icon on the Trap Information palette to display an explanation of the **Default Trap** setting. Here, the names of the two colors are listed; the Edit Trap or Trap Preferences dialog box is listed as the source of the trap decision (the **Source of Trap Values**); and the significant trap option (Property) is also singled out.*

1 *In this example, the text only partially overlaps a background color.*

What follows are guidelines for common trapping situations that may occur.

Trapping type

When it comes to trapping, a text box is treated like a single foreground object. The text box color will trap to the background color based on the current trap settings. When a text box with a background of None is on top of a background color, QuarkXPress will trap the type, even if the type itself is not overlapping the background color **1**. This can occur with type that appears inside a large text box.

To control how text traps, select the text and set it to Overprint or Knockout via the Trap Information palette. You can also highlight individual characters or words and apply a unique trap setting to them that's different from the remaining characters in the box. Any box that's layered on top of a text box will trap to the background color of the text box—not the type itself.

QuarkXPress regards type that is partially on top of a paragraph rule as trapping to an indeterminate background color. If the type is completely within the paragraph rule, then the type is trapped based on the type color-to-rule color relationship from the Edit > Colors trap settings. This relationship can only be changed using Edit > Colors > Edit Trap.

Trapping a frame

A frame is layered on top of the contents of the box the frame is attached to. Using the Trap Information palette, different trapping settings can be applied to the inside, middle, and outside parts of a single line or multi-line frame, and to the gaps in a dashed frame.

Trapping imported pictures

In QuarkXPress, a picture can't be spread or choked to a background color.

Trapping adjustments that are made to a vector (object-oriented) picture in a drawing program, such as Adobe Illustrator, will output successfully from QuarkXPress. The Trap Information palette provides no trapping controls for the picture itself. But don't scale an imported vector picture that was created with built-in trapping, because such scaling will also resize the trapping areas in the picture.

You can specify that a raster (bitmap) picture knock out or overprint a background color using the Trap Information palette. Using the Trap Information palette, you can set the image of a picture to overprint or knock out a background. This is helpful if you're colorizing a Grayscale TIFF picture in QuarkXPress. Click on a picture, then choose Overprint or Knockout from the Picture pop-up menu on the Trap Information palette—whichever your commercial printer tells you to choose.

A line art (black and white) picture that has been colored black in QuarkXPress with a shade of black equal or greater than the overprint limit will overprint any background color(s) it is positioned on top of. Use the Trap Information palette to set the picture to knock out, if desired.

Lines and boxes in QuarkXPress can knock out, overprint, or trap to pictures that are underneath them. Use the Trap Information palette to set the type of trap. Type can knock out, overprint, or spread to a picture underneath it.

Trapping bitmaps

You can apply trapping to some types of bitmap pictures via the Trap Information palette, including:

> Grayscale TIFF (8-bit)
>
> Black & white TIFF (1-bit)
>
> RGB TIFF
>
> CMYK TIFF
>
> Colorized Grayscale TIFF

Trapping cannot be applied to an EPS in QuarkXPress.

Just a start

From this introductory chapter to XML, you will get a glimpse of the many roles XML plays. XML is very complex, though, and worthy of many books on its own. When you're ready to learn more, check out these sources:

XML for the World Wide Web Visual QuickStart Guide, by Elizabeth Castro, Peachpit Press, 2001.

www.w3.org, the Web site for the World Wide Web Consortium, which is the main standards body for any and all things Web.

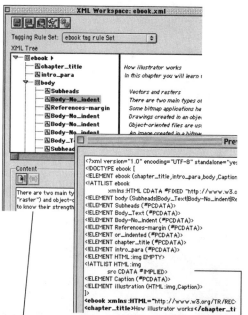

1 *The **XML Workspace** palette lets you view XML elements and their content. Here, the elements match the style sheets used in a QuarkXPress file. The palette can display the actual XML code.*

XML in QuarkXPress 5

QuarkXPress 5 includes the avenue.quark XTension, which converts QuarkXPress content into XML format. **XML** (Extensible Markup Language) is a simple structured language that helps manage information by identifying data, be it data you enter directly into the XML file or data in a text or database file. Once identified, that data can be selectively extracted and placed in other files and organized in ways that differ from the original source. XML data can be output as HTML files for the Web or can be used for print output.

In this chapter you will be working with **elements**, which are fields of text or data. Each element holds a specific piece of information (e.g., name, address, zip code). XML is used to define elements and the relationship among those elements. Each element is assigned a name, and that name in turn is used to label (tag) the contents of a QuarkXPress file, item by item. Specific elements can be selected, organized, and used to generate output.

In QuarkXPress, style sheets are applied to different categories of text (header, intro paragraph, body, caption, etc.). The job of the avenue.quark XTension is to gather into an element the text from a print document that specific style sheets are applied to. Once it's in an element, you control which text is output by choosing which elements are output **1**.

(Continued on the following page)

Elements are assigned a specific order in which the content is to be displayed in its output form (presentation), whether it's print, the Web, or CD-ROM. By separating the content of a QuarkXPress file (text and pictures) from the structure of the file (e.g., fields on a form or the arrangement of style sheets on a page in a print document), XML makes it possible to display that content in a variety of output settings.

For QuarkXPress users, the power of XML is that it can automatically tag and extract text from any QuarkXPress document in which style sheets have been assigned. Then the XML file can be translated into **HTML** and displayed in a browser.

The appearance of text in an HTML document can be controlled by **CSS** (cascading style sheet) files, which apply formatting information to HTML text. CSS files can be created using QuarkXPress 5. They control the color, fonts, and style attributes of the elements (and the QuarkXPress content for those elements) in an XML file.

And finally, a dynamic link can be set up between an XML file and the original QuarkXPress file. With this link in place, if the QuarkXPress file is edited, the elements that hold the text in the XML file will update automatically.

XML blues

Currently, only the latest versions of the **Internet Explorer 5** and **Netscape 6** Web browsers can translate XML code into properly styled, readable content. These browsers, though, don't always comprehend all the XML code (read: lots of alert error boxes), and neither browser supports the XML code that references external picture files. So even if the XML text does display, no pictures will display on an XML page. Sorry.

XML in QuarkXPress 5

Using elements

Elements in a **DTD** are similar to fields in a database. The more specific the fields are, the more specific will be the data they contain, and the more varied the ways the data can be extracted and organized into different reports or presentations in an HTML or print document.

For comparison, think of a mail merge function, where each line of an address is defined as an individual element. Rearranging the elements would alter how the individual lines of the address could be displayed. Specified lines of the address could be used in an output document (say, using just names and business titles) without using the remaining lines of the address. All this rearranging and reorganizing is controlled using elements in an XML file.

XML and DTDs

A **DTD** (short for "document type definition") is a plain text file that is created with a simple text editor. A DTD specifies which **elements** will be in an XML file, the kind of information that can be put into an element, the order of the elements in the XML file, and which elements can contain **subelements** (nested elements). A DTD, while not required for XML creation, controls the relationships between elements and helps keep elements consistent between documents.

Complex DTDs are usually created by specialized administrative or technical support personnel. For the individual designer using QuarkXPress, a variation of an existing DTD can serve as a framework for creating individual DTDs for each type of QuarkXPress file that will be translated into HTML.

The XML format is best suited for extracting and transferring text from multiple QuarkXPress files that follow a specific style sheet structure or form fields layout. For small, individual HTML projects, you can create a new Web document in QuarkXPress 5 or drag-and-drop existing QuarkXPress picture boxes and text boxes into a new Web document. So this whole XML step in between may be overkill for a small project. The decision is yours.

Starting out with XML

Before you can create an XML file and tag existing content in a QuarkXPress file, you have to define a DTD. To make things easier, you can base the new DTD on an existing one. A simple DTD need only contain, for example, elements that represent the style sheet names used in an existing QuarkXPress file. You will also create a **container element** to define the order and interrelationship of the elements in the XML file.

(Continued on the following page)

In QuarkXPress, DTD elements display on the **XML Tree**, which is located on the **XML Workspace** palette. On the XML Tree, elements are displayed hierarchically, from top level to sublevel, as defined in the DTD file.

Key parts of a DTD

The DTD references a **root element**, which is the overall keyword that categorizes all the data to be contained in the XML elements. Technically, the XML file will specify the root element, but the DTD should reference a root element in an opening comment for clarity to users of the DTD.

Each element must be **declared** (defined) in order to establish what kind of content information it can contain. If an element can contain **child elements** (subelements of the parent element), those child elements must be listed in the declaration of the parent element. The parent element is a container element, and child elements are nested under the parent element on the XML Tree on the XML Workspace palette.

If content from the QuarkXPress file is to be arranged in a particular sequence, the container element declares the order of its child elements in the resulting XML file. This order can either be the exact order of content in the QuarkXPress file or it can be given a flexible structure so it can differ from the order of content in the QuarkXPress file.

Only one paragraph of text can be stored in an element. If the element is declared to contain child elements, then multiple paragraphs can be stored in each of the child elements. The DTD you'll create by following the instructions on the next page will include a parent element, which in turn will be used to tag a story that contains more than one paragraph style sheet.

Mind your p's and q's

XML and DTD element names are case-sensitive. Switching between capital and lowercase letters for different occurrences of an element name will cause an XML parser (the software that interprets XML data) to interpret each occurrence as a different element. XML and DTD element names must begin with a **letter** or an **underscore** (_); the remaining characters in the name can be **letters, underscores, numbers, colons, hyphens,** or **periods**—but NOT spaces or tabs!

Parent and child elements

- Declaring an element as a container element makes it a parent and determines which elements are nested within (are children of) that parent element.

- The XML Tree on the XML Workspace palette represents element relationships as defined in the DTD. On the XML Tree, a parent element occupies a higher position (is less indented), and each child element is nested below its parent.

- Sibling elements reside on the same indent level on the tree.

- The topmost element on the tree is usually the root element. All elements that are declared within this element in the DTD will occupy the next level on the tree.

```
☐ ▦▦▦▦▦ vqs-to-ebookbold.dtd ▦▦▦▦▦ 凹▤
<!-- NAME:        vqs to e-book     -->
<!-- Root element is ebook          -->
<!ELEMENT ebook (chapter_title, intro_para, body,
      illustration)>
<!ATTLIST ebook xmlns:HTML CDATA #FIXED
      "http://www.w3.org/TR/REC-html40">
<!ELEMENT body (Subheads I Body_Text I Body-No_indent I
      References-margin I or_indented I Body_bold )*>
<!ELEMENT Subheads (#PCDATA)>
<!ELEMENT Body_Text (#PCDATA)>
<!ELEMENT Body-No_indent (#PCDATA)>
<!ELEMENT References-margin (#PCDATA)>
<!ELEMENT or_indented (#PCDATA)>
<!ELEMENT Body_bold (#PCDATA)>
<!ELEMENT chapter_title (#PCDATA)>
<!ELEMENT intro_para (#PCDATA)>
<!ELEMENT HTML:img  EMPTY>
<!ATTLIST HTML:img  src CDATA #IMPLIED>
<!ELEMENT Caption (#PCDATA)>
<!ELEMENT illustration  (HTML:img, Caption)>
```

1 *This is **DTD code** that was created in SimpleText.
The element name (the word after <!ELEMENT) was
declared using style sheet names from our document
(Subheads, Body_Text, Body-No_indent, References-
margin, or_indented, Body_bold, chapter_title,
intro_para, Caption). You should use style sheet
names from your document as the element names.*

```
<!-- Root element is ebook        -->
```
2

```
<!ELEMENT ebook (chapter_title, intro_para, body,
      illustration)>
```
3

```
<!ELEMENT chapter_title (#PCDATA)>
<!ELEMENT intro_para (#PCDATA)>

<!ELEMENT illustration (HTML:img, Caption)>
```
4

Note: Before you create a DTD, make sure
your QuarkXPress file contains various
paragraph style sheets for different categories of text, such as a title style sheet and
an intro paragraph style sheet, and make
sure those style sheets are applied to the
appropriate text. A picture box and a caption style sheet are also referenced in the
DTD in our instructions. **1** Substitute your
style sheet names for the element names in
the following steps.

To create a simple DTD:

1. Open a plain-text editor, such as
    SimpleText (Mac) or WordPad
    (Windows). Don't use Microsoft Word,
    as it won't save the file as plain text,
    and some characters may be changed
    upon saving.

2. Type a comment line stating what the
    root element will be. Comment lines
    are written as follows: <!-- comment
    text here --> **2**.

3. Declare (define) the root element as
    an element, and, in parentheses after
    the root element name, include the
    elements (your primary style sheet
    names) that are to become the next
    top level on the XML Tree on the XML
    Workspace palette. All elements are
    contained in the root element, and
    are expected to match content in the
    QuarkXPress file **3**.

    All elements must be enclosed, mean-
    ing that the line of code must start with
    "<!" and end with ">".

4. Declare the elements that were listed in
    the parentheses in the previous step.
    End each non-container element line
    with "(#PCDATA)" (parsed character
    data) to tell the XML parser (the soft-
    ware that interprets XML data) that
    those elements can contain text and/or
    entity references or processing instruc-
    tions. The elements can be declared in
    any order within the DTD **4**.

(Continued on the following page)

Create a DTD

5. For an instance like a story that contains different paragraph style sheets within it, declare a body element. Then, in parentheses, list all the child elements (the paragraph and character style sheet names from your story text) that you want to be contained within that element (body) **1**.

The vertical bar "|" represents an either/or option. Any one of these style choices can be present in the story. The exact order and presence of style sheets in the story isn't important, because the body element will use any one of those styles in its container of elements.

An asterisk "*" symbol after the closing parenthesis indicates that zero (none), one, or more than one occurrence of an element may occur in body text. (This code symbol helps prevent XML parsing errors.) By placing the symbol outside the parentheses, the body element can have none, one, or all the listed style sheet names present, in any order, and in any frequency, when the content of the QuarkXPress file is tagged. If an asterisk is inserted after an element, it will apply only to that element.

6. Declare the child elements, as listed in the previous step **2**. In the Quark-XPress file whose content you want to include, make sure all the paragraph and character style sheets are declared in one of these locations: the first element line, the body element line, or another container element line. The first element line must contain either all the elements or all the parent elements, with the parent elements themselves being declared in subsequent lines to show their child elements. You can only declare an element that has been referenced in the first element line or a parent container line.

DTD symbols

When placed at the end of an element name, the DTD symbols listed below indicate how many times that nested element will occur within the main element above it. These symbols provide greater flexibility for handling the order and frequency of content to be tagged into elements. They also display on the DTD Tree in the Edit Tagging Rules dialog box (see page 439).

Symbol	Indicates
No symbol	only one time
?	zero (none) or one time
+	one or more times
*	zero (none), one, or more times

```
<!ELEMENT body (Subheads | Body_Text | Body-No_indent |
    References-margin | or_indented | Body_bold )*>
```

1 *The **body element** is declared as a **container** element, and is the parent to the child elements that are listed within the parentheses. These child elements will match style sheets with the same name in the QuarkXPress story. On the XML Tree on the XML Workspace palette, the child elements will be nested under the parent body element.*

```
<!ELEMENT Subheads (#PCDATA)>
<!ELEMENT Body_Text (#PCDATA)>
<!ELEMENT Body-No_indent (#PCDATA)>
<!ELEMENT References-margin (#PCDATA)>
<!ELEMENT or_indented (#PCDATA)>
<!ELEMENT Body_bold (#PCDATA)>
```

2 *Declare the **child elements** (listed in the body element) that will hold content from style sheets with the same name in the QuarkXPress story. In our example, the Body_bold element was created to handle words in the story text that have been styled with the Body bold **character** style sheet.*

What is HTML:img?

Technically, the term HTML is being declared as a prefix—an abbreviation for the XML namespace. The full name of a namespace takes the form of a URL, thus ensuring that it's a unique term. The URL is not used to point to a specific Web page! The XML parser will now understand the term HTML (as used in the <!ATTLIST lines).

```
<!ATTLIST ebook xmlns:HTML CDATA #FIXED
    "http://www.w3.org/TR/REC-html40">
```
1

```
<!ELEMENT HTML:img EMPTY>
<!ATTLIST HTML:img src CDATA #IMPLIED>
```
2

```
<!ELEMENT illustration (HTML:img, Caption)>
```
3

7. Include the <!ATTLIST ... > line (an attribute declaration). This code enables your browser to display the images that are referenced by the XML file. If you're not technically oriented, just copy the code in **1**.

If you want to know the details, continue reading this step. Define the elementName (ebook), attributeName (xmlns:HTML signifies that the HTML term is using the XML namespace), attributeType (CDATA signifies character data; #FIXED signifies the content must be set to the value that immediately follows), and DefaultValue (the URL). This whole line of code tells a browser (e.g., Microsoft Internet Explorer) to interpret the element (HTML:img) that was declared in step 8 as an HTML <IMG> tag.

8. Declare the element HTML:img as EMPTY, since it will contain no text content. Next, declare another <!ATTLIST... > to define element HTML:img to have an attribute of src (the abbreviation for source) **2**. The attribute is a reference to an unparsed, external entity. This allows QuarkXPress picture items to be tagged to an element that contains an attribute, which holds the address and title of a picture file.

The container element "illustration" is declared to contain the HTML:img and Caption elements **3**. We could have written <!ELEMENT illustration (HTML:img) > and included a caption child element, since they are in separate boxes. How these elements are declared in the DTD will determine how the item is dragged onto the XML Tree when content is tagged. (Tagging is discussed on page 442.)

9. Make sure your file matches the structure of our DTD example and uses your style sheet names. Then save the file as plain text with a .dtd extension.

Now you'll incorporate the DTD file into a new XML file.

To create an XML file:

1. Open the QuarkXPress print document that is to be tagged.

2. Choose File > New > XML (Cmd-Shift-X/Ctrl-Shift-X).

3. Click Custom.xmt on the Template list to create an XML document from scratch **1**.

or

Click an existing XML template file (.xmt) from the Template list on which to base the new XML document. Read more about templates on page 440.

4. Click Import, locate your DTD file, then click Open.

5. Make sure the root element you referenced in the DTD is chosen from the Root Element pop-up menu.

6. Click OK. The XML Workspace palette will open **3**. Leave this palette open and proceed with the next set of instructions.

TIP Once you click OK, you can't change which DTD or root element is assigned to this XML file. You would have to make a new XML file in order to choose a different DTD or root element.

TIP On the XML Tree on the XML Workspace palette, click the arrowhead to the left of an element to expand the outline and view its nested child elements, if any. Click the arrowhead again to collapse the outline.

To open an existing XML document or template:

1. Choose File > Open.

2. Locate the .xml file, then click Open. Any QuarkXPress document associated (tagged) with the XML document will also open.

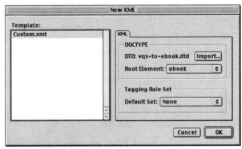

1 *The **New XML** dialog box*

XML tree symbols

A An element defined as (**#PCDATA**)

回 A **parent** element

□ An **empty** element

... **Attribute** of an element

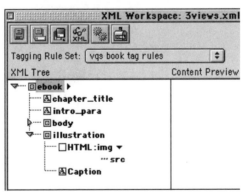

2 *Buttons on the **XML Workspace** palette*

Save   Save as   Revert to Saved   Preview XML   Synchronize Content   Post

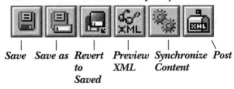

3 *The **XML Tree** on the **XML Workspace** palette takes its structure from the DTD, with the root element at the top and the elements contained in the root element declaration below. In our example, the "illustration" container element has two child elements; the HTML:img element has an "src" attribute.*

The Tagging Rules dialog boxes are used to tag paragraph and character style sheet names in a QuarkXPress file to elements that have been defined in a DTD, as listed on the XML tree on the XML Workspace palette. QuarkXPress style sheets are used to organize content for XML elements.

To create tagging rules:

1. With your QuarkXPress print document open, choose Edit > Tagging Rules.

2. Click New Set.

3. Type a Name for the rule set **1**.

4. Click an element name on the DTD Tree, click Add Rule, check Style Sheet in the Rule Settings area, then choose the correct paragraph style sheet name from the pop-up menu. *Optional:* With the same element still selected, you could click Add Rule again, check Style Sheet, then assign any character style sheet to that element.

5. Check "New tag for each paragraph" to have avenue.quark tag each paragraph style sheet occurrence as a separate element in the XML file. Leave this box unchecked for character style sheets.

Where the DTD tree comes from

The DTD tree shown in the Edit Tagging Rules dialog box derives from the parent and child elements as defined in the DTD. To change what's listed on the DTD tree, you would have to redefine (rewrite) the elements in the DTD file.

6. Repeat steps 4 and 5 for all the other elements that are going to represent the style sheet names. At any time, you can click Duplicate to duplicate the currently selected rule or click Delete to delete the currently selected rule.

7. Click OK.

8. Click Save to save the rule set. The new tagging rule set will be listed on the Tagging Rule Set pop-up menu on the XML Workspace palette.

TIP The DTD and <root element> used by the current XML document will appear in the DOCTYPE: field in the Tagging Rules dialog box and on the title bar of the Edit Tagging Rules dialog box.

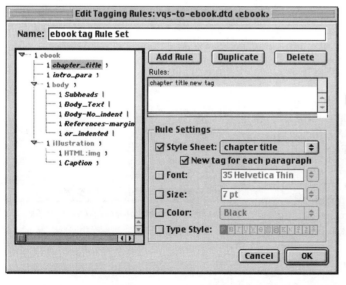

1 *In the Edit Tagging Rules dialog box for our file, the chapter_title element has a rule setting, which is linked to the chapter title style sheet. The words "new tag" appear because New tag for each paragraph is checked.*

Once a relationship is established between QuarkXPress style sheets and XML elements (as defined in the tagging rule set), then any QuarkXPress file that uses a style sheet with the same name can be quickly translated into the organization of that particular XML file. XML files can be converted into HTML, and by controlling what elements are used in an XML file, you can control what QuarkXPress information will be converted to HTML. The original content of the QuarkXPress file is preserved and is used as the content source.

To save an XML file:

1. Click the Save (first) button 🖬 on the XML Workspace palette.

2. Enter a name and choose a location **1**.

3. From the Type pop-up menu, choose "XML Document" or "avenue.quark Template."

4. From the Encoding pop-up menu, choose UTF-8 (this is a Unicode specification that includes European and Asian font characters).

5. Check Save XML as Standalone to embed the DTD code into the XML file. If this option is left unchecked, then the external DTD associated with this XML file must be available to avenue.quark in order for the XML file to be reopened.

Technical note: This option affects the status of the standalone=yes/no declaration in the first line of XML code, and affects whether the DTD code is stored internally in the XML file or externally as a separate file.

6. *Optional:* Check Exclude avenue.quark Processing Instruction to save the XML file without the extra avenue.quark code. You won't be able to reopen the XML file in avenue.quark, though.

7. Click Save.

DTD tree symbols

The symbols that appear to the left of element names on the DTD tree in the Edit Tagging Rules dialog box signify how many times that nested element will occur within the main parent element above it. (For a definition of each symbol, see page 436.)

■ If an element name is bold and black, tagging rules can be created for it.

■ If the element name is bold, black, *and* italic, at least one tagging rule has already been set for that element.

The character next to an element name (the "," or "|") is the same character that was used to separate elements that were declared in a container element in the DTD. The container element defines what the child elements are and how frequently they occur.

XML templates

New XML files can be based on an existing setup using an **XML template** (such files have an .xmt extension). The new file won't write over the template. By default, XML templates are saved to the QuarkXPress application > Templates folder.

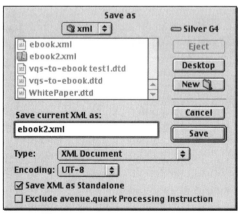

1 *The Save/Save as dialog box for an XML file*

Preview XML tips

- You can select and/or copy lines of text in the Preview XML dialog box, but you can't edit any code or content.

- A preview of the XML code in our example of a DTD would show a **<body>** tag, followed by a child tag named for the style sheet that's applied to the first paragraph in the story. The child's text content would be surrounded by "< >" brackets. The **</body>** tag marks the end of the body element.

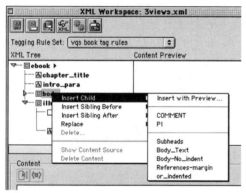

1 *The XML Tree submenus, showing options for modifying the XML Tree*

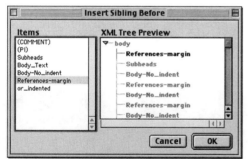

2 *This dialog box opens after choosing the Insert Sibling Before dialog box and the Insert With Preview option. Choose an element to insert from the list on the left; the XML Tree previews on the right.*

TIP To save a variation of an XML file, click the Save As (second) button 🖫 on the XML Workspace palette. Change the name and/or location, change any of the options in steps 3–5 above, then click Save.

To preview an XML document:

Click the Preview XML button 🔯 on the XML Workspace palette. XML code, the code from the DTD, and any tagged content will be listed in the dialog box. Click OK when you're done.

To edit the XML Tree:

1. On the XML Workspace palette, click an element on the XML Tree.

2. Control-click/Right-click the element, then from the XML Tree submenu, choose one of these options **1**:

   Insert Child—a nested element will be inserted.

   Insert Sibling Before or **Insert Sibling After**—an element on the same level of the tree will be inserted.

   Replace—the selected element will be replaced by another element.

   Delete—the selected element will be deleted.

   Show Content Source—the selected element's content will be highlighted in the current QuarkXPress document.

Then:

   From one of the Insert [   ] submenus or the Replace submenu:

   Choose **Insert** (or **Replace**) **with Preview** to preview the edit on the XML Tree. Elements that are available for insertion or replacement will be listed on the left side of the dialog box **2**. Click OK to accept the change (or click Cancel to reject the change).
   or

(Continued on the following page)

Choose an element from the list at the bottom of the submenu to have that element be inserted or replaced at the selected point on the tree.

The XML Tree will update accordingly.

TIP To revert an XML file to its last saved state, click the Revert to Saved button ⊞ on the XML Workspace palette.

To close an XML document:

Click the close box in the upper-left corner (Mac OS)/upper-right corner (Windows) of the XML Workspace palette.

Your next step is to tag the QuarkXPress content to the elements in the XML file. avenue.quark will read through an existing QuarkXPress file and match the style sheet name found in the text with the tagging rules you just assigned to elements defined in the DTD, and that are contained in the XML file. The process is automatic: All you have to do is Cmd-drag/Ctrl-drag the selected text box onto an element on the XML Tree on the XML Workspace palette, and avenue.quark will do the rest.

To tag the content of a QuarkXPress file:

1. Open an XML document and the QuarkXPress file that you're going to use as the content source for that XML document.

2. Choose the Item tool, click in a text box, then Cmd-drag/Ctrl-drag the box over an element name on the XML Tree **1**. A + (plus) icon will display as you drag. Release the mouse when a rectangular selection frame appears around the element name. (For a picture box, see page 445.)

The contents of the selected element will display in the Content field on the XML Workspace palette.

Multiple palettes

More than one XML file can be open at a time, and each file will have its own XML Workspace palette. The palette title bar will indicate to which file the palette belongs. The currently active XML Workspace palette has an edit icon 🖉 in its upper-right corner.

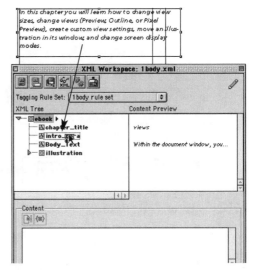

1 *Cmd-drag/Ctrl-drag a text box onto the appropriate element name on the **XML Tree**. The first few words of content will display in the **Content Preview** panel.*

Note: If the element or attribute already contains text, then that existing text will be replaced by the newly-tagged text.

TIP Tagged QuarkXPress text is enclosed within [and] brackets, which display when Invisibles are showing (View > Show Invisibles).

To remove the content of an element:

1. Click an element on the XML Tree.

2. Control-click/Right-click, then from the Replace submenu, choose the same element name to remove its current content (e.g., to remove the intro_text element content, choose intro_text from the submenu). Re-tag to add new content to the element.

TIP The Delete Content option on the context menu is available only for elements for which the content was manually typed into the Content field on the XML Workspace palette (see page 446).

Remove Content of Element

The method described below is the fastest way to convert QuarkXPress text content into XML. *Note:* In order for a paragraph with an applied style sheet to become the source of content for a declared element, you first have to create a rule linking the style sheet to an element name in the tagging rule set.

To tag a story that is styled using several different style sheets:

1. Make sure the correct tagging rule set is chosen from the Tagging Rule Set pop-up menu on the XML Workspace palette **2**. The Tagging Rules command created connections (links) between the style sheet names and the XML elements.

2. Click in a story (text box) in an open QuarkXPress print document.

3. Cmd-drag/Ctrl-drag the text box over the desired element on the XML Tree (the "body" element in our example gained nested child subelements on the XML Tree) **3**. Each subelement represents a style sheet that was declared in the DTD, specified as a rule in the tagging rule set, and found in the story in the QuarkXPress file. (We specified that these subelements were to be organized within the body container element in the DTD.)

TIP More than one story can be tagged to the same parent element. The subelements of the second story will display on the palette following the elements of the first story that was tagged, regardless of the location of the stories in the QuarkXPress file.

Tagging alert!

If an element has been defined with tagging rules that include both paragraph and character style sheets, then the Choose Rule/Position dialog box will open when you tag a story **1**. You will have to choose the correct element (based on the tagging rule link between style sheets and an element) to contain the text. ***Beware!*** If you use a different element for text styled with a character style sheet, that text will be placed into a different element from the rest of the paragraph. At least for now, local character styling in a QuarkXPress file isn't easily incorporated into XML.

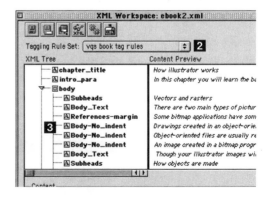

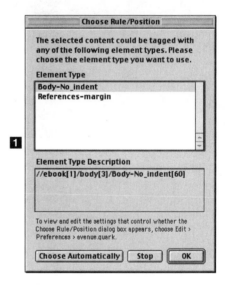

Do you know where your pictures are?

Remember to keep the actual picture file in the same folder as the XML file, otherwise the picture won't display in the browser!

Note: As of this writing, neither Internet Explorer nor Netscape Navigator can interpret XML code used to reference external picture files, which means that no pictures will display on the XML page in those browsers.

Guidelines for tagging a picture box or caption box

The following comments apply to the elements we declared in the DTD code that we used as an example (see page 435).

- When tagging a caption text box to the XML Tree, you can drag the box over the nested caption element or over the parent element "illustration" **1**.

- You can't drag the picture box onto the HTML:img element (or the "illustration" element, for that matter), because the HTML:img element was declared as an empty element.

- Picture boxes must be dragged to the nested "src" attribute **2** because the DTD designated that the picture file name be embedded as an attribute value. You can add an attribute to an empty element if you want the attribute to store the location of that element's content.

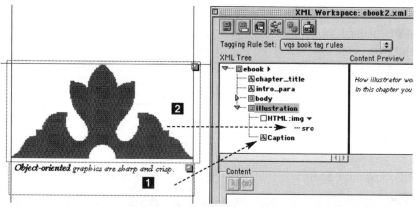

In this illustration, picture and caption items are being tagged using our DTD structure. The caption content will be contained in the "Caption" child element. The picture file name and path will be contained as an attribute ("src") for the "HTML:img" child element.

Text in a QuarkXPress file that has been tagged to elements in XML is dynamically linked, meaning if you edit the text in the QuarkXPress file, the element content will update automatically. To manually update the content in the XML document to match the current content of the QuarkXPress file, click the Synchronize Content button on the XML Workspace palette ■, then click Yes. You'll need to manually update if you choose Revert to Saved in the QuarkXPress file.

Beware! You can't undo the Break Dynamic Link command, which you'll learn to use in these instructions. What you can do instead is use the Replace command on the context menu to remove any text content, and then re-tag the QuarkXPress text to the element to reestablish a dynamic link.

To break the link between an element and its content:

1. On the XML Tree on the XML Workspace palette, click the element you want to break the link from ■.

2. Click the Break Dynamic Link button ▣ in the lower part of the palette ■. The Enable Dynamic Content Update option can be turned on or off in Edit > Preferences > Preferences > Application–avenue.quark.

For elements on the XML Tree that don't contain content from a QuarkXPress document, content can be added manually.

To enter content in an element manually:

1. Click an element or Control-click/ Right-click and use the Insert [   ] submenu ■ to insert a new element.

2. Type the content in the Content field on the XML Workspace palette.

3. When you're done entering content, press Tab to exit the Content field.

■ *Synchronize Content* button

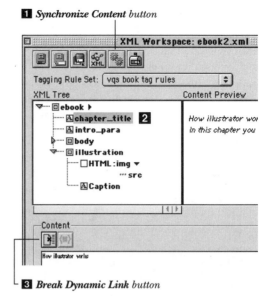

■ *Break Dynamic Link* button

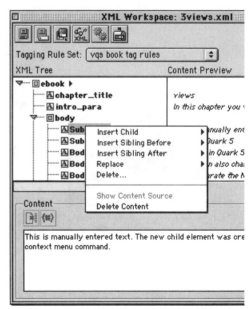

■ *To delete manually entered text for a selected element, choose* **Delete Content** *from the bottom of the context menu.*

Sequences

The Sequences palette enables you to create a sequence (list) of items in a QuarkXPress document and then tag the sequence as a single unit in a single step.

To create a new sequence:

1. Open a QuarkXPress print document.

2. Open the Sequences palette, then click the New Sequence button 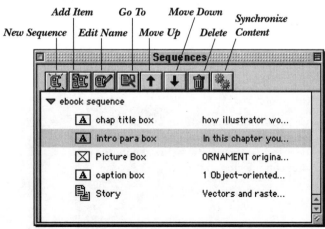 **❶**.

3. Leave the sequence name selected on the palette.

4. Select an item in the QuarkXPress document.

5. Click the Add Item button on the Sequences palette to add the item to the newly-named sequence. This button is only available when a sequence or item name is selected on the palette list and an item is selected in a QuarkXPress document.

6. Repeat steps 4–5 to add other items to the sequence.

TIP To delete an individual item or an entire sequence from the list, click the applicable name, then click the Delete button. This can't be undone.

Add Item   Go To   Move Down
New Sequence | Edit Name | Move Up | Delete | Synchronize Content

❶ *The **Sequences** palette, showing a sequence of items: The first few words of text or the picture title are listed next to each item.*

Create Sequence

To rename a sequence or any item on the list:

1. Click a Sequence or item name on the Sequences palette, then click the Edit Name button. 📝

   or

   Cmd-click/Ctrl-click an item name on the list.

2. Type the desired name **1**, then click OK.

1 *Use the **Edit Name** dialog box to **rename** an item or sequence.*

The order in which items are selected and added to the sequence determines their order on the list and in the XML document. The position of any item on the list can be changed.

To move an item to a different position on the list:

1. Click an item name on the Sequences palette list **2**.

2. Click the Move Up ⬆ or Move Down button ⬇ on the palette **3** to move the item one step upward or downward at a time. Keep clicking the arrow, if desired, to move the item further upward or downward.

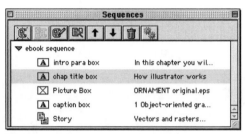

2 *Click an item name on the **Sequences** palette.*

To add an item to a sequence:

1. Expand a sequence name list on the Sequences palette.

2. Click the name of the item on the sequence list below which you want the new item to be added.

3. Select an item in the QuarkXPress document.

4. Click the Add Item button 🖳 on the Sequences palette. The new item will be listed on the palette below the item that you selected in step 2.

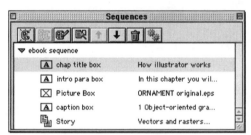

3 *Clicking the **Move Up** button causes the selected item to move upward on the list.*

Rename Sequence; Move, Add Item

Getting the pictures

Picture boxes aren't tagged automatically when the instructions on this page are followed. You have to manually **Cmd-drag/Ctrl** drag each picture box item from the Sequences palette over the appropriate element or attribute name on the XML Tree. Be sure to keep the actual picture file in the same folder as the XML file, though, otherwise the picture won't display in the browser. We are looking forward to a time when the browsers will be capable of displaying XML picture data.

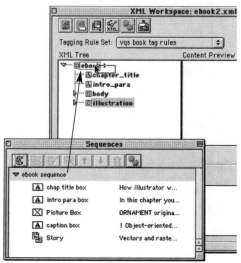

1 *Cmd-drag/Ctrl-drag a sequence name over the topmost element on the **XML Tree** on the XML Workspace palette.*

Before a sequence can be tagged, a tagging rule set must be chosen for the current XML document. The rules define the associations between the style sheets in the QuarkXPress document and the elements in the XML document.

To tag a sequence:

1. Make sure the Sequences palette, the XML Workspace palette, and the relevant QuarkXPress document are open.

2. Make sure the appropriate Tagging Rule Set is chosen from the pop-up menu on the XML Workspace palette.

3. Cmd-drag/Ctrl-drag the sequence name from the Sequences palette over the topmost element on the XML Tree on the XML Workspace palette **1**. avenue.quark will automatically tag all the items listed.

TIP Nested child elements are created automatically for text items that are associated with multiple style sheets, if two conditions are met: First, a DTD container element was declared that defines which child elements can be contained within the parent element, and second, the style sheets were associated with the appropriate DTD elements via a Tagging Rule set.

You can use the Sequences palette to navigate through an open QuarkXPress file.

To go to an item in a document:

Click an item name on the Sequences palette list, then click the Go To button **1**. 📑

or

Double-click an item name on the palette.

The chosen item will become selected, and it will be displayed in the current QuarkXPress document window.

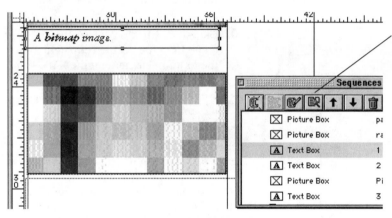

1 *Click the* **Go To** *button on the* **Sequences** *palette to display that item in the document.*

After a sequence of items has been created in a QuarkXPress document, you can automatically update the item content listed on the Sequences palette with the current contents of the QuarkXPress file.

Note: Even if you don't synchronize the content that is displayed for an item in a sequence, the most current QuarkXPress content will be used when the sequence is tagged to the XML elements.

To synchronize the contents of a QuarkXPress file with items in a sequence:

With the QuarkXPress file open, on the Sequences palette, click the Synchronize Content button 🞉. The content that is displayed for all the items in the sequence will be updated with the current content of the QuarkXPress file.

Special characters A

Zapf Dingbats: Mac OS and Windows

Dingbat	Key Combo Mac/Win	ASCII		Dingbat	Key Combo Mac/Win	ASCII
	space	32		✠	: (Shift-;)	58
✂	! (Shift-1)	33		✢	;	59
✄	" (Shift-')	34		✣	< (Shift-,)	60
✁	# (Shift-3)	35		†	=	61
✆	$ (Shift-4)	36		✞	> (Shift-.)	62
☎	% (Shift-5)	37		✟	? (Shift-/)	63
✇	& (Shift-7)	38		✠	@ (Shift-2)	64
✈	'	39		✡	A	65
✈	((Shift-0)	40		✢	B	66
✉	) (Shift-9)	41		✣	C	67
☛	* (Shift-8)	42		✤	D	68
☞	+ (Shift-=)	43		✥	E	69
✌	,	44		✦	F	70
✍	-	45		✧	G	71
✎	.	46		★	H	72
✏	/	47		☆	I	73
✐	0	48		✪	J	74
✑	1	49		✫	K	75
✒	2	50		✬	L	76
✓	3	51		✭	M	77
✔	4	52		✮	N	78
✕	5	53		✯	O	79
✖	6	54		✰	P	80
✗	7	55		✱	Q	81
✘	8	56		✲	R	82
✚	9	57		✳	S	83

451

Dingbat	Key Combo Mac/Win	ASCII
✳	T	84
✳	U	85
✳	V	86
✳	W	87
✳	X	88
✳	Y	89
✳	Z	90
✳	[	91
✳	\	92
✳	]	93
✿	^ (Shift-6)	94
✿	_ (Shift--)	95
✿	`	96
✿	a	97
✿	b	98
✳	c	99
✳	d	100
✳	e	101
✳	f	102
✳	g	103
✳	h	104
✳	i	105
✳	j	106
✳	k	107
●	l	108
○	m	109
■	n	110
❑	o	111
❒	p	112
❑	q	113
❑	r	114
▲	s	115

Dingbat	Key Combo Mac	Key Combo Win
▼	t	116
◆	u	117
❖	v	118
◗	w	119
❘	x	120
❙	y	121
❚	z	122
❛	{	123
❜	|	124
❝	}	125
❞	~	126
❨	Opt-U Shift-A	Alt+0128
❩	Opt-Shift-A	Alt+0129
❪	Opt-Shift-C	Alt+0130
❫	Opt-E Shift-E	Alt+0131
❬	Opt-N Shift-N	Alt+0132
❭	Opt-U Shift-O	Alt+0133
❮	Opt-U Shift-U	Alt+0134
❯	Opt-E, A	Alt+0135
❨	Opt-`, A	Alt+0136
❩	Opt-i, A	Alt+0137
❲	Opt-U, A	Alt+0138
❳	Opt-N, A	Alt+0139
❴	Opt-A	Alt+0140
❵	Opt-C	Alt+0141
❡	Opt-Shift-8	Alt+0161
❢	Opt-4	Alt+0162
❣	Opt-3	Alt+0163
❤	Opt-6	Alt+0164
❥	Opt-8	Alt+0165
❦	Opt-7	Alt+0166
❧	Opt-S	Alt+0167

Dingbat	Key Combo Mac	Key Combo Win	Dingbat	Key Combo Mac	Key Combo Win
♣	Opt-R	Alt+0168	⑨	Opt-Shift-\	Alt+0200
♦	Opt-G	Alt+0169	⑩	Opt-;	Alt+0201
♥	Opt-2	Alt+0170	❶	Opt-space	Alt+0202
♠	Opt-E	Alt+0171	❷	Opt-`, Shift-A	Alt+0203
①	Opt-U	Alt+0172	❸	Opt-N, Shift-A	Alt+0204
②	Opt-=	Alt+0173	❹	Opt-N, Shift-O	Alt+0205
③	Opt-Shift-'	Alt+0174	❺	Opt-Shift-Q	Alt+0206
④	Opt-Shift-O	Alt+0175	❻	Opt-Q	Alt+0207
⑤	Opt-5	Alt+0176	❼	Opt-hyphen	Alt+0208
⑥	Opt-Shift-=	Alt+0177	❽	Opt-Shift-hyphen	Alt+0209
⑦	Opt-,	Alt+0178	❾	Opt-[	Alt+0210
⑧	Opt-.	Alt+0179	❿	Opt-Shift-[	Alt+0211
⑨	Opt-Y	Alt+0180	→	Opt-]	Alt+0212
⑩	Opt-M	Alt+0181	→	Opt-Shift-]	Alt+0213
❶	Opt-D	Alt+0182	↔	Opt-/	Alt+0214
❷	Opt-W	Alt+0183	↕	Opt-Shift-V	Alt+0215
❸	Opt-Shift-P	Alt+0184	↘	Opt-u, Y	Alt+0216
❹	Opt-P	Alt+0185	→	Opt-U, Shift-Y	Alt+0217
❺	Opt-B	Alt+0186	↗	Opt-Shift-1	Alt+0218
❻	Opt-9	Alt+0187	→	Opt-Shift-2	Alt+0219
❼	Opt-0	Alt+0188	→	Opt-Shift-3	Alt+0220
❽	Opt-Z	Alt+0189	→	Opt-Shift-4	Alt+0221
❾	Opt-'	Alt+0190	→	Opt-Shift-5	Alt+0222
❿	Opt-O	Alt+0191	⇒	Opt-Shift-6	Alt+0223
①	Opt-Shift-/	Alt+0192	⇒	Opt-Shift-7	Alt+0224
②	Opt-1	Alt+0193	➡	Opt-Shift-9	Alt+0225
③	Opt-L	Alt+0194	➤	Opt-Shift-0	Alt+0226
④	Opt-V	Alt+0195	➤	Opt-Shift-W	Alt+0227
⑤	Opt-F	Alt+0196	➤	Opt-Shift-R	Alt+0228
⑥	Opt-X	Alt+0197	➥	Opt-I, Shift-A	Alt+0229
⑦	Opt-J	Alt+0198	➡	Opt-I, Shift-E	Alt+0230
⑧	Opt-\	Alt+0199	➤	Opt-E, Shift-A	Alt+0231

Dingbat	Key Combo Mac	Key Combo Win
➡	Opt-U, Shift-E	Alt+0232
⇨	Opt-`, Shift-E	Alt+0233
⇨	Opt-E, Shift-I	Alt+0234
⇌	Opt-I, Shift-I	Alt+0235
⇨	Opt-U, Shift-I	Alt+0236
⇨	Opt-`, Shift-I	Alt+0237
⇨	Opt-E, Shift-O	Alt+0238
⇨	Opt-I, Shift-O	Alt+0239
[not used]	Opt-Shift-K	Alt+0240
⇨	Opt-`, Shift-O	Alt+0241
⊃	Opt-E, Shift-U	Alt+0242
⇉	Opt-I, Shift-U	Alt+0243

Dingbat	Key Combo Mac	Key Combo Win
↘	Opt-`, Shift-U	Alt+0244
⇥	Opt-Shift-B	Alt+0245
↗	Opt-I, space	Alt+0246
↘	Opt-N, space	Alt+0247
⇢	Opt-Shift-,	Alt+0248
↗	Opt-Shift-.	Alt+0249
→	Opt-H	Alt+0250
↔	Opt-K	Alt+0251
⇢	Opt-Shift-Z	Alt+0252
⇥	Opt-Shift-G	Alt+0253
⇒	Opt-Shift-X	Alt+0254

Special Characters: Mac OS *(not font specific)*

Character	Key Combo	ASCII Code
Ä	Opt-U, Shift-A	0128
Å	Opt-Shift-A	0129
Ç	Opt-Shift-C	0130
É	Opt-E, Shift-E	0131
Ñ	Opt-N, Shift-N	0132
Ö	Opt-U, Shift-O	0133
Ü	Opt-U, Shift-U	0134
á	Opt-E, A	0135
à	Opt-`, A	0136
â	Opt-i, A	0137
ä	Opt-U, A	0138
ã	Opt-N, A	0139
å	Opt-A	0140
ç	Opt-C	0141
é	Opt-E, E	0142
è	Opt-`, E	0143

Character	Key Combo	ASCII Code
ê	Opt-I, E	0144
ë	Opt-U, E	0145
í	Opt-E, I	0146
ì	Opt-`, I	0147
î	Opt-I, I	0148
ï	Opt-U, I	0149
ñ	Opt-N, N	0150
ó	Opt-E, O	0151
ò	Opt`, O	0152
ô	Opt-I, O	0153
ö	Opt-U, O	0154
õ	Opt-N, O	0155
ú	Opt-E, U	0156
ù	Opt`, U	0157
û	Opt-I, U	0158

Zapf Dingbats; Special Characters

Special Characters: Mac OS

Character	Key Combo	ASCII Code
ü	Opt-U, U	0159
†	Opt-T	0160
°	Opt-Shift-8	0161
¢	Opt-4	0162
£	Opt-3	0163
§	Opt-6	0164
•	Opt-8	0165
¶	Opt-7	0166
ß	Opt-S	0167
®	Opt-R	0168
©	Opt-G	0169
™	Opt-2	0170
´	Opt-E, space	0171
¨	Opt-U, space	0172
≠	Opt-=	0173
Æ	Opt-Shift-'	0174
Ø	Opt-Shift-O	0175
∞	Opt-5	0176
±	Opt-Shift-=	0177
≤	Opt-,	0178
≥	Opt-.	0179
¥	Opt-Y	0180
μ	Opt-M	0181
∂	Opt-D	0182
Σ	Opt-W	0183
∏	Opt-Shift-P	0184
π	Opt-P	0185
∫	Opt-B	0186
ª	Opt-9	0187
º	Opt-0	0188

Character	Key Combo	ASCII Code
Ω	Opt-Z	0189
æ	Opt-'	0190
ø	Opt-O	0191
¿	Opt-Shift-/	0192
¡	Opt-1	0193
¬	Opt-L	0194
√	Opt-V	0195
ƒ	Opt-F	0196
≈	Opt-X	0197
Δ	Opt-J	0198
«	Opt-\	0199
»	Opt-Shift-\	0200
…	Opt-;	0201
non-brk space	Opt-space	0202
À	Opt-`, Shift-A	0203
Ã	Opt-N, Shift-A	0204
Õ	Opt-N, Shift-O	0205
Œ	Opt-Shift-Q	0206
œ	Opt-Q	0207
–	Opt-hyphen	0208
—	Opt-Shift-hyphen	0209
"	Opt-[	0210
"	Opt-Shift-[	0211
'	Opt-]	0212
'	Opt-Shift-]	0213
÷	Opt-/	0214
◊	Opt-Shift-V	0215
ÿ	Opt-u, Y	0216
Ÿ	Opt-U, Shift-Y	0217
⁄	Opt-Shift-1	0218

Special Characters: Mac OS

Character	Key Combo	ASCII Code
€	Opt-Shift-2	0219
‹	Opt-Shift-3	0220
›	Opt-Shift-4	0221
fi	Opt-Shift-5	0222
fl	Opt-Shift-6	0223
‡	Opt-Shift-7	0224
·	Opt-Shift-9	0225
‚	Opt-Shift-0*	0226
„	Opt-Shift-W	0227
‰	Opt-Shift-R	0228
Â	Opt-I, Shift-A	0229
Ê	Opt-I, Shift-E	0230
Á	Opt-E, Shift-A	0231
Ë	Opt-U, Shift-E	0232
È	Opt-`, Shift-E	0233
Í	Opt-E, Shift-I	0234
Î	Opt-I, Shift-I	0235
Ï	Opt-U, Shift-I	0236
Ì	Opt-`, Shift-I	0237

Character	Key Combo	ASCII Code
Ó	Opt-E, Shift-O	0238
Ô	Opt-I, Shift-O	0239
	Opt-Shift-K	0240
Ò	Opt-`, Shift-O	0241
Ú	Opt-E, Shift-U	0242
Û	Opt-I, Shift-U	0243
Ù	Opt-`, Shift-U	0244
ı	Opt-Shift-B	0245
^	Opt-I, space	0246
˜	Opt-N, space	0247
¯	Opt-Shift-,	0248
˘	Opt-Shift-.	0249
˙	Opt-H	0250
°	Opt-K	0251
¸	Opt-Shift-Z	0252
˝	Opt-Shift-G	0253
˛	Opt-Shift-X	0254
ˇ	Opt-Shift-T	0255

Special Characters: Windows *(not font specific)*

Character	Key Combo (Alt+ANSI code)	Character	Key Combo (Alt+ANSI code)
€	Alt+0128	[*not used*]	Alt+0160
[*not used*]	Alt+0129	¡	Alt+0161
‚	Alt+0130	¢	Alt+0162
ƒ	Alt+0131	£	Alt+0163
„	Alt+0132	¤	Alt+0164
…	Alt+0133	¥	Alt+0165
†	Alt+0134	¦	Alt+0166
‡	Alt+0135	§	Alt+0167
ˆ	Alt+0136	¨	Alt+0168
‰	Alt+0137	©	Alt+0169
Š	Alt+0138	ª	Alt+0170
‹	Alt+0139	«	Alt+0171
Œ	Alt+0140	¬	Alt+0172
[*not used*]	Alt+0141	-	Alt+0173
Ž	Alt+0142	®	Alt+0174
[*not used*]	Alt+0143	¯	Alt+0175
[*not used*]	Alt+0144	°	Alt+0176
‘	Alt+0145	±	Alt+0177
’	Alt+0146	²	Alt+0178
“	Alt+0147	³	Alt+0179
”	Alt+0148	´	Alt+0180
•	Alt+0149	µ	Alt+0181
–	Alt+0150	¶	Alt+0182
—	Alt+0151	·	Alt+0183
˜	Alt+0152	¸	Alt+0184
™	Alt+0153	¹	Alt+0185
š	Alt+0154	º	Alt+0186
›	Alt+0155	»	Alt+0187
œ	Alt+0156	¼	Alt+0188
[*not used*]	Alt+0157	½	Alt+0189
ž	Alt+0158	¾	Alt+0190
Ÿ	Alt+0159	¿	Alt+0191

Special Characters: Windows

Character	Key Combo (Alt+ANSI code)	Character	Key Combo (Alt+ANSI code)
À	Alt+0192	à	Alt+0224
Á	Alt+0193	á	Alt+0225
Â	Alt+0194	â	Alt+0226
Ã	Alt+0195	ã	Alt+0227
Ä	Alt+0196	ä	Alt+0228
Å	Alt+0197	å	Alt+0229
Æ	Alt+0198	æ	Alt+0230
Ç	Alt+0199	ç	Alt+0231
È	Alt+0200	è	Alt+0232
É	Alt+0201	é	Alt+0233
Ê	Alt+0202	ê	Alt+0234
Ë	Alt+0203	ë	Alt+0235
Ì	Alt+0204	ì	Alt+0236
Í	Alt+0205	í	Alt+0237
Î	Alt+0206	î	Alt+0238
Ï	Alt+0207	ï	Alt+0239
Ð	Alt+0208	ð	Alt+0240
Ñ	Alt+0209	ñ	Alt+0241
Ò	Alt+0210	ò	Alt+0242
Ó	Alt+0211	ó	Alt+0243
Ô	Alt+0212	ô	Alt+0244
Õ	Alt+0213	õ	Alt+0245
Ö	Alt+0214	ö	Alt+0246
×	Alt+0215	÷	Alt+0247
Ø	Alt+0216	ø	Alt+0248
Ù	Alt+0217	ù	Alt+0249
Ú	Alt+0218	ú	Alt+0250
Û	Alt+0219	û	Alt+0251
Ü	Alt+0220	ü	Alt+0252
Ý	Alt+0221	ý	Alt+0253
Þ	Alt+0222	þ	Alt+0254
ß	Alt+0223	ÿ	Alt+0255

Keyboard shortcuts

	Mac OS	**Windows**
Display/hide palettes		
Tools	F8	F8
Measurements	F9	F9
Document Layout	F10	F4
Style Sheets	F11	F11
Colors	F12	F12
Find/Change	Cmd-F	Ctrl+F
Trap Information	Option-F12	Ctrl+F12
Font Usage	F13	F2
Picture Usage	Option-F13	
Lists	Option-F11	Ctrl+F11
Dialog boxes		
OK (or heavy bordered button)	Return	Enter
Display next tab	Cmd-Option-Tab	Ctrl+Tab
Display previous tab	Cmd-Option-Shift-Tab	Ctrl+Shift+Tab
Cancel	Cmd-. (period) *or* Esc	Esc
Apply	Cmd-A	Alt+A
Continuous apply (not Space/Align) (toggles on/off)	Cmd-Option-A *or* Option-click Apply	Alt+A
Yes	Cmd-Y	Y
No	Cmd-N	N
Highlight field	Double-click	Double-click
Dialog boxes and palettes		
Highlight next field	Tab	Tab
Highlight previous field	Shift-Tab	Shift+Tab
Add	+	+
Subtract	-	-
Multiply	*	*
Divide	/	/
Revert to original values	Cmd-Z or F1	Ctrl+Shift+Z

	Mac OS	**Windows**
Tools palette		
Show Tools or select next tool	Cmd-Option-Tab	Ctrl+Alt+Tab
Show Tools or select previous tool	Cmd-Option-Shift-Tab	Ctrl+Alt+Shift+Tab
Item tool/Content tool toggle	Shift-F8	Shift+F8
Keep a tool selected	Option-click tool	Alt+click+tool
Measurements palette		
Display Measurements palette and highlight first field	Cmd-Option-M	Ctrl+Alt+M
Display measurements palette/ highlight font field	Cmd-Option-Shift-M *or* Shift-F9	Ctrl+Alt+Shift+M *or* Shift+F9
Clipboard		
Cut	Cmd-X *or* F2	Ctrl+X
Copy	Cmd-C *or* F3	Ctrl+C
Paste	Cmd-V *or* F4	Ctrl+V
Whole document		
New...	Cmd-N	Ctrl+N
New Library	Cmd-Option-N	Ctrl+Alt+N
New Web Document	Cmd-Option-Shift-N	Ctrl+Alt+Shift+N
Open...	Cmd-O	Ctrl+O
Save	Cmd-S	Ctrl+S
Save As...	Cmd-Option-S	Ctrl+Alt+S
Quit/Exit	Cmd-Q	Ctrl+Q or Alt+F4
Append	Cmd-Option-A	Ctrl+Alt+A
Revert to last Auto Save	Option-Revert to Saved	Alt+Revert to Saved
Document Setup	Cmd-Option-Shift-P	Ctrl+Alt+Shift+P
Undo		
Undo	Cmd-Z *or* F1	Ctrl+Z
Display		
Fit in Window view	Cmd-0 (zero)	Ctrl+0 (zero)
Fit largest spread in window	Option-Fit in Window view *or* Cmd-Option-0 (zero)	Alt+Fit in Window *or* Ctrl+Alt+0 (zero)
Actual Size view	Cmd-1	Ctrl+1
Zoom in	Control-Shift-click *or* drag	Ctrl+Space bar click *or* drag
Zoom out	Control-Option-Shift-click	Ctrl+Alt+Space bar click
Highlight view percent field	Control V	Ctrl+Alt+V
Thumbnails	Shift-F6 *or* enter "T" in view percent field (press Return/Enter)	Shift F6 *or* enter "T" in view percent field (press Return/Enter)

	Mac OS	**Windows**
Halt redraw	Cmd-. (period)	Esc
Force redraw	Cmd-Option-. (period)	Shift+Esc
Show/hide Baseline Grid	Option-F7	Ctrl+F7

Rulers and guides

	Mac OS	**Windows**
Show/hide Guides	F7	F7
Snap to Guides	Shift-F7	Shift+F7
Show/hide Rulers	Cmd-R	Ctrl+R
Delete all horizontal ruler guides (no pasteboard showing)	Option-click horizontal ruler	Alt+click horizontal ruler
Delete all vertical ruler guides (no pasteboard showing)	Option-click vertical ruler	Alt+click vertical ruler

Document windows

	Mac OS	**Windows**
Close active document	Cmd-W	Ctrl+F4
Close all documents	Cmd-Option-W *or* Option-click close box	No Win equivalent listed No Win equivalent listed
Stack or tile windows (Windows users: Cascade or tile)	Shift-press document title bar and choose Stack or Tile	Windows > Cascade, *or* Tile Horizontally, *or* Tile Vertically
Stack or tile at Actual Size view *(Windows users: Cascade or tile)*	Control-Stack/Tile	Ctrl+Alt+Cascade/Tile
Stack or tile at Fit in Window view *(Windows users: Cascade or tile)*	Cmd-Stack/Tile	Ctrl+Cascade/Tile
Stack or tile at Thumbnails view *(Windows users: Cascade or tile)*	Option-Stack/Tile	Alt+Cascade/Tile
Maximize document window		F3

Navigate through a document

	Mac OS	**Windows**
Go To Page...	Cmd-J	Ctrl+J
Page properties (Web documents)	Cmd-Option-Shift-A	Ctrl-Alt-Shift-A
Start of story	Control A *or* Home	Ctrl+Home
End of story	Control D *or* End	Ctrl+End
Up one screen	Control K *or* Page Up	Page Up
Down one screen	Control L *or* Page Down	Page Down
To first page	Control Shift-A *or* Shift-Home	Ctrl+Page Up
To last page	Shift-End	Ctrl+Page Down
To previous page	Shift-Page Up	Shift+Page Up
To next page	Shift-Page Down	Shift+Page Down
Page Grabber Hand	Option-drag	Alt+drag

Keyboard Shortcuts

	Mac OS	**Windows**
Toggle master/document page display	Shift-F10	Shift+F4
Display next master page	Option-F10	Ctrl+Shift+F4
Display previous master page	Option-Shift-F10	Ctrl+Shift+F3
Enable Live Scroll (Interactive Preference off) or Disable Live Scroll (Interactive Preference on)	Option-drag scroll box	Alt+drag scroll box

Items

Frame...	Cmd-B	Ctrl+B
Modify...	Cmd-M *or* double-click item with Item tool	Ctrl+M
Lock/Unlock	F6	F6
Delete item	Cmd-K	Ctrl+K
Constrain rotation to 0°, 45°, 90°	Shift-click with Rotation tool	Shift+while rotating
Move item (Content tool)	Cmd-drag	Ctrl+drag
Nudge item 1 point	Arrow keys	Arrow keys
Nudge item ⅒ point	Option-arrow keys	Alt+Arrow keys
Constrain movement to horizontal/vertical (Item tool)	Shift-drag	Shift-drag
Constrain movement to horizontal/vertical (Content tool)	Cmd-Shift-drag	Ctrl+Shift+drag

Select text

Show/Hide Invisibles	Cmd-I	Ctrl+I
One word (no punctuation mark)	Double-click	Double-click
One word (with punctuation mark)	Double-click between word and punctuation	Double-click between word and punctuation
One line	Triple-click	Triple-click
One paragraph	Click four times quickly	Click four times quickly
Entire story (Select All) Content tool	Click five times quickly *or* Cmd-A	Click five times quickly *or* Ctrl-A
Previous character	Shift-left arrow	Shift+left arrow
Next character	Shift-right arrow	Shift+right arrow
Previous line	Shift-up arrow	Shift+up arrow
Next line	Down arrow	Shift+down arrow
Previous word	Cmd-Shift-left arrow	Ctrl+Shift+left arrow
Next word	Cmd-Shift-right arrow	Ctrl+Shift+right arrow

	Mac OS	Windows
From the insertion point to:		
Start of paragraph	Cmd-Shift-up arrow	Ctrl+Shift+up arrow
End of paragraph	Cmd-Shift-down arrow	Ctrl+Shift+down arrow
Start of line	Cmd-Option-Shift-left arrow	Ctrl+Alt+Shift+left arrow *or* Shift+Home
End of line	Cmd-Option-Shift-right arrow	Ctrl+Alt+Shift+right arrow *or* Shift+End
Start of story	Cmd-Option-Shift-up arrow	Ctrl+Alt+Shift+up arrow *or* Ctrl+Shift+Home
End of story	Cmd-Option-Shift-down arrow	Ctrl+Alt+Shift+down *or* Ctrl+Shift+End

Move the text insertion point

	Mac OS	Windows
Character-by-character	Left and right arrows	Left and right arrows
Line-by-line	Up and down arrows	Up and down arrows
Word-by-word	Cmd-left and right arrows	Ctrl+left and right arrows
Paragraph-by-paragraph	Cmd-up and down arrows	Ctrl+up and down arrows
Start of line	Cmd-Option-left arrow	Ctrl+Alt+left arrow *or* Home
End of line	Cmd-Option-right arrow	Ctrl+Alt+right arrow *or* End
Start of story	Cmd-Option-up arrow	Ctrl+Alt+up arrow *or* Ctrl+Home
End of story	Cmd-Option-down arrow	Ctrl+Alt+down arrow Ctrl+End

Drag and drop text

	Mac OS	Windows
Drag-move	Drag	Drag
Drag-copy (Interactive Preference on)	Shift-drag	Shift+drag

Delete text

	Mac OS	Windows
Previous character	Delete	Backspace
Next character	Shift-Delete	Delete *or* Shift+Backspace
Previous word	Cmd Delete	Ctrl+Backspace
Next word	Cmd-Shift-Delete	Ctrl+Delete *or* Ctrl+Shift+Backspace
Selected characters	Delete	Delete

Resize text interactively

	Mac OS	Windows
Resize text and box	Cmd-drag handle	Ctrl+drag handle
Resize text and box proportionally	Cmd-Option-Shift-drag handle	Ctrl+Alt+Shift+drag handle

	Mac OS	**Windows**
Text flow		
Get text...	Cmd-E	Ctrl+E
Current page number (use on master page or document page)	Cmd-3	Ctrl+3
Previous text box page number	Cmd-2	Ctrl+2
Next text box page number	Cmd-4	Ctrl+4
Next column	Enter	Enter
Next box	Shift-Enter	Shift+Keypad Enter
Save Text	Cmd-Option-E	Ctrl+Alt+E
Open Section dialog box for currently displayed page	Click page number in lower left corner of Document Layout palette	Click page number in lower left corner of Document Layout palette
Open Insert Pages dialog box	Option-drag master page into document page area	Alt+drag master page into document page area
Paragraph formats		
Formats...	Cmd-Shift-F	Ctrl+Shift+F
Leading...	Cmd-Shift-E	Ctrl+Shift+E
Tabs...	Cmd-Shift-T	Ctrl+Shift+T
Rules...	Cmd-Shift-N	Ctrl+Shift+N
Increase leading 1 point	Cmd-Shift-"	Ctrl+Shift+"
Decrease leading 1 point	Cmd-Shift-:	Ctrl+Shift+:
Increase leading 1/10 point	Cmd-Option-Shift-"	Ctrl+Alt+Shift+"
Decrease leading 1/10 point	Cmd-Option-Shift-:	Ctrl+Alt+Shift+:
Delete all tab stops	Option-click tabs ruler	Alt+click tabs ruler
Right-indent tab	Option-Tab (in text box)	Shift+Tab
Suggested Hyphenation	Cmd-H	Ctrl+H
Set button in Tabs pane in Paragraph Attributes dialog box	Cmd-S	Alt+S
H&Js	Cmd-Option-H *or* Option-Shift-F11	Ctrl+Shift+F11 *or* Ctrl+Alt+H
Copy formats from one paragraph to another in the same story	Select paragraph to be formatted, then Option-Shift-click in source paragraph	Select paragraph to be formatted, then Alt+Shift+click in source paragraph
Fonts		
Character...	Cmd-Shift-D *or* Cmd-Shift-\	Ctrl+Shift+D *or* Ctrl+Shift+\
Select next font	Highlight text, then Option-F9	Highlight text, then Ctrl+F9

	Mac OS	**Windows**
Select previous font	Highlight text, then Option-Shift-F9	Highlight text, then Ctrl+Shift+F9
Insert one Zapf Dingbats character	Cmd-Shift-Z, then type character	Ctrl+Shift+Z, then type character
Insert one Symbol character	Cmd-Shift-Q, then type character	Ctrl+Shift+Q, then type character

Baseline shift

Baseline Shift-up 1 point	Cmd-Option-Shift-+ (plus)	Ctrl+Alt+Shift+0 (zero)
Baseline Shift-down 1 point	Cmd-Option-Shift-- (hyphen)	Ctrl+Alt+Shift+9

Style text

Plain text	Cmd-Shift-P	Ctrl+Shift+P
Bold	Cmd-Shift-B	Ctrl+Shift+B
Italic	Cmd-Shift-I	Ctrl+Shift+I
Underline	Cmd-Shift-U	Ctrl+Shift+U
Word Underline	Cmd-Shift-W	Ctrl+Shift+W
Outline	Cmd-Shift-O	Ctrl+Shift+O
Shadow	Cmd-Shift-S	Ctrl+Shift+S
All Caps	Cmd-Shift-K	Ctrl+Shift+K
Small Caps	Cmd-Shift-H	Ctrl+Shift+H
Strike Thru	Cmd-Shift-/	Ctrl+Shift+/
Superscript	Cmd-Shift-+ (plus)	Ctrl+Shift+0 (zero)
Subscript	Cmd-Shift– (hyphen)	Ctrl+Shift+9
Superior	Cmd-Shift-V	Ctrl+Shift+V

Horizontal alignment of text

Left alignment	Cmd-Shift-L	Ctrl+Shift+L
Right alignment	Cmd-Shift-R	Ctrl+Shift+R
Center alignment	Cmd-Shift-C	Ctrl+Shift+C
Justified alignment	Cmd-Shift-J	Ctrl+Shift+J
Forced justify	Cmd-Option-Shift-J	Ctrl+Alt+Shift+J

Tracking and kerning

Increase Kerning/Tracking 10 units	Cmd-Shift-]	Ctrl+Shift+]
Decrease Kerning/Tracking 10 units	Cmd-Shift-[	Ctrl+Shift+[
Increase Kerning/Tracking 1 unit	Cmd-Option-Shift-]	Ctrl+Alt+Shift+]
Decrease Kerning/Tracking 1 unit	Cmd-Option-Shift-[	Ctrl+Alt+Shift+[

Horizontal/vertical type scale

Decrease scale 5%	Cmd-[	Ctrl+[
Increase scale 5%	Cmd-]	Ctrl+]

	Mac OS	**Windows**
Decrease scale 1%	Cmd-Option-[	Ctrl+Alt+[
Increase scale 1%	Cmd-Option-]	Ctrl+Alt+]

Word space tracking

Increase Word Space 10 units	Cmd-Shift-Control]	Ctrl+Shift+]
Decrease Word Space 10 units	Cmd-Shift-Control [	Ctrl+Shift+[
Increase Word Space 1 unit	Cmd-Option-Shift-Control]	Ctrl+Alt+Shift+]
Decrease Word Space 1 unit	Cmd-Option-Shift-Control [	Ctrl+Alt+Shift+[

Special text characters

New paragraph	Return	Enter
New line	Shift-Return	Shift+Enter
Indent here	Cmd-\	Ctrl+\
Discretionary new line	Cmd-Return	Ctrl+Enter
Discretionary hyphen	Cmd-- (hyphen)	Ctrl+- (hyphen)
Nonbreaking standard hyphen	Cmd-=	Ctrl+=
Nonbreaking standard space	Cmd-Space bar *or* Cmd-5	Ctrl+5
Breaking en space	Option-Space bar	Ctrl+Shift+6
Nonbreaking en space	Cmd-Option-Space bar *or* Cmd-Option-5	Ctrl+Alt+Shift+6
Breaking flex space	Option-Shift-Space bar	Ctrl+Shift+5
Nonbreaking flex space	Cmd-Option-Shift-Space bar	Ctrl+Alt+Shift+5
Nonbreaking em dash	Cmd-Option-=	Ctrl+Alt+Shift+=
Breaking em dash	Option-Shift-- (hyphen)	Ctrl+Shift+=
Nonbreaking en dash	Option– (hyphen)	Ctrl+Alt+Shift+- (hyphen)
Break at discretionary hyphen only	Cmd-- (hyphen) before first character in word	Ctrl+-(hyphen) before first character in word
Breaking punctuation space	Shift-Space bar	Shift+Space
Nonbreaking punctuation space	Cmd-Shift-Space bar	Ctrl+Shift+Space

Tables

Resize table, rows, and columns (not content) non-proportionally	No modifier keys	
Resize table, rows, and columns (not content) proportionally	Option-Shift	Alt-Shift
Resize table, rows, columns, and content non-proportionally	Cmd	Ctrl
Resize table to a square; content doesn't resize	Shift	Shift
Resize table, rows, columns, and content proportionally	Cmd-Option-Shift	Ctrl-Alt-Shift

	Mac OS	Windows
Import a picture		
Get Picture...(Item or Content tool)	Cmd-E	Ctrl+E
TIFF, GIF, JPEG:		
line art to grayscale	Option-Open	Alt+ Open
grayscale to black-and-white	Cmd-Open	Ctrl+ Open
color to grayscale	Cmd-Open	Ctrl+ Open
Pictures and picture boxes or Béziers		
Center picture in box	Cmd-Shift-M	Ctrl+Shift+M
Move picture in box 1 point	Arrow keys	Arrow keys
Move picture in box ⅒ point	Option-arrow keys	Alt+arrow keys
Fit picture to box	Cmd-Shift-F	Ctrl+Shift+F
Fit picture to box (maintain aspect ratio)	Cmd-Option-Shift-F	Ctrl+Alt+Shift+F Victortest
Enlarge picture in 5% increments	Cmd-Option-Shift->	Ctrl+Alt+Shift+>
Reduce picture in 5% increments	Cmd-Option-Shift-<	Ctrl+Alt+Shift+<
Constrain box to square or circle	Shift-drag	Shift+drag
Resize box (maintain aspect ratio)	Option-Shift-drag	Alt+Shift+drag
Resize picture and box (Item > Edit > Shape off for Béziers)	Cmd-drag	Ctrl+drag
Resize picture and box (constrain proportions of box, not picture)	Cmd-Shift-drag	Ctrl+Shift+drag
Resize picture and box (maintain aspect ratio)	Cmd-Option-Shift-drag	Ctrl+Alt+Shift+drag
Picture styling		
Picture Contrast...	Cmd-Shift-C	Ctrl+Shift+C
Negative	Cmd-Shift–(hyphen)	Ctrl+Shift+- (hyphen)
Halftone (grayscale, line art only)	Cmd-Shift-H	Ctrl+Shift+H
Runaround/clipping		
Runaround...	Cmd-T	Ctrl+T
Edit runaround	Option-F4	Ctrl+F10
Clipping...	Cmd-Option-T	Ctrl+Alt+T
Edit clipping path	Option-Shift-F4	Ctrl+Shift+F10
Bézier box or line (or clipping path)		
Add a point	Option-click line segment	Alt+click line segment
Delete a point	Option-click point	Alt+click point *or* Backspace (Item tool)
Delete selected Bézier point while drawing shape	Delete	Backspace
Edit Bézier while drawing it	Cmd	Ctrl

	Mac OS	**Windows**
Constrain line, point, or handle movement to 0°, 45°, 90°	Shift-drag	Shift+drag
Temporarily suspend text reflow	Space bar	Space bar
Retract one curve handle	Option-click handle	Alt+ click handle
Retract both curve handles	Control-shift-click point	Ctrl+Shift+click point
Expose/create curve handle	Control-shift-drag point	Ctrl+Shift+drag point
Select all points in active item (combined paths/items)	Cmd-Shift-A *or* triple-click point	Ctrl+Shift+A *or* triple-click point
Select all points in active item (single path)	Double-click point *or* Cmd-Shift-A	Ctrl+Shift+A *or* double-click point
Convert Bézier line to filled-center Bézier box	Option-Item menu > Shape > 🌑	Alt+item menu > Shape > 🌑
Edit Shape	Shift-F4	F10

Convert Bézier point

To a corner point	Option-F1	Ctrl+F1
To a smooth point	Option-F2	Ctrl+F2
To a symmetrical point	Option-F3	Ctrl+F3
Corner to smooth/smooth to corner	Control-Shift-drag curve handle	Ctrl+Shift+drag curve handle
Smooth to corner while drawing shape	Cmd-Control drag curve handle	Ctrl+click point, then press Ctrl+F1

Convert Bézier segment

Curved to a straight segment	Option-Shift-F1	Ctrl+Shift+F1
Straight to a curved segment	Option-Shift-F2	Ctrl+Shift+F2

Line or text

Increase width/size to preset size	Cmd-Shift->	Ctrl+Shift+>
Decrease width/size to preset size	Cmd-Shift-<	Ctrl+Shift+<
Increase width/size by 1 point	Cmd-Option-Shift->	Ctrl+Alt+Shift+>
Decrease width/size by 1 point	Cmd-Option-Shift-<	Ctrl+Alt+Shift+<
Other width & Other size	Cmd-Shift-\	Ctrl+Shift+\
Constrain resize/rotate to 0°, 45°, 90°	Shift-drag	Shift+drag
Constrain to original angle	Option-Shift-drag	Alt+Shift+drag

Style sheets

Display Palette	F11	F11
Open Edit Style Sheet dialog box	Cmd-click style sheet with Content tool	Ctrl+click style sheet with Content tool
Display Edit Style Sheet menu	Ctrl-click style sheet name	Right+click style sheet name
Apply No Style, then style sheet	Option-click style name on Style Sheets palette	Alt+click style name on Style Sheets palette

Keyboard Shortcuts

	Mac OS	**Windows**
Color		
Colors...	Cmd-click color on Colors palette *or* Shift-F12	Ctrl+click color on Color palette *or* Shift+F12
Multiple items		
Select All (Item tool)	Cmd-A	Ctrl+A
Select multiple items (Item tool)	Shift-click *or* marquee	Shift+click *or* marquee
Group	Cmd-G	Ctrl+G
Ungroup	Cmd-U	Ctrl+U
Duplicate	Cmd-D	Ctrl+D
Step and Repeat...	Cmd-Option-D	Ctrl+Alt+D
Select behind other items	Cmd-Option-Shift-click	Ctrl+Alt+Shift+click
Bring to Front	F5	F5
Send to Back	Shift-F5	Shift+F5
Bring Forward one level	Option-Item menu-Bring Forward *or* Option-F5	Ctrl+F5
Send Backward one level	Option-Item menu- Send Backward *or* Option-Shift-F5	Ctrl+Shift+F5
Space/Align...	Cmd-, (comma)	Ctrl+, (comma)
Anchored boxes		
Text to box (anchor box and delete text)	Option-choose Style menu > Text to Box	Alt+choose Style menu > Text to Box
Check spelling		
Check Word	Cmd-L	Ctrl+W
Check Story	Cmd-Option-L	Ctrl+Alt+W
Check Document	Cmd-Option-Shift-L	Ctrl+Alt+Shift+W
Lookup	Cmd-L	Alt+L
Skip	Cmd-S	Alt+S
Add	Cmd-A	Alt+A
Add all suspect words to current auxiliary dictionary	Option-Shift-click Done button	Alt+Shift+click Close button
Find/Change		
Find/Change...	Option-F	Ctrl-F
Change Find Next button to Find First	Option-Find Next (in Find/Change dialog box)	Alt+Find Next (in Find/Change dialog box)
Close Find/Change	Cmd-Option-F	Ctrl+Alt+F
Wild card (Find what)	Cmd-?	Ctrl+?
Space	Space bar	Space bar
Tab	\t	\t *or* Ctrl+Tab

	Mac OS	**Windows**
New paragraph	Cmd-Return *or* \p	Ctrl+Enter *or* \p
New line	Cmd-Shift-Return *or* \n	Ctrl+Shift+Enter *or* \n
New column	Cmd-Enter *or* \c	\c
New box	Cmd-Shift-Enter *or* \b	\b
Punctuation space	Cmd-. (period) *or* \	Ctrl+. (period) *or* \
Flex space	Cmd-Shift-F *or* \f	Ctrl+Shift+F *or* \f
Backslash	Cmd-\ *or* \\	Ctrl+\ *or* \\
Previous box page number	Cmd-2 *or* \2	Ctrl+2 *or* \2
Current box page number	Cmd-3 *or* \3	Ctrl+3 *or* \3
Next box page number	Cmd-4 *or* \4	Ctrl+4 *or* \4

Indexing

Display palette	Cmd-Option-I	
Highlight text field	Cmd-Option-I	
Add highlighted entry	Cmd-Option-Shift-I	
Edit highlighted index entry	Double-click	

Compare components

Compare two style sheets, colors, lists, H&Js, dashes & stripes, print styles	Open dialog box from Edit menu, Cmd-click two components, then Option-click Append (Import button in Print Styles)	Open dialog box from Edit menu, Crtl-click two components, then Alt click Append (Import button in Print Styles)

Preferences

Document Preferences...	Cmd-Y	Ctrl+Y
Document > Paragraph	Cmd-Option-Y	Ctrl+Alt+Y
Document > Trapping	Option-Shift-F12	Ctrl+Shift+F12
Tool Preferences	Double-click item creation *or* Zoom tool	Double-click item creation *or* Zoom tool
Application Preferences	Cmd-Option-Shift-Y	Ctrl+Alt+Shift+Y

Output

Page Setup	Cmd-Option-P	Ctrl+Alt+P
Print	Cmd-P	Ctrl+P
Save Page as EPS	Cmd-Option-Shift-S	Ctrl+Alt+Shift+S

Note: If you choose an F key as a Keyboard Equivalent
for a style sheet, it will override the default F key command.

Index

Index

Index

Index

Index

Index